PRACTICAL COOKERY

Uses of meringue: (top) large vacherin; (foreground) small vacherin and examples of presenting meringues

Practical COOKERY

Victor Ceserani MBE, CPA, MBA, FHCIMA

Formerly Head of
The School of Hotelkeeping and Catering,
Ealing College of Higher Education

Ronald Kinton BEd (Hons), FHCIMA

Formerly of
Garnett College, College of Education
for Teachers in Further and Higher Education

Editorial Consultant: David Foskett BEd (Hons), MHCIMA

Director of Hospitality, Education and Training
at the Polytechnic of West London

Seventh Edition

Hodder & Stoughton

LONDON SYDNEY AUCKLAND TORONTO

ISBN 0 340 52683 1

First published 1962
Second edition 1967
Third edition 1972
Fourth edition 1974
Fifth edition 1981
Sixth edition 1987
Seventh edition 1990
Fifth impression 1992

Typeset by Wearside Tradespools, Fulwell, Sunderland
Printed in Great Britain for Hodder and Stoughton Educational, a division of Hodder and Stoughton Ltd, Mill Road, Dunton Green, Sevenoaks, Kent by William Clowes Limited, Beccles and London.

Contents

Acknowledgments

The authors wish to acknowledge and thank the following:

- The publishers for enabling this book to be illustrated
- David Foskett, their editorial consultant, for his help and advice throughout the book and for providing the vegetarian chapter
- Jane Cliff Bsc (Nutrition), and Jenny Poulter, BSc, PhD, for their section on nutrition/healthy eating in Chapter 2 and for the nutritional data supplied alongside many of the recipes
- Wendy Doyle, Research Nutritionist for her help with the nutritional analysis

The authors and publishers would like to thank the following:

- The photographer Ian O'Leary and his assistant Tim Ridley for their helpful advice and co-operation
- David Foskett for the use of the kitchens and help of staff at Ealing College of Higher Education
- Glynn Johnson, Cert Ed, and Frank McDowall, Cert Ed, MHCIMA, for the interest, helpful suggestion and care taken in the preparation and presentation of the food required for the photographs
- The Milk Marketing Board for generously sponsoring the work of Jane Cliff, Jenny Poulter and Wendy Doyle.
- The Health Education Authority for permission to reproduce the diagram on page 27, from their *Guide to Healthy Eating*.

Preface

The Milk Marketing Board was delighted to contribute towards the major task of providing nutritional data on selected recipes in this latest edition of *Practical Cookery*.

The study of nutrition has always been an essential element of a caterer's training. However, with increasing public interest in nutrition and the move towards pre-prepared food, the caterers' role in helping their customers select a healthy diet has intensified. The Dairy Industry has responded to this by adding to their traditional range of dairy products a number of reduced fat products, thus offering alternatives for those who need or wish to make use of them. This wider selection extends the versatility, taste and opportunity for caterers and their customers.

The Board has enjoyed a long-standing relationship with caterers and the Catering Industry through extensive promotional activities, and also with catering colleges during its ten year co-sponsorship of the 'Taste of Britain Student Caterers Competition'.

We are pleased to strengthen this relationship still further by our association with this prestigious publication.

Bob Steven, Chairman
Milk Marketing Board, England and Wales
December 1989

Introduction to the Seventh Edition

The purpose of this book is to provide a sound foundation of professional cookery for students taking City and Guilds of London Catering Courses 705 and 706/1, 706/2 and 706/3; also the BTEC Courses Certificate and Diploma, Higher Certificate and Higher Diploma Courses, the examinations of the Hotel, Catering and Institutional Management Association and Caterbase programmes. We also think that the book will assist students of catering other than those taking these courses and examinations.

As in previous editions account has been taken of trends towards a more positive attitude to eating for the benefit of health. Included is a chapter on vegetarian dishes and suggested alternatives to certain ingredients to meet this demand. Furthermore, an important new dimension to this edition is the inclusion of nutritional data so that students may know at a glance the nutritional content of certain recipes.

We hope that the addition of illustrations in this edition will serve to interest and motivate students by assisting in the preparation of certain foods and dishes, and help in improving their standards of presentation.

Account is taken of the continuing changes in syllabus that are taking place (such as the demand for knowledge of nutritional data), whilst retaining what we consider to be a clear format for learning and in preparation for industry.

Students need to know what is expected of them and to know if they have achieved these expectations. Many courses have their requirements stated in objective terms so that both students and teachers know what is expected of them. The intention of this book is to assist students to realise their objectives.

Objectives may be expressed generally or specifically. General objectives will be those indicating understanding, knowing, appreciating, awareness; specific objectives are those which can be measured, where there is some tangible proof that the intention or objective has been realised. This may be in both the theoretical and in the practical situation; for example, it is possible to write a list of points to observe when deep frying; it is also possible in practice to apply these points in practical situations.

The following important objectives are appropriate throughout the student's learning of the theory and practice of professional cookery. In addition each chapter is also preceded by relevant objectives.

1 To develop a professional attitude and appearance to the job. To acquire professional skills and to behave in a professional manner.
2 To understand the methods of cookery and be able to produce a variety of dishes using these methods in all kinds of establishments.

3 To know the principles underlying the selection of ingredients and their cost; and to be able to evaluate quality of materials and be able to compare fresh, part-prepared, commercial and convenience items.
4 To understand recipe balance and be able to follow recipes to produce dishes of the required standard of quality, colour, consistency, seasoning, flavour, temperature and presentation.
5 To know where, when and how specific foods and dishes would be served and, where appropriate, be able to understand and use basic French culinary terms.
6 To be able to select and correctly use utensils and equipment for both large and small kitchens.
7 For health, safety and economic reasons to understand and practise at all times safe, hygienic and methodical work procedures.
8 To be able to adjust recipes where required to meet current trends.

To check if the learning objectives of the theoretical aspects have been achieved students are recommended to use *Questions on Practical Cookery* which is published in conjunction with this book. However, the achievement of the practical objectives can only be evaluated in a practical situation.

Although the recipes are for four portions unless stated otherwise, the nutritional information given in certain recipes is for one portion only.

We recommend the use of the following books: *Le Repertoire de la Cuisine* by L. Saulnier, *The Larder Chef* by Leto and Bode, *The Vegetarian Cookbook* by Sarah Brown, *Contemporary Cookery* by V. Ceserani, R. Kinton and D. Foskett and *The Theory of Catering*, 6 edn. by R. Kinton and V. Ceserani.

In the preparation of this edition we have been assisted by David Foskett, BEd (Hons) MHCIMA, Dean of the Faculty of Hospitality Studies and Head of Department of Hotelkeeping and Catering Operations, Ealing College. David Foskett trained at Westminster Technical College, gained hotel experience at the Dorchester and Savoy, and industrial catering experience at the Head Office of British Petroleum. He has qualifications in food technology and as a Chef Technologist has worked in test kitchens for food manufacturers.

Knife grinder, palette knife, vegetable peeler, small knife, fork, boning knife, trussing needle, large knife, steel, carving knife

I

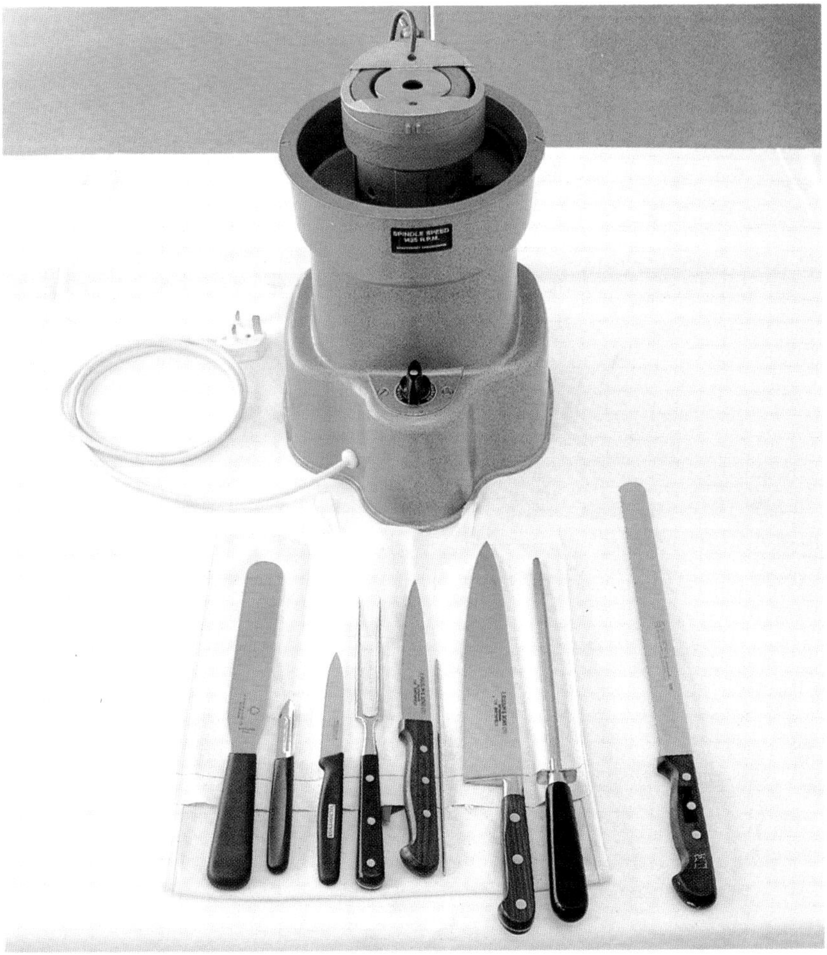

SELECTION, USE AND CARE OF KNIVES AND SMALL EQUIPMENT

General objectives
Chefs and cooks should be able to understand which tools should be selected for a particular purpose, to know how to use them correctly and to take care of them.

Specific objectives
Having read this section the reader will be able to state the purpose of the tools, describe their care and explain how to use them safely.

In the practical situation this knowledge and understanding would then be applied.

Knives must be handled with respect, used correctly and taken care of so that a professional performance can be achieved. Blunt knives are likely to be the cause of accidents since more pressure has to be applied than if a sharp knife is used. Sharp knives enable the work to be completed more quickly with less expenditure of energy and with better finish, thus giving greater job satisfaction.

Safety rules

Always observe the rules of safety for the benefit of yourself and others.

1. If carried, the knife point must be held downwards.
2. Knives on the table must be placed flat so that the blade is not exposed upwards.
3. Do not allow knives to project over the edge of the table.
4. When using knives keep your mind and eye on the job in hand.
5. Use the correct knife for the correct purpose.
6. Always keep knives sharp.
7. After use always wipe the knife with the blade away from the hand.
8. Keep the handle of the knife clean when in use.
9. Never leave knives lying in the sink.
10. Never misuse knives; a good knife is a good friend but it can be a dangerous weapon.

Selecting the right knife for the correct purpose

Specific tools have been designed for certain functions to be performed in the kitchen so that work can be done successfully. A basic set of tools could comprise:

1 vegetable peeler	peeling vegetables and fruit
2 vegetable knife 4″ blade	general use, vegetables and fruit

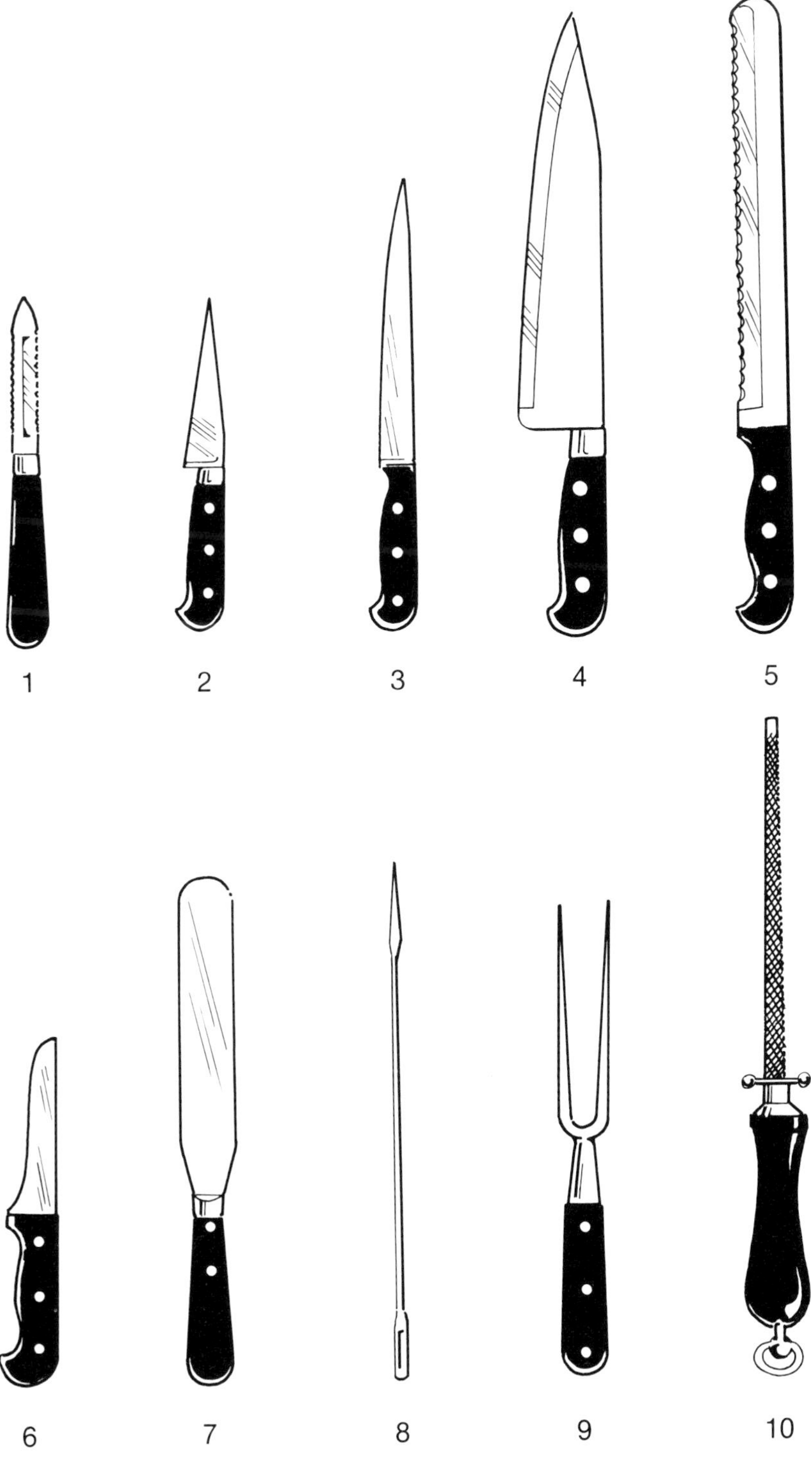
1
2
3
4
5
6
7
8
9
10

3	filleting knife 6″ blade (flexible)	filleting fish
4	medium large knife 10″ blade	shredding, slicing, chopping
5	carving knife } in addition when and if needed	carving
6	boning knife } in addition when and if needed	butchery
7	palette knife	spreading, turning items over and lifting
8	trussing needle	trussing poultry and game
9	fork	lifting and holding joints of meat
10	steel	sharpening knives

Having chosen the correct tool there are occasions when extra care needs to be taken.

1 When using a knife to cut side ways there is less control than when cutting downwards, e.g. cross cuts when chopping onion or slicing long sandwich loaves lengthwise.
2 When shredding or chopping it is necessary to keep the finger tips and nails clear of the blade since they are not visible all the time. When chopping, keep the fingers of the hand not holding the handle – on top of the blade.
3 Never bone out or fillet frozen meat or fish in the frozen state; however, when thawed the centre may still be very cold and cause the fingertips to be numbed. Cuts are then more likely to occur.
4 When using a large knife use the thumb and first finger on the sides of the blade near the handle so as to control the sideways as well as the downward movement of the knife.
5 When using a trussing needle take extra care when drawing the needle and string upwards towards the face.
6 When scoring pork rind take care lest the surface being scored offers varying degrees of resistance, causing the knife to go out of control.

Sharpening

Two tools are available for sharpening knives, a steel which should be well grooved and a carborundum stone, which should not be too coarse as a saw edge may result. Periodically knives will require to be ground which is usually done by a knife grinder.

When using a stone *always* draw the blade of the knife away from the hand holding the stone because few stones are provided with a guard.

When using a steel, for preference use one with a guard. Should you however have a steel with no guard *always* draw the knife being sharpened away from you. When using a stone or a steel, angle the blade of the knife to 45° and sharpen alternate sides of the knife using considerable pressure and drawing almost the whole length of the blade edge along the stone or steel. Having used the stone always follow up by using the steel and then wipe the knife on a cloth before use. The reason for drawing the knife across at an angle is to produce an edge to the blade, and to obtain a sharp edge it is necessary to apply both sides of the blade to the steel or stone. As the stone produces a rough edge it is necessary to follow with a steel to provide a smooth sharp edge. The knife must be wiped after using the stone since small particles of the stone will adhere to the blade.

The steel may be used in three ways. Whichever way is chosen, care must be taken to sharpen the knife safely.

1 Holding the steel in one hand and the knife in the other (right-handed people will hold the knife in the right hand), draw the blade down the steel at an angle of 45° some six or seven times on each side of the steel (thus both sides of the blade), exerting pressure. Before doing so, *check* that the steel has a guard. See below.

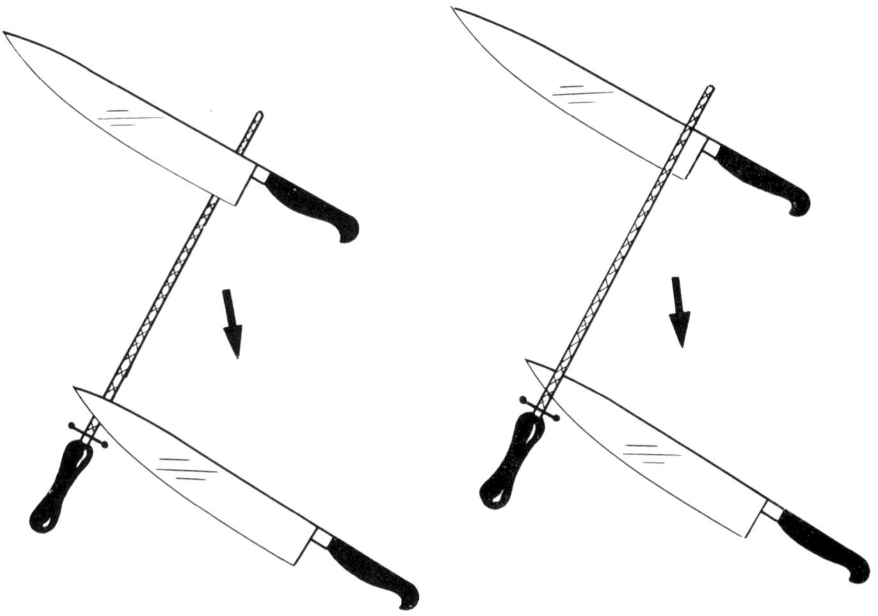

2 Holding the steel and knife as (1), draw the knife away from you towards the end of the steel at an angle of 45° some six or seven times on each side of the steel (thus both sides of the blade), exerting pressure. See below.

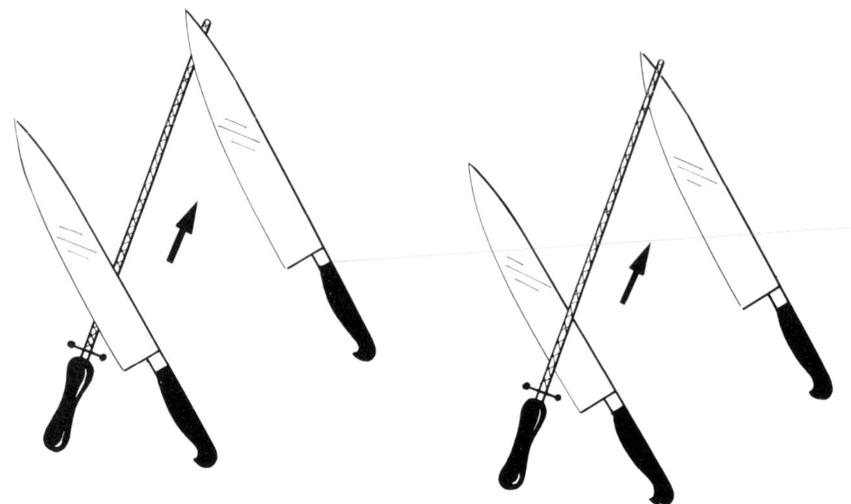

3 Placing the pointed end of the steel on the wooden block or heavy board, draw the knife downwards towards the block at an angle of 45° exerting pressure and making certain the steel does not slip. As with the two previous methods, both sides of the blade are drawn down the steel some six or seven times for each side. See below.

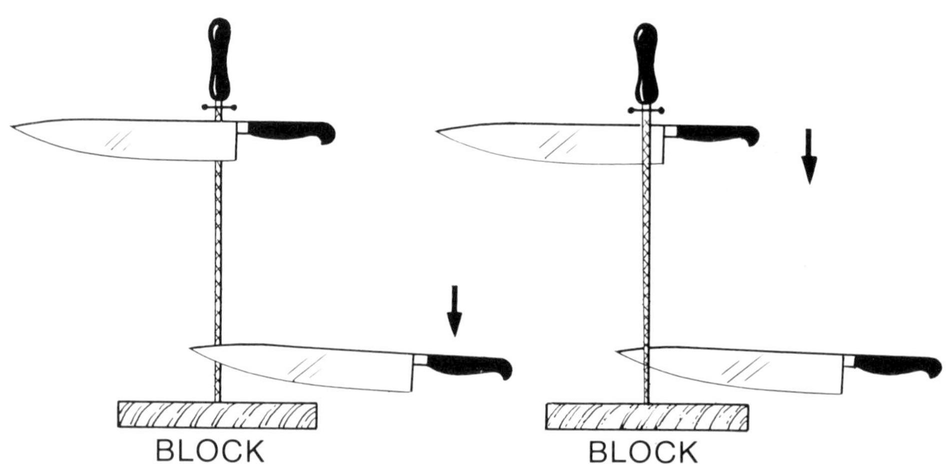

To test for the sharpness, the skin of a tomato is a good indicator. To retain sharpness always use a wooden surface or suitable cutting surface of a cutting board. Never cut on stainless steel. Clean knives during and after use and particularly after using on acid items such as lemon. Stains on the blade can be cleaned with a fine cleaning powder or abrasive pad.

Stainless steel knives for professional cooks are available which may need less sharpening as they retain their sharpness and of course do not stain.

It should be remembered that a good craftsman or craftswoman never blames their tools, since they always take care of them.

Small equipment

In addition to the range of chef's knives, there are a number of other small implements in general use. It is important always to buy good quality equipment and to wash and dry it thoroughly after each use. Some examples include:

Cook's forks

These are obtainable in several shapes and sizes and are used:

a) for holding hot and cold meats in place whilst carving. It is sensible practice to use a fork with a guard for this purpose in case the knife should slip;
b) for turning large pieces of meat or poultry being roasted or braised. Do not pierce the meat if possible otherwise the meat juices will seep out, resulting in loss of flavour and moisture.

Cook's tongs

These are used:

a) for turning small pieces of food during cooking;
b) in place of hands or forks when removing foods for dressing-up ready for service. Tongs are more efficient than forks for handling small items of food and, in addition, there is no risk of piercing the foods.

Vegetable peelers

These are obtainable in several patterns, e.g.

a) fixed blade English type;
b) fixed blade French type – this usually removes a thinner skin from the vegetable or fruit;

c) swivel blade – this takes a little practice to use effectively but, once mastered, it can be used very swiftly and economically;
d) combined peeler and apple corer.

Vegetable groovers

These are usually obtainable in two types:

a) top cutter
b) side cutter

Use: for grooving and decorating lemons, oranges, limes, carrots.

Vegetable cutters

These are scoop-shaped implements obtainable usually in four sizes:

a) pea-shaped round (referred to as a Solferino cutter);
b) small ball-shaped round (referred to as a Parisienne cutter);
c) slightly larger ball-shaped round (referred to as a Noisette cutter);
d) plain oval shaped (referred to as an Olivette cutter);
e) fluted oval shaped.

The last four are generally used for cutting potatoes, hence Parisienne, Noisette and Olivette potatoes.

Trussing and larding needles

These are obtainable in several sizes suitable for large and small joints of meat or different sizes of poultry or game (e.g. 20 kg (40 lb) turkey, 500 g (1 lb) grouse).

Kitchen scissors and secateurs

Scissors are chiefly used for trimming fish and secateurs for jointing game and poultry.

Pastry cutting wheels

These are obtainable with plain or fluted edges and are used for cutting raviolis, cannelonis and other pastry shapes.

Citrus fruit zesters

These are obtainable in several types and used for removing the zest-filled top layer of citrus skin in ribbons ranging in width from fine filaments to thicker sized twists.

Frying: basket, spider, skimmer, draining trays

USEFUL INFORMATION AND HEALTHY EATING IN PRACTICE

Metric equivalents

	Approx. equivalent	Exact equivalent
¼ oz	5 g	7.0 g
½ oz	10 g	14.1 g
1 oz	25 g	28.3 g
2 oz	50 g	56.6 g
3 oz	75 g	84.9 g
4 oz	100 g	113.2 g
5 oz	125 g	141.5 g
6 oz	150 g	169.8 g
7 oz	175 g	198.1 g
8 oz	200 g	227.0 g
9 oz	225 g	255.3 g
10 oz	250 g	283.0 g
11 oz	275 g	311.3 g
12 oz	300 g	340.0 g
13 oz	325 g	368.3 g
14 oz	350 g	396.6 g
15 oz	375 g	424.0 g
16 oz	400 g	454.0 g
2 lb	1 kg	908.0 g
¼ pt	125 ml	142 ml
½ pt	250 ml (¼ litre)	284 ml
¾ pt	375 ml	426 ml
1 pt	500 ml (½ litre)	568 ml
1½ pt	750 ml (¾ litre)	852 ml
2 pt (1 qt)	1000 ml (1 litre)	1.13 litre
2 qt	2000 ml (2 litre)	2.26 litre
1 gal	(4½ litre)	4.54 litre

Approx. measurements	
½ cm = ¼ in	10 cm = 4 in
1 cm = ½ in	12 cm = 5 in
2 cm = 1 in	15 cm = 6 in
4 cm = 1½ in	16 cm = 6½ in
5 cm = 2 in	18 cm = 7 in
6 cm = 2½ in	30 cm = 12 in
8 cm = 3 in	45 cm = 18 in

Oven Temperature Chart

	Degrees C	Regulo	Degrees F
Slow (cool)	110	¼	225
	130	½	250
	140	1	275
	150	2	300
	160	3	325
Moderate	180	4	350
	190	5	375
	200	6	400
Hot	220	7	425
	230	8	450
Very hot	250	9	500

Oils and Fats

This chart indicates which cooking oils, margarines and fats are healthiest, i.e. the ones with the smallest percentage of saturated fats.

Oil/fat	Saturated %	Mono-unsaturated %	Poly-unsaturated %
Coconut oil	85	7	2
Butter	60	32	3
Palm oil	45	42	8
Lard	43	42	9
Beef dripping	40	49	4
Margarine, hard (vegetable oil only)	37	47	12
Margarine, hard (mixed oils)	37	43	17
Margarine, soft	32	42	22
Margarine, soft (mixed oils)	30	45	19
Low-fat spread	27	38	30
Margarine, polyunsaturated	24	22	54
Ground nut oil	19	48	28
Maize oil	16	29	49
Wheatgerm oil	14	11	45
Soya bean oil	14	24	57
Olive oil	14	70	11
Sunflower seed oil	13	32	50
Safflower seed oil	10	13	72
Rape seed oil	7	64	32

Ingredients and ingredient substitutes

Traditional ingredients have been tried and tested in recipes and have given satisfactory results. However, many new ingredients and ingredient substitutes may need to be adopted for reasons such as cost reduction, healthy eating, and problems with sources of supply. When using a new ingredient, the recipe may need to be modified and adapted. This process of modification and adaptation requires skill and knowledge developed through experimentation.

Food manufacturers are constantly launching new products in response to market research, identifying caterers' needs. Such products are often claimed to be better and, in some cases, healthier than existing lines. These may well be technological innovations and could enhance and improve existing recipes, but it will be the chef who will make the final decision on the acceptability of the ingredient. The chef is required to use his/her judgement and creativity, together with his/her skill in experimenting with any new ingredient, based on previous knowledge.

It is important always to follow, where possible, the food manufacturer's recommendations. For example, there are several non-dairy creamers available. Some are produced specifically for pastry work and so, being sweetened, are unsuitable for savoury recipes. However, there are also various unsweetened products that may be used in place of fresh cream for soups, sauces etc. It is important to determine the heat suitability of these products before use, for example by testing whether or not they will withstand boiling without detriment to the product.

Healthy eating in practice

Food fulfils many functions. People enjoy eating for many reasons and in many different environments: food excites the senses; it can provide a focus for social events, and can be used as a reward, for bribery or for comfort. It is also a fuel supply for the body and has an important role to play in promoting health. The nutritional aspects of food are important but no caterer can afford to lose sight of the basic qualities which ensure enjoyment of the food. All food should:

a look inviting,
b smell appetising,
c taste pleasing with regard to flavour, seasoning and texture.

What do all the experts say?

Health professionals all agree that there are strong and sound reasons why we should change what we eat – particularly how much fat, sugar, fibre and salt we consume. The strength of evidence is startling and suggests that, together with smoking and lack of exercise, our unhealthy diet significantly contributes to our high rates of coronary heart disease and other related problems. For many of us simple changes in the food we eat may significantly lower the risk of developing obesity, heart disease, some cancers and some diseases of the digestive system.

The 1983 NACNE (National Advisory Committee on Nutrition Education) and 1984 COMA (Committee on Medical Aspects of Food Policy) reports are the most important documents on dietary advice to be published in the last decade. The NACNE document was much broader in the advice that it gave than COMA, which only looked at diet and heart disease. The recommendations give clear practical guidelines for adults to shape their eating patterns for the future:

What NACNE says

- Energy (Calorie) intake should be enough to maintain optimum body weight[1] and adequate exercise
- Total fat should be no more than 80–85 g/day
- Saturated fat should be no more than 20–23 g/day[2]
- Sugar should be no more than 50 g/day
- Dietary fibre should be increased from an average of 20 g to 30 g/day
- Salt should be no more than 5 g/day

[1] see 'Are you a healthy weight?', p. 25.
[2] for someone eating approximately 2200 kcals/day

For caterers, therefore, these recommendations now provide a yardstick against which the meals prepared can be assessed for their nutritional content and hence their healthiness.

Are you a healthy weight?

The right weight for your height can give a rough check on your eating habits. The chart on page 25, taken from the Health Education Authority's *Guide to Healthy Eating*, shows ranges of weights for a particular height. This accounts for different builds and body frames.

Find out where your height and weight lines cross on the chart opposite and use the guidelines below it to check your weight:

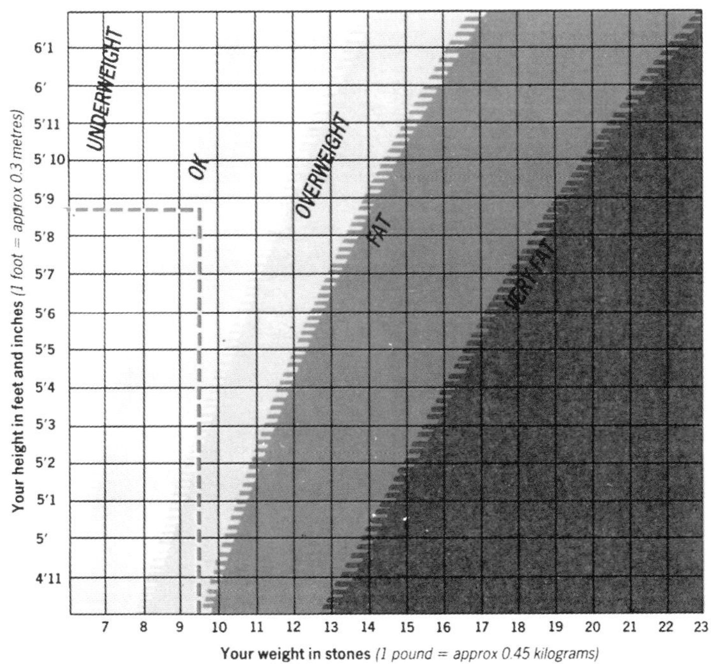

Underweight	–	Check that you're eating enough
OK	–	You're eating the right amount of food, but check that you're eating the right type of food
Overweight	–	Your health would benefit if you lost weight
Fat	–	For your health you need to lose weight
Very Fat	–	You urgently need to lose weight. Your doctor might advise you to see a dietitian

Our health in the caterers' hands

Caterers have a major role in maintaining the nation's health. As professionals, caterers have the skills and knowledge to make healthier food options more appetising and inspiring. In the UK, about one-third of all meals eaten each day are prepared by caterers. There is a widespread belief held by providers of food that there are no bad foods only bad eating patterns. This can encourage caterers to think that it is acceptable to provide dishes loaded with fat and sugar because their ill-effects will be balanced by the food customers eat at home. This is bad-practice. Every meal counts. However, this does not necessarily mean that every meal must be a perfect nutritional mix.

The scope for caterers is enormous. There is an increasing consumer demand for healthier meals and the response by some sectors of the catering industry has been highly imaginative. However, these shining examples of good practice are by no means the norm.

Integrating healthy changes into a catering operation involves a complex series of stages (see diagram opposite), but these are not insurmountable. Menus, recipes, production and service techniques often require revision; the type and range of food items procured have to be reviewed and steps taken to market healthier food choices to consumers. The following table is an example of how traditional recipe ingredients may be replaced by healthier ones:

Instead of	Choose
Whole milk	Skimmed milk (or semi-skimmed)
Butter or hard margarine	Polyunsaturated margarine
Lard, hard vegetable fats	Pure vegetable oils, e.g. corn oil, sunflower oil
Full-fat cheeses e.g. Cheddar	Low-fat cheeses, e.g. low-fat Cheddar has half the fat
Fatty meats	Lean meat (smaller portion) or chicken or fish
Cream	Plain yoghurt, quark

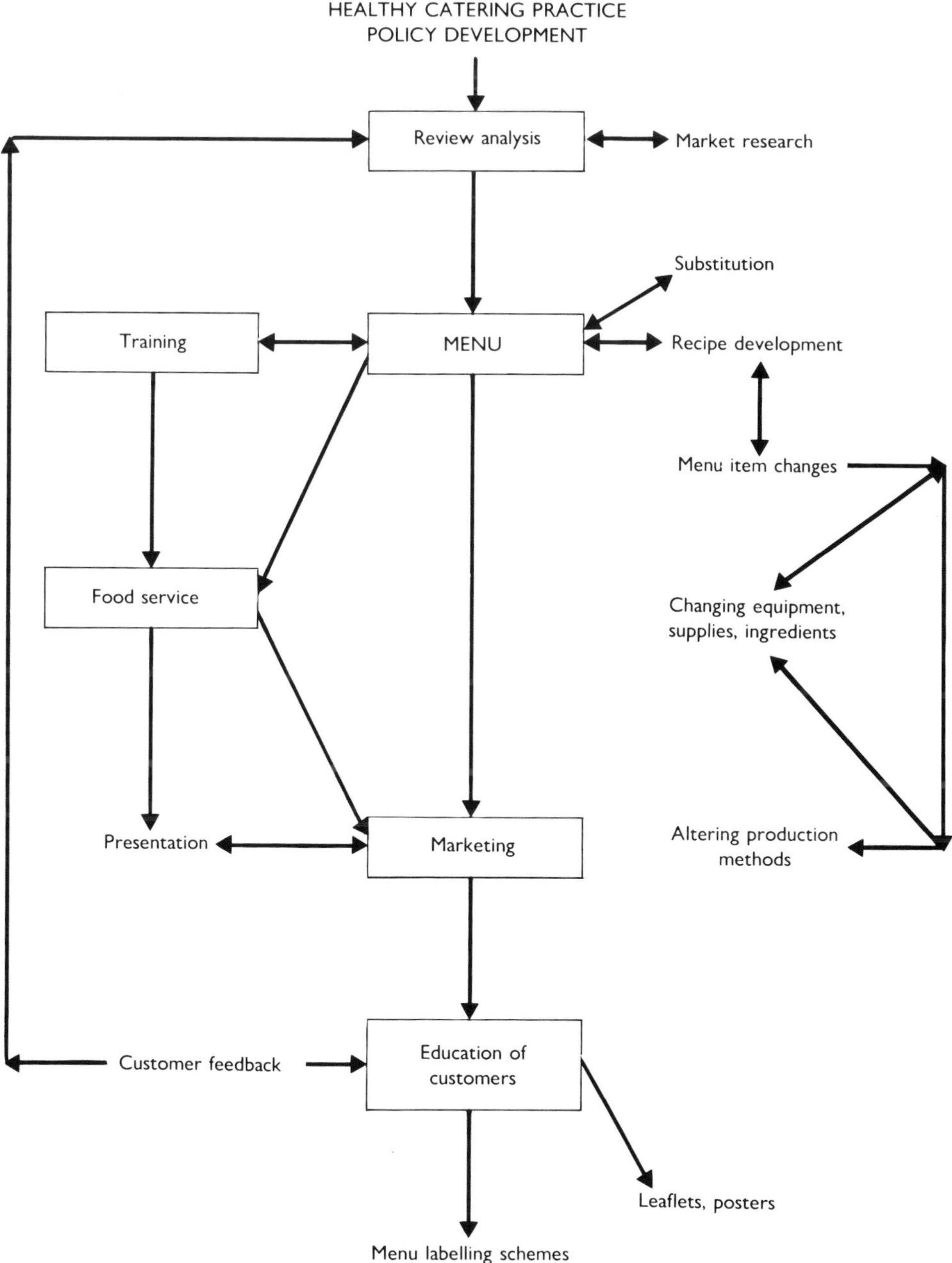
HEALTHY CATERING PRACTICE
POLICY DEVELOPMENT
Review analysis
Market research
Substitution
Training
MENU
Recipe development
Menu item changes
Food service
Changing equipment, supplies, ingredients
Presentation
Marketing
Altering production methods
Customer feedback
Education of customers
Leaflets, posters
Menu labelling schemes

In addition, policies need to be developed to ensure that a blue-print for coordinated action is available to all within an organization (see diagram on page 27). The analysis of recipes for their nutritional content is often the starting point for many of these changes to occur. More and more, recipes are published alongside a nutritional analysis or with some other indication of their nutritional quality. There is a vast repertoire of healthy recipes and some of these have been developed for catering operations. (A selection of these is given in the 'Further Information' section at the end of this Chapter.)

The nutritional analysis of meals is usually a 'book exercise', in which the nutritional content of different foods used in the recipes are selected from standard food composition tables devised by McCance and Widdowson. For the computer literate there are also several easy programs on the market which give a portion of a dish in terms of calories, grams of fat, fibre, salt and much more. A word of caution is required, however, since these analyses provide only an *approximate* estimate of the nutritional content of meals and so should be interpreted accordingly. Very few foods have a constant composition and variations occur for a number of reasons. For example, the fat content of a lamb cutlet will vary according to the breed of the animal or how it is fed or butchered. The values in the tables or data bases of the computer programs are, in the main, analytical results obtained from the chemical analysis of representative samples of cutlets. The lamb cutlet that you choose for a particular recipe may well have a different composition.

The analysis

Over a third of the recipes given in subsequent chapters have been analysed to show their content of the more important components. The nutritional information is presented alongside the relevant recipes using the following format:

Format for nutritional information

1 portion provides	(States whether analysis is given per portion or per recipe)
350 kcals/1452 kJ	(Energy content expressed as kilocalories or kilojoules)
11.7 g fat **of which 5.2 g saturated**	(Total fat is listed together with its saturated fat – this is most prevalent in animal products)
23.0 g carbohydrate **of which 2.9 g sugars**	(The aim is to eat more starchy carbohydrate and less sugar)
7.6 g protein	(Intake of protein is not generally a problem in the UK)
1.0 g fibre	(An important part of the foods we eat – found especially in cereals, pulses, vegetables and fruit)

The nutritional analysis for each recipe is based on the ingredients listed in the individual recipe. In other words no garnishes or serving suggestions have been included in the calculations. If the type or quantity of ingredients are altered then the nutritional analysis quoted should not be used. The addition or substitution of different ingredients can change the nutritional value of a recipe enormously. For example, adding prawns to a soup will, amongst other things, increase the protein content; enriching a sauce with cream and egg yolks will increase the fat content, particularly the level of saturated fat.

Nutritional information is presented for all the basic recipes within the text, together with other popular dishes. In carrying out the nutritional analyses of these recipes several assumptions were made:

Fat

Many recipes cite the option of two or three different types of fat, some of which can be better than others in terms of health (see Oils and Fats chart, page 22). As a general rule, the higher the degree of saturation, the poorer the health rating of the particular fat. Thus the choice of fat used in a recipe can influence the nutritional quality of the finished dish substantially:

Look at the differences that fats make

	Fried eggs cooked in:	
Butter	**Hard margarine**	**Sunflower oil**
	Each portion provides	
127 kcals/536 kJ	127 kcals/536 kJ	127 kcals/536 kJ
10.7 g fat of which 4.1 g saturated	10.7 g fat of which 3.4 g saturated	10.7 g fat of which 2.6 g saturated
– g carbohydrate of which – g sugars	– g carbohydrate of which – g sugars	– g carbohydrate of which – g sugars
7.8 g protein	7.8 g protein	7.8 g protein
– g fibre	– g fibre	– g fibre

Milk

It has been assumed that whole milk (3.8% fat) has been used unless the recipe specifically states semi-skimmed (1.6% fat) or skimmed milk (0.1% fat).

Salt

Chefs often add salt to taste. It is therefore difficult to quantify amounts of salt for each recipe and, as a consequence, no analytical data is given for salt or sodium content. However a general reduction is recommended – but this should not be considered detrimental to overall quality.

Rice, flour, bread

Analysis has been carried out for white varieties unless the recipe specifically states wholegrain varieties.

Portion sizes

In some cases recipes are quoted for 4–6 portions, and in these instances analyses has been based on 4 portions only. If more or fewer portions are served from a recipe, then the nutritional content will be different.

What do the analyses tell the caterer?

To the trained eye nutritional data can be a goldmine. An idea of what the information can reveal is shown below:

What do nutritional analyses reveal?

Veal escalope cordon bleu

1 portion provides:	
627 kcals/2632 kJ	(A chef may need 2600 to 2900 kcals daily)
48.1 g fat of which 16.3 g saturated	(The maximum recommended amount of fat for the average person is 80–85 g daily. Add a portion of roast potatoes to this dish and you could be eating 56 g fat)
12.0 g carbohydrate of which 1.3 g sugars	(The starch and sugar content of this dish is low)
37.1 g protein	(A chef may need about 75 g of protein each day. Most people have no problem achieving this)
0.7 g fibre	(Negligible fibre content. This dish contributes little toward the 30 g per day which is recommended for health)

The sample recipe of Veal escalope cordon bleu (see page 311) has 48.1 g (nearly 2 oz) of *fat* per portion, which is high, and over one third of this is saturated. The *energy* (Calories) supplied per portion is high and about three quarters of this energy is from fat. A glance at the recipe shows where it all comes from: ham and cheese are added to the meat which is then breaded and fried in butter and oil. The dish is served with more butter. It may be possible to make significant reductions in the fat content without forfeiting too much in terms of flavour, texture or appearance of the finished entrée.

The recipe is also low in *carbohydrate* and *dietary fibre* because meat has virtually none of these; the amounts from the breadcrumbs and seasoned flour being insignificant. The dish may be eaten with vegetables, like potatoes and broccoli, which would boost the starch and fibre content of the meal and at the same time dilute its fat content.

In general, by adding or augmenting dishes with different accompaniments the nutritional profile of the resulting complete meal can change and may shift towards something more healthy. The aim is to provide proportionately more calories from starchy carbohydrates and fewer from fats and sugars. In food terms this means more potatoes, pasta, rice or bread on the plate, together with greater quantities of vegetables, particularly pulses – a change in meal concept for many people. The addition of a jacket potato and a portion of peas to the braised beef recipe below shows the important effects that these accompaniments have, particularly as most of the energy is now coming from the carbohydrate rather than from fat. Carbohydrate has, as a consequence, increased from 2 g to 37.8 g, and the fibre content has improved.

Energy from carbohydrates rather than fats

Braised beef	Braised beef served with jacket potato and peas
1 portion provides:	
175 kcals/717 kJ	380 kcals/1595 kJ
13.9 g fat of which 3.3 g saturated	14.5 g fat of which 3.4 g saturated
2.0 g carbohydrate of which 1.9 g sugars	37.8 g carbohydrate of which 0.3 g sugars
18.1 g protein	26.9 g protein
0.6 g fibre	4.6 g fibre

How can the analyses be used?

By comparing the nutritional content of individual recipes with the recommendations put forward in the NACNE and COMA reports, it is possible to interpret their value in terms of health. However it can still be difficult to tell whether the levels of fat, fibre or sugar are 'high' or 'low'. The Coronary Prevention Group has developed an ingenious scheme which can help us do just this. Their system of banding the nutrients in foods into categories of high, medium and low when compared to a set of suggested criteria involves a number of fairly complicated calculations which are best done with help from a trained dietitian. Once this type of banding has been done the information can be used in many different ways, particularly with a view to providing customer information. This will enable customers to choose a healthy combination of items from any menu. Consumers are becoming more interested in the nutritional breakdown of the foods on offer and, if caterers provide this information, it must be accurate and presented in an understandable way.

Nutritional analysis of recipes can be used to provide:

- menu labelling schemes, such as the 'traffic light' scheme, which has been used in schools to register the fat and sugar content of foods. This system has been successfully introduced where the colour coding is explained in class and used in the schools meals service,
- recipe cards or handouts for customers which include the nutritional breakdown,
- posters and leaflets detailing nutritional information for customers,
- articles for in-house company magazines, local or national press,
- healthier standard recipes,
- specific marketing initiatives, such as healthy eating days, healthy eating promotion buffets, etc, which help to consolidate healthy catering practice.

Further information

Department of Health (COMA) (1984) *Diet and Cardiovascular Disease*, London: HMSO

Health Education Authority (NACNE) (1983) *Proposals for Nutritional Guidelines for Health Education in Britain*, London: HEA

Health Education Authority (1987) *Guide to Healthy Eating*, London: HEA

Paul, A A and Southgate, D A T (1978) *McCance and Widdowson's: The Composition of Foods*, 4th ed, London: HMSO

A selection of healthy catering recipes

Department of Health (1989) *Catering for Health, Recipe File*, London: HMSO

Robbins, C (1989) *The Healthy Catering Manual*, London: Dorling Kindersley

Stevenson, D and Scobie, P (1987) *Catering for Health*, London: Hutchinson

Examples of various foods deep fried with different coatings (clockwise from top): apple fritters (p. 503); French fried onions (p. 427); croquette potatoes (p. 439)

3

METHODS OF COOKERY

Having read the chapter these general and specific objectives should be achieved.

General objectives
To have a knowledge and understanding of the methods or processes of cookery and to be aware of the simple scientific, artistic and commercial implications to be considered regarding food preparation.

Specific objectives
To be able to state which, why and how foods are cooked by the various methods, to explain why this is so in relation to nutritional, menu and economic factors. To select suitable equipment to use for each process.

The transference of heat to food

All methods of cooking depend on one or more of the following principles.

Radiation

Heat passes from its source in direct rays until it falls on an object in its path, e.g. grilling.

Conduction

This is the transferring of heat through a solid object by contact. Some materials, e.g. metal used for pans, transfer heat more quickly than say wood used for wooden spoons. Conduction is the principle involved in the use of solid electric hot plate.

Convection

This is the movement of heated particles of gases or liquids. On heating, the particles expand, become less dense and rise. The colder particles sink to take their place, thus causing convection currents which distribute heat. This principle is used in heating a gas oven and in the heating of liquids.

The effect of heat on food

Protein

Protein is coagulated by heat. The process is gradual, for example when heat is applied to egg white it thickens, becomes opaque and then firm. Over-heating will harden the protein, making it tough, unpalatable and shrunken. This characteristic coagulation of protein when heated is employed in its use as a coating for deep and shallow fried foods and in the development of crust in bread formed by the protein gluten in wheat.

Carbohydrates

Effect of *moist heat* on starch: moist heat causes the starch grains to soften and swell. Near boiling point the cellulose framework bursts, releasing the starch which thickens the liquid.

Effect of *dry heat* on starch: the starch changes colour from creamy white to brown and after prolonged heat will carbonise and burn. Water is given off during heating and the starch on the surface is changed to dextrin, a form of sugar, e.g. toast.

Effect of *moist heat* on sugar: sugar dissolves in water – more rapidly in hot water than in cold. On heating it becomes syrup; on further heating it colours then caramelises and will eventually turn to carbon and ash.

Effect of *dry heat* on sugar: sugar will quickly caramelise and burn.

Fats

Fats melt to oils when heated. Water is given off with a bubbling noise as heating continues. When all the water has been driven off a faint blue haze appears, further heating will result in smoking and burning. The unpleasant smell of burning fat is caused by the presence of fatty acids.

Vitamins

Vitamin A and *carotene* are insoluble in water so they are not lost by moist methods of cooking, such as boiling and steaming, or by soaking. Therefore boiled vegetables contain the same amount of carotene as raw vegetables.

Vitamin D is not destroyed by heat or lost by solubility.

Thiamine, vitamin B_1, is very soluble in water and about 50% will dissolve in the cooking liquid. High temperatures, e.g. pressure cooking, destroy vitamin B_1 and alkali (baking powder) will cause some destruction.

Riboflavin, vitamin B_2, is soluble in water and will dissolve out in the cooking liquid, some is lost in normal cooking but more losses occur in pressure cooking.

Nicotinic acid, or *niacin*, is soluble in water and dissolves to some extent in the cooking liquid. It is stable in the presence of heat but is easily oxidised, which means that the chemical process of the products is adversely affected by taking in oxygen.

Vitamin C is lost or destroyed very easily in cooking and care must be taken to preserve it as much as possible. It is soluble in water and is easily dissolved in cleaning and cooking water; therefore vegetables containing vitamin C should not be soaked in water and cooking liquid should be made use of. It is best to cook in small quantities and as quickly as possible as vitamin C is destroyed by heat. Raw fruit and vegetables contain most vitamin C.

Vitamin C oxidises (see nicotinic acid) to form a substance which is useless to the body, to minimise oxidation cook with a lid on; also food containing vitamin C should only be stored for short periods and must be used as fresh as possible.

There is an enzyme present with Vitamin C in foods which, once the cells of the plant are damaged by bruising or cutting, begins to destroy the vitamin by oxidising it. The optimum or most favourable condition for destruction of the enzyme is between 65 °–88 °C so if the vegetable is put into boiling water the enzyme activity will be quickly destroyed.

Ways of cooking food

1 Boiling
2 Poaching
3 Stewing
4 Braising
5 Steaming
6 Baking
7 Roasting
8 Grilling
9 Frying (shallow and deep)
10 Paper bag (en papillotte)
11 Microwave
12 Pot roasting (*poêlé*)

Included in each method of cookery are examples of food cooked by that method, with the page number. To locate other recipes use the chapter or main index.

Variations in definition and classification of cookery processes occur because certain words used in English may not correspond exactly with French words. For example,

a) Boiled turbot in English, *Turbot poché* in French;
b) Boiled chicken in English, *Poulet poché* in French;
c) Stewed or poached fruits in English, *Compote des fruits* in French.

Boiling

Definition

Boiling is the cooking of prepared foods in a liquid at boiling point. This could be water, court-bouillon, milk or stock.

Purpose

The purpose of boiling is to cook food so that it is:

a) Pleasant to eat with an agreeable flavour,
b) Suitable texture, tender or slightly firm according to the food,
c) Easy to digest,
d) Safe to eat.

Methods

There are two ways of boiling:

i) Place the food into boiling liquid, reboil, then reduce the heat for gentle boiling to take place, this is known as simmering;
ii) Cover food with cold liquid, bring to the boil, then reduce heat to allow food to simmer.

Examples of foods cooked by boiling

Stocks – beef, mutton, chicken, fish p. 91.
Glazes – p. 92, fish, meat p. 92.
Sauces – brown p. 98, white p. 94, curry p. 104, jam p. 526.
Soups – tomato p. 160, Scotch broth p. 156.
Eggs – pp. 180–2.
Farinaceous – spaghetti p. 193, noodles p. 196.
Fish – skate p. 231, turbot p. 223, cod p. 224, salmon p. 224.
Meats – beef silverside p. 279, leg of mutton p. 252, leg of pork p. 325, bacon p. 333.
Chicken – p. 359.
Vegetables – cabbage p. 415, carrots p. 413.
Potatoes – pp. 437 and 449.
Sweets and pastry – milk pudding p. 513, sugar p. 537.

Boiling crab (p. 126)

Effects of boiling

Gentle boiling helps to break down the tough fibrous structure of certain foods which would be less tender if cooked by other methods. When boiling meats for long periods the soluble meat extracts are dissolved in the cooking liquid. Cooking must be slow in order to give time for the connective tissue in tough meat to be changed into soluble gelatine, so releasing the fibres and making the meat tender. If the connective tissue gelatinises too quickly the meat fibres fall apart and the meat will be tough and stringy. Gentle heat will ensure coagulation of the protein without hardening.

Advantages of boiling

1 Older, tougher, cheaper joints of meat and poultry can be made palatable and digestible.
2 It is appropriate for large scale cookery and is economic on fuel.
3 Nutritious, well-flavoured stock can be produced.
4 Labour saving, as boiling needs little attention.
5 It is a safe, quick and simple procedure to add the required amount of liquid.

The advantages of food started slowly in cold liquid, brought to the boil and allowed to boil gently:

1 Helps to tenderise the fibrous structure (meat), extracts starch (vegetable soups) and flavour from certain foods (stocks).
2 Can avoid damage to foods which would lose their shape if added to boiling liquid, e.g. whole fish.

The advantages of adding food to boiling liquid:

1 Suitable for green vegetables as maximum colour and nutritive value are retained, provided boiling is restricted to the minimum time.
2 Seals in the natural juices as with meat.

Time and temperature control

Temperature must be controlled so that the liquid is brought to the boil, or reboil, then adjusted in order that gentle boiling takes place until the food is cooked to the required degree. Stocks, soups and sauces must only simmer, spaghetti cooked slightly firm (al dente), meat and poultry well cooked and tender; vegetables should not be overcooked.

Although approximate cooking times are given for most foods, the age, quality and size of various foods will nevertheless affect the cooking time required.

Techniques associated with boiling

Soaking

Prior to boiling, this is the covering in cold water of certain foods, e.g. dried vegetables, to soften them; salted meats, to extract some of the salt.

Skimming

This is the removal of scum, grease and other impurities from the surface of the liquid.

Blanching and refreshing

i) in cold water – place foods, e.g. bones, in cold water, bring to boil and wash off under cold running water until clean;
ii) in hot water – plunge into boiling water and refresh, e.g. for removing skins from tomatoes.

Equipment

Examples of equipment used for boiling include stock pots, saucepans, boiling pans and bratt pans. Thoroughly wash with hot detergent, water rinse with hot water and dry. Equipment with moving parts should be greased occasionally. Further information: refer to *The Theory of Catering* (6th edn.) p. 207.

Handle equipment carefully to avoid damage and store pans upside-down on clean racks. Check that equipment is clean before use and that the handles are not loose. Copper pans *must* be completely tinned inside.

Any faults, particularly with large equipment, must be reported.

General rules

a) Select pans which are neither too small or large.
b) When cooking in boiling liquid ensure there is sufficient liquid and that it is at boiling point before adding food.
c) Frequently skim during the cooking.
d) Simmer whenever possible so as to minimise evaporation, maintain volume of liquid and minimise shrinkage.

Safety

1 Select containers of the right capacity – if too small there is danger of boiling liquid splashing over, forming steam and causing scalds.
2 Always move pans of boiling liquid on the stove with care.
3 Position pan handles so that they do not protrude from stove or become hot over the heat.
4 Extra care is required when adding or removing foods from containers of boiling liquid.

Poaching

Poaching an egg (p. 183)

Definition

The cooking of foods in the required amount of liquid at just below boiling point.

Purpose

The purpose of poaching food is to cook food so that it is:

a) Easy to digest;
b) A suitable tender texture;
c) Safe to eat;
d) Pleasant to eat because, where appropriate, an agreeable sauce is made with the cooking liquid.

Methods

There are two ways of poaching: a) shallow and b) deep.

a) Shallow poaching. Foods, e.g. cuts of fish and chicken, to be cooked by this method are cooked in the minimum of liquid, that is, water, stock, milk or wine. The liquid should never be allowed to boil but kept at a temperature as near to boiling point as possible.
To prevent the liquid boiling, bring to the boil on top of the stove and complete the cooking in a moderate hot oven, approximately 180 °C.

b) Deep poaching. Eggs are cooked in approximately 8 cm (3 in) of gently simmering water. (The practice of poaching eggs in individual shallow metal pans over boiling water is cooking by steaming.) The English term boiling is frequently used for what in French is called *poché* (poached). Boiled cod, salmon, turbot and chicken are referred to as boiled in English and poché in French. Whole fish and chicken are covered in cold liquid, brought to the boil and allowed to simmer gently until cooked. Cuts of fish on the bone, e.g. fish steaks (tronçon and darne) are placed into simmering liquid and cooked gently.

Examples of foods which are poached

Eggs – poached, p. 183.
Farinaceous – gnocchi parisienne, p. 199.

Fish – shallow poaching, pp. 225–30.
deep poaching (boiled), pp. 223–5.
Poultry – p. 359.
Fruits – fresh and dried, p. 509.

Effects of poaching

Poaching helps to tenderise the fibrous structure of the food, and the raw texture of the food becomes edible by chemical action.

Techniques associated with poaching

Cutting and tying

This is the cutting of foods in even pieces and tying to retain shape and give ease of handling.

Folding

Certain foods, e.g. fish fillets, are made neater and smaller by folding in half or in three.

Draining

This is to dry off all the cooking liquid from the food before being served or coated with a sauce.

Reducing for sauce

This is to strain off the cooking liquor after the food is cooked. Then by rapid boiling, the cooking liquor is reduced and added to, or used as the basis for, the accompanying or coating sauce.

Holding for service

Means keeping food hot after it is cooked until it is ready to be served.

Time and temperature control

a) Temperature must be controlled so that the cooking liquor does not fall below, or exceed, the correct degree required:
shallow poaching, just below simmering point;
deep poaching, just below gentle simmering.
b) Time – to ensure the food is correctly cooked. It is important that the food is neither undercooked, therefore unpalatable, or overcooked, when it will break up and also lose nutritive value.
c) The various types and qualities of food will affect both time and temperature needed to achieve successful poaching.

Equipment

Suitable-sized trays, pans or ovenproof dishes are used for poaching. They should be washed immediately after use in hot detergent water, rinsed in clean hot water and dried.

When handling, use equipment carefully to avoid damage or breakage; do not use excessive heat or plunge hot pans or dishes into cold water. Store pans and trays upside-down on clean racks and ovenproof dishes on clean cupboard shelves.

Always check equipment is clean before use, do not use cracked ovenproof dishes, as they may break in the oven. Report any faulty dishes and breakages.

Safety

1 Select suitable-sized pans to prevent spillage and possible scalding.
2 Move trays etc. carefully on and off stove, or from the oven, as tilting or jarring may cause spillage.
3 Carefully place food in the pan when adding to simmering liquid.
4 When a hot container is removed from the oven, sprinkle with a little flour to warn that it is hot.

Stewing

Definition

Stewing is the slow cooking of food cut into pieces and cooked in the minimum amount of liquid (water, stock or sauce); the food and liquid are served together.

Purpose

Because stewing is both economical and nutritional, cheaper cuts of meat and poultry, which would be unsuitable for roasting and grilling, can be made tender and palatable.

Stewing also produces an acceptable flavour, texture and eating quality.

Methods of stewing

All stews have a thickened consistency achieved by:

a) The unpassed ingredients in the stew, e.g. Irish stew;
b) Thickening of the cooking liquor, e.g. *blanquette* (white stew);
c) Cooking in the sauce, e.g. brown stew.

Stewed foods can be cooked in a covered pan on the stove or in a moderate oven.

Foods cooked by stewing

Fish – bouillabaisse (French soup/stew).
Meat – goulash p. 287, minced beef p. 293, haricot mutton p. 260, Irish stew p. 258, brown stew of veal p. 306, white stew of veal p. 306.
Poultry – chicken fricassée p. 364, curried chicken p. 367, tripe and onions p. 295, jugged hare p. 373.
Vegetables – marrow provençale p. 420, ratatouille p. 411.

Effects of stewing

In the slow process of cooking in gentle heat the connective tissue in meat and poultry is converted into a gelatinous substance so that the fibres fall apart easily and become digestible. The protein is coagulated without being toughened. Unlike boiling, less liquid is used and the cooking temperature is approximately 5 °C lower.

See also 'effects of boiling' p. 40 as this also applies to stewing.

Advantages

a) The meat juices which escape from the meat during cooking are retained in the liquid which is part of the stew.
b) Correct slow cooking results in very little evaporation.
c) Nutrients are conserved.
d) Tenderises tough foods.
e) Economical in labour because foods can be cooked in bulk.

Temperature and time control

1 Temperature control is essential to the slow cooking required for efficient stewing, therefore the liquid must barely simmer.
2 A tight fitting lid is used to retain steam which helps maintain temperature and reduce evaporation.
3 Time will vary according to the quality of the food used.
4 The ideal cooking temperature for stewing on top of the stove is approximately 82 °C (simmering temperature); cooking in the oven at gas mark 3, 170 °C.

Techniques associated with stewing

Blanching and refreshing

When food is covered with cold water, brought to the boil, and rinsed until clean under cold water.

Preparation for Irish stew (p. 258)

Setting and browning

Rapid shallow frying of food in oil or fat to *seal in* the goodness, and enhance the flavour and colour.

Blending in the liquid

The gradual mixing of the warm liquid to the other ingredients of the stew.

Equipment

Examples of equipment used for stewing include saucepans, boiling pans and bratt pans. Ovenproof dishes can be used for stewing in the oven.

Care and cleanliness

Thoroughly wash with hot detergent water, rinse with hot water and dry. Moving parts of large-scale equipment should be greased occasionally. Store pans upside-down on clean racks. Check that handles are not loose and that copper pans are completely tinned. Any faults with large equipment should be reported.

General rules

1 Stews should not be over-thickened: the sauce should be light in consistency, therefore correct ratios of thickening agents are essential.
2 Adjustment to the consistency should be made as required during cooking.
3 Overcooking causes: (a) evaporation of liquid; (b) breaking up of the food; (c) discoloration; and (d) spoilage of flavour.

Safety

1 Select suitable-sized pans.
2 Care is essential when removing hot pans from the oven.
3 When removing lids be careful of escaping steam, which may cause scalds.
4 Sprinkle flour on hot pans and lids after removal from the oven as a warning that they are hot.
5 Move pans of hot food with care.
6 Ensure that pan handles are not over heat or sticking out from the stove.
7 Carefully remove food from pans of hot liquid.

Braising

Definition

Braising is a method of cooking in the oven; unlike roasting or baking the food is cooked in liquid in a covered pan, casserole or cocotte. It is a combination of stewing and pot roasting.

Purpose

a) To give variety to the menu and the diet.
b) To make food tender, digestible, palatable and safe to eat.
c) To produce and enhance flavour, texture and eating quality.

Preparation for braised beef (p. 290)

Methods of braising

There are two methods: brown braising, used for joints and portion-sized cuts of meat; white braising, used for vegetables and sweetbreads.

1 Brown braising:
   a) Joints, e.g. beef, venison, are marinaded and may be larded then sealed quickly by browning on all sides in a hot oven or in a pan on the stove. Sealing the joints helps retain flavour, nutritive value and gives a good brown colour. Joints are then placed on a bed of roots in a braising pan, with the liquid and other flavourings, covered with a lid and cooked slowly in the oven.
   b) Cuts, e.g. steaks, chops, liver. The brown braising of cuts of meat is similar to that of joints.
2 White braising: e.g. celery, cabbage and sweetbreads. These are blanched, refreshed, cooked on a bed of roots with white stock in a covered container in the oven.

Examples of foods which are braised

Farinaceous – rice p. 201.
Meat: lamb – hearts p. 264, chops p. 250.
  beef – olives p. 292, joints p. 290, liver p. 297.
  veal – shoulder p. 309.
Poultry – duck p. 368.
Vegetables – celery p. 414, onions p. 427.

Effects of braising

Cooking by braising causes the breakdown of the tissue fibre in the structure of certain foods which softens the texture, thus making it tender and edible. The texture is also improved by being cooked in the braising liquid.

Advantages

1 Tougher, less expensive meats and poultry can be used.
2 Maximum flavour and nutritional value are retained.
3 Variety of presentation and flavour is given to the menu.

Time and temperature control

1 Slow cooking is essential for efficient braising, the liquid must barely simmer.
2 To reduce evaporation and maintain temperature use a tight-fitting lid.
3 Time needed for braising will vary according to the quality of the food.
4 Ideal oven temperature for braising is 160 °C, gas mark 3.

Techniques associated with braising

Sealing

Applying heat to the surface of the meat to prevent the escape of natural juices.

Larding

Inserting strips of fat bacon into meat.

Marinating

Steeping food in a richly spiced pickling liquid to give flavour and to assist in tenderising.

Sweating

The extraction of flavour without colouring; e.g. vegetables in fat.

Basting

Frequent spooning of cooking liquid over meat to moisten.

Blending

To bring together different flavours and textures, e.g. mixing cornflour and milk; adding marinade to the sauce.

Refreshing

To make cold under running cold water.

Browning

The application of heat to colour the surface.

Equipment

Thick-bottomed pans or ovenproof dishes with tight-fitting lids and handles are essential for braising. Bratt pans and jacket boilers may be used in large-scale catering.

Steeping (soaking in warm water) may be necessary to assist cleaning. Thoroughly wash with hot detergent water, rinse with hot water and dry.

Handle equipment carefully to avoid damage and store pans upside-down on clean racks. Ensure that equipment is clean before use and that the handles are secure.

General rules

These are the same as for stewing. However, if the joint is to be served whole, the lid is removed three-quarters of the way through cooking. The joint is then frequently basted to give a glaze for presentation.

Safety

1 Select a suitable size pan with tight-fitting lid and handles.
2 Care is required when removing hot pans from the oven and when removing the lid.
3 Immediately sprinkle flour on hot pans and lids as a warning.

Steaming

Definition

Steaming is the cooking of prepared foods by steam (moist heat) under varying degrees of pressure.

Purpose

The purpose of steaming food is to cook it so that it is:

a) Easy to digest;
b) Of an edible texture and pleasant to eat;
c) Safe to eat;
d) As nutritious as possible (steaming minimises nutritive loss).

Preparation for steamed sponge pudding (p. 499)

Methods of steaming

1 Atmospheric or low pressure steaming – food may be cooked by direct or indirect contact with the steam:
   a) direct, in a steamer or in a pan of boiling water, e.g. steak and kidney pudding;
   b) indirect, between two plates over a pan of boiling water.
2 High pressure steaming in purpose-built equipment, which does not allow the steam to escape, therefore enabling steam pressure to build up, thus increasing the temperature and reducing cooking time.

Vacuum cooking in a pouch

Known as *sous-vide*, this is a method of cooking in which food contained in vacuum-sealed plastic pouches is cooked by steam (see also *The Theory of Catering*, Ch. 6). The advantages of sous-vide cooking of food are:

1 Minimal change of texture and weight loss;
2 No drying out and very little colour loss;
3 Dishes can be garnished and decorated before the vacuum packing and cooking process;
4 The food cooks in its own natural juices;
5 Labour saving;
6 Uniformity of standard.

Method for vacuum cooking

Raw food products, e.g. cuts of fish, breast of chicken or duck, are lightly seasoned and any required cut vegetables, herbs, spices, stock or wine added and placed into specially developed plastic pouches.

A vacuum packing machine seals the pouch, which is then cooked in a temperature-controlled convection steam cooker. The length of cooking time must be carefully controlled. Once cooked, the pouch is quickly cooled and kept at a temperature of 3 °C.

When required for service the pouches are either placed in boiling water or a steam oven.

Examples of foods suitable for steaming

Fish – which is boiled or poached may be steamed. Recipes pp. 223–30.
Meat – tongue p. 296, ham and bacon pp. 334–6, meat pudding p. 285.
Vegetables – potatoes in jackets p. 441. Almost all vegetables can be cooked by this method using very high pressure steamers.
Sweet puddings – suet p. 497, sponge p. 499.

Effects of steaming

When food is steamed the structure and texture is changed by chemical action and becomes edible. The texture will vary according to the type of food, type of steamer and degree of heat, e.g. sponges and puddings are lighter in texture if steamed rather than baked.

Advantages of steaming

1 Retention of goodness (nutritional value).
2 Makes some foods lighter and easy to digest, e.g. suitable for invalids.
3 Low pressure steaming reduces risk of overcooking protein.
4 High pressure steaming enables food to be cooked or reheated quickly because steam is forced through the food, thus cooking it rapidly.

5 Labour-saving and suitable for large-scale cookery.
6 High-speed steamers used for 'batch' cooking enable the frequent cooking of small quantities of vegetables throughout the service. The advantage is that the vegetables are freshly cooked – retaining colour, flavour and nutritive value.
7 With steamed fish, the natural juices can be retained by serving with the fish or in making the accompanying sauce.
8 Steaming is economical on fuel as a low heat is needed and a multi-tiered steamer can be used.

Time and temperature control

Foods should be placed in the steamer when the pressure gauge indicates the required degree of pressure. This will ensure that the necessary cooking temperature has been reached.

Cooking times will vary according to the equipment used and the type, size and quality of food to be steamed. Manufacturers' instructions are an essential guide to successful steaming.

Techniques associated with steaming

Preparation of container

Ensure inside of container or mould is clean and lightly coated with fat or oil, known as *greasing*.

Moulding

The placing of prepared food into prepared moulds.

Traying up

The filling of trays with moulds or containers to facilitate handling.

Loading

The placing of the trays in the steamer.

Covering and waterproofing

The efficient protection of foods cooked in moulds, using protective paper and foil to prevent penetration of moisture which would make the product soggy.

Equipment

In addition to the plate and perforated container there are four types of steamer – atmospheric, pressure, high pressure and pressureless convection. See page 215 *The Theory of Catering*.

Cleaning

The inside of the steamer, trays and runners are washed in hot detergent water, rinsed and dried. Where applicable the water-generating chamber should be drained, cleaned and refilled. Door controls should be lightly greased occasionally and the door left open slightly to allow air to circulate when the steamer is not in use.

Before use check that the steamer is clean and safe to use. Any fault must be reported immediately.

Metal containers, e.g. sleeves and basins, may be thoroughly cleaned with kitchen paper or a clean cloth; other containers must be washed in hot detergent water, rinsed in hot water and dried. Containers are stored in closed cupboards.

Specific points

Puddings – meat and sweet. Basins must be greased, then after being filled, efficiently covered with greased greaseproof or silicone paper and foil to prevent moisture penetrating and resulting in a soggy pudding.

Safety factors

1 Where applicable, check that the water in the water well is at the correct level and that the ball-valve arm moves freely.
2 Before opening steamer door allow steam pressure to be reduced.
3 Take extra care when opening the door, use it as a shield from escaping steam as a severe scald may result.
4 Follow manufacturers' instructions at all times regarding cleaning and operating procedures.

Baking

Definition

Baking is the cooking of food by dry heat in an oven in which the action of the dry convection heat is modified by steam.

Purpose

a) To make food digestible, palatable and safe to eat.
b) To create eye-appeal through colour and texture and produce an enjoyable eating quality.
c) Baked goods lend variety to the menu and are popular in the diet.

Methods

Note Ovens must be pre-heated prior to baking.

1 Dry baking: when baking, steam arises from the water content of the food; this steam combines with the dry heat of the oven to cook the food, e.g. cakes, pastry, baked jacket potatoes.
2 Baking with increased humidity: when baking certain foods, e.g. bread, the oven humidity is increased by placing a bowl of water or injection steam into the oven, thus increasing the water content of the food and so improving eating quality.
3 Baking with heat modification: placing food in a container of water (bain-marie), e.g. baked egg custard, modifies the heat so that the food cooks more slowly, does not over-heat and lessens the possibility of the egg mixture overcooking.

Examples of foods cooked by baking

Eggs – in cocottes p. 179.
Meat – Steak and kidney pie p. 289.
  Toad in the hole p. 328.
  Cornish pasties p. 259.
  Shepherds pie p. 261.
Chicken vol-au-vent p. 361.
Baked jacket potatoes p. 440.
Baked apples p. 505.
Fruit flans p. 479.
Baked egg custard p. 515.
Fruit buns p. 473.
Cakes p. 463.

Flan and band baked blind (p. 479)

Effect of baking

Chemical action caused by the effect of heat on certain ingredients, e.g. yeast, baking powder, changes the raw structure of many foods to an edible texture, e.g. pastry, cakes. However, different ingredients, methods of mixing, and types of product required will cause many variations.

Advantages of baking

1 A wide variety of sweet and savoury foods can be produced.
2 Bakery products yield appetising goods with eye-appeal and mouth-watering aromas.
3 Bulk cooking can be achieved with uniformity of colour and degree of cooking.

4 Baking ovens have effective manual or automatic temperature controls.
5 There is straightforward access for loading and removal of items.

Time and temperature control

1 Ovens must always be heated to the required temperature before the food is added.
2 In general purpose ovens, shelves must be placed according to the food being cooked, because the hotter part of the oven is at the top. With convection ovens the heat is evenly distributed.
3 Accurate timing and temperature control are essential to baking. The required oven temperature must be reached before each additional batch of goods is placed in the oven. This is known as recovery time.

Techniques associated with baking

Greasing

Trays and tins are usually greased to prevent food sticking.

Marking

Some goods are marked with a sharp blade to indicate portions prior to baking. The cooked portions can then be evenly divided. Marking may be for decoration and to assist even cooking, e.g. bread.

Loading

This is the economic use of oven space to ensure the maximum amount of food is organised to be baked, thus minimising time and use of energy.

Brushing

This may occur before, during or after baking:
Before – eggwash on pastry, e.g. sausage rolls to colour.
During – milk wash on breadrolls, to improve appearance.
After – sugar wash on fruit buns to give gloss.

Cooling

This is the placing of baked goods on wire grids or racks so that air circulates and prevents the base becoming soggy.

Finishing

This is the final operation on certain baked goods to improve presentation, e.g. (a) bun wash on hot cross buns, (b) using sugar sprinkled on cooked puff pastry and returned to a very hot oven to caramelise the sugar to give a gloss finish – this is known as *glazing*.

Recovery time

This is the time required for the oven temperature to reach the correct degree before cooking each batch of food.

Dusting

This is the light sprinkling of flour, which occurs:

1 Prior to baking
   a) when rolling or moulding pastry goods;
   b) onto trays for certain bread and rolls; or
   c) onto certain bread and rolls;
2 After baking, e.g. using sugar on puff pastry.

Equipment

Refer to *The Theory of Catering* pp. 208–210. Pastry ovens are specially designed for the baking of pastry goods. They are shallow in height and obtainable in one, two, three or four decks.

Small equipment

Baking sheets are made of black wrought steel. The less they are washed the less likely they are to cause foods to stick. New baking sheets should be heated in a hot oven, wiped clean and lightly oiled. Before use, lightly grease. After use, while still warm, clean by scraping and dry wiping. If washing is necessary use hot detergent water, rinse in hot water and dry.

Tartlet moulds and cake tins should be cared for in the same way. For further information on utensils see *The Theory of Catering* pp. 233–242.

General rules

1 Always pre-heat ovens so that the required cooking temperature is immediately applied to the product, otherwise the product will be spoiled.
2 Accuracy is essential in weighing, measuring and controlling temperature.
3 Trays and moulds must be correctly prepared.
4 Minimise the opening of oven doors as draughts may affect the quality of the product, and oven temperature is reduced.
5 Utilise oven space efficiently.
6 Avoid jarring of products before and during baking as the quality may be affected, e.g. fruit cake, sponges, soufflés.

Safety

1 Use thick, dry, sound oven cloths for handling hot trays etc.
2 Jacket sleeves should be rolled down to prevent burns from hot trays and ovens.
3 Trays and ovens should not be overloaded.
4 Extra care is needed to balance and handle loaded trays in and out of the oven.

Roasting

Definition

Roasting is cooking in dry heat with the aid of fat or oil in an oven or on a spit. Radiant heat is the means of cooking when using a spit; oven roasting is a combination of convection and radiation.

Purpose

The purpose of roasting is to cook food so that it is tender, easy to digest, safe to eat, and palatable. Also to give variety to the menu and the diet.

Methods

1 Placing prepared foods e.g. meat, poultry, on a rotating spit over or in front of fierce radiated heat.
2 Placing prepared foods in an oven with either:
   a) applied dry heat;
   b) forced air-convected heat;
   c) convected heat combined with microwave energy.

Examples of foods suitable for roasting

Meat: lamb – best-end p. 248.
  beef – sirloin p. 278.
  pork – leg p. 325.
  veal – stuffed breast p. 314.
Poultry and game – chicken p. 351, duck p. 369, pheasant p. 376.
Vegetables – potatoes p. 447, parsnips p. 432.

Effects of roasting

The surface protein of the food is sealed by the initial heat of the oven, thus sealing it and preventing the escape of too many natural juices. When the food is lightly browned, oven temperature is reduced to cook the inside without hardening the surface of the food.

Advantages

1 Good quality meat and poultry is tender and succulent when roasted.
2 Meat juices issuing from the joint are used for gravy and enhance flavour.
3 By careful use both energy and oven temperature can be controlled.
4 Ovens with transparent doors enable cooking to be observed.
5 Access, adjustment and removal of items is straightforward.
6 Minimal fire risk.

Spit roasting

1 Skill and techniques can be displayed to the customer.
2 Continual basting with the meat juice over the carcass or joint on the revolving spit give a distinctive flavour, depending on the fuel used e.g. wood, charcoal.

Time and temperature control

1 Ovens must be preheated.
2 Oven temperature and shelf settings in recipes must be followed.
3 Shape, size, type, bone proportion and quality of food will affect the cooking time.
4 Meat thermometers or probes can be inserted to determine the exact temperature in the centre of the joint.
5 See table of approximate cooking times:

	Approximate cooking times	**Degree of cooking**
Beef	15 min per ½ kg (1 lb) and 15 min over	Underdone
Lamb	20 min per ½ kg (1 lb) and 20 min over	Cooked through
Lamb	15 min per ½ kg (1 lb) and 15 min over	Cooked pink
Mutton	20 min per ½ kg (1 lb) and 20 min over	Cooked through
Veal	20 min per ½ kg (1 lb) and 25 min over	Cooked through
Pork	25 min per ½ kg (1 lb) and 25 min over	Thoroughly cooked

Techniques associated with roasting

Boning out

The removal of bones from raw meat to facilitate carving.

Tying

The securing of meat with string to retain shape.

Trussing

The tying of poultry with string to keep in shape.

Metal trivet

A trivet (or grid) is used to raise the joint from the fat in the roasting tray to prevent the joint from frying.

Basting

This is the frequent spooning of the melted fat and juices over the food during cooking to keep it moist, and assist in colouring.

Basting best-end of lamb during roasting (p. 248)

Testing for cooking

To test if cooked, press the surface of the meat and squeeze out some meat juice. If the juice runs:

a) red – meat is underdone;
b) pink – meat is medium cooked;
c) clear – meat is cooked through.

Equipment

See *The Theory of Catering* p. 208 for general purpose oven, forced air convection and combined forced air/microwave.

Spits are either independent or built into an oven. Meat or poultry are impaled and secured on a rod which is continuously revolved over, or in front of, heat, e.g. wood, gas, electricity or charcoal.

Meat probes are thermometers designed to be pierced into the centre of joints to give a reading of the internal temperature.

Trays used for roasting must be strong, with handles, and kept in good repair.

Ovens should be cleaned whilst warm, using hot detergent water and a mild abrasive if necessary. Rinse with hot water. Steep trays and removable parts of spit if necessary, wash in hot detergent water, rinse and dry thoroughly and store upside-down on clean racks. Clean and grease moving parts of spits.

Any faults must be reported immediately and ovens must be inspected and serviced regularly.

Safety

Roasting trays should be of the suitable size: if too small, basting becomes difficult and dangerous; if too large, fat in the tray will burn – spoiling the flavour of meat and gravy.

Handle hot roasting trays carefully at all times, using a thick dry sound cloth.

Ensure food is securely held before removing from roasting tray.

Grilling

Definition

This is a fast method of cooking by radiant heat sometimes known as broiling.

Purpose

a) To make foods digestible, palatable and safe to eat.
b) To utilise the speed of the cooking process to produce a distinctive flavour, colour, texture and eating quality.
c) To bring variety to the menu and to introduce into the diet simple, uncomplicated dishes.

Methods of grilling

Grilled foods can be cooked:
a) Over heat – e.g. charcoal, barbecues, gas or electric heated grills;
b) Under heat – gas or electric salamanders (overfired grills);
c) Between heat – electrically heated grill bars or plates.

Over heat

Grill bars must be preheated and brushed with oil prior to use, otherwise food will stick. The bars should char the food on both sides to give the distinctive appearance and flavour of grilling. Most foods are started on the hottest part of the grill and moved to a cooler part to complete the cooking. The thickness of the food and the heat of the grill determine the cooking time, which is learned by experience.

Degrees of cooking grills		Appearance of juice issuing from the meat when pressed
Rare	*au bleu*	Red and bloody
Underdone	*saignant*	Reddish pink
Just done	*à point*	Pink
Well done	*bien cuit*	Clear

Under heat (Salamander)

1 Cooking on the salamander bars; the salamander should be preheated and the bars greased. Steaks, chops and items that are likely to slip between the grill bars may be cooked under the salamander.
2 Cooking between a double wire grid; food items that are difficult to handle because they may easily break up may be placed in between a well-greased, centre-hinged, double wire grid with a handle, making it both easy and swift to cook the food, e.g. whole sole, whole plaice.
3 Cooking on a flat tray with a rim: tomatoes, mushrooms, bacon, sausages, and kidneys may be grilled under a salamander. A rim is required on the tray to prevent spillage of fat and articles of food sliding from the tray.
4 The salamander can also be used for browning, gratinating and glazing certain dishes, e.g. duchess potato border, macaroni au gratin, filets de sole bonne femme, and for toasting.

Between heat

This is grilling between electrically heated grill bars or plates and is applied to small cuts of meat.

Examples of food cooked by grilling

Fish – cod p. 216, herring p. 217, mackerel p. 217, plaice p. 218.
Meat – brochette p. 253, mixed grill p. 251, veal cutlets p. 308, chops p. 326, kidneys p. 263, chicken p. 356, beef steak p. 282.
Vegetables – mushrooms p. 415, tomatoes p. 430.
Savouries – Welsh rarebit p. 550, mushrooms and bacon p. 551.
Toasted items e.g. bread, tea cakes, muffins.

Effects of grilling

Because of the speed of cooking there is maximum retention of nutrients and flavour.

Meat – because of the rapid cooking and intense heat, grilling is only suitable for certain cuts of best quality meat; inferior meat would be tough and inedible. The effect of fierce heat on the surface of the meat rapidly coagulates and seals the surface protein, thus helping to retain the meat juices. Grilled meats lose less of their juices than meat cooked by any other method provided they are not pierced with a fork while cooking.

Advantages

1 Speed of grilling enables food to be quickly cooked to order.
2 Charring foods gives a distinctive appearance and improves flavour.
3 Control of cooking is aided because food is visible whilst being grilled.
4 Variety is given to menu and diet.
5 Grills may be situated in view of the customer.

Techniques associated with grilling

Oiling, greasing and basting

The grill bar must be oiled before, during and after use and trays lightly greased. Foods are brushed with oil before being placed on grill bars or they will stick. *Brushing* with oil during grilling, known as *basting* prevents food drying out.

Flouring

This is the passing of fish through seasoned flour.

Crumbing

Fish may be passed through
a) flour, egg and crumbs, or
b) melted butter or margarine and crumbs, then placed on greased trays – this is known as *traying up*.

Charring or searing

These are the dark brown marks on foods caused by contact with the very hot grill bars. Charring gives the distinctive flavour to grilled foods.

Equipment

The salamander, or grill heated from above, uses gas or electricity. The salamander bars and drip tray should be cleaned with hot detergent water, rinsed and replaced and the salamander lit for a few minutes to dry the bars.

Under-fired grill bars are heated using gas, charcoal or a coke product. Care must be taken with the fire bricks lining the grill as they are easily broken. After use, the burned charcoal or coke is removed, or the gas turned off, and grill bars thoroughly cleaned and lightly greased.

Although the salamander is often used for toasted products there is special equipment designed for toasting. Toasters must be kept clean and free from crumbs.

Tongs, slices and palette knives are used for handling and turning grilled foods. Skewers are used to keep foods together, e.g. kebabs, or to keep foods open, e.g. kidneys, and for ease of handling. All small equipment should be washed in hot detergent water, rinsed and dried and stored in clean drawers or cupboards.

Check that equipment is clean and in safe condition for use; any faults must be reported immediately.

All gas and electrical equipment should be inspected and serviced regularly.

Grilling steak (p. 282)

General rules for efficient grilling

1 Smaller, thinner items require cooking quickly.
2 Seal and colour food on the hot part of the grill then move to a cooler part to complete cooking.
3 Slow cooking results in the food drying out.
4 Basting of food and oiling of bars prevents dryness.
5 Tongs are used for turning and lifting, e.g. cutlets and steaks. Palette knives and slices are used for turning and lifting from trays, e.g. tomatoes, mushrooms, whole or cut fish.

Safety

1 Take extra care when moving salamander and grill bars, when grilling.
2 Trays used for grilling must have raised edges and not be overloaded.
3 Never place trays on the top surface of the heated salamander.
4 Take care when removing foods from grills and salamanders.

Shallow frying

Definition

Shallow frying is the cooking of food in a small quantity of pre-heated fat or oil in a shallow pan or on a flat surface (griddle plate).

Purpose

a) To give variety to the menu and the diet, by making food palatable, digestible and safe to eat.
b) To brown food giving it a different colour and an interesting and attractive flavour.

Methods

There are four methods of frying using a shallow amount of fat or oil: shallow fry; sauté; griddle; and stir fry.

1 *Shallow fry* – the cooking of food in a small amount of fat or oil in a frying pan or sauté pan. The presentation side of the food should be fried first, as this side will have the better appearance because the fat is clean, then turned so that both sides are cooked and coloured. This applies to small cuts of fish, meat and poultry, also small whole fish (up to 400 g/1 lb). Eggs, pancakes and certain vegetables are cooked by this method. The term *meunière* refers to shallow-fried fish which is passed through seasoned flour, shallow fried and finished with lemon juice, nut-brown butter and chopped parsley.
2 *Sauté* – this term is used:
   a) when cooking tender cuts of meat and poultry in a sauté or frying pan. After the food is cooked on both sides it is removed from the pan, the fat is discarded and the pan deglazed with stock or wine. This then forms an important part of the finished sauce. When the term 'sauté' is used for a dish of meat or poultry, e.g. Rognon sauté, poulet sauté, boeuf sauté, the meat should be completely cooked, the sauce finished and the two only combined for serving. Only tender foods can be used and misunderstanding of the term has come about as inferior meats have been used which need stewing. Therefore the term *ragoût* should be used when the meat and sauce are stewed together. A common example of this error is Sauté de boeuf using stewing beef when it should be called Ragoût de boeuf.
   b) Sauté is also used when cooking, for example, potatoes, onions, or kidneys when they are cut into slices or pieces and tossed (*sauter* means to jump or toss) in hot shallow fat or oil in a frying pan till golden brown and cooked.

3 *Griddle* – foods cooked on a griddle (a solid metal plate), e.g. hamburgers, sausages, sliced onions, are placed on a lightly oiled pre-heated griddle and turned frequently during cooking. Pancakes may be cooked this way but are turned only once.
4 *Stir fry* – fast frying in a wok or frying pan in a little fat or oil, e.g. vegetables, strips of beef, chicken, etc.

Examples of foods which are shallow fried

Eggs – omelettes p. 186, fried p. 182.
Fish – meunière p. 215, sole, plaice, trout, cod, herring.
Meat – lamb noisettes p. 255, kidneys p. 264, beef Stroganoff p. 286, steak bordelaise p. 284, veal escalope viennoise p. 310.
Poultry – chicken sauté chasseur p. 354, chicken Parmentier p. 358.
Vegetables – cauliflower p. 419, onions p. 427, chicory p. 422.
Potatoes – macaire p. 446, sauté p. 442, Byron p. 446.
Sweets and pastries – jam omelette p. 512, pancakes p. 504.
Savouries – croque monsieur p. 543.

Effects

The high temperature used in shallow frying produces almost instant coagulation of the surface protein of the food and prevents the escape of the natural juices.

Some of the frying medium will be absorbed by the food being fried, which will change the nutritional content.

Advantages

It is a quick method of cooking prime cuts of meat and poultry as suitable fats or oils can be raised to a high temperature without burning. As the food is in direct contact with the fat it cooks rapidly.

Time and temperature control

This is particularly important as all shallow-fried foods should have an appetising golden brown colour on both sides. This can only be achieved by careful control of the temperature, which should be initially hot, then reducing the heat and turning the food when required.

Techniques associated with shallow frying

Proving

This is the preparation of frying pans (not sauté pans) when new before being used. They are lightly oiled, well heated on the stove or in the oven for 10–15 minutes, then wiped firmly with a clean cloth or paper and the pan finished with a little oil.

Browning

This is the appetising brown colour given to food by:

1 Careful attention to selection of a suitable pan;
2 Choice of cooking oil or fat;
3 Control of the cooking temperature.

Tossing

This is the turning over of the contents of the pan by means of wrist and hand manipulation.

Turning

This is the turning over of the food onto the second side after the presentation side is cooked to a golden brown.

Holding for service

This means keeping food warm after being cooked.

Preparation for sauté potatoes (p. 442)

Equipment

Pans suitable for shallow frying include:

frying pans – general purpose;
frying pans – omelette and oval-shaped for fish;
woks, and sauté pans;
bratt pans and griddles for large scale cooking.

For information regarding the cleaning and handling of this equipment see page 208 of *The Theory of Catering*.

All small equipment when cleaned should be thoroughly dried and stored on clean racks. Faulty pans should not be used but reported immediately.

General rules

1 When shallow frying continuously over a busy period it is essential to prepare and cook in a systematic way.

2 Pans should be cleaned after every use.
3 New pans used for frying (except sauté pans) must be proved before being used.

Safety

1 Select the correct type and size of pan: not too small, as food will not brown evenly and may break up, e.g. fish; not too large, as areas not covered by food will burn and spoil the flavour of the food being cooked.
2 Always keep sleeves rolled down as splashing fat may burn the forearm.
3 Avoid being splashed by hot fat when placing food in the pan – add it carefully away from you.
4 Use a thick, clean, dry cloth when handling pans.
5 Move pans carefully in case they jar and tip fat onto the stove.

Deep frying

Definition

This is the cooking of food in pre-heated deep oil or clarified fat.

Purpose

a) To cook appetising foods of various kinds thus giving variety to the diet and the menu.
b) To produce food with an appetising golden brown colour, crisp, palatable and safe to eat.

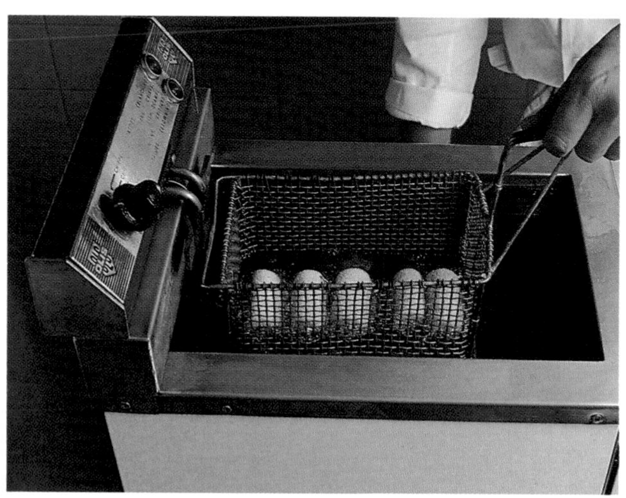

Frying croquette potatoes (p. 439)

Methods

1 Conventional deep-fried foods, with the exception of potatoes, are coated with milk and flour, egg and crumbs, batter or pastry to:
  a) protect the surface of the food from intense heat;
  b) prevent the escape of moisture and nutrients;
  c) modify the rapid penetration of the intense heat.

  The food is carefully placed into deep pre-heated oil or fat, fried until cooked and golden brown, well drained and served.

2 Partial deep-frying is known as blanching and may be applied to chipped potatoes. The purpose is to partly cook in advance of service and to complete the cooking to order. With certain types of potatoes this gives an eating quality of a floury inside and crisp exterior to the chips.

Examples of deep-fried foods

Eggs – Scotch eggs p. 186, French-fried eggs p. 183.
Fish – scampi p. 223, fish cakes p. 232.
Chicken – cutlets p. 362.
Savoury – cheese fritters p. 551.
Potatoes – croquette p. 439, chips p. 443, almond potatoes p. 440.
Vegetables – onions p. 427.
Pastry and sweets – apple fritters p. 503, doughnuts p. 474.

Effects of deep frying

The effect of deep frying on coated items is that the surface is sealed by coagulation of the protein, e.g. milk or eggs, with the minimum absorption of fat. However, the interior may be raw, e.g. apple fritters and will require to be cooked. With a cooked interior, e.g. croquette potatoes, it only needs to be heated through. The coating, e.g. batter etc., does need to be cooked. With uncoated items, e.g. chipped potatoes, the food absorbs a large amount of fat thus affecting the texture and nutritional content.

The effect of deep frying on the structure of the item being cooked will vary according to the nature of the food.

Advantages

1 Blanching, or partial cooking, enables certain foods to be held for cooking later, which helps during busy service and saves time.
2 Coating foods enables a wide variety to be cooked by this method.
3 Foods can be cooked quickly and easily handled for service.
4 Coated foods are quickly sealed, thus preventing the enclosed food becoming greasy.

Temperature and time control

With deep fat frying it is essential for fat temperatures to be maintained at the correct degree. When quantities of food are being continuously fried, after the removal of one batch the temperature of the fat must be allowed to recover before the next batch is cooked. If this is not done the food will be pale and insipid in appearance and soggy to eat.

Timing is important; if thicker pieces of food are being cooked, the temperature must be lowered to allow for sufficient cooking time otherwise the food will be over-coloured and under-cooked. The reverse is also true – the smaller the pieces of food the hotter the frying temperature and a shorter cooking time.

Techniques associated with deep frying

Coating

This is the protection of foods before frying, as for shallow frying.

Blanching

This is the half- or pre-cooking of potatoes with the minimum of colour.

Clarifying

This is the slow cooking of beef fat to remove all water and any impurities so that when strained it is suitable for frying.

Draining

This means allowing all fat or oil to drain off the food on wire racks or in the basket after cooking.

Holding for service

This means keeping food hot, without losing crispness, until required. This time should be kept to a minimum otherwise food will not be served in its best condition.

Equipment

Spiders

These are specially designed wire slices used for removing food from fryers, e.g. fish in batter, fritters.

Frying baskets

These are used for frying certain foods, usually leaving the food in the basket during cooking, e.g. croquettes, fish cakes.

For details of frying equipment, their care and cleaning see pages 217–218 in *The Theory of Catering*.

There is a variety of equipment available: fritures with straight sides and deep; flat-bottomed pans for use on stove tops; free-standing single or multi-pan units with manual or computerised control; pressure fryers; and continuous fryers with automatic time and temperature control.

Fritures must be kept clean and in efficient working condition at all times and any faults must be reported immediately.

Efficiency

1 Systematic preparation and cooking are essential.
2 Never overfill fryers with fat or oil or food to be cooked.
3 When using free-standing fryers without a thermometer never allow smoke to rise from the fat, this will give a disagreeable taste and smell to food being fried.
4 The normal frying temperature is between 175 °C and 195 °C (350–380 °F), this is indicated by a slight heat haze rising from the fat.
5 Do not attempt to fry too much food at one time.
6 Allow fat to recover its heat before adding the next batch of food.
7 Ensure a correct oil/fat ratio to food. If too much food is cooked in too little fat, even if the initial temperature of the fat is correct, the effect of a large amount of food will reduce the temperature drastically and spoil the food.
8 Reduce frying temperatures during slack periods to conserve fuel.
9 Restrict holding time to a minimim – fried foods soon lose their crispness.
10 Oil and fat should be strained after use, otherwise remaining food particles will burn when the fat is next heated thus spoiling the appearance and flavour of the food.
11 Always cover oil or fat when not in use to prevent oxidation.

Safety

1 Always only half-fill fryers with fat or oil.
2 Never overload fryers with food.
3 Dry foods thoroughly before frying, e.g. potatoes, otherwise they will splutter and cause burns.
4 Always carefully place food in the fryer *away* from you. If it is added towards you hot fat could splash and burn.
5 Always have a frying basket and spider to hand in case food is required to be lifted out of the fryer quickly. A combination of the fats being too hot, fat almost ready for discarding and the food being damp can result

in the fat boiling over. If it is a free-standing friture on the stove then there is a risk of fire.

6 Move free-standing fryers with great care so as not to jar them and spill fat on the stove.
7 Ensure that correct fire prevention equipment is to hand and that you are familiar with the fire drill procedure.
8 Keep sleeves rolled down at all times when handling fryers.
9 Use clean, dry, thick, sound cloths when handling fritures.
10 Allow fat to cool before straining.

Paper bag cooking

Known as *en papillotte*, this is method of cookery in which food is tightly sealed in oiled greaseproof paper or foil so that during cooking no steam escapes and maximum natural flavour and nutritive value is retained.

Thick items of food, e.g. veal chops, red mullet, may be partly and quickly pre-cooked, usually by grilling or shallow frying, then finely cut vegetables, herbs and spices can be added. The bags are tightly sealed, placed on a lightly greased tray and cooked in a hot oven. When cooked, the food is served in the bag and opened by or in front of the customer.

Microwave cooking

Definition

This is a method of cooking and re-heating food using a high frequency power in a microwave oven powered by electricity. The microwaves are similar to those which carry television from the transmitter to the receiver but are at a higher frequency. The microwaves activate the water molecules or particles of food and agitate them, causing heat by friction which cooks or re-heats the food.

Purpose

a) Raw, pre-prepared or pre-cooked foods are cooked quickly and made palatable and digestible.
b) Foods are safer to eat, particularly re-heated foods, because the total food is heated at the same time.

Application

Microwave cooking can be used for cooking raw food, re-heating cooked food and de-frosting frozen foods.

Advantages

1 A saving of between 50 to 70 per cent over conventional cooking times on certain foods.
2 A quick way to cook and re-heat foods.
3 A fast method of de-frosting foods.
4 Economical on:
   a) electricity – less energy required;
   b) labour – less washing up as foods can be cooked in serving dishes.
5 Hot meals can be available 24 hours a day and completely operated on a self-service basis, thereby increasing consumer satisfaction and reducing costs.
6 Food is cooked in its own juices so flavour and goodness are retained.
7 Minimises food shrinkage and drying-out.
8 When used with conventional cooking methods production can be more flexible.

Disadvantages

1 Not suitable for all foods.
2 Limited oven space restricts use to small quantities.
3 Many microwave ovens do not brown food, although browning elements are available within certain models.
4 Not all containers are suitable for use.
5 Microwaves can only penetrate 5 cm (1½ inches) into food (from all sides).

Special points for attention

a) Correct selection of cooking and time controls according to the manufacturer's intructions is essential.
b) Certain foods must be removed when underdone to finish cooking, so standing time is important; during this time for example fish turns from opaque to flaky, scrambled eggs turn creamy. Tender, crisp vegetables do not need to stand.

Techniques associated with microwave cookery

Baked potatoes and whole unpeeled apples must have the skin pierced in order to release pressure and prevent them bursting. Eggs must not be cooked in their shells or they will burst.

Cover foods when possible to reduce condensation and spluttering.

Factors which affect efficient cooking

1 Only use suitable containers: glass, china, plastic. Only use metal or foil if the particular cooker has been developed to take metal without

causing damage. For the best results use straight-sided, round, shallow containers.

2 Even-shaped items cook uniformly, arrange uneven-shaped items with the thickest part to the outside of the dish.
3 Keep food as level as possible, do not pile into mounds.
4 Allow sufficient space to stir or mix e.g. vegetables, sauces.
5 Turn items such as corn on the cob during cooking because dense items take longer to cook then porous items.
6 Foods with higher water content cook faster than those which are drier.
7 Most foods should be covered when cooked in a microwave oven. Microwave clingfilm is available to cover food.

Examples of food used in a microwave

Fish – e.g. smoked haddock, cod steak.
Vegetables – e.g. carrots, cauliflower, courgettes.
Reheated dishes – e.g. shepherds pie, beef stew.
Defrosting – e.g. cakes, vegetables, prawns, meat.

Equipment

All microwave ovens consist of a basic unit of different sizes with varying levels of power. Additions to the standard model include defrosting, browning elements, stay-hot controls and a revolving turntable. There is also a microwave cooker combined with forced air convection which can be used for microwave or convection or both together. This gives the advantage of both speed and colouration. For this combined oven, metal containers can be used without damage to the cooker.

Cleaning and care

Prior to cleaning, disconnect from the electricity supply. Use a damp cloth to clean both the inside and outside of the oven. If the oven is greasy use a solution of washing-up liquid. After damp cleaning finish with a soft dry cloth. All small equipment should be washed in hot detergent water, dried and stored in clean cupboards.

Small equipment

Suitable cooking dishes are those made from ceramic, glass, wood, paper and plastic materials. Metal or foil dishes must never be used other than on specified cookers otherwise they will cause damage.

Special microwave thermometers are available which can be left in meat or poultry during cooking; ordinary meat thermometers must not be used.

Separating rings can be used to stack three plates one above the other. There must be air space between each and the top plate must be covered.

Special utensils include browning dishes designed to brown foods. A whole range of containers is available, specifically designed for microwave use.

Safety

1. Should the door seal be damaged do not use the oven. This should be reported to the employer immediately.
2. Do not operate the oven when it is empty.
3. Remember to pierce foods and covers that are likely to burst.
4. Regular inspection is essential and manufacturer's instructions must be followed.

Pot roasting

Definition

Pot roasting is cooking on a bed of root vegetables in a covered pan. Known as *poêlé*, this method retains maximum flavour of all ingredients.

Preparation for pot roasted chicken (p. 365)

Method

Place the food on a bed of roots and herbs, coat generously with butter or oil, cover with a lid and cook in an oven.

Examples of foods cooked by pot roasting

Fillet of beef; chicken (e.g. p. 365); pheasant.

Equipment

Casseroles, cocottes, braising pans – all with tight-fitting lids.

General rules

a) Select pans neither too large nor too small.
b) Use the vegetables and herbs with a good stock as base for the sauce.

Cold preparations

Preparing dressed crab (p. 127)

Definition

The preparation of raw and/or cooked foods into a wide variety of cold items.

Purpose

1 To add variety to the menu and diet by preparing food that has eye-appeal, is palatable and digestible.
2 To produce a variety of flavours and textures and provide food that is particularly suitable for hot weather.
3 To prepare food that can be conveniently wrapped for take-aways.

Types of cold work

a) The preparation and presentation of single or combined foods as hors-d'oeuvre, salads, dressings and cold sauces.
b) Processing of prepared foods for cold buffets, cafeterias, bars, counters and take-aways.
c) Other preparations include marinades and forcemeat stuffings, see pages 328, 372.

Examples of cold food preparations

Hors-d'oeuvre, salads, sandwiches p. 145.
Sauces-vinaigrette, mayonnaise p. 118.

Cold buffet items – dressed crab p. 127, liver paté p. 121, smoked mackerel mousse p. 128, salmon mayonnaise p. 233, cold roast beef p. 278, roast chicken p. 351, veal and ham pie p. 314.
Sweet items suitable for cold buffets – fresh fruit salad p. 506, bavarois p. 519, trifle p. 508, chocolate gâteau p. 468.

Cold food characteristics

a) Appearance must be clean and fresh. Presentation should be eye appealing, neither too colourful or over-decorative, therefore stimulating the appetite.
b) Nutritional value is obtained because of the mixture of raw and cooked foods.

Hygiene, handling and storage

Correct hygiene practices regarding personal habits, food and equipment is essential at all times, particularly when dealing with cold food. Refer to *The Theory of Catering* pages 332–371.

Techniques associated with cold preparation

Peeling

This is the removal of the outer skin of fruit or vegetables using a peeler or small knife, according to the thickness of the skin.

Chopping

This is cutting into very small pieces, e.g. parsley, onions.

Cutting

This is using a knife to divide food into required shapes and sizes.

Carving

This means cutting meat or poultry into slices.

Seasoning

This is the addition of salt and pepper.

Dressing

a) Salad dressing, e.g. vinaigrette.
b) The arrangement of food for presentation on plates, dishes or buffets.

Garnishing

This is the final addition to the dish, e.g. quarters of tomato added to egg mayonnaise.

Marinade

A richly spiced pickling liquid used to give flavour and to assist in tenderising meats, e.g. venison.

Equipment

Bowls, basins, whisks, spoons, etc. as well as food processors, mixing machines and blenders are used in cold preparations. For further information refer to *The Theory of Catering*, pp. 222–242.

Preparation for cold work

Well planned organisation is essential to ensure adequate pre-preparation (*mise-en-place*), so that foods are assembled with a good work flow and ready on time.

Before, during and after assembling, and before final garnishing, foods must be kept in a cool place, cold room or refrigerator so as to minimise risk of food contamination. Garnishing and final decoration should take place as close to serving time as possible.

General rules

1 To be aware of the texture and flavour of many raw foods that can be mixed together or combined with cooked foods, e.g. coleslaw, meat salad.
2 To understand what combination of foods, for example salads, are best suited to be served with other foods, e.g. cold meat or poultry.
3 To develop simple artistic skills which require the minimum of time required for preparation and assembly.
4 To provide an attractive presentation of food at all times.

Safety

Personal, food and equipment hygiene practice of the highest order must be observed with all cold work. Refer to *The Theory of Catering*, pp. 332–371.

Cuts of bread (clockwise from left): heart-shaped croûtons; croûtons; croûtes; triangular croûtons

4

CULINARY TERMS

General objectives	*Specific objectives*
To know and understand the basic terms used in cookery.	To be able to explain the commonly used terms listed and to be able to use them correctly.

Abatis de volaille	Poultry offal – giblets, etc.
Abats	Offal, heads, hearts, liver, kidneys, etc.
Accompaniments	Items offered separately with a dish of food
Agar-agar	A gelatine substitute obtained from seaweed
Aile	Wing of poultry or game birds
à la	In the style of
à la carte	Dishes prepared to order and priced individually
à la française	In the French style
Aloyau de boeuf	Sirloin of beef
Amino acid	Organic acids found in proteins
Appareil	Prepared mixture
Aromates	Aromatic herbs, spices
Arroser	To baste as in roasting
Ascorbic acid	Known as vitamin C found in citrus fruits and blackcurrants. Necessary for growth and maintenance of health.
Aspic	A savoury jelly mainly used for decorative larder work
Assaisonner	To season
Assorti	An assortment
Au bleu	When applied to meat it means very underdone
Au four	Baked in the oven
Au gratin	Sprinkled with cheese or breadcrumbs and browned
Au vin blanc	With white wine
Bacteria	Single-celled micro-organisms some of which are harmful, e.g. cause food poisoning. Others are useful, e.g. in cheese-making. Bacteria – plural Bacterium – singular
Bain-marie	(i) A container of water to keep foods hot without fear of burning (ii) A shallow container of water for cooking foods in order to prevent them burning (iii) A deep, narrow container for storing hot sauces, soups and gravies
Barder	To bard. The covering of the breasts of birds with thin slices of fat bacon before roasting
Barquette	A boat-shaped pastry tartlet
Basting	Spooning the melted fat over the food during cooking to keep the food moist

Bat out	To flatten slices of raw meat with a cutlet bat
Bean sprouts	Young shoots of dried beans
Beignets	Fritters, sweet or savoury
Au beurre	With butter
Beurre fondu	Melted butter, e.g. asperges, beurre fondu
Beurre manié	Equal quantities of flour and butter used for thickening sauces, e.g. moules marinière
Beurre noir	Black butter e.g. raie au beurre noir
Beurre noisette	Nut-brown butter as used with fish meunière
Blanc	A cooking liquor of water, lemon juice, flour and salt. Also applied to the white of chicken, breast and wings
Blanchir	To blanch a) To make white as in the case of bones and meat b) To retain colour as in the case of vegetables c) To skin as for tomatoes d) To make limp as for certain braised vegetables e) To cook without colour as for the first frying of potatoes
Blanquette	A white stew cooked in stock from which the sauce is made e.g. blanquette de veau
Bombe	An ice-cream speciality of different flavours in bomb shape
Bouchée	Small puff paste case, literally 'a mouthful'
Bouillon	Unclarified stock
Bouquet garni	A faggot of herbs: parsley, thyme and bay leaf usually tied inside pieces of leek and celery
Brine	A preserving solution of water, salt, saltpetre and aromates used for meats, e.g. silverside, brisket, tongue
Brunoise	Small dice
Buttermilk	Liquid remaining from the churning of butter
Calcium	A mineral required for building bones and teeth. Obtained from cheese and milk
Calorie	A unit of heat or energy to be known as kilocalorie
Canapé	A cushion of bread on which are served various foods, hot and cold
Carbohydrate	This is a nutrient which has three groups, sugar, starch and cellulose. The first two provide the body with energy
Carbon dioxide	A gas produced by all raising agents
Carte du jour	Menu for the day
Casserole	An earthenware fireproof dish with a lid
Cellulose	The coarse structure of fruit, vegetables and cereals which is not digested but used as roughage (dietary fibre)
Chapelure	Crumbs made from dry bread
Chateaubriand	Head of the fillet of beef
Chaud-froid	A demi-glace or creamed velouté with gelatine or aspic added, used for masking cold dishes
Chauffant	Pan of hot salted water for reheating foods

Chinois	A conical strainer
Chlorophyll	The green colour in vegetables
Civet	A brown stew of game, usually hare
Clarification	To make clear, e.g. fat, stock, jelly
Clostridium perfringens	Food poisoning bacteria found in the soil, vegetables and meat
Clouté	Studded, e.g. clove in an onion
Coagulation	The solidification of a protein which is irreversible, e.g. fried egg, cooking of meat
Cocotte	Porcelain or earthenware fireproof dish
Collagen and elastin	Proteins in connective tissue, e.g. gristle. Found in large quantities in tough cuts of beef which, when braised or stewed, is tenderised
Compote	Stewed fruit, e.g. compote de fruits
Concassée	Coarsely-chopped, e.g. parsley, tomatoes
Consommé	Basic clear soup
Contrefilet	Boned sirloin of beef
Cook out	The process of cooking the flour in a roux, soup or sauce
Cordon	A thread or thin line of sauce
Coriander leaves	Leaves of an aromatic plant used for flavouring
Correcting	To adjust the seasoning, consistency and colour
Côte	A rib or chop, e.g. côte de veau
Côtelette	Cutlet, e.g. côtelette d'agneau
Cottage cheese	A soft cheese made from skimmed milk
Coupé	Cut
Coupe	An individual serving bowl
Court-bouillon	A well-flavoured cooking liquor for fish
Crème fraîche	Whipping cream and buttermilk heated to 24–29 °C
Crêpes	Pancakes
Croquettes	Cooked foods moulded cylinder shape, egg and crumbed and deep fried
Cross-contamination	Transfer of micro-organisms from contaminated to uncontaminated hands or equipment
Croûtons	Cubes of fried bread served with soup, also triangular pieces with spinach and heart-shaped with certain vegetables and entrées
Crudités	Small neat pieces of raw vegetables
Cuisse de poulet	Chicken leg
Cullis (coulis)	Sauce made from fruit or vegetable puree, e.g. raspberry, tomato
Curd cheese	A low-fat soft cheese approximately 11% fat
Dariole	A small mould as used for cream caramel
Darne	A slice of round fish on the bone
Déglacer	To swill out a pan in which food has been fried, with wine, stock or water in order to use the sediment for the acompanying sauce or gravy
Dégraisser	To skim fat off liquid
Demi-glace	Equal quantities of espagnole and brown stock reduced by half

Désosser	To bone out meat
Dilute	To mix a powder, e.g. cornflour, with a liquid
Dish paper	A plain dish paper
Doily	A fancy dish paper
Drain	Placing food in a colander, allowing liquid to seep out
Duxelle	Finely chopped mushrooms cooked with chopped shallots
Egg wash	Beaten egg (with a little milk or water)
Emulsion	A mixture of oil and water which does not separate on standing, e.g. mayonnaise, hollandaise
Entrecôte	A steak cut from the boned sirloin
Escalope	Thin slice, e.g. escalope de veau
Espagnole	Basic brown sauce
Estouffade	Brown stock
Farce	Stuffing
Fécule	Fine potato flour
Feuilletage	Puff paste
Fines herbes	Chopped parsley, tarragon, chervil
Flake	To break into natural segments, e.g. cooked fish
Flan	Open fruit tart
Fleurons	Small crescent-shaped pieces of puff pastry
Flute	A 2 cm (1 in) diameter French bread used for soup garnishes
Frappé	Chilled, e.g. melon frappé
Friandises	Petits fours or sweetmeats
Fricassée	A white stew in which the meat, fish or poultry is cooked in the sauce, e.g. fricassée de volaille
Friture	A pan that contains deep fat
Fromage blanc	Fat-free skimmed milk fresh cheese
Fumé	Smoked, e.g. saumon fumé
Garam masala	A combination of spices
Garnish	Garniture – trimmings on the dish
Gâteau	A cake of more than one portion
Gelatine	A soluble protein used for setting foods, e.g. bavarois
Gibier	Game, e.g. farce de gibier
Glace	Ice or ice-cream, e.g. glace vanille
To glaze	a) To colour a dish under the salamander, e.g. filet de sole bonne femme b) To finish a flan or tartlet, e.g. with apricot jam c) To finish certain vegetables, e.g. carottes glacées
Gluten	This is formed from protein present in flour when mixed with water.
Gomasio	A mixture of toasted sesame seeds and salt
Haché	Finely chopped or minced

Herb salt	A salt flavoured with herbs
Hors-d'oeuvre	Appetising first-course dishes
Jardinière	Vegetables cut into batons
Julienne	Cut into fine strips
Jus-lié	Thickened gravy
Larder	To insert strips of fat bacon into meat
Lardons	Batons of thick streaky bacon
Liaison	A thickening or binding
Macédoine	a) A mixture – fruit or vegetables b) Cut in ½ cm (¼ in) dice
Magnetron	The device which generates microwaves in a microwave oven
Marinade	A richly spiced pickling liquid used to give flavour and to assist in tenderising meats, e.g. beef, venison
Marmite	Stockpot
Petite marmite	A small earthenware pot in which soup is made and served
Menu	Bill of fare
Micro-organisms	Very small living plants or animals, e.g. bacteria, yeasts, moulds
Mignonette	Coarsely-ground pepper
Mill pepper	Pepper from the pepper mill
Mineral salts	These are mineral elements, small quantities of which are essential for health
à la minute	Cooked to order
Mirepoix	Roughly-cut onion, carrots, celery; a sprig of thyme and a bay leaf
Mise-en-place	Basic preparations prior to serving
Miso	Seasoning made from fermented soya beans
Mono-sodium glutamate	A flavouring added to food products to increase flavour
Mousse	A dish of light consistency, hot or cold
Napper	To coat or mask with sauce
Natives	A menu term denoting English oysters
Navarin	Brown stew of lamb or mutton
Niacin	Part of vitamin B found in liver, kidney, meat extract, bacon
Noisette	A cut from a boned-out loin of lamb, e.g. noisette d'agneau
Nutrients	These are the components of food required for health (protein, fats, carbohydrates, vitamins, mineral salts, water)
Oxidation	The chemical process whereby the product is affected by taking in oxygen

Palatable	Pleasant to the taste
Pané	Passed through seasoned flour, beaten egg and white breadcrumbs
Parsley butter	Butter containing lemon juice and chopped parsley
Pass	To cause to go through a sieve or strainer
Pathogens	Bacteria which cause disease
Paupiette	A stuffed and rolled strip of fish or meat
Paysanne	To cut into even, thin pieces, triangular, round or square
Persillé	Garnished with chopped parsley
Petits fours	Very small pastries, biscuits, sweets, etc.
pH value	A scale indicating acidity or alkalinity in food
Phosphorus	A mineral element found in fish. Required for building bones and teeth
Picked parsley	Sprig of parsley
Piquant	Sharply flavoured
Piqué	Studded, e.g. clove in an onion
Plat du jour	Special dish of the day
Polenta	An Italian dish using coarsely ground cornmeal
Printanière	Garnish of spring vegetables
Protein	The nutrient which is needed for growth and repair
Prove	To allow a yeast dough to rest in a warm place so that it can rise and expand
Pulses	Vegetables grown in pods (dried)
Quark	Salt-free soft cheese made from semi-skimmed milk
Ragoût	Stew, e.g. ragoût de boeuf
Réchauffer	To reheat
Reduce	To concentrate a liquid by boiling
Refresh	To make cold under running cold water
Riboflavin	Part of vitamin B known as B2. Sources – yeast, liver, egg, cheese
Rissoler	To fry to a golden brown
Root ginger	The root from the ginger plant
Roux	A thickening of cooked flour and fat
Sabayon	Yolks of eggs and a little water cooked until creamy
Saccharometer	Instrument used for measuring density of sugar syrup
Salamander	This is a type of grill heated from above
Salmonella	Food poisoning bacterium found in meat and poultry
Sauté	a) To toss in fat, e.g. pommes sautées b) To cook quickly in a sauté or frying pan c) A brown stew of a specific type, e.g. sauté de veau
Seal	To set the surface of meat in a hot oven or pan to colour and retain juices
Seasoned flour	Flour seasoned with salt and pepper
Set	To seal the outside surface

Shredded	Cut in fine strips, e.g. lettuce, sorrel, onion
Silicone paper	Non-stick paper
Singe	To brown or colour
Smetana	A low-fat product, a cross between soured cream and yoghurt
Sodium	Mineral element in the form of salt, e.g. sodium chloride. Found in cheese, bacon, fish, meat
Soufflé	A very light dish, either sweet or savoury, hot or cold
Staphylococcus	Food poisoning bacterium found in the human throat and nose, also in septic cuts
Starch	A carbohydrate found in cereals, certain vegetables, farinaceous foods
Strain	To separate the liquid from the solids by passing through a strainer
Studded onion	Onion studded with a clove and bay leaf
Sweat	To cook in fat under a lid without colour
Syneresis	The squeezing out of liquid from an overcooked protein and liquid mixture, e.g. scrambled egg, egg custard
Table d'hôte	A meal at a fixed price
Tahini	A strong flavoured sesame seed paste
Terrine	An earthenware dish used for cooking and serving pâté
Thiamine	Part of vitamin B known as B1, it assists the nervous system. Source – yeast, bacon, wholemeal bread
Timbale	A double service dish
Tofu	Low-fat bean curd made from soya beans
Tourné	Turned, to shape in barrels or large olives
Tranche	A slice
Tronçon	A slice of flat fish on the bone
T.V.P.	Textured vegetable protein, is derived from soya beans, oats etc.
Vegan	A person who does not eat fish, meat, poultry, game, dairy products and eggs
Vegetarian	A vegetarian does not eat fish, meat, poultry or game
Velouté	a) A basic sauce b) A soup of velvet or smooth consistency
Vitamins	These are chemical substances which assist the regulation of body processes
Vol-au-vent	A large puff pastry case
Wok	A round-bottomed frying pan used extensively in Chinese cookery
Yeast extract	A mixture of brewer's yeast and salt, high in flavour and protein
Yoghurt	Easily digested fermented milk product

Roast chicken and bacon (p. 351) with roast gravy (p. 104) and bread sauce (p. 106)

5

STOCKS AND SAUCES

General objectives
To appreciate the value of stock and to know the principles of its production and use.

To understand the purpose of sauces and to know the various types, hot and cold, and how they are made.

Specific objectives
To state the proportions required, to explain the care needed to prepare clear stock and the hygienic treatment of it. To use it to advantage in the kitchen.

To state when and how sauces are made and to explain with what they are served. To demonstrate the production of each sauce to a satisfactory standard with particular regard to consistency. To list the derivatives of the basic sauces.

Cold Sauces

Stocks

Stock is a liquid containing some of the soluble nutrients and flavours of food which are extracted by prolonged and gentle simmering (with the exception of fish stock, which requires only 20 minutes); such liquid is the foundation of soups, sauces and gravies. Stocks are the foundation of many important kitchen preparations; therefore the greatest possible care should be taken in their production.

1 Unsound meat or bones and decaying vegetables will give stock an unpleasant flavour and cause it to deteriorate quickly.
2 Scum should be removed, otherwise it will boil into the stock and spoil the colour and flavour.
3 Fat should be skimmed, otherwise, it will taste greasy.
4 Stock should always simmer gently, for if it is allowed to boil quickly, it will evaporate and go cloudy.
5 It should not be allowed to go off the boil, otherwise, in hot weather, there is a danger of its going sour.
6 Salt should not be added to stock.
7 When making chicken stock, if raw bones are not available, then a boiling fowl can be used.
8 If stock is to be kept, strain, reboil, cool quickly and place in the refrigerator.

THE STOCKS	LES FONDS
1 · **White beef stock**	*Fond blanc or fond de marmite*
2 · **White mutton stock**	*Fond blanc de mouton*
3 · **White veal stock**	*Fond blanc de veau*
4 · **White chicken stock**	*Fond blanc de volaille*

[*Uses of the above: white soups, sauces and stews.*]

5 · **Brown beef stock**	*Fond brun or estouffade*
6 · **Brown mutton stock**	*Fond brun de mouton*
7 · **Brown veal stock**	*Fond brun de veau*
8 · **Brown chicken stock**	*Fond brun de volaille*
9 · **Brown game stock**	*Fond de gibier*

[*Uses of the above: brown soups, sauces, gravies and stews.*]

10 · General proportions of ingredients for all stocks except fish stock

2 kg	4 lb	raw bones
4 litres	1 gal	water
½ kg	1 lb	vegetables (onion, carrot, celery, leek)
		bouquet garni (thyme, bay leaf, parsley stalks)
		12 peppercorns

General method for all white stocks (except fish stock)

1 Chop up the bones, remove any fat or marrow.
2 Place in a stock pot, add the cold water and bring to the boil.
3 If the scum is dirty then blanch and wash off the bones, re-cover with cold water and re-boil.
4 Skim, wipe round sides of the pot and simmer gently.
5 Add the washed, peeled, whole vegetables, bouquet garni and peppercorns.
6 Simmer 6–8 hours. Skim and strain.

During the cooking a certain amount of evaporation must take place, therefore add ½ litre (1 pt) cold water just before boiling point is reached. This will also help to throw the scum to the surface and make it easier to skim.

General method for all brown stocks

1 Chop the bones and brown well on all sides either by:
   a) placing in a roasting tin in the oven, or
   b) carefully browning in a little fat in a frying-pan.
2 Drain off any fat and place the bones in stock pot.
3 Brown any sediment that may be in the bottom of the tray, deglaze (swill out) with ½ litre (1 pt) of boiling water, simmer for a few minutes and add to the bones.
4 Add the cold water, bring to the boil and skim.
5 Wash, peel and roughly cut the vegetables, fry in a little fat till brown, strain and add to the bones.
6 Add the bouquet garni and peppercorns.
7 Simmer for 6–8 hours. Skim and strain.

For brown stocks a few squashed tomatoes and washed mushroom trimmings may also be added to improve the flavour.

11 · **Fish stock** *Fumet de poisson* (see page 212)

12 · **Vegetable stocks, white and brown** (see page 381)

13 · **Meat glaze** *Glace de viande*

14 · **Fish glaze** *Glace de poisson*

Glazes are made by boiling steadily white or brown beef stock or fish stock and allowing them to reduce to a sticky or gelatinous consistency. They are then stored in jars and when cold kept in the refrigerator for up to one week. If they are to be deep frozen then place into small preserving jars which have been sterilised for one hour. The glaze can then be kept for several months.

Glazes are used to improve the flavour of a prepared sauce which may be lacking in strength. They may also be used as a base for sauces, e.g. fish glaze for fish white wine sauce.

Sauces

A sauce is a liquid which has been thickened by

a) roux,
b) beurre manié (kneaded butter),
c) cornflour, arrowroot or fécule,
d) egg yolks,
e) cream, and/or butter added to reduced stock.

All sauces should be smooth, glossy in appearance, definite in taste and light in texture – the thickening medium should be used in moderation.

15 The roux

A roux is a combination of fat and flour which are cooked together. There are three degrees to which a roux may be cooked, namely
(i) white roux,
(ii) blond roux,
(iii) brown roux.

A boiling liquid should never be added to a hot roux as the result may be lumpy and the person making the sauce may be scalded by the steam produced. If allowed to stand for a time over a moderate heat a sauce made with a roux may become thin due to chemical change (dextrinisation) in the flour.

White roux

Uses: béchamel sauce (white sauce), soups.

Equal quantities of margarine or butter and flour cooked together without colouring for a few minutes to a sandy texture.

Alternatively, use polyunsaturated vegetable margarine or make a roux with vegetable oil, using equal quantities of oil to flour. This does give a slack roux but enables the liquid to be easily incorporated.

Blond roux

Uses: veloutés, tomato sauce, soups.

Equal quantities of margarine, butter or vegetable oil and flour cooked for a little longer than a white roux, but without colouring, to a sandy texture.

Brown roux

Uses: espagnole (brown sauce), soups.

200 g (8 oz) dripping or vegetable oil to 250 g (10 oz) flour per 4 litres (gallon) of stock, cooked together slowly to a light-brown colour. Overcooking of brown roux causes the starch to change chemically (dextrinise) and lose some of its thickening property. This will cause the fat to separate from the roux and rise to the surface of the soup or sauce being made. It will also cause too much roux to be used to achieve the required thickness and will give an unpleasant flavour.

16 Other thickening agents for sauces

Cornflour, arrowroot or fécule

Uses: jus-lié and sauces.

These are diluted with water, stock or milk, then stirred into the boiling liquid and allowed to re-boil for a few minutes. For large-scale cooking and economy, flour may be used.

Beurre manié

Uses: chiefly fish sauces.
Equal quantities of butter or margarine and flour kneaded to a smooth paste and mixed into a boiling liquid.

Egg yolks

Uses: mayonnaise, hollandaise and custard sauces.
Refer to the appropriate recipe as the yolks are used in a different manner for each sauce.

Vegetables or fruit

Fruit or vegetable purée known as a cullis (*coulis*). No other thickening agent is used.

Blood

Use: jugged hare (see page 373).

Glazes

Fish or meat glazes can be made into sauces by the addition of butter and/or cream.

Basic sauce recipes for 1 litre (1 quart)

Basic Sauces: béchamel; velouté; espagnole; demi-glace; sauce tomate; sauce hollandaise.

17 · **White sauce** *Béchamel*

This is a basic white sauce made from milk and a white roux.

100 g	4 oz	margarine or butter
100 g	4 oz	flour
1 litre	1 qt	milk
		1 studded onion

Using whole milk/hard margarine
This recipe provides:

1721 kcals/7228 kJ
120.3 g fat of which 59.5 g saturated
124.8 g carbohydrate of which 48.6 g sugars
42.5 g protein
3.6 g fibre

Using skimmed milk/hard margarine
This recipe provides:

1401 kcals/5884 kJ
83.3 g fat of which 36.1 g saturated
127.8 g carbohydrate of which 51.6 g sugars
43.5 g protein
3.6 g fibre

1 Melt the margarine or butter in a thick-bottomed pan.
2 Add the flour and mix in.
3 Cook for a few minutes over a gentle heat without colouring.
4 Remove from heat to cool the roux.
5 Gradually add the warmed milk and stir till smooth.
6 Add the onion studded with a clove.
7 Allow to simmer for 30 min.
8 Remove the onion, pass the sauce through a conical strainer.
9 Cover with a film of butter or margarine to prevent a skin forming.

1 litre (1 quart)

Sauces made from béchamel

(Quantities for ½ litre (1 pt): 8–12 portions)

	Sauce	Served with	Additions per ½ litre (1 pt)
18	**Anchovy** Sauce anchois	Poached or fried or boiled fish	1 tablespn anchovy essence
19	**Egg** Sauce aux oeufs	Poached fish or boiled fish	2 hard-boiled eggs in small dice
20	**Cheese** Sauce Mornay	Fish or vegetables	50 g (2 oz) grated cheese, 1 egg yolk. Mix well in boiling sauce, remove from heat. Strain if necessary but do not allow to reboil
21	**Onion** Sauce aux oignons	Roast mutton	100 g (4 oz) chopped or diced onions cooked without colour either by boiling or sweating in butter
22	**Soubise** Sauce Soubise	Roast mutton	As for onion sauce but passed through a strainer
23	**Parsley** Sauce persil	Poached or boiled fish and vegetables	1 tablespn chopped parsley
24	**Cream** Sauce crème	Poached fish and boiled vegetables	Add cream, milk, natural yoghurt or fromage blanc to give the consistency of double cream
25	**Mustard** Sauce moutarde	Grilled herrings	Add diluted English or Continental mustard to make a fairly hot sauce

26 Velouté (chicken, veal, fish, mutton)

This is a basic white sauce made from white stock and a blond roux.

100 g	4 oz	margarine, butter or oil
100 g	4 oz	flour
1 litre	1 qt	stock (chicken, veal, fish, mutton) as required

Using hard margarine
This recipe provides:

1094 kcals/4594 kJ
82.6 g fat of which 35.4 g saturated
79.0 g carbohydrate of which 1.6 g sugars
13.3 g protein
3.6 g fibre

Using sunflower oil
This recipe provides:

1263 kcals/5304 kJ
101.5 g fat of which 13.3 g saturated
78.9 g carbohydrate of which 1.5 g sugars
13.2 g protein
3.6 g fibre

1. Melt the fat or oil in a thick-bottomed pan.
2. Add the flour and mix in.
3. Cook out to a sandy texture over gentle heat without colour.
4. Allow the roux to cool.
5. Gradually add the boiling stock.
6. Stir until smooth and boiling.
7. Allow to simmer approx. 1 hour.
8. Pass through a fine conical strainer.

A velouté sauce for chicken, veal or fish dishes is usually finished with cream and in some cases, also egg yolks.

1 litre (1 quart)

Sauces made from veloutés

27 Caper sauce *Sauce aux câpres*

Use: served with boiled leg of mutton.

This is a velouté sauce made from mutton stock with the addition of 2 tablespns capers per ½ litre (1 pt) of sauce.

½ litre (1 pint) 8–12 portions

28 Supreme sauce *Sauce suprême*

Uses: served hot with boiled chicken, vol-au-vent, etc., and also for white chaud-froid sauce.

This is a velouté made from chicken stock flavoured with well-washed mushroom trimmings.

½ litre	1 pt	chicken velouté
25 g	1 oz	mushroom trimmings (white)
60 ml	⅛ pt	cream
		1 yolk
		2–3 drops lemon juice

1 Allow the velouté to cook out with the mushroom trimmings.
2 Pass through a fine strainer. Re-boil.
3 Mix the cream and yolk in a basin (liaison).
4 Add a little of the boiling sauce to the liaison.
5 Return all to the sauce – do not reboil.
6 Mix, finish with lemon sauce and correct the seasoning.

½ litre (1 pint) 8–12 portions

29 · **Aurore sauce** *Sauce aurore*

Use: boiled chicken, poached eggs, chaud-froid sauce, etc.

Proceed as for sauce suprême, add 1 tablespn tomato purée to the sauce. This should give a pink and slightly tomato-flavoured sauce.

½ litre (1 pint) 8–12 portions

30 · **Mushroom sauce** *Sauce aux champignons*

Uses: boiled chicken, sweetbreads, etc.

Proceed as for sauce suprême, add 100 g (4 oz) well-washed, sliced, sweated white button mushrooms after the velouté has been strained. Simmer for 10 min and finish with yolk and cream.

½ litre (1 pint) 8–12 portions

31 · **Ivory sauce** *Sauce ivoire*

To the sauce suprême add a little meat glaze to give an ivory colour. Used with boiled chicken.

Uses of veal velouté
An example of veal velouté is the sauce prepared in a blanquette of veal.

Uses of fish velouté
Refer to fish section (page 213).

32 · **Brown sauce** *Sauce espagnole*

50 g	2 oz	good dripping or oil
60 g	2½ oz	flour
25 g	1 oz	tomato purée
1 litre	1 qt	brown stock
100 g	4 oz	carrot
100 g	4 oz	onion
50 g	2 oz	celery

Using hard margarine
This recipe provides:

686 kcals/2881 kJ
42.0 g fat of which 17.8 g saturated
67.2 g carbohydrate of which 20.2 g sugars
14.0 g protein
8.6 g fibre

Using sunflower oil
This recipe provides:

771 kcals/3236 kJ
51.5 g fat of which 6.8 g saturated
67.1 g carbohydrate of which 20.2 g sugars
13.9 g protein
8.6 g fibre

1 Heat the dripping or oil in a thick-bottomed pan.
2 Add the flour, cook out slowly to a light brown colour, stirring frequently.
3 Cool and mix in the tomato purée.
4 Gradually mix in the boiling stock. Bring to the boil.
5 Wash, peel and roughly cut the vegetables.
6 Lightly brown in a little fat or oil in a frying-pan.
7 Drain off the fat and add to the sauce.
8 Simmer gently 4–6 hours. Skim when necessary. Strain.

Care should be taken when making the brown roux not to allow it to cook too quickly, otherwise the starch in the flour (which is the thickening agent) will burn, and its thickening properties weaken. Over-browning should also be avoided as this tends to make the sauce taste bitter.

1 litre (1 quart)

33 · **Demi-glace sauce** *Sauce demi-glace*

This is a refined espagnole and is made by simmering 1 litre (1 qt) espagnole and 1 litre (1 qt) brown stock and reducing by a half. Skim off all impurities as they rise to the surface during cooking. Pass through a fine chinois (conical strainer), re-boil, correct the seasoning.

1 litre (1 quart)

Using sunflower oil
This recipe provides:

720 kcals/3010 kJ
51.0 g fat of which 6.6 g saturated
52.0 g carbohydrate of which 3.7 g sugars
15.0 g protein
2.1 g fibre

Using hard margarine
This recipe provides:

630 kcals/2634 kJ
42.0 g fat of which 17.5 g saturated
52.0 g carbohydrate of which 3.8 g sugars
15.0 g protein
2.1 g fibre

Sauces made from demi-glace

(Recipe for ¼ litre (½ pint))

34 · **Bordelaise sauce** *Sauce bordelaise*

50 g	2 oz	chopped shallots	reduction
125 ml	¼ pt	red wine	reduction
		pinch mignonette pepper	reduction
		sprig of thyme	reduction
		bay leaf	reduction
250 ml	½ pt	demi-glace	

1 Place reduction in a small sauteuse.
2 Allow to boil until reduced to a quarter
3 Add the demi-glace. Simmer 20–30 min.
4 Correct the seasoning. Pass through a fine strainer.

This sauce traditionally includes poached beef marrow either:
a) in dice poached and added to the sauce; or
b) cut in slices, poached and placed on meat before being sauced over.

Usually served with fried steaks, e.g. Entrecôte bordelaise.

¼ litre (½ pint) 4–6 portions

35 · **Chasseur sauce** *Sauce chasseur*

25 g	1 oz	butter
10 g	½ oz	chopped shallots
		1 small clove chopped garlic (optional)
50 g	2 oz	sliced button mushrooms
60 ml	⅛ pt	white wine (dry)
100 g	4 oz	tomatoes, skinned, deseeded, diced
250 ml	½ pt	demi-glace
		chopped parsley and tarragon

1 Melt the butter in a small sauteuse.
2 Add the shallots and cook gently for 2–3 min without colour.
3 Add the garlic and the mushrooms, cover, gently cook 2–3 min.
4 Strain off the fat.
5 Add the wine and reduce by half.
6 Add the tomatoes.
7 Add the demi-glace, simmer 5–10 min.
8 Correct the seasoning and add the tarragon and parsley.

Usually served with fried steaks, chops, chicken, etc., e.g. Noisette d'agneau chasseur.

¼ litre (½ pint) 4–6 portions

36 Devilled sauce *Sauce diable*

50 g	2 oz	chopped shallot or onion	reduction
5 g	¼ oz	mignonette pepper	
		tablespn white wine	
		tablespn vinegar	
		cayenne pepper	
250 ml	½ pt	demi-glace	

1 Boil the reduction and reduce by half.
2 Add the demi-glace. Simmer 5–10 min.
3 Season liberally with cayenne.
4 Pass through a fine chinois. Correct seasoning.

May be served with grilled or fried fish or meats e.g. Jambon grillé, sauce diable.

¼ litre (½ pint) 4–6 portions

37 Poivrade sauce *Sauce poivrade*

25 g	1 oz	margarine, butter or oil	
50 g	2 oz	onion	mirepoix
50 g	2 oz	carrot	
50 g	2 oz	celery	
		1 bay leaf	
		sprig of thyme	
		2 tablespns white wine	
		2 tablespns vinegar	
5 g	¼ oz	mignonette pepper	
250 ml	½ pt	demi-glace	

1 Melt the fat or oil in a small sauteuse.
2 Add the mirepoix and allow to brown.
3 Pour off the fat.
4 Add the wine, vinegar and pepper.
5 Reduce by half. Add the demi-glace.
6 Simmer 20–30 min. Correct the seasoning.
7 Pass through a fine chinois.

Usually served with venison.

¼ litre (½ pint) 4–6 portions

38 Italian sauce *Sauce italienne*

25 g	1 oz	margarine, oil or butter	duxelle
10 g	½ oz	chopped shallots	
50 g	2 oz	chopped mushrooms	
250 ml	½ pt	demi-glace	
25 g	1 oz	chopped lean ham	
100 g	4 oz	tomatoes, skinned, deseeded, diced	
		chopped parsley, chervil and tarragon	

1 Melt the fat or oil in a small sauteuse.

2 Add the shallots and gently cook 2–3 min.
3 Add the mushrooms and gently cook 2–3 min.
4 Add the demi-glace, ham and tomatoes.
5 Simmer 5–10 min. Correct the seasoning.
6 Add the chopped herbs.

Usually served with fried cuts of veal or lamb, e.g. Escalope de veau italienne.

¼ litre (½ pint) 4–6 portions

39 **Brown onion sauce** *Sauce lyonnaise*

25 g	1 oz	margarine, oil or butter
100 g	4 oz	sliced onions
		2 tablespns vinegar
250 ml	½ pt	demi-glace

1 Melt the fat or oil in a sauteuse.
2 Add the onions, cover with a lid.
3 Cook gently till tender.
4 Remove the lid and colour lightly.
5 Add the vinegar and completely reduce.
6 Add the demi-glace, simmer 5–10 min.
7 Skim and correct the seasoning.

May be served with Vienna steaks or fried liver.

¼ litre (½ pint) 4–6 portions

40 **Madeira sauce** *Sauce Madère*

250 ml	½ pt	demi-glace
		2 tablespns Madeira wine
25 g	1 oz	butter

1 Boil the demi-glace in a small sauteuse.
2 Add the Madeira, re-boil. Correct the seasoning.
3 Pass through a fine chinois. Gradually mix in the butter.

May be served with braised ox tongue (Langue braisé au madère).

¼ litre (½ pint) 4–6 portions

41 **Sherry sauce** *Sauce Xérès*

42 **Port wine sauce** *Sauce porto*

are made in the same way as Madeira sauce, using dry sherry or port wine as indicated

43 · **Piquant sauce** *Sauce piquante*

60 ml	⅛ pt	vinegar	reduction
50 g	2 oz	chopped shallots	
250 ml	½ pt	demiglace	
25 g	1 oz	chopped gherkins	
10 g	½ oz	chopped capers	
		½ tablespn chopped chervil, tarragon and parsley	

1 Place vinegar and shallots in a small sauteuse and reduce by half.
2 Add demi-glace, simmer 15–20 min.
3 Add the rest of the ingredients.
4 Skim and correct the seasoning.

May be served with made-up dishes and grilled meats.

¼ litre (½ pint) 4–6 portions

44 · **Robert sauce** *Sauce Robert*

10 g	½ oz	margarine, oil or butter
50 g	2 oz	onions
60 ml	⅛ pt	vinegar
250 ml	½ pt	demi-glace
		1 level tablespoon English or Continental mustard
		¼ level tablespoon castor sugar

1 Melt the fat or oil in a small sauteuse.
2 Add the finely chopped onion.
3 Cook gently without colour.
4 Add the vinegar and reduce completely.
5 Add the demi-glace, simmer 5–10 min.
6 Remove from the heat and add the mustard diluted with a little water and the sugar, do not boil.
7 Skim and correct the seasoning.

May be served with fried pork chop, e.g. Côte de porc, sauce Robert.

¼ litre (½ pint) 4–6 portions

45 · **Charcutière sauce** *Sauce charcutière*

Proceed as for sauce Robert and finally add 25 g (1 oz) sliced or julienne gherkins.

May also be served with pork chop.

¼ litre (½ pint) 4–6 portions

46 · Reform sauce *Sauce Réforme*

25 g	1 oz	carrot	mirepoix
25 g	1 oz	onion	
10 g	½ oz	celery	
		½ bay leaf	
		sprig of thyme	
10 g	½ oz	margarine or butter	
		½ tablespn vinegar	
		½ tablespoon redcurrant jelly	
		6 peppercorns	
250 ml	½ pt	demi-glace	
50 g	2 oz	julienne of cooked beetroot, white of egg, gherkin, mushroom, truffle, tongue	

1 Fry off the mirepoix in the fat in a sauteuse.
2 Drain off the fat.
3 Add the crushed peppercorns and vinegar and reduce by two-thirds.
4 Add the demi-glace. Simmer for 30 min.
5 Skim. Add the redcurrant jelly.
6 Re-boil and strain through a chinois.
7 Add the garnish.

Served with lamb cutlet, e.g. Côtelette d'agneau Réforme.

¼ litre (½ pint) 4–6 portions

Roast gravy (p. 104) and bread sauce (p. 106)

Miscellaneous sauces

47 · Curry sauce *Sauce kari*

50 g	2 oz	chopped onion
		¼ clove of garlic
10 g	½ oz	oil, butter or margarine
10 g	½ oz	flour
5 g	¼ oz	curry powder
5 g	¼ oz	tomato purée
375 ml	¾ pt	stock
25 g	1 oz	chopped apple
		1 tablespn chopped chutney
5 g	¼ oz	desiccated coconut
10 g	½ oz	sultanas
10 g	½ oz	grated ginger root or
5 g	¼ oz	ground ginger
		salt

Using sunflower oil
This recipe provides:

260 kcals/1092 kJ
14.1 g fat of which 4.1 g saturated
30.3 g carbohydrate of which 19.9 g sugars
4.9 g protein
4.1 g fibre

1. Gently cook the onion and garlic in the fat in a small sauteuse without colouring.
2. Mix in the flour and curry powder.
3. Cook gently to a sandy mixture.
4. Mix in the tomato purée, cool.
5. Gradually add the boiling stock and mix to a smooth sauce.
6. Add the remainder of the ingredients, season with salt.
7. Simmer 30 min.
8. Skim and correct the seasoning.

This sauce has a wide range of uses, e.g. with prawns, shrimps, vegetables, eggs, etc.

For poached or soft-boiled eggs it may be strained and for all purposes it may be finished with 2–3 tablespns cream or natural yoghurt.

¼ litre (½ pint) 4–6 portions

48 · Roast gravy *Jus rôti*

200 g	8 oz	raw bones
250 ml	1 pt	stock or water
50 g	2 oz	onion
25 g	1 oz	celery
50 g	2 oz	carrot

Using sunflower oil
This recipe provides:

120 kcals/504 kJ
10.0 g fat of which 1.3 g saturated
1.8 g carbohydrate of which 0.0 g sugars
5.6 g protein
0.0 g fibre

For preference use beef bones for roast beef gravy and the appropriate bones for lamb, veal, mutton and pork.

1 Chop bones and brown in the oven or brown in a little fat on top of the stove in a frying-pan.
2 Drain off all fat.
3 Place in saucepan with the stock or water.
4 Bring to boil, skim and allow to simmer.
5 Add the lightly browned mirepoix which may be fried in a little fat in a frying-pan, or added to the bones when partly browned.
6 Simmer 1½–2 hr.
7 Remove the joint from the roasting tin when cooked.
8 Return the tray to a low heat to allow the sediment to settle.
9 Carefully strain off the fat, leaving the sediment in the tin.
10 Return to the stove and brown carefully, deglaze with the brown stock.
11 Allow to simmer for a few minutes.
12 Correct the colour and seasoning. Strain and skim.

This sauce is illustrated on pages 85 and 105.

¼ litre (½ pint) 4–6 portions

49 Thickened gravy *Jus-lié*

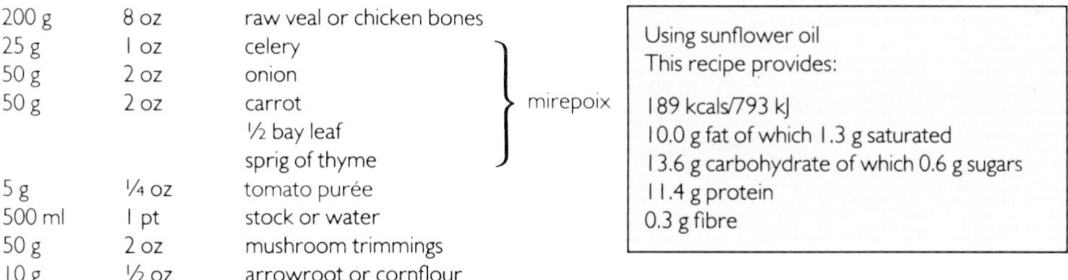

200 g	8 oz	raw veal or chicken bones	
25 g	1 oz	celery	mirepoix
50 g	2 oz	onion	mirepoix
50 g	2 oz	carrot	mirepoix
		½ bay leaf	mirepoix
		sprig of thyme	mirepoix
5 g	¼ oz	tomato purée	
500 ml	1 pt	stock or water	
50 g	2 oz	mushroom trimmings	
10 g	½ oz	arrowroot or cornflour	

Using sunflower oil
This recipe provides:

189 kcals/793 kJ
10.0 g fat of which 1.3 g saturated
13.6 g carbohydrate of which 0.6 g sugars
11.4 g protein
0.3 g fibre

1 Chop the bones and brown in the oven or in a little fat in a sauteuse on top of the stove.
2 Add mirepoix, brown well.
3 Mix in the tomato purée and stock.
4 Simmer 2 hr. Add mushroom trimmings.
5 Dilute the arrowroot in a little cold water.
6 Pour into the boiling stock, stirring continuously until it re-boils.
7 Simmer 10–15 min. Correct the seasoning.
8 Pass through a fine strainer.

¼ litre (½ pint) 4–6 portions

50 · Bread sauce

375 ml	¾ pt	milk
		small onion studded with a clove
25 g	1 oz	fresh white breadcrumbs
		salt, cayenne
10 g	½ oz	butter

1 Infuse the simmering milk with the studded onion for 15 min.
2 Remove the onion, mix in the crumbs. Simmer 2–3 min.
3 Season, correct the consistency.
4 Add the butter on top of the sauce to prevent a skin forming.
5 Mix well when serving.

Served with roast chicken and roast game. (Illustrated on page 85.)

¼ litre (½ pint)   4–6 portions

51 · Apple sauce

400 g	1 lb	cooking apples
25 g	1 oz	sugar
25 g	1 oz	margarine or butter

1 Peel, core and wash the apples.
2 Place with the sugar, margarine or butter and a little water in a saucepan with a tight-fitting lid.
3 Cook to a purée.
4 Pass through a sieve or liquidise.

Served with roast pork, duck and goose. *¼ litre (½ pint)   4–6 portions*

52 · Cranberry sauce *Sauce airelles*

400 g	1 lb	cranberries
60–100 ml	⅛–¼ pt	water
50 g	2 oz	sugar

Boil together in a suitable pan (not iron or aluminium because the interior coating of the pan will cause the cranberries to discolour) until soft, liquidise or sieve if required.

Traditionally served with roast turkey. *¼ litre (½ pint)   4–6 portions*

53 · Tomato sauce *Sauce tomate*

10 g	½ oz	margarine or butter	
50 g	2 oz	onion	mirepoix
50 g	2 oz	carrot	mirepoix
25 g	1 oz	celery	mirepoix
		½ bay leaf	mirepoix
		sprig of thyme	mirepoix
10 g	½ oz	bacon scraps	

Using hard margarine
This recipe provides:

221 kcals/931 kJ
12.5 g fat of which 5.1 g saturated
20.2 g carbohydrate of which 11.5 g sugars
8.5 g protein
2.9 g fibre

10 g	½ oz	flour
50 g	2 oz	tomato purée
375 ml	¾ pt	stock
		½ clove garlic
		salt, pepper

Using butter
This recipe provides:

223 kcals/936 kJ
12.6 g fat of which 6.7 g saturated
20.2 g carbohydrate of which 11.5 g sugars
8.5 g protein
2.9 g fibre

1 Melt the margarine or butter in a small sauteuse.
2 Add the mirepoix and bacon scraps and brown slightly.
3 Mix in the flour and cook to a sandy texture. Allow to colour slightly.
4 Mix in the tomato purée, allow to cool.
5 Gradually add the boiling stock, stir to the boil.
6 Add the garlic, season. Simmer, 1 hr.
7 Correct the seasoning and cool.
8 Pass through a fine chinois.

This sauce has many uses, e.g. served with spaghetti, eggs, fish, meats, etc. (See page 203 for an illustration of service of tomato sauce.)

¼ litre (½ pint) 4–6 portions

54 · **Smitaine sauce** *Sauce smitaine*

25 g	1 oz	butter or margarine
50 g	2 oz	finely chopped onion
60 ml	⅛ pt	white wine
½ litre	1 pint	sour cream
		seasoning
		juice of ¼ of a lemon

1 Melt butter or margarine in a sauteuse and cook onion without colour.
2 Add the white wine and reduce by half.
3 Add sour cream and season lightly, reduce by one-third.
4 Pass through a fine strainer and finish with lemon juice.

55 · **Melted butter** *Beurre fondu*

200 g	8 oz	butter
		2 tablespns water or white wine

Method I

Boil the butter and water gently together till combined, then pass through a fine strainer.

Method II

Melt the butter and carefully strain off the fat leaving the water and sediment in the pan.

Usually served with boiled fish and certain vegetables, e.g. blue trout, salmon; asparagus and sea kale.

¼ litre (½ pint) 4–6 portions

56 Hollandaise sauce *Sauce hollandaise*

		6 crushed peppercorns	reduction (optional)
		1 tablespn vinegar	
		2 egg yolks	
200 g	8 oz	butter	
		salt, cayenne	

This recipe provides:

1616 kcals/6789 kJ
176.2 g fat of which 107.9 g saturated
0.1 g carbohydrate of which 0.1 g sugars
7.3 g protein
0.0 g fibre

1. Place the peppercorns and vinegar in a small sauteuse or stainless steel pan and reduce to one-third.
2. Add 1 tablespn cold water, allow to cool.
3. Mix in the yolks with a whisk.
4. Return to a gentle heat and whisking continuously cook to a sabayon (this is the cooking of the yolks to a thickened consistency, like cream, sufficient to show the mark of the whisk).
5. Remove from the heat and cool slightly.
6. Whisk in gradually the melted warm butter until thoroughly combined.
7. Correct the seasoning. If reduction is not used, add a few drops of lemon juice.
8. Pass through a muslin, tammy cloth, or fine chinois.
9. The sauce should be kept at only a slightly warm temperature until served.
10. Serve in a slightly warm sauceboat.

The cause of hollandaise sauce curdling is either because the butter has been added too quickly, or because of excess heat which will cause the albumen in the eggs to harden, shrink and separate from the liquid.

Should the sauce curdle, place a teaspoon of boiling water in a clean sauteuse and gradually whisk in the curdled sauce. If this fails to reconstitute the sauce then place an egg yolk in a clean sauteuse with a dessertspoon of water. Whisk lightly over gentle heat until slightly thickened. Remove from heat and gradually add the curdled sauce whisking continuously. To stabilise the sauce during service, 60 ml (1/8 pint) thick béchamel may be added before straining.

Served with hot fish (salmon, trout, turbot), and vegetables (asparagus, cauliflower, broccoli).

1/4 litre (1/2 pint) 4–6 portions

57 **Béarnaise sauce** *Sauce béarnaise*

10 g	½ oz	chopped shallots
		6 crushed peppercorns
5 g	¼ oz	tarragon
		1 tablespn tarragon vinegar
		3 egg yolks
200 g	8 oz	butter
		sprig chopped chervil

1 Make a reduction with the shallots, peppercorns, tarragon stalks and vinegar.
2 Proceed as for hollandaise sauce.
3 After passing add the chopped tarragon leaves and chervil.

Usually served with grilled meat and fish, e.g. Chateaubriand grillé, sauce béarnaise. This sauce should be twice as thick as hollandaise.

¼ litre (½ pint) 4–6 portions

Compound butter sauces

58 **Parsley butter** *Beurre maître d'hôtel*

50 g	2 oz	butter
		juice of ¼ lemon
		¼ teaspn chopped parsley
		salt, pepper

1 portion provides:

93 kcals/389 kJ
10.3 g fat of which 6.5 g saturated
– g carbohydrate of which – g sugars
0.1 g protein
– g fibre

Note To reduce risk of Salmonella infection use pasteurised egg yolks, do not keep the same longer than two hours then discard. This applies to both Hollandaise and Bearnaise sauces.

1 Combine all the ingredients.
2 Shape into a roll 2 cm (1 in) diam.
3 Place in wet greaseproof paper or foil.
4 Harden in the refrigerator.
5 Cut into ½ cm (¼ in) slices.

May be served with grilled meats and fish and fried fish (Sole Colbert).

4 portions

59 **Anchovy butter** *Beurre d'anchois*

50 g	2 oz	butter
		salt, pepper
		few drops anchovy essence

Proceed as for parsley butter.
May be served with grilled and fried fish, e.g. grilled lemon sole.

4 portions

60 · **Shrimp butter** *Beurre des crevettes*

50 g	2 oz	cooked shrimps
50 g	2 oz	butter

1 Finely chop or pound the shrimps in a mortar.
2 Add the butter and mix well.
3 Proceed as for parsley butter points 2–5.

May be served with grilled or fried fish, e.g. grilled plaice.

4 portions

Cold sauces Les sauces froides

61 · **Mayonnaise sauce** *Sauce mayonnaise*

This is a basic cold sauce and has a wide variety of uses, particularly in hors-d'oeuvre dishes. It should always be available on any cold buffet.

If during the making of the sauce, it should become too thick, then a little vinegar or water may be added. Mayonnaise will turn or curdle for several reasons:

1 If the oil is added too quickly.
2 If the oil is too cold.
3 If the sauce is insufficiently whisked.
4 If the yolk is stale and therefore weak.

		2 egg yolks
		2 teaspns vinegar
		salt, ground white pepper
		⅛ teaspn English or Continental mustard
250 ml	½ pt	olive or other good quality oil
		1 teaspn boiling water (approx.)

This recipe provides:

2388 kcals/10 030 kJ
262.2 g fat of which 38.9 g saturated
0.3 g carbohydrate of which 0.1 g sugars
6.8 g protein
0.0 g fibre

1 Place yolks, vinegar and seasoning in a bowl and whisk well.
2 Gradually pour on the oil very slowly, whisking continuously.
3 Add the boiling water whisking well.
4 Correct the seasoning.

The method of rethickening a turned mayonnaise is either

a) by taking a clean basin, adding 1 teaspn boiling water and gradually whisking in the curdled sauce, or
b) by taking another yolk thinned with ½ teaspn cold water whisked well, then gradually whisking in the curdled sauce.

¼ litre (½ pint)   8 portions approx.

Cold salmon (p. 234) with mayonnaise sauce

62 · **Andalusian sauce** *Sauce andalouse*

Add to 1/4 litre (1/2 pt) of mayonnaise, 2 tablespns tomato juice or ketchup and 1 tablespn pimento cut in julienne.

May be served with cold salads.

1/4 litre (1/2 pint)

63 · **Green sauce** *Sauce verte*

50 g	2 oz	spinach, tarragon, chervil, chives, watercress
250 ml	½ pt	mayonnaise

1 Pick, wash, blanch and refresh the green leaves.
2 Squeeze dry.
3 Pass through a very fine sieve.
4 Mix with the mayonnaise.

May be served with cold salmon or salmon trout.

1/4 litre (1/2 pint) 8 portions approx.

64 · **Tartare sauce** *Sauce tartare*

250 ml	½ pt	mayonnaise	
25 g	1 oz	capers	chopped
50 g	2 oz	gherkins	chopped
		sprig of parsley	chopped

Combine all the ingredients.

Usually served with deep fried fish. (See page 203 for an illustration of service of this sauce.)

1/4 litre (1/2 pint) 8 portions approx.

65 · **Remoulade sauce** *Sauce remoulade*

Prepare as for tartare sauce adding 1 teaspoon of anchovy essence and mixing thoroughly.

This sauce may be served with fried fish.

1/8 litre (1/4 pint)

66 Tyrolienne sauce *Sauce tyrolienne*

5 g	¼ oz	shallots
30 ml	¼ pt	oil
50 g	2 oz	tomatoes
⅛ litre	¼ pt	mayonnaise
		¼ bay leaf
		small sprig of thyme
		½ teaspn parsley, chervil, tarragon

1 Finely chop the shallots.
2 Cook without colour in the oil.
3 Peel, de-seed and dice the tomatoes.
4 Add to the shallots.
5 Cook until soft and dry.
6 Pass the tomatoes and shallots through fine sieve.
7 Allow to cool.
8 Mix in with the mayonnaise and chopped parsley, chervil and tarragon (fines herbes).

This sauce may be served with fried fish or cold meats.

⅛ litre (¼ pint)

67 Horseradish sauce *Sauce raifort*

25 g	1 oz	grated horseradish
		1 tablespn vinegar
		salt, pepper
125 ml	½ pt	lightly whipped cream

This recipe provides:

430 kcals/1807 kJ
43.8 g fat of which 27.8 g saturated
6.0 g carbohydrate of which 5.0 g sugars
3.6 g protein
2.1 g fibre

1 Wash, peel and re-wash the horseradish.
2 Grate finely.
3 Mix all the ingredients together.

Serve with roast beef, smoked trout.

⅛ litre (¼ pint) 8 portions

68 Mint sauce

		2–3 tablespns mint
		1 dessertspn castor sugar
125 ml	¼ pt	vinegar

This recipe provides:

49 kcals/204 kJ
0.0 g fat of which 0.0 g saturated
11.3 g carbohydrate of which 11.3 g sugars
1.5 g protein
1.8 g fibre

1 Chop the washed, picked mint with the sugar.
2 Place in a china basin and add the vinegar.
3 If the vinegar is too sharp dilute with a little water.

Serve with roast lamb. (Illustrated on page 239.)

Note A less acid sauce can be produced by dissolving the sugar in 125 ml (¼ pt) boiling water and, when cold, adding the chopped mint and 1–2 tablespns vinegar to taste.

⅛ litre (¼ pint) 8 portions

69 · Cumberland sauce

100 ml	3/16 pt	redcurrant jelly
5 g	¼ oz	chopped shallots
		juice of ¼ lemon
		2 tablespns port
		juice of 1 orange
		¼ level teaspn of English mustard

This recipe provides:
336 kcals/1410 kJ
0.3 g fat of which 0.0 g saturated
78.8 g carbohydrate of which 78.6 g sugars
1.1 g protein
1.2 g fibre

1. Warm and melt the jelly.
2. Blanch the shallots well and refresh.
3. Add the shallots to the jelly with the remainder of the ingredients.
4. Cut a little fine julienne of orange zest, blanch, refresh and add to the sauce.

May be served with cold ham.

⅛ litre (¼ pint) 8 portions

70 · Oxford sauce

As for Cumberland sauce, using chopped blanched orange and lemon zest instead of julienne of orange.

Chaud-froid sauces and aspic jelly

Chaud-froid sauces and aspic jelly are basic larder preparations. Chaud-froid sauces are derived from béchamel, velouté or demi-glace to which aspic jelly or gelatine is added so as to help them to set when cold. They are used to mask fish, meat, poultry and game, either whole, or cut in pieces, for cold buffets, which are then usually decorated and finally coated with aspic.

Aspic is a savoury jelly which may be used on cold egg, fish, meat, poultry, game and vegetable dishes that are prepared for cold buffets so as to give them an attractive appearance. For meat dishes a beef or veal stock is made; for fowl, chicken stock; and for fish, fish stock.

71 · Chaud-froid sauce *White*

50 g	2 oz	leaf gelatine
1 litre	1 qt	béchamel or velouté
125 ml	¼ pt	cream (if necessary to improve the colour of the sauce)

This recipe provides:
2449 kcals/10 285 kJ
180.6 g fat of which 97.7 g saturated
127.3 g carbohydrate of which 51.2 g sugars
86.6 g protein
3.6 g fibre

1 Soak the gelatine in cold water.
2 Bring the sauce to the boil.
3 Remove from the heat.
4 Add the well-squeezed gelatine and stir until dissolved, and correct the seasoning.
5 Pass through a tammy cloth or fine strainer.
6 When the sauce is half cooled mix in the cream.

1 litre (1 quart)

Brown

1 litre	1 qt	demi-glace
50 g	2 oz	leaf gelatine

Using sunflower oil
This recipe provides:
863 kcals/3624 kJ
51.1 g fat of which 6.6 g saturated
50.7 g carbohydrate of which 3.8 g sugars
53.2 g protein
2.2 g fibre

Proceed as above, omitting the cream.

72 · Aspic jelly *Gelée d'aspic*

		2–3 whites of eggs
1 litre	1 qt	strong, fat-free, seasoned stock (as required poultry, meat, game or fish)
		1 tablespn vinegar
		2 sprigs tarragon
75 g	3 oz	leaf gelatine (approx. 24 leaves)

This recipe provides:
397 kcals/1668 kJ
0.0 g fat of which 0.0 g saturated
7.4 g carbohydrate of which 0.1 g sugars
91.3 g protein
0.0 g fibre

1 Whisk the whites in a thick-bottomed pan with ¼ litre (½ pt) of the cold stock and the vinegar and tarragon.
2 Heat the rest of the stock, add the gelatine (previously soaked for 20 minutes in cold water) and whisk till dissolved.
3 Add the stock and dissolved gelatine into the thick-bottomed pan. Whisk well.
4 Place on the stove and allow to come gently to the boil until clarified.
5 Strain through a muslin.
6 Repeat if necessary, using egg whites only to give a crystal-clear aspic.

For further information see *The Larder Chef*, Leto and Bode and *Contemporary Cookery*, Ceserani, Kinton and Foskett.

1 litre (1 quart)

Green salad (p. 141); mixed salad (p. 141); French salad (p. 141) with vinaigrette (p. 119)

6

HORS-D'OEUVRE, SALADS AND SANDWICHES

General objectives
To know when, where and how hors-d'oeuvre and salads are served and to be aware of the need for variety. To understand the principles related to single and composite hors-d'oeuvre and single and composite salads. To appreciate the need for attractive presentation and correct utilisation of food.

To know the kinds of sandwiches and fillings available.

Specific objectives
To be able to list and prepare a wide variety of foods which may be used and to demonstrate presentation showing a high degree of artistic ability. To pay particular attention to seasoning and variation of colour, texture and ingredients. To describe and demonstrate various ways of serving salads, paying due attention to freshness and presentation. To be able to list and produce a variety of salad dressings.

To list a variety of ingredients which may be used on their own or combined as sandwich fillings. To state and demonstrate different ways of presenting a variety of sandwiches.

The choice of a wide variety of foods, combination of foods and recipes is available for preparation and services as hors-d'oeuvre and salads.

Hors-d'oeuvre can be divided into three categories:

a) single cold food items e.g. smoked salmon, pâté, melon etc.,
b) a selection of well seasoned cold dishes,
c) well seasoned hot dishes.

Hors-d'oeuvre may be served for luncheon, dinner or supper and the wide choice, colour appeal and versatility of the dishes makes many items and combinations of items suitable for snacks and salads at any time of day.

Salads may be served as an accompaniment to hot and cold foods and as dishes in their own right. They can be served for lunch, tea, high tea, dinner, supper and snack meals. Salads may be divided in two sections:

a) simple – using one ingredient;
b) mixed or composite – using more than one ingredient.

Some salads may form part of a composite hors-d'oeuvre.

Single food hors-d'oeuvre

1 **Salad dressings**

1 Vinaigrette 2 Mayonnaise

3 Acidulated cream 4 Natural yoghurt

These dressings may be varied by the addition of other ingredients.

Vinaigrette

3–6 tablespns	olive oil, according to taste	combine
1 teaspn	French mustard	
1 tablespn	vinegar	
	salt, mill pepper	

Using 3 tablespns oil
This recipe provides:

415 kcals/1740 kJ
45.5 g fat of which 6.3 g saturated
0.5 g carbohydrate of which 0.1 g sugars
0.6 g protein
0.0 g fibre

Illustrated on page 115.

Variations to vinaigrette

Using 6 tablespns oil
This recipe provides:

819 kcals/3439 kJ
90.5 g fat of which 12.6 g saturated
0.5 g carbohydrate of which 0.1 g sugars
0.6 g protein
0.0 g fibre

a) English mustard in place of French mustard;
b) chopped herbs (chives, parsley, tarragon, etc.);
c) chopped hard-boiled egg;
d) lemon juice in place of vinegar (lemon dressing).

Roquefort dressing

50 g	2 oz	Roquefort cheese
125 ml	¼ pt	vinaigrette

This recipe provides:

662 kcals/2779 kJ
67.7 g fat of which 16.6 g saturated
0.7 g carbohydrate of which 0.1 g sugars
12.4 g protein
0.0 g fibre

1 Purée the cheese.
2 Gradually add the vinaigrette mixing continuously.

Thousand island dressing

		salt, pepper
		3–4 drops tabasco
125 ml	¼ pt	vinegar
375 ml	¾ pt	oil
50 g	2 oz	red pimento
50 g	2 oz	green pimento
		chopped parsley
		2 hard boiled eggs
2 tablespns		tomato ketchup (optional)

This recipe provides:

3584 kcals/15 055 kJ
387.0 g fat of which 56.5 g saturated
10.2 g carbohydrate of which 9.8 g sugars
16.1 g protein
1.8 g fibre

1 Place salt, pepper, tabasco and vinegar in a basin.
2 Mix well.
3 Mix in the oil.
4 Add the chopped pimentos and parsley.
5 Mix in the sieved hard-boiled eggs.

Mayonnaise

See page 110.

Acidulated cream

	juice of ¼ lemon
4 tablespns	cream

Gently stir the juice into the cream at the last moment before serving.

> This recipe provides:
>
> 200 kcals/838 kJ
> 21.0 g fat of which 13.3 g saturated
> 1.6 g carbohydrate of which 1.6 g sugars
> 1.2 g protein
> 0.0 g fibre

2 · **Oysters** *Les huîtres*

The shells should be tightly shut to indicate freshness. The oysters should be carefully opened with a special oyster knife so as to avoid scratching the inside shell, then turned and arranged neatly in the deep shell and served on a bed of crushed ice on a plate. They should not be washed unless gritty and the natural juices should always be left in the deep shell.

Accompaniments – brown bread and butter and lemon. It is usual to serve six oysters as a portion.

3 · **Caviar** *Caviar*

This is the prepared roe of the sturgeon, a very expensive imported commodity usually served in its original tin or jar, in a timbale of crushed ice. One spoonful, 25 g (1 oz), represents a portion.

Accompaniment – brown bread and butter.

4 · **Smoked salmon** *Saumon fumé*

Before service, a side of smoked salmon must be carefully trimmed to remove the dry outside surface. All bones must be removed; a pair of pliers are found useful for this. The salmon is carved as thinly as possible on the slant and neatly dressed, overlapping, on a plate or dish, decorated with sprigs of parsley 35–50 g (1½–2 oz) per portion.

Accompaniments – brown bread and butter and lemon.

Illustrated as part of a plated hors-d'oeuvre on page 131.)

> 1 portion (25 g) provides:
>
> 36 kcals/149 kJ
> 1.1 g fat of which 0.3 g saturated
> 0.0 g carbohydrate of which 0.0 g sugars
> 6.4 g protein
> 0.0 g fibre

> 1 portion (35 g) provides:
>
> 50 kcals/209 kJ
> 1.6 g fat of which 0.4 g saturated
> 0.0 g carbohydrate of which 0.0 g sugars
> 8.9 g protein
> 0.0 g fibre

Other smoked fish served as hors-d'oeuvre include halibut, eel, conger eel, trout, mackerel, herring (buckling), cod's roe, sprats.

5 · Gulls' eggs *Oeufs de mouettes*

These eggs are hard-boiled, then served cold, and may be dressed on a bed of mustard and cress. It is usual to serve two per portion.

Accompaniment – brown bread and butter.

6 · Foie gras *Foie gras*

This is a ready-prepared delicacy made from goose liver, and it may be served in its original dish. If tinned, it should be thoroughly chilled, removed from the tin and cut into 1 cm (½ in) slices.

Serve garnished with a little chopped aspic jelly.

7 · Liver pâté *Pâté de foie*

This is a home-made preparation often seen on the menu as pâté maison. A typical recipe is:

100 g	4 oz	liver (chicken, pigs, calves, lambs, etc.)
25 g	1 oz	butter, oil or margarine
10 g	½ oz	chopped onion
		½ clove garlic
		sprig of thyme, parsley, chervil
50 g	2 oz	fat pork
50 g	2 oz	lean pork
		salt, pepper
25 g	1 oz	fat bacon

1 portion provides:

213 kcals/896 kJ
19.1 g fat of which 8.5 g saturated
0.7 g carbohydrate of which 0.1 g sugars
9.8 g protein
– g fibre

1 Cut the liver in 2 cm (1 in) pieces.
2 Toss quickly in the butter in a frying-pan over a fierce heat for a few seconds with the onion, garlic and herbs.
3 Allow to cool.
4 Pass with the pork, twice through a mincer. Season.
5 Line an earthenware terrine with wafer-thin slices of fat bacon.
6 Place in the mixture. Cover with fat bacon.
7 Stand in a tray half full of water and bring to simmering point.
8 Cook in a moderate oven for 1 hr.

When quite cold cut in ½ cm (¼ in) slices and serve on lettuce leaves on a plate or dish.

Usually accompanied with freshly made toast. *4 portions*

8 and 9 · Salami and assorted cooked or smoked sausages *Saucisson*

These are ready-bought sausages usually prepared from pork by specialist butchers. Most countries have their own specialities, and a variety of them are exported. They are thinly sliced and either served individually or an assortment may be offered. Mortadella, garlic sausage and zungenwurst are other examples of this type of sausage.

(Illustrated as part of a plated hors-d'oeuvre on page 131.)

10 · Potted shrimps

These are a bought, prepared dish consisting of peeled shrimps cooked and served in butter. They may be served on their own or with smoked salmon.

Accompaniment – brown bread and butter.

11 · Grapefruit *Pamplemousse*

These are halved, the segments are individually cut with a small knife, then they are chilled. Serve with a maraschino cherry in the centre. The common practice of sprinkling with castor sugar is incorrect, as some customers prefer their grapefruit without sugar.

Serve half a grapefruit per portion in a coupe.

Clockwise from top left: half grapefruit; orange cocktail; Florida cocktail; orange cocktail in coupe

12 · Grapefruit cocktail

Allow ½–1 grapefruit per head.

The fruit should be peeled with a sharp knife in order to remove all white pith and yellow skin. Cut into segments and remove all the pips. The segments and the juice should then be dressed in a cocktail glass or grapefruit coupe and chilled. A cherry may be added.

Preparation of grapefruit, orange and Florida cocktails

13 · Grapefruit and orange cocktail

Allow half an orange and half a grapefruit per head.

Prepare segments as for grapefruit cocktail and arrange in a coupe. A cherry may be added. Serve chilled. Sometimes known as Florida cocktail.

14 · Orange cocktail

As for grapefruit cocktail, using oranges in place of grapefruit.

15 · Florida cocktail

This is a mixture of grapefruit, orange and pineapple segments.

16 · Avocado pear *l'Avocat*

Allow ½ a pear per portion.

The pears must be ripe (test by pressing gently, the pear should give slightly).

1 Cut in half lengthwise. Remove the stone.
2 Serve garnished with lettuce accompanied by vinaigrette (page 119) or variations on vinaigrette.

Preparation and presentation of avocado pear

Avocado pears are sometimes filled with shrimps or crabmeat bound with a shellfish cocktail sauce or other similar fillings, and may be served hot or cold using a variety of fillings and sauces.

Avocado pear may also be halved lengthwise, the stone removed, the skin peeled and the pear sliced and fanned onto a plate, and garnished with a simple or composed salad.

17 · Fruit cocktail

Allow ½ kg (1 lb) unprepared fruit for 4 portions.

This is a mixture of fruits such as apples, pears, pineapples, grapes, cherries, etc., washed, peeled and cut into neat segments or dice and added to a syrup (100 g (4 oz) sugar to ¼ litre (½ pt) water) and the juice of half a lemon. Neatly place in cocktail glasses and chill.

18 · Tropical fruit cocktail

As for fruit cocktail, using a variety of fruits, e.g. mango, passion fruit, lychees, pineapple, kiwi fruit.

19 · Melon cocktail

Approximately half a melon for 4 portions.

The melon, which must be ripe, is peeled, then cut into neat segments or dice or scopped out with a parisienne spoon, dressed in cocktail glasses and chilled. A little liqueur, e.g. crème de menthe, maraschino, may also be added.

20 · Chilled melon *Melon frappé*

Approximately half a honeydew or cantaloup melon for 4 portions.

1 portion provides:

20 kcals/82 kJ
0.0 g fat of which 0.0 g saturated
4.7 g carbohydrate of which 4.7 g sugars
0.6 g protein
0.9 g fibre

Cut the melon in half, remove the pips and cut into thick slices. Cut a piece off the skin so that the slice will stand firm and serve on crushed ice.

Accompaniment – castor sugar and ground ginger.

21 · Charentais melon *Melon de Charente*

1 melon per portion.

1 Cut a slice from the top of the melon to form a lid.
2 Remove the seeds.
3 Replace the lid and serve chilled.

22 · Charentais melon with port *Melon de Charente au porto*

As for previous recipe adding ½ glass of port to the inside of each melon approximately 15 min before service.

23 Charentais melon with raspberries

Melon de Charente aux framboises

As for recipe 20 adding 50 g (2 oz) picked and washed raspberries. (Strawberries may be used as a variation.)

24 Fruit juice

Pineapple, orange, grapefruit.

This is usually bought ready prepared, but may be made from the fresh fruit.

25 Tomato juice *Jus de tomate*

½ kg (1 lb) tomatoes for 4 portions.

1 portion provides:

18 kcals/74 kJ
0.0 g fat of which 0.0 g saturated
3.5 g carbohydrate of which 3.5 g sugars
1.1 g protein
0.0 g fibre

Fresh ripe tomatoes must be used. Wash, remove the eyes, then liquidise and pass through a strainer. The juice is then served in cocktail glasses and chilled. Offer Worcester sauce when serving.

26 Shellfish cocktails: crab *Cocktail de crabe*; lobster *homard*; shrimp *crevettes*; prawn *crevettes roses*

		½ lettuce
100–150 g	4–6 oz	prepared shellfish
125 ml	¼ pt	shellfish cocktail sauce

1 portion provides:

230 kcals/966 kJ
21.0 g fat of which 3.2 g saturated
0.6 g carbohydrate of which 0.6 g sugars
9.6 g protein
0.3 g fibre

1 Wash, drain well and finely shred the lettuce.
2 Place about 2 cm (1 in) deep in cocktail glasses or dishes.
3 Add the prepared shellfish.
   a) crab (shredded white meat only).
   b) lobster (cut in ½ cm (¼ in) dice).
   c) shrimps (peeled and washed).
   d) prawns (peeled, washed, and if large cut into two or three pieces).
4 Coat with sauce.
5 Decorate with an appropriate piece of the content, e.g. prawn, with the shell on the tail removed, on the edge of the glass of a prawn-cocktail.

4 portions

Shellfish Cocktail Sauce

Method I

	1 egg yolk	mayonnaise
1 dessertspn	vinegar	mayonnaise
	salt, pepper, mustard	mayonnaise
5 tablespns	olive oil or sunflower oil	mayonnaise
3 tablespns	tomato juice or ketchup to taste	
2–3 drops	Worcester sauce (optional)	

Make the mayonnaise as on page 110.

Combine with the tomato juice and Worcester sauce (if using).

Method II

5 tablespns	lightly whipped cream or unsweetened non-dairy cream
3 tablespns	tomato juice or ketchup to taste
	salt, pepper
	few drops of lemon juice

Mix all the ingredients together.

Fresh or tinned tomato juice or diluted tomato ketchup may be used for both the above methods, but the use of tinned tomato purée gives an unpleasant flavour.

1/8 litre (1/4 pint)

27 · Dressed crab

When buying crabs, care should be taken to see that they have both claws and that they are heavy in comparison to their size. When possible they should be bought alive to ensure freshness.

Place the crabs in boiling salted water with a little vinegar added. Allow to boil for approx 15–30 min according to size; these times apply to crabs weighing from 1/2–2 1/2 kg (1–5 lb). Allow to cool in the cooling liquor.

Dressed crab

Preparation of dressed crab

To dress

1 Remove large claws and sever at the joints.
2 Remove the flexible pincer from the claw.
3 Crack or saw carefully and remove all flesh.
4 Remove flesh from two remaining joints with handle of spoon.
5 Carefully remove the soft under-shell.
6 Discard the gills (dead man's fingers) and the sac behind the eyes.
7 Scrape out all the inside of the shell and pass through sieve.
8 Season with salt, pepper, Worcester sauce and a little mayonnaise sauce, thicken lightly with fresh white breadcrumbs.
9 Trim the shell by tapping carefully along the natural line.
10 Scrub the shell thoroughly and leave to dry.
11 Dress the brown meat down the centre of the shell.
12 Shred the white meat, taking care to remove any small pieces of shell.
13 Dress neatly on either side of the brown meat.
14 Decorate as desired, using any of the following: chopped parsley, hard-boiled white and yolk of egg, anchovies, capers, olives.
15 Serve the crab on a flat dish, garnish with lettuce leaves, quarters of tomato and the legs.

Serve a vinaigrette or mayonnaise sauce separately.

Allow 200–300 g (8–12 oz) unprepared crab per portion

28 Soused herring or mackerel

		2 herrings or mackerel
		salt, pepper
25 g	1 oz	button onions
25 g	1 oz	carrots, peeled and fluted
		½ bay leaf
		6 peppercorns
		sprig of thyme
60 ml	⅛ pt	vinegar

This recipe provides:
576 kcals/2419 kJ
44.5 g fat of which 9.4 g saturated
3.0 g carbohydrate of which 3.0 g sugars
41.0 g protein
1.1 g fibre

1. Clean, scale and fillet the fish.
2. Wash fillets well, season with salt and pepper.
3. Roll up with the skin outside.
4. Place in an earthenware dish.
5. Peel and wash the onion.
6. Cut onion and carrot into neat thin rings.
7. Blanch for 2–3 min.
8. Add to the fish with the remainder of the ingredients.
9. Cover with greaseproof paper and cook in a moderate oven for 15–20 min.
10. Allow to cool, place in a dish with the onion and carrot.
11. Garnish with picked parsley.

29 Smoked mackerel mousse

200 g	8 oz	smoked mackerel, free from bone and skin
		optional seasoning: pepper, chopped parsley, fennel or chervil, tablespn tomato ketchup, two ripe tomatoes free from skin and pips.
90 ml	3½ fluid oz	double cream (or non-dairy cream)

1. Ensure that the mackerel is completely free from skin and bones.
2. Place with required seasoning in liquidiser.
3. Three quarter whip the cream.
4. Remove mackerel from liquidiser and fold into the cream. Correct the seasoning.
5. Serve in individual dishes accompanied with hot toast.

This recipe can be used for smoked trout or smoked salmon trimmings. It can also be used for fresh salmon, in which case 50 g (2 oz) of cucumber can be incorporated with the selected seasoning.

8 portions

Assorted hors-d'oeuvre Hors-d'oeuvre variés

Recipe numbers 30 to 58 may be served in four ways unless otherwise indicated:

a) as a single hors-d'oeuvre
b) as part of a composite hors-d'oeuvre
c) as a main course when it will be suitably garnished with salad items
d) as an accompaniment to a main course.

30 **Anchovies** *Anchois*

As an hors-d'oeuvre only.

Remove from the tin and dress in raviers, pour over a little oil and decorate if desired with any of the following:

capers, sprigs of parsley, chopped hard-boiled white and yolk of egg.

31 **Sardines** *Sardines à l'huile*

Not as accompaniment to a main course.

Remove carefully from the tin, dress neatly in raviers and add a little oil. The sardines may be decorated with picked parsley and lemon.

(Illustrated on page 131.)

32 **Tunny** *Thon*

Not as an accompaniment to a main course.

Remove from the tin, dress neatly, cut or flaked, in raviers, decorate as desired.

33 **Stuffed eggs** *Oeufs farcis*

		2 hard-boiled eggs
25 g	1 oz	butter
		4 tablespns mayonnaise or natural yoghurt
		salt, pepper

1 Quarter or halve the eggs.
2 Remove the yolks and pass through a sieve.
3 Mix the yolks with butter and mayonnaise and correct the seasoning.
4 Place in a piping bag with a star tube.
5 Pipe neatly back into the egg whites.
6 Dress on a bed of shredded lettuce or lettuce leaves.

For variation add a little tomato ketchup, spinach juice, duxelle or anchovy essence, to the egg yolks.

34 **Egg mayonnaise** *Oeuf mayonnaise*

1 portion provides:
182 kcals/763 kJ
15.7 g fat of which 3.4 g saturated
2.4 g carbohydrate of which 2.4 g sugars
8.1 g protein
1.6 g fibre

To cook hard-boiled eggs.

1 Place the eggs in boiling water.
2 Re-boil and simmer for 8–10 min.
3 Refresh until cold.

Note When started in cold water cook for 12 minutes.

If eggs are over-cooked, iron in the yolk and sulphur compounds in the white are released to form the blackish ring (ferrous sulphide) around the yolk. This will also occur if the eggs are not refreshed immediately they are cooked.

Egg mayonnaise (clockwise from bottom right): as part of a selection of hors-d'oeuvre; as an individual hors-d'oeuvre; as a main dish

As part of a selection for hors-d'oeuvre

Cut the hard-boiled eggs in quarters or slices, neatly dress in raviers and coat with mayonnaise.

As an individual hors-d'oeuvre

Allow one hard-boiled egg per portion, cut in half and dress on a leaf of lettuce, coat with mayonnaise, garnish with quarters of tomatoes, slices of cucumber.

As a main dish

Allow two hard-boiled eggs per portion, cut in halves and dress on a plate, coat with mayonnaise sauce. Surround with a portion of lettuce, tomato, cucumber, potato salad, vegetable salad, beetroot or coleslaw.

35 **Shellfish mayonnaise**

Shrimp, prawn, crab, lobster
As an hors-d'oeuvre allow 25–35 g (1–1½ oz) prepared shellfish per portion

		1 lettuce
100–150 g	4–6 oz	prepared shellfish
125 ml	¼ pint	mayonnaise sauce or natural yoghurt
		capers, anchovies
		parsley or fennel for decoration

1 Shred the lettuce finely and place in a ravier.
2 Add the shellfish cut as for shellfish cocktail.
3 Coat with mayonnaise sauce. Decorate as desired.

This may also be served as a fish or a main course, in which case the amount of shellfish is doubled and the other ingredients are slightly increased.

Plated hors-d'oeuvre: sardine (p. 129); potato salad (p. 132); salami (p. 121); rice salad (p. 136); tomato salad (p. 135), fish salad (p. 133); smoked salmon (p. 120); meat salad (p. 134); egg mayonnaise (p. 130)

Selection of hors-d'oeuvre (clockwise from top left): potato salad (p. 132); Niçoise salad (p. 137); fish salad (p. 133); cucumber salad (p. 135); tomato salad (p. 135); rice salad (p. 136); meat salad (p. 134); cauliflower à la greque (p. 139); egg mayonnaise (p. 130)

36 **Potato salad** *Salade de pommes de terre*

Not usually a single hors-d'oeuvre or main course.

200 g	8 oz	cooked potatoes
		1 tablespn vinaigrette, salt, pepper
10 g	½ oz	chopped onion or chive (optional)
60 ml	¼ pt	mayonnaise or natural yoghurt
		chopped parsley or mixed fresh herbs

Using mayonnaise
This recipe provides:

479 kcals/2013 kJ
34.9 g fat of which 5.1 g saturated
40.0 g carbohydrate of which 1.3 g sugars
4.0 g protein
2.6 g fibre

1 Cut the potatoes in ½–1 cm (¼–½ in) dice, sprinkle with vinaigrette.
2 Mix with the onion or chive, add the mayonnaise and correct the seasoning. (The onion may be blanched to reduce the harshness.)
3 Dress neatly in a ravier. Sprinkle with chopped parsley.

(Illustrated on page 131.)

37 **Potato and egg salad** *Salade de pommes de terre aux oeufs*

As for recipe 36 with the addition of 2 chopped hard-boiled eggs.

38 **Potato and watercress salad** *Salade cressonnière*

400 g	1 lb	small cooked potatoes
		1 bunch watercress
		4 tablespns vinaigrette
		1 hard-boiled egg
		chopped parsley or mixed fresh herbs

1 Cut potatoes into 2 mm (⅛ in) slices.
2 Mix with picked watercress leaves and vinaigrette.
3 Dress in serving dish.
4 Sprinkle with sieved hard-boiled egg and chopped parsley.

39 **Potato and apple salad**

As for recipe 36 with the addition of 100 g (4 oz) of peeled diced dessert apple mixed with lemon juice.

40 **Vegetable salad** *Salade de légumes*

Recipe 1 (Russian Salad) (Salade russe)

100 g	4 oz	carrots
50 g	2 oz	turnips
50 g	2 oz	French beans
50 g	2 oz	peas
		1 tablespn vinaigrette
60 ml	¼ pt	mayonnaise or natural yoghurt
		salt, pepper

Using mayonnaise
This recipe provides:

373 kcals/1566 kJ
35.0 g fat of which 5.2 g saturated
10.1 g carbohydrate of which 8.2 g sugars
5.0 g protein
11.9 g fibre

1 Peel and wash the carrots and turnips.
2 Cut into ½ cm (¼ in) dice or batons.
3 Cook separately in salted water.
4 Refresh and drain well.
5 Top and tail the beans.
6 Cut in ½ cm (¼ in) dice, cook, refresh and drain well.
7 Cook the peas, and refresh and drain well.
8 Mix all the well-drained vegetables with vinaigrette and then mayonnaise.
9 Correct the seasoning. Dress neatly in a ravier.

Recipe 2 (Vegetable salad)

Arrange neat bouquets of cooked vegetables, e.g. carrots, turnips, peas, beans, etc. around bunch of cooked cauliflowers or broccoli buds. Serve vinaigrette and mayonnaise separately.

41 **Fish salad** *Salade de poisson*

Not usually an accompaniment to a main course.

100 g	4 oz	cooked fish (free from skin and bone)
		1 hard-boiled egg
50 g	2 oz	cucumber (optional)
		chopped parsley or fennel
		salt, pepper
		1 tablespn vinaigrette
		¼ lettuce

This recipe provides:

233 kcals/978 kJ
13.5 g fat of which 3.0 g saturated
1.5 g carbohydrate of which 1.4 g sugars
26.4 g protein
1.3 g fibre

1 Flake the fish.
2 Cut the egg and cucumber in ½ cm (¼ in) dice.
3 Finely shred the lettuce.
4 Mix ingredients together, add the parsley.
5 Correct the seasoning. Mix with the vinaigrette.
6 Dress neatly in a ravier.
7 May be decorated with lettuce, anchovies and capers.

(Illustrated on page 131.)

42 **Fish mayonnaise** *Mayonnaise de poisson*

The method is the same as for shellfish mayonnaise (page 130) using cooked flaked fish in place of shellfish.

43 Meat salad *Salade de viande*

Not usually an accompaniment to a main course.

200 g	8 oz	cooked lean meat
25 g	1 oz	gherkins
50 g	2 oz	cooked French beans
50 g	2 oz	tomatoes
5 g	¼ oz	chopped onion or chives (optional)
		1 tablespn vinaigrette
		chopped parsley or mixed fresh herbs

This recipe provides:

385 kcals/1616 kJ
15.2 g fat of which 4.8 g saturated
2.7 g carbohydrate of which 2.5 g sugars
59.7 g protein
2.7 g fibre

1 Cut the meat and gherkins in ½ cm (¼ in) dice.
2 Cut the beans into ½ cm (¼ in) dice.
3 Skin tomatoes, remove seeds.
4 Cut into ½ cm (¼ in) dice.
5 Mix with remainder of the ingredients, blanching the onions if required.
6 Correct the seasoning.
7 Dress neatly in a ravier.
8 Decorate with lettuce leaves, tomatoes and fans of gherkins.

Well-cooked braised or boiled meat is ideal for this salad.

Meat salad

44 Beetroot *Betterave*

Not as a main course.

Wash and cook the beetroot in a steamer or in gently simmering water till tender (test by skinning), cool and peel. Cut into ½ cm (¼ in) dice or ½×1 cm (¼×½ in) batons. Beetroot may be served a) plain, b) with vinegar or c) sprinkled with vinaigrette.

45 Beetroot salad *Salade de betterave*

Recipe 1

Not as a main course.

200 g	8 oz	neatly cut or sliced beetroot
		chopped parsley
10 g	½ oz	chopped onion or chive (optional)
		1 tablespn vinaigrette

1 Combine all the ingredients, blanching the onion if required.
2 Dress neatly in a ravier. Sprinkle with chopped parsley.

Recipe 2

As for recipe 1, bound with 60–120 ml (1/8–1/4 pint) mayonnaise or natural yoghurt in place of vinaigrette.

46 · **Cucumber** *Concombre*

Not as a single hors-d'oeuvre or main course.

Peel the cucumber if desired; cut into thin slices and dress neatly in a ravier.

47 · **Cucumber salad** *Salade de concombres*

Not as a main course.

½ cucumber
chopped parsley or mixed fresh herbs
1 tablespn vinaigrette

1 Peel and slice the cucumber.
2 Sprinkle with vinaigrette and parsley.
3 Alternatively cucumber may be diced ½ cm (¼ in), bound with mayonnaise or yoghurt.

To remove indigestible juices from the cucumber, slice and lightly sprinkle with salt. allow the salt to draw out the water for approximately 1 hour, wash well under cold water and drain. This will make the cucumber limp.

48 · **Tomato** *Tomate*

If of good quality, the tomatoes need not be skinned.

Wash, remove the eyes, slice thinly or cut into segments. Dress neatly in a ravier.

49 · **Tomato salad** *Salade de tomates*

200 g	(approx. 8 oz)	4 tomatoes
		¼ lettuce
		1 tablespn vinaigrette
10 g	½ oz	chopped onion or chive (optional)
		chopped parsley or mixed fresh herbs

This recipe provides:

94 kcals/394 kJ
6.6 g fat of which 1.1 g saturated
6.7 g carbohydrate of which 6.6 g sugars
2.5 g protein
3.9 g fibre

1 Peel tomatoes if required. Slice thinly.
2 Arrange neatly on lettuce leaves.
3 Sprinkle with vinaigrette, onion, blanched if required, and parsley.

(Illustrated on page 131.)

50 Tomato and cucumber salad *Salade de tomates et de comcombres*

2 tomatoes
¼ cucumber
1 tablespn vinaigrette
chopped parsley or mixed fresh herbs

1 Alternate slices of tomato and cucumber.
2 Sprinkle with vinaigrette and parsley.

51 Rice salad *Salade de riz*

100 g	4 oz	2 tomatoes
100 g	4 oz	cooked rice
50 g	2 oz	peas, cooked
		1 tablespn vinaigrette
		salt, pepper

This recipe provides:

216 kcals/906 kJ
6.9 g fat of which 1.1 g saturated
34.6 g carbohydrate of which 3.3 g sugars
5.9 g protein
8.3 g fibre

1 Skin and remove seeds from tomatoes.
2 Cut in ½ cm (¼ in) dice.
3 Mix with the rice and peas.
4 Add the vinaigrette and correct the seasoning.
5 Dress neatly in a ravier.

(Illustrated on page 131.)

52 Celery *Céleri*

Trim and thoroughly wash the celery. Remove any discoloured outer stalks. Serve stalks whole or cut into strips.

53 Celeriac *Céleri-rave*

200 g	8 oz	celeriac
		½ lemon
		1 level teaspn English or Continental mustard
		salt, pepper
60 ml	¼ pt	mayonnaise, cream or natural yoghurt

1 Wash and peel celeriac. Cut into fine julienne.
2 Combine with lemon juice and remainder of the ingredients.
3 Dress in a ravier.

54 French bean salad *Salade de haricots verts*

200 g	8 oz	cooked French beans
		1 tablespn vinaigrette
		salt, pepper

Combine all the ingredients and dress in a ravier.

55 · Niçoise salad *Salade niçoise*

100 g	4 oz	tomatoes
200 g	8 oz	cooked French beans
100 g	4 oz	cooked diced potatoes
		salt, pepper
		1 tablespn vinaigrette
10 g	½ oz	anchovy fillets
5 g	¼ oz	capers
10 g	½ oz	stoned olives

This recipe provides:

207 kcals/867 kJ
9.6 g fat of which 1.5 g saturated
25.0 g carbohydrate of which 4.9 g sugars
6.9 g protein
9.9 g fibre

1 Peel tomatoes, remove seeds. Cut into neat segments.
2 Dress the beans, tomato and potatoes neatly in a ravier.
3 Season with salt and pepper. Add the vinaigrette.
4 Decorate with anchovies, capers and olives.

(Illustrated on page 131.)

56 · Waldorf salad *Salade Waldorf*

Dice of celery or celeriac and crisp russet apples mixed with shelled and peeled walnuts bound with a mayonnaise and dressed on quarters or leaves of lettuce. This may also be served in hollowed-out apples.

57 · Haricot bean salad *Salade de haricots blancs*

200 g	8 oz	haricot beans, cooked
		1 tablespn vinaigrette
		chopped parsley
10 g	½ oz	chopped onion, blanched if required, or chive (optional)
		salt, pepper

Combine all the ingredients and dress in a ravier.

This recipe can be used for any type of dried bean.

58 · Three-bean salad

Use 200 g (½ lb) of three different dried beans, e.g. red kidney, black-eyed, flageolet, etc. Proceed as for recipe 57.

This recipe provides:

440 kcals/1849 kJ
8.7 g fat of which 1.1 g saturated
63.4 g carbohydrate of which 6.3 g sugars
30.9 g protein
36.0 g fibre

59 · Orange salad *Salade d'orange*

Not usually as a main course.

Segments of orange cut as recipe 61 with a little of the orange juice, neatly dressed in a salad dish.

60 · Coleslaw

125 ml	¼ pt	mayonnaise or natural yoghurt
200 g	8 oz	white or Chinese cabbage
50 g	2 oz	carrot
25 g	1 oz	onion (optional)

Using mayonnaise
This recipe provides:

599 kcals/2514 kJ
59.0 g fat of which 8.8 g saturated
11.7 g carbohydrate of which 11.4 g sugars
5.9 g protein
7.2 g fibre

1 Trim off the outside leaves of the cabbage.
2 Cut into quarters. Remove the centre stalk.
3 Wash the cabbage, shred finely and drain well.
4 Mix with a fine julienne of raw carrot and shredded raw onion. To lessen the harshness of raw onion, blanch and refresh.
5 Bind with mayonnaise sauce, natural yoghurt or vinaigrette.

61 · Florida salad *Salade Florida*

Allow ¼ lettuce and ½ large orange per portion.

1 Remove the orange zest with a peeler.
2 Cut into fine julienne.
3 Blanch for 2–3 min and refresh.
4 Peel the oranges and remove all the white skin.
5 Cut into segments between the white pith and remove all the pips.
6 Dress the lettuce in a bowl, keeping it in quarters if possible.
7 Arrange 3 or 4 orange segments in each portion.
8 Sprinkle with a little orange zest.
9 Serve an acidulated cream dressing separately.

62 · Japanese salad *Salade japonaise*

Dice of tomato, pineapple, orange and apple bound with acidulated cream dressing and served on leaves or with quarters of lettuce.

63 · Manon salad *Salade Manon*

Allow ¼ lettuce and ½ grapefruit per portion.

Peel the grapefruit and cut into segments. Dress neatly on leaves of lettuce or on quarters of lettuce.

Serve a vinaigrette with a little lemon juice and sugar added.

64 · Mimosa salad *Salade mimosa*

Segments of oranges, slices of banana, skinned and pipped grapes mixed with acidulated cream and dressed on leaves or quarters of lettuce.

Hors-d'oeuvre à la grecque

All vegetables cooked *à la grecque* are cooked in the following liquid:

250 ml	½ pt	water
60 ml	⅛ pt	olive oil
		juice of 1 lemon
		½ bay leaf
		sprig of thyme
		6 peppercorns
		6 coriander seeds
		salt

65 · **Artichokes** *Artichauts à la grecque*

1 Peel and trim six artichokes.
2 Cut the leaves short. Remove the chokes.
3 Blanch the artichokes in water with a little lemon juice for 10 min.
4 Refresh the artichokes. Place in cooking liquid. Simmer 15–20 min.
5 Serve cold in a ravier with a little of the unstrained cooking liquid.

66 · **Onions (button)** *Oignons à la grecque*

1 Peel and wash 200 g (8 oz) button onions.
2 Blanch for approx. 5 min. and refresh.
3 Place onions in the cooking liquor. Simmer till tender.
4 Serve cold with unstrained cooking liquor.

67 · **Cauliflower** *Chou-fleur à la grecque*

1 Trim and wash one medium cauliflower.
2 Break into small sprigs about the size of a cherry.
3 Blanch for approx. 5 min. and refresh.
4 Simmer in the cooking liquor 5–10 min. Keep the cauliflower slightly undercooked, and crisp.
5 Serve cold with unstrained cooking liquor.

Cauliflower à la greque

68 · **Celery** *Céleri à la grecque*

1 Wash and clean two heads of celery.
2 Blanch in lemon water for 5 min. Refresh. Cut into 2 cm (1 in) pieces.
3 Place in a shallow pan. Add the cooking liquor, simmer till tender.
4 Serve cold with unstrained cooking liquor.

69 Leeks *Poireaux à la grecque*

This recipe provides:

639 kcals/2641 kJ
60.0 g fat of which 8.4 g saturated
19.3 g carbohydrate of which 19.3 g sugars
7.6 g protein
16.4 g fibre

1 Trim and clean ½ kg (1 lb) leeks.
2 Tie into a neat bundle.
3 Blanch for approx. 5 min. and refresh.
4 Cut into 2 cm (1 in) lengths and place in a shallow pan.
5 Cover with the cooking liquor. Simmer till tender.
6 Serve cold with unstrained cooking liquor.

70 Hors-d'oeuvre à la portugaise

All the vegetables prepared à la grecque may also be prepared à la portugaise. They are prepared and blanched in the same way then cooked in the following liquid:

		1 chopped onion
		1 tablespn olive oil
400 g	1 lb	tomatoes
		1 clove garlic
		½ bay leaf
		chopped parsley
		sprig of thyme
25 g	1 oz	tomato purée
		salt, pepper

1 Sweat the onion in the oil.
2 Skin and remove the seeds from tomatoes. Roughly chop.
3 Add to the onion with the remainder of the ingredients.
4 Correct the seasoning.
5 Add the vegetable and simmer till tender, with the exception of the cauliflower which should be left crisp.
6 Serve hot or cold with the unstrained cooking liquor.

71 Chicory *Endive belge*

Trim off the root end. Cut into 1 cm (½ in) lengths, wash well and drain.

72 Curled chicory *Endive frisée*

Thoroughly wash and trim off the stalk. Drain well.

73 Lettuce and iceberg lettuce *Laitue*

Trim off the root and remove the outside leaves. Wash thoroughly and drain well. The outer leaves can be pulled off and the hearts cut into quarters.

74 **Cos lettuce** *Laitue romaine*

Trim off the root end and remove the outside leaves. Wash thoroughly and drain well. Cut into quarters.

75 **Mustard and cress**

Trim off the stalk ends of the cress. Wash well and lift out of the water so as to leave the seed cases behind. Drain well.

76 **Radishes** *Radis*

The green stems should be trimmed to about 2 cm (1 in) long, the root end cut off.

Wash well, drain and dress in a ravier.

77 **Watercress** *Cresson*

Trim off the stalk ends, discard any discoloured leaves, thoroughly wash and drain.

78 **Mixed salad** *Salade panachée*

Neatly arrange in a salad bowl. A typical mixed salad would consist of lettuce, tomato, cucumber, watercress, radishes, etc. Almost any kind of salad vegetable can be used.

Offer a vinaigrette separately.

Illustrated on page 115.

79 **Green salad** *Salade verte*

Any of the green salads, lettuce, cos lettuce, lambs lettuce (also known as corn salad or mâche), curled chicory, or any combination of green salads may be used, and a few leaves of raddichio. Neatly arranged in a salad bowl, serve with vinaigrette separately.

Illustrated on page 115.

80 **French salad** *Salade française*

The usual ingredients are lettuce, tomato and cucumber, but these may be varied with other salad vegetables, in some cases with quarters of egg. A vinaigrette made with French mustard (French dressing) should be offered.

Illustrated on page 115.

Mixed salad

Cocktail canapé ingredients

81 Cocktail canapés *Canapés à la russe*

These are small items of food, hot or cold, which are served at cocktail parties, buffet receptions and may be offered as an accompaniment to drinks before any meal (luncheon, dinner or supper). Typical items for cocktail parties and light buffets are:

1 Hot savoury pastry patties of lobster, chicken, crab, salmon, mushroom, ham, etc. small pizzas, quiches, brochettes, hamburgers.
2 Hot sausages (chipolatas), various fillings, such as chicken livers, prunes, mushrooms, tomatoes, gherkins, etc., wrapped in bacon and skewered and cooked under the salamander. Fried goujons of fish.
3 Savoury finger toast to include any of the cold canapés. These may also be prepared on biscuits or shaped pieces of pastry. On the bases the following may be used: salami, ham, tongue, thinly sliced cooked meats, smoked salmon, caviar, mock caviar, sardine, eggs, etc.
4 Game chips, gaufrette potatoes, fried fish balls, celery stalks spread with cheese.
5 Sandwiches, bridge rolls – open or closed but always small.
6 Sweets such as trifles, charlottes, jellies, bavarois, fruit salad, gâteaux, strawberries and raspberries with fresh cream, ice creams, pastries.
7 Beverages, coffee, tea, fruit-cup, punch-bowl, iced coffee.

Preparation of cocktail canapés

Canapés are served on neat pieces of buttered toast or puff or short pastry. A variety of foods may be used – slices of hard-boiled egg, thin slices of cooked meats, smoked sausages, fish, anchovies, prawns, mussels, etc. They may be left plain, or decorated with piped butter and coated with aspic jelly.

The size of a canapé should be suitable for a mouthful.

Tray of cocktail canapés (10p piece to indicate size)

82 Bouchées

Prepare the puff pastry cases according to the instructions on page 488.

Bouchée fillings are numerous as bouchées are served both hot and cold. They may be served as cocktail savouries, or as a first course, a fish course or as a savoury. All fillings should be bound with a suitable sauce, for example:

Mushroom	— chicken velouté or béchamel
Shrimp	— fish velouté or béchamel or curry
Prawn	— fish velouté or béchamel or curry
Chicken	— chicken velouté
Ham	— chicken velouté or béchamel or curry
Lobster	— fish velouté or béchamel or mayonnaise
Vegetable	— mayonnaise, natural yoghurt, fromage frais, quark or béchamel

83 Savouries using barquettes and tartlets

There are a variety of savouries which may be served either as hot appetisers (at a cocktail reception) or as the last course of an evening meal. The tartlet or barquette may be made from thinly rolled short paste and cooked blind.

Examples of fillings

Shrimps in curry sauce,
chicken livers in demi-glace or devilled sauce,
Mushrooms in béchamel, suprême or aurora sauce,
Poached soft roes with devilled sauce, e.g. barquette méphisto,
Poached soft roes covered with cheese soufflé mixture and baked, e.g. barquette Charles V.

The cooked tartlets or barquettes should be warmed through before service, the filling prepared separately and neatly placed in them, garnished with a sprig of parsley.

For further information read *The Larder Chef* (Leto and Bode), *Contemporary Cookery* (Ceserani, Kinton and Foskett).

Sandwiches

Sandwiches are one of the most varied types of food produced. They may be made from every kind of bread, fresh or toasted, in a variety of shapes and with an almost endless assortment of fillings.

Types of bread	*Types of filling*	
White	Ham	Tomato
Brown	Tongue	Cucumber
Caraway seed	Beef	Cress
Rye	Chicken	Lettuce
Granary	Smoked fish	Watercress
Wholemeal	Tinned fish	Egg
French sticks	Fish and meat paste	Cheese
Rolls and baps		

Examples of combination fillings

Fish and lettuce	Roast beef and coleslaw
Cheese and tomato	Roast pork and apple sauce
Cucumber and egg	Tuna fish and cucumber
Apple and chutney	Chopped ham, celery and apple

Seasonings to flavour sandwiches

Mayonnaise (egg, salmon, etc)
Vinaigrette (crab, lobster, fish, egg)
English mustard (ham, beef)
French mustard (cheese, tongue)
Chutney (cheese, tinned meat)
Pickles

Types of spread

Butter
Margarine
Peanut butter

Where sandwiches are required in large quantities, one method is to use large sandwich loaves and remove the crusts from three sides and one end. The bread is then cut in thin slices across the loaf, using a sharp carving knife (a serrated knife will be found ideal). (The bread may be buttered before being cut.)

The slices of bread are stacked neatly, one on top of the other, resting on a crust of bread. When the bread is cut it is then buttered (unless this has been done before each slice is cut) and the prepared fillings are added quickly and efficiently and the complete loaf is made into long sandwiches. If they are to be kept for any length of time the crusts are replaced and wrapped in clean cloth or greaseproof paper or foil. When required for service the sandwiches are easily and quickly cut into any required size or shape, neatly dressed on a doily on a flat dish and sprinkled with washed and drained mustard and cress. A typical set of fillings for a loaf could be, ham, tongue, smoked salmon, tomato, cucumber, egg.

Using wholem bread, polyunsat marg
1 portion provides:

237 kcals/995 kJ
9.9 g fat of which 1.8 g saturated
25.2 g carbohydrate of which 1.3 g sugars
13.4 g protein
4.5 g fibre

Using white bread, butter
1 portion provides:

338 kcals/1421 kJ
19.4 g fat of which 11.9 g saturated
30.1 g carbohydrate of which 2.1 g sugars
13.1 g protein
2.6 g fibre

84 **Sandwiches**

Toasted sandwiches

These are made by inserting a variety of savoury fillings between two slices of hot, freshly buttered toast, e.g. scrambled egg, bacon, fried egg, scrambled egg with chopped ham, or by inserting two slices of buttered bread with the required filling into a sandwich toaster.

Club sandwich

This is made by placing between two slices of hot buttered toast a filling of lettuce, grilled bacon, slices of hard-boiled egg, mayonnaise and slices of chicken.

Bookmaker sandwich

This is an underdone minute steak between two slices of hot buttered toast.

Double-decker and treble-decker sandwiches

Toasted and untoasted bread can be made into double-decker sandwiches, using three slices of bread with two separate fillings. Treble and quadro-decker sandwiches may also be prepared. They may be served hot or cold.

Open sandwich or Scandinavian smorrëbrod

This is prepared from a buttered slice of any bread garnished with any type of meat, fish, eggs, vegetables, salads, etc.

The varieties of open sandwich can include some of the following:

1 Smoked salmon, lettuce, potted shrimps, slice of lemon.
2 Scrambled egg, asparagus tips, chopped tomato.
3 Grilled bacon, cold fried egg, tomato sauce, mushrooms.
4 Cold sliced beef, sliced tomato, fans of gherkins.
5 Shredded lettuce, sliced hard-boiled egg, mayonnaise, cucumber.
6 Cold boiled rice, cold curried chicken, chutney.
7 Minced raw beef, anchovy fillet, raw egg yolk, chopped horseradish, onion and parsley.
8 Pickled herring, chopped gherkin, capers sieved, hard-boiled egg.

When serving open sandwiches it is usual to offer a good choice. Care should be taken with finishing touches, using parsley, sliced radishes, gherkins, pickles, capers, etc., to give a neat clean look to the dish. Presentation is important.

Consommé with profiteroles (p. 153); brown onion soup (p. 167)

7

SOUPS

General objectives	*Specific objectives*
To know the characteristics of soups and understand the principles of their production.	To be able to explain where, when and how each soup would be served. To produce each soup to a satisfactory standard with particular attention to the consistency of thick soups and clarity of clear soups. To compare soups made with fresh ingredients with commercial products.

Soup Les Soupes

Soups are served for luncheon, dinner, supper and snack meals.

A portion is usually between 200–250 ml (1/3–1/2 pt), depending on the type of soup and the number of courses to follow.

Soup Classification	Base	Passed or Unpassed	Finish	Example
Clear	Stock	Strained	Usually garnished	Consommé
Broth	Stock Cut vegetables	Unpassed	Chopped parsley	Scotch broth Minestroni
Purée	Stock Fresh vegetables Pulses	Passed	Croûtons	Lentil soup Potato soup
Velouté	Blond roux Vegetables Stock	Passed	Liaison of yolk and cream	Velouté of chicken
Cream	a) Stock and vegetables b) Vegetable purée and bechámel c) Velouté	Passed	Cream, milk or yoghurt	Cream of vegetable Cream of fresh pea Cream of tomato
Bisque	Shellfish Fish stock	Passed	Cream	Lobster soup Crab soup
Miscellaneous	Soups which are not classified under the other headings			Mulligatawny Kidney

1 · Clear soup (basic recipe) *Consommé*

Ingredients for, and clarification of, consommé

1 portion provides:
30 kcals/126 kJ
0.0 g fat of which 0.0 g saturated
1.8 g carbohydrate of which 0.0 g sugars
5.6 g protein
0.0 g fibre

200 g	8 oz	chopped or minced beef
		salt
		1 to 2 egg whites
1 litre	1 qt	cold, white or brown beef stock
100 g	4 oz	mixed vetables (onion, carrot, celery, leek)
		bouquet garni
		3–4 peppercorns

1. Thoroughly mix the beef, salt, egg white and ¼ litre (½ pt) cold stock in a thick-bottomed pan.
2. Peel, wash and finely chop the vegetables.
3. Add to the beef with the remainder of the stock, the bouquet garni and the peppercorns.
4. Place over a gentle heat and bring slowly to the boil stirring occasionally.
5. Allow to boil rapidly for 5–10 sec. Give a final stir.
6. Lower the heat so that the consommé is simmering very gently.
7. Cook for 1½–2 hr without stirring.
8. Strain carefully through a double muslin.
9. Remove all fat, using both sides of 8 cm (3 in) square pieces of kitchen paper.
10. Correct the seasoning and colour, which should be a delicate amber.
11. Degrease again, if necessary. Bring to the boil and serve.

A consommé should be crystal clear. The clarification process is caused by the albumen of the egg white and meat coagulating, rising to the top of the liquid and carrying other solid ingredients. The remaining liquid beneath the coagulated surface should be gently simmering.

Cloudiness is due to some or all of the following:

a) poor quality stock
b) greasy stock
c) unstrained stock
d) imperfect coagulation of the clearing agent
e) whisking after boiling point is reached, whereby the impurities mix with the liquid
f) not allowing the soup to settle before straining
g) lack of cleanliness of pan or cloth
h) any trace of grease or starch

Consommés are varied in many ways by altering the stock, e.g. chicken, chicken and beef, etc. Also by the addition of numerous garnishes. Certain consommés are also served cold and are popular in very hot weather for luncheon, dinner or supper.

4 portions

2 · Royal *Royale*

A royal is a savoury egg custard used for garnishing consommé, it should be firm but tender, the texture smooth, not porous. When cut, no moisture (syneresis) should be apparent; when this happens it is a sign of overcooking.

1 Whisk up 1 egg; season with salt and pepper and add the same amount of stock or milk.
2 Pass through a fine strainer.
3 Pour into a buttered dariole mould.
4 Stand the mould in a pan half full of water.
5 Allow to cook gently in a moderate oven until set, approx. 15–20 min.
6 Remove when cooked, when quite cold turn out carefully.
7 Trim the edges and cut into neat slices 1 cm (½ in) thick, then into squares or diamonds.

3 · Clear soup royal *Consommé royale*

1 Prepare royal as above.
2 When ready for service place the royale in the tureen, plate or bowl and carefully pour on the boiling consommé.

4 · Clear soup julienne *Consommé julienne*

Basic consommé with a garnish of 50 g (2 oz) carrot, turnip and leek cut in 2 cm (1 in) long fine julienne which has been previously cooked in a little salted water, then refreshed to preserve the colour. The garnish must be added to the consommé at the last moment before serving.

5 · **Clear soup brunoise** *Consommé brunoise*

Basic consommé with a garnish of 50 g (2 oz) carrot, turnip and leek cut into 2 mm (1/12 in) dice, cooked as for julienne. Add to the consommé at the last minute before serving.

6 · **Clear soup Celestine** *Consommé Célestine*

Basic consommé with the addition of fine 2 cm (1 in) long julienne of pancake. The pancakes are made from basic pancake mixture, page 502, seasoned with salt and pepper and with chopped parsley, tarragon and chervil added. Add to the consommé at the last moment before serving.

7 · **Clear soup with vermicelli** *Consommé vermicelle*

Cook 25 g (1 oz) vermicelli in boiling salted water until tender. Refresh and wash well under slowly running water. Drain in a strainer and add to the consommé at the last moment before serving.

8 · **Clear soup with profiteroles** *Consommé aux profiteroles*

Use 30 ml (1/8 pt) choux paste, see page 462, place in a piping bag with a 3 mm (1/8 in) plain tube. Pipe out pea-sized pieces on a lightly greased baking sheet. Bake in a moderate oven approx. 5 min. Add to the consommé at the last moment or serve separately. (Do not add sugar to the choux paste.)

(The service of this dish is illustrated on page 147.)

9 · **Cold clear soup** *Consommé en tasse*

This is a basic consommé lightly jellied and served in cups. The basic ingredients should be strong enough to effect the jelling, failing this a little gelatine may be added.

10 · **Cold clear soup with tomato** *Consommé Madrilène*

This is a basic consommé, well-flavoured with tomato and celery and served with a garnish of neatly cut 3 mm (1/8 in) dice of tomato (peeled and seeds removed).

11 · Petite marmite *Petite marmite*

This is a double-strength consommé garnished with neat pieces of chicken winglet, cubes of beef, turned carrots and turnips and squares of celery, leek and cabbage. The traditional method of preparation is for the marmites to be cooked in special earthenware or porcelain pots ranging in size from 1–6 portions. Petite marmite should be accompanied by thin toasted slices of flute, grated Parmesan cheese and a slice or two of poached beef marrow.

		4 chicken winglets
50 g	2 oz	lean beef (cut in 1 cm dice)
1 litre	2 pt	good strength beef consommé
100 g	4 oz	carrots
50 g	2 oz	celery
100 g	4 oz	leeks
25 g	1 oz	cabbage
100 g	4 oz	turnips
		8 slices of boof-bone marrow
50 g	2 oz	toasted slices of flute
25 g	1 oz	Parmesan cheese (grated)

1 portion provides:

261 kcals/1098 kJ
16.2 g fat of which 7.1 g saturated
13.0 g carbohydrate of which 4.4 g sugars
16.5 g protein
3.2 g fibre

1. Trim chicken winglets and cut in halves.
2. Blanch and refresh chicken winglets and the squares of beef.
3. Place the consommé into the marmite or marmites.
4. Add the squares of beef. Allow to simmer 1 hour.
5. Add the winglet pieces, turned carrots and squares of celery.
6. Allow to simmer 15 min.
7. Add the leek, cabbage and turned turnips, allow to simmer gently until all the ingredients are tender. Correct seasoning.
8. Degrease thoroughly using both sides of 8 cm (3 in) square pieces of kitchen paper.
9. Add the slices of beef bone marrow just before serving.
10. Serve the marmite on a dish paper or a round flat dish accompanied by the toasted flutes (see page 167) and grated cheese.

4 portions

12 · Turtle soup *Tortue clair*

Real turtle soup is produced by food manufacturers, however a substitute can be made as follows.

50 g	2 oz	dried turtle meat
1 litre	2 pt	good strength consommé
		a sachet turtle herbs
25 g	1 oz	arrowroot
60 ml	⅛ pt	dry sherry or Madeira

1. Soak the turtle meat in cold water for at least 24 hours.
2. Remove the turtle meat from the water, place in a little white stock and allow to simmer until tender.

3 Cut the turtle meat into 1 cm dice.
4 Bring the consommé to a gentle simmer.
5 Add the turtle herbs ensuring that they are securely wrapped in a piece of cloth.
6 Allow the turtle herbs to infuse for 5–10 mins, then remove.
7 Dilute the arrowroot in a little cold water.
8 Slowly add the diluted arrowroot to the gently simmering consommé, stirring continuously until the consommé reboils. Correct the seasoning.
9 Strain the consommé into a clean pan, reboil, add the diced cooked turtle meat and pour into a hot soup tureen.
10 Add the sherry or Madeira and immediately place the lid on the soup tureen.
11 The turtle soup should be accompanied with cheese straws and quarters of lemon.

Turtle herbs are bought ready prepared and usually comprise a blend of basil, sage, thyme, coriander, marjoram, rosemary, bay-leaf and peppercorns.

4 portions

13 **Mutton broth**

200 g	8 oz	scrag end of mutton
1 litre	2 pt	water or mutton or lamb stock
25 g	1 oz	barley
200 g	8 oz	vegetables (carrot, turnip, leek, celery, onion)
		bouquet garni
		salt, pepper
		chopped parsley

1 Place the mutton in a saucepan and cover with cold water.
2 Bring to the boil, immediately wash off under running water.
3 Clean the pan, replace the meat, cover with cold water, bring to the boil, skim.
4 Add the washed barley, simmer for 1 hr.
5 Add the vegetables, cut as for Scotch broth, bouquet garni and season.
6 Skim when necessary, simmer till tender, approx. 30 min.
7 Remove the meat, allow to cool and cut from the bone, remove all fat, and cut the meat into neat dice the same size as the vegetables, add to the broth.
8 Correct the seasoning, skim, add the chopped parsley and serve.

4 portions

14 Scotch broth

25 g	1 oz	barley
1 litre	2 pt	white beef stock
200 g	8 oz	vegetables (carrot, turnip, leek, celery, onion)
		bouquet garni
		salt, pepper
		chopped parsley

1 portion provides:

48 kcals/204 kJ
0.2 g fat of which – g saturated
9.7 g carbohydrate of which 4.2 g sugars
2.5 g protein
2.4 g fibre

1 Wash the barley. Simmer in the stock for approx. 1 hr.
2 Peel and wash the vegetables and cut into neat 3 mm (1/8 in) dice.
3 Add to the stock with a bouquet garni and season.
4 Bring to the boil, skim and simmer until tender, approx. 30 min.
5 Correct the seasoning, skim, remove the bouquet garni, add the chopped parsley and serve.

4 portions

15 Chicken broth

		1/4 of a boiling fowl
1 litre	2 pt	water
200 g	8 oz	vegetables (celery, turnip, carrot, leek)
		bouquet garni
		salt, pepper
25 g	1 oz	rice
		chopped parsley

1 Place the fowl in a saucepan, add the cold water, bring to the boil and skim. Simmer for 1 hr.
2 Add the vegetables, prepared as for Scotch broth, bouquet garni and season. Simmer until almost cooked.
3 Add the washed rice and continue cooking.
4 Remove all skin and bone from the chicken and cut into neat dice the same size as the vegetables, add to the broth.
6 Skim, correct the seasoning, add the chopped parsley and serve.

4 portions

16 Green pea soup (with dried peas) *Purée St. Germain*

200 g	8 oz	green split peas (soaked overnight if necessary)
1 1/2 litres	3 pt	white stock or water
50 g	2 oz	carrot (whole)
		bouquet garni
25 g	1 oz	green of leek
50 g	2 oz	onion
50 g	2 oz	knuckle of ham or bacon
		salt, pepper
		1 slice stale bread } croûtons
50 g	2 oz	butter } croûtons

1 portion provides:

277 kcals/1 164 kJ
11.2 g fat of which 6.8 g saturated
33.3 g carbohydrate of which 2.3 g sugars
13.0 g protein
6.7 g fibre

1 Pick and wash the peas.
2 Place in a thick-bottomed pan, cover with cold water or stock.
3 Bring to the boil and skim.
4 Add the remainder of the ingredients and season.
5 Simmer until tender, skim when necessary.
6 Remove the bouquet garni, carrot and ham.
7 Pass through a sieve or liquidise.
8 Pass through a medium conical strainer.
9 Return to a clean saucepan, re-boil, correct the seasoning and consistency. Skim if necessary.

Serve accompanied by ½ cm (¼ in) diced bread croûtons, shallow fried in butter, drained and served in a sauceboat.

4 portions

17 **Haricot bean soup** *Purée soissonnaise*

200 g	8 oz	white haricot beans (soaked overnight if necessary)
1½ litres	3 pt	white stock or water
50 g	2 oz	carrot
		bouquet garni
50 g	2 oz	onion
50 g	2 oz	knuckle of ham or bacon
		salt, pepper
		1 slice stale bread } *croûtons*
50 g	2 oz	butter } *croûtons*

Method of cooking as for green pea soup (recipe 16).

4 portions

18 **Yellow pea soup (dried peas)** *Purée egyptienne*

Proceed as for green pea soup (recipe 16) using yellow split peas and omitting the leek. The carrot need not be removed and can be sieved or liquidised with the peas.

19 **Lentil soup** *Purée de lentilles*

200 g	8 oz	lentils
1 litre	2 pt	white stock or water
50 g	2 oz	carrot
		bouquet garni
50 g	2 oz	onion
50 g	2 oz	knuckle of ham or bacon
		salt, pepper
		1 teaspn tomato purée
		1 slice stale bread } *croûtons*
50 g	2 oz	butter } *croûtons*

1 portion provides:

283 kcals/1191 kJ
12.4 g fat of which 6.8 g saturated
31.2 g carbohydrate of which 2.2 g sugars
13.7 g protein
6.4 g fibre

Method of cooking and serving as for green pea soup (recipe 16).

20 · **Cream of green pea soup (fresh peas)** *Crème St. Germain*

Basic Recipe

25 g	1 oz	onion
25 g	1 oz	leek
25 g	1 oz	celery
25 g	1 oz	butter
250 ml	½ pt	peas (shelled)
500 ml	1 pt	water or white stock
		sprig of mint
		bouquet garni
500 ml	1 pt	thin béchamel
60 ml	⅛ pt	cream

1 portion provides:

323 kcals/1356 kJ
23.6 g fat of which 12.8 g saturated
19.6 g carbohydrate of which 8.0 g sugars
9.3 g protein
8.3 g fibre

1 Sweat onion, leek and celery in the butter.
2 Moisten with water or stock and bring to boil.
3 Add peas, mint and bouquet garni, and allow to boil approx. 5 min.
4 Remove bouquet garni, add béchamel and bring to boil.
5 Remove from heat and liquidise or pass through a sieve.
6 Correct seasoning, pass through medium strainer.
7 Finish with cream.

4 portions

21 · **Green pea soup with tapioca** *Crème Lamballe*

As recipe 20 with a garnish of 25 g (1 oz) cooked and washed tapioca added at the same time as the cream.

22 · **Green pea soup with vermicelli and sorrel** *Crème longchamps*

Crème St. Germain (recipe 20) garnished with 25 g (1 oz) cooked and washed vermicelli and julienne of sorrel cooked in butter.

23 · **Potato soup** *Purée Parmentier*

25 g	1 oz	butter or margarine	
50 g	2 oz	onion	
50 g	2 oz	white of leek	
1 litre	2 pt	white stock or water	
400 g	1 lb	peeled potatoes	
		bouquet garni	
		salt, pepper	
		chopped parsley	
		1 slice stale bread	*croûtons*
50 g	2 oz	butter	*croûtons*

Using butter
1 portion provides:

253 kcals/1063 kJ
15.7 g fat of which 9.8 g saturated
26.1 g carbohydrate of which 2.1 g sugars
3.6 g protein
2.9 g fibre

1 Melt the butter or margarine in a thick-bottomed pan.
2 Add the peeled and washed sliced onion and leek, cook for a few minutes without colour with a lid on.

3 Add the stock and the peeled, washed, sliced potatoes and the bouquet garni and season.
4 Simmer for approx. 30 min. Remove the bouquet garni, skim.
5 Pass the soup firmly through a sieve then pass through a medium conical strainer or liquidise.
6 Return to a clean pan, re-boil, correct the seasoning and consistency and serve.

Sprinkle with chopped parsley. Serve fried or toasted croûtons separately.

4 portions

24 · Potato and watercress soup *Purée cressonnière*

1 Ingredients as for potato soup plus a small bunch of watercress.
2 Pick off 12 neat leaves of watercress, plunge into a small pan of boiling water for 1–2 sec. Refresh under cold water immediately, these leaves are to garnish the finished soup.
3 Add the remainder of the picked and washed watercress, including the stalks, to the soup at the same time as the potatoes.
4 Finish as for potato soup.

25 · Chive and potato soup *Vichyssoise*

25 g	1 oz	butter or margarine
50 g	2 oz	onion
50 g	2 oz	white of leek
1 litre	2 pt	white stock
400 g	1 lb	peeled potatoes
		bouquet garni
		salt, pepper
125–250 ml	¼–½ pt	cream
		chopped chives

1 Melt the butter or margarine in a thick-bottomed pan.
2 Add the peeled and washed sliced onion and leek, cook for a few minutes without colour with a lid on.
3 Add the stock and the peeled, washed, sliced potatoes and the bouquet garni and season.
4 Simmer for approx. 30 min. Remove the bouquet garni, skim.
5 Pass the soup firmly through a sieve then pass through a medium conical strainer or liquidise.
6 Return to a clean pan, re-boil, correct the seasoning and consistency.
7 Finish with cream and garnish with chopped chives, either raw or cooked in a little butter. Usually served chilled.

4 portions

26 · Tomato soup *Potage de tomates*

50 g	2 oz	butter or margarine	
25 g	1 oz	bacon trimmings	*mirepoix*
100 g	4 oz	onion	
100 g	4 oz	carrot	
50 g	2 oz	flour	
100 g	4 oz	tomato purée	
1¼ litres	2½ pt	stock	
		bouquet garni	
		salt, pepper	
		1 slice stale bread	*croûtons*
50 g	2 oz	butter	

Using hard margarine
1 portion provides:

274 kcals/1150 kJ
21.3 g fat of which 11.2 g saturated
17.1 g carbohydrate of which 3.7 g sugars
4.6 g protein
1.0 g fibre

1 Melt the butter or margarine in a thick-bottomed pan.
2 Add the bacon, rough diced onion and carrot, brown lightly.
3 Mix in the flour and cook to a sandy texture.
4 Remove from the heat, mix in the tomato purée.
5 Return to heat. Gradually add the hot stock.
6 Stir to the boil. Add the bouquet garni, season lightly.
7 Simmer for approximately 1 hr. Skim when required.
8 Remove the bouquet garni and mirepoix.
9 Pass firmly through a sieve then through a conical strainer.
10 Return to a clean pan, correct the seasoning, and consistency. Bring to the boil.
11 Serve fried or toasted croûtons separately.

Note If a slight sweet/sour flavour is required, reduce 100 ml (3/16 pt) vinegar and 35 g (1½ oz) castor sugar to a light caramel and mix into the completed soup.

4 portions

27 · Cream of tomato soup *Crème de tomates*

1 Prepare soup as for tomato soup using only 1 litre (2 pt) stock.
2 When finally re-boiling the finished soup add ¼ litre (½ pt) of milk or ⅛ litre (¼ pt) of cream or yoghurt.

28 · Cream of tomato soup with rice *Crème portugaise*

Cream of tomato with a garnish of 12 g (½ oz) plain boiled rice.

29 Cream of tomato and potato soup *Crème Solférino*

1 Half cream of tomato and half potato soup mixed together and garnished with small balls of carrots and potatoes, cooked separately in a little salted water, refreshed and added to the soup just before serving.
2 Recipe 26 with the addition of 200 g (8 oz) of sliced, peeled potatoes with the stock (6 portions).

30 Tomato soup (using fresh tomatoes) *Crème de tomates fraîches*

1 Prepare the soup as recipe 26, using 1 litre (2 pt) stock.
2 Substitute 1–1½ kg (2–3 lb) fresh ripe tomatoes for the tomato purée.
3 Remove the eyes from the tomatoes, wash them well and squeeze them into the soup after the stock has been added and has come to the boil.
4 If colour is lacking, add a little tomato purée soon after the soup comes to the boil.

31 Mushroom soup *Crème de champignons*

100 g	4 oz	onion, leek and celery
50 g	2 oz	margarine or butter
50 g	2 oz	flour
1 litre	2 pt	white stock (preferably chicken)
200 g	8 oz	white mushrooms
		bouquet garni
		salt, pepper
125 ml or 60 ml	¼ pt	milk or ⅛ pt cream

Using hard margarine
1 portion provides:

170 kcals/712 kJ
11.8 g fat of which 5.2 g saturated
12.6 g carbohydrate of which 3.0 sugars
3.8 g protein
1.6 g fibre

1 Gently cook the sliced onions, leek and celery in the margarine or butter in a thick-bottomed pan without colouring.
2 Mix in the flour, cook over a gentle heat to a sandy texture without colouring.
3 Remove from the heat, cool slightly.
4 Gradually mix in the hot stock. Stir to the boil.
5 Add the well-washed, chopped mushrooms, bouquet garni and season.
6 Simmer 30–45 min. Skim when necessary.
7 Remove the bouquet garni. Pass through a sieve or liquidise.
8 Pass through a medium strainer. Return to a clean saucepan.
9 Re-boil, correct the seasoning and consistency, add the milk or cream.

Note Natural yoghurt, skimmed milk or non-dairy cream may be used in place of dairy cream.

4 portions

32 · Chicken soup *Crème de volaille or Crème reine*

100 g	4 oz	onion, leek and celery
50 g	2 oz	butter or margarine
50 g	2 oz	flour
1 litre	2 pt	chicken stock
		bouquet garni
		salt, pepper
250 ml	½ pt	milk or 25 ml (¼ pt) cream
25 g	1 oz	cooked dice of chicken (garnish)

Using hard margarine
1 portion provides:

199 kcals/836 kJ
13.6 g fat of which 6.2 g saturated
14.0 g carbohydrate of which 4.2 g sugars
5.9 g protein
1.0 g fibre

1 Gently cook the sliced onions, leek and celery in a thick-bottomed pan, in the butter or margarine without colouring.
2 Mix in the flour, cook over a gentle heat to a sandy texture without colouring.
3 Cook slightly, gradually mix in the hot stock. Stir to the boil.
4 Add the bouquet garni and season.
5 Simmer 30–45 min, skim when necessary.
6 Remove the bouquet garni.
7 Pass firmly through a fine strainer or liquidise.
8 Return to a clean pan, re-boil and finish with milk or cream and correct the seasoning.
9 Add the garnish and serve.

Note Natural yoghurt, skimmed milk or non-dairy cream may be used in place of dairy cream.

4 portions

33 · Vegetable soup *Purée de légumes*

300 g	12 oz	mixed vegetables (onion, carrot, turnip, leek, celery)	
50 g	2 oz	butter or margarine	
25 g	1 oz	flour (white or wholemeal)	
1 litre	2 pt	white stock	
100 g	4 oz	potatoes	
		bouquet garni	
		salt, pepper	
		1 slice stale bread	*croûtons*
50 g	2 oz	butter	*croûtons*

Using hard margarine
1 portion provides:

263 kcals/1105 kJ
20.7 g fat of which 11.1 g saturated
17.2 g carbohydrate of which 3.7 g sugars
3.1 g protein
2.8 g fibre

1 Peel, wash and slice all the vegetables (except the potatoes).
2 Cook gently in the butter or margarine in a pan with the lid on, without colouring.
3 Mix in the flour, cook slowly for a few minutes without colouring, cool slightly.
4 Mix in the hot stock.

5 Stir and bring to the boil.
6 Add the sliced potatoes, bouquet garni and season. Simmer for 30–45 min, skim when necessary.
7 Remove the bouquet garni.
8 Pass through a sieve and then through a medium strainer or liquidise.
9 Return to a clean pan, re-boil, correct the seasoning and the consistency.
10 Serve with croûtons separately.

4 portions

34 · Cream of vegetable soup *Crème de légumes*

Ingredients and method as for vegetable soup (recipe 33), but: a) in place of ½ litre (1 pt) stock use ½ litre (1 pt) thin béchamel; or b) finish with milk or ⅛ litre (¼ pt) cream (see note recipe 31), simmer for 5 min and serve as for vegetable soup.

35 · Carrot soup *Purée de carottes*

50 g	2 oz	onion	
50 g	2 oz	celery	
400 g	1 lb	carrots	
50 g	2 oz	leek	
50 g	2 oz	butter or margarine	
25 g	1 oz	flour (white or wholemeal)	
		½ teaspn tomato purée	
1 litre	2 pt	white stock or water	
		bouquet garni	
		salt, pepper	
		1 slice stale bread	*croûtons*
50 g	2 oz	butter	*croûtons*

1 Gently cook the sliced vegetables in the butter or margarine with a lid on the pan, without colour, until soft. Mix in the flour.
2 Cook over a gentle heat for a few minutes without colouring.
3 Mix in the tomato purée.
4 Gradually add the hot stock. Stir to the boil.
5 Add the bouquet garni and season.
6 Simmer 45–60 min. Skim when necessary.
7 Remove the bouquet garni and pass firmly through a sieve, then through a medium strainer or liquidise.
8 Return to a clean pan, re-boil, correct the seasoning and consistency.
9 Serve croûtons separately.

4 portions

36 · Cream of carrot soup *Crème de carottes*

Method A

Make as for carrot soup (recipe 35), using 1/8–1/4 litre (1/4–1/2 pt) less stock and finish with 1/4 litre (1/2 pt) milk or 1/8 litre (1/4 pt) of cream. (See note recipe 31).

Method B

As for carrot soup, but use only 1/2 litre (1 pt) stock and 1/2 litre (1 pt) béchamel.

37 · Cream of carrot soup with rice *Crème Crecy*

Cream of carrot soup garnished with 12 g (1/2 oz) plain boiled and well-washed rice.

38 · Basic soup recipe (for recipes 39 to 52)

100 g	4 oz	sliced onions, leek and celery
200 g	8 oz	named soup vegetable sliced
50 g	2 oz	butter or margarine
50 g	2 oz	flour
1 litre	2 pt	white stock or water
		bouquet garni
		salt, pepper

Using hard margarine
1 portion provides:

143 kcals/601 kJ
10.3 g fat of which 4.4 g saturated
11.4 g carbohydrate of which 1.8 g sugars
1.9 g protein
1.9 g fibre

1. Gently cook all the sliced vegetables, in the fat under a lid, without colour.
2. Mix in the flour and cook slowly for a few minutes without colour. Cool slightly.
3. Gradually mix in the hot stock. Stir to the boil.
4. Add the bouquet garni and season.
5. Simmer for 45 min approx., skim when necessary.
6. Remove the bouquet garni, pass firmly through the sieve and through a medium strainer or liquidise.
7. Return to a clean pan, re-boil and correct the seasoning and consistency.
8. For cream soups see note recipe 31.

4 portions

39 · Cauliflower soup *Purée de chou-fleur*

As basic recipe 38 garnished with small sprigs of cauliflower cooked in salted water.

40 · **Cream of cauliflower soup** *Crème Dubarry*

As basic recipe 38 but in place of ½ litre (1 pt) stock use ½ litre (1 pt) thin béchamel or use ⅛–¼ litre (¼–½ pt) less stock and finish with ¼ litre (½ pt) milk or ⅛ litre (¼ pt) of cream and garnish as for cauliflower soup (recipe 39).

Using hard margarine
1 portion provides:

361 kcals/1515 kJ
25.3 g fat of which 11.9 g saturated
27.1 g carbohydrate of which 8.1 g sugars
7.7 g protein
2.5 g fibre

41 · **Celery soup** *Purée de céleri*

As basic recipe 38 garnished with 2 cm (1 in) lengths of fine julienne of celery cooked in salted water.

42 · **Cream of celery soup** *Crème de céleri*

As recipe 40 garnished as for celery soup (recipe 41).

43 · **Leek soup** *Purée de poireaux*

As basic recipe 38 garnished with 2 cm (1 in) lengths of fine julienne of leek cooked in salted water.

44 · **Cream of leek soup** *Crème de poireaux*

As recipe 40 garnished as for leek soup (recipe 43).

45 · **Onion soup (white)** *Purée d'oignons*

As basic recipe 38.

46 · **Cream of onion soup** *Crème d'oignons*

As recipe 40.

47 · **Turnip soup** *Purée de navets*

As basic recipe 38.

48 · **Cream of turnip soup** *Crème de navets*

As recipe 40.

49 · **Artichoke soup** *Purée d'artichauts*

As basic recipe 38.

50 · Cream of artichoke soup *Crème palestine*

As recipe 40.

51 · Potato and turnip soup *Purée freneuse*

As basic recipe 38.

52 · Cream of potato and turnip soup *Crème freneuse*

As recipe 40.

53 · Asparagus soup *Crème d'asperges*

50 g	2 oz	onion
50 g	2 oz	celery
50 g	2 oz	butter or margarine
50 g	2 oz	flour
1 litre	2 pt	white stock (preferably chicken)
400 g	½ lb	asparagus stalk trimmings or
150 g	6 oz	tin of asparagus
		bouquet garni
		salt, pepper
250 ml or 125 ml	½ pt or ¼ pt	milk or cream (see note recipe 31)

1 Gently sweat the sliced onions and celery, without colouring, in the butter or margarine.
2 Remove from the heat, mix in the flour, return to a low heat and cook out, without colouring, for a few minutes. Cool.
3 Gradually add the hot stock. Stir to the boil.
4 Add the well-washed asparagus trimmings or the tin of asparagus, bouquet garni and season with salt.
5 Simmer 30–40 min. Remove the bouquet garni.
6 Pass through a sieve, then a fine chinois, but do not push the asparagus fibres through the mesh or liquidise.
7 Return to a clean pan, re-boil, correct the seasoning and consistency.
8 Add the milk or cream and serve.

4 portions

54 · Brown onion soup *Soupe à l'oignon*

600 g	1 ½ lb	onions
25 g	1 oz	butter or margarine
		1 clove of garlic, chopped (optional)
10 g	½ oz	flour, white or wholemeal
1 litre	2 pt	brown stock
		salt, mill pepper
		¼ of a flute
50 g	2 oz	grated cheese

Using butter
1 portion provides:

197 kcals/827 kJ
9.7 g fat of which 5.8 g saturated
20.4 g carbohydrate of which 8.1 g sugars
8.3 g protein
3.1 g fibre

Above: ingredients for brown onion soup; Right: preparation and service of brown onion soup

1. Peel the onions, halve and slice finely.
2. Melt the butter in a thick-bottomed pan, add the onions and garlic and cook steadily over a good heat until cooked and well browned.
3. Mix in the flour and cook over a gentle heat, browning slightly.
4. Gradually mix in the stock, bring to the boil, skim and season.
5. Simmer approx. 10 min until the onion is soft. Correct the seasoning.
6. Pour into an earthenware tureen or casserole or individual dishes.
7. Cut the flute (French loaf, 2 cm (1 in) diameter) into slices and toast on both sides.
8. Sprinkle the toasted slices of bread liberally over the top.
9. Sprinkle with grated cheese and brown under the salamander.
10. Place on a dish and serve.

(The service of this dish is also illustrated on page 147.)

4 portions

55 Mulligatawny *Molegoo Tunee*

100 g	4 oz	chopped onion
		½ clove of garlic (chopped)
50 g	2 oz	butter, margarine or oil
50 g	2 oz	flour, white or wholemeal
		1 dessertspn curry powder
		1 dessertspn tomato purée
1 litre	2 pt	brown stock
25 g	1 oz	chopped apple
6 g	¼ oz	ground ginger
		1 dessertspn chopped chutney
25 g	1 oz	desiccated coconut
		salt
10g	½ oz	cooked rice, white or wholegrain

Using sunflower oil
1 portion provides:

227 kcals/952 kJ
17.1 g fat of which 5.0 g saturated
16.3 g carbohydrate of which 4.1 g sugars
3.3 g protein
2.6 g fibre

1 Lightly brown the onion and garlic in the fat or oil.
2 Mix in the flour and curry powder, cook out for a few minutes, browning slightly.
3 Mix in the tomato purée. Cool slightly.
4 Gradually mix in the brown stock. Stir to the boil.
5 Add the remainder of the ingredients and season with salt.
6 Simmer 30–45 min.
7 Pass firmly through a medium strainer or liquidise.
8 Return to a clean pan, re-boil.
9 Correct the seasoning and consistency.
10 Place the rice in a warm soup tureen and pour in the soup.

4 portions

56 Kidney soup *Soupe aux rognons*

50 g	2 oz	good dripping or oil
50 g	2 oz	flour, white or wholemeal
10 g	½ oz	tomato purée
1½ litres	3 pt	brown stock
200 g	8 oz	kidney (usually ox)
100 g	4 oz	carrot } diced
100 g	4 oz	onion } diced
		bouquet garni
		salt, pepper

1 Melt the fat in a thick-bottomed pan, mix in the flour.
2 Cook slowly to a brown roux. Cool slightly.
3 Mix in the tomato purée.
4 Gradually mix in the hot stock. Stir to the boil.
5 Remove the skin and gristle from the kidney and cut into ½ cm (¼ in) dice.
6 Quickly fry the kidney in a little hot fat in a frying-pan for a minute,

then add the carrot and onion and lightly brown together. Drain off all fat and add to the soup.
7 Add the bouquet garni and seasoning.
8 Simmer 1½–2 hr, skim when necessary.
9 Remove bouquet garni, pass the soup through a fine strainer or liquidise.
10 Return to a clean pan, re-boil.
11 Correct the seasoning and consistency and serve.
12 This soup may be garnished with a little of the diced kidney.

4 portions

57 Thick oxtail soup *Queue de boeuf lié*

		½ oxtail
50 g	2 oz	oil or fat
100 g	4 oz	onion
		½ clove garlic (optional)
100 g	4 oz	carrot and turnip
50 g	2 oz	flour, white or wholemeal
10 g	½ oz	tomato purée
1½ litres	3 pt	brown stock
		bouquet garni
		salt and mill pepper
100 g	4 oz	carrot and turnip for garnish

Using sunflower oil
1 portion provides:
238 kcals/1001 kJ
16.6 g fat of which 3.2 g saturated
13.7 g carbohydrate of which 4.1 g sugars
9.4 g protein
2.2 g fibre

1 Cut the oxtail into pieces through the natural joints.
2 Quickly fry in the hot oil or fat till lightly brown.
3 Add the diced onion, garlic (if using) and carrot and turnip and brown well together.
4 Mix in the flour and cook to a brown roux over gentle heat or in the oven.
5 Cool slightly. Mix in the tomato purée.
6 Gradually mix in the hot stock. Stir to the boil and skim.
7 Add the bouquet garni and seasoning. Simmer 3–4 hr.
8 Remove the bouquet garni and pieces of oxtail.
9 Pass the soup through a fine strainer.
10 Remove flesh from the oxtail and liquidise with the soup.
11 Return to a clean pan, re-boil, correct the seasoning and consistency.
12 Garnish with the extreme tip of the tail cut into rounds, and a little carrot and turnip turned in small balls with a solferino spoon, or cut into 2 mm ($^1/_{12}$ in) dice and cooked in salted water.
13 This soup may be finished with 2 tablespns sherry.

4 portions

58 · **Clear oxtail soup** *Queue de boeuf clair*

1 As recipe 57 without using any flour.
2 Drain off all the fat before adding to the stock.
3 Before adding the garnish add 25 g (1 oz) diluted arrowroot to the soup, re-boil until clear, and strain.
4 Finish and serve for thick oxtail soup.

4 portions

59 · **Cock-a-leekie**

½ litre (1 pt) good chicken stock and ½ litre (1 pt) good veal stock garnished with a julienne of prunes, white of chicken and leek.

60 · **Leek and potato soup** *Potage de poireaux et pommes*

400 g	1 lb	leeks (trimmed and washed)
25 g	1 oz	butter or margarine
750 ml	1½ pt	white stock
		bouquet garni
200 g	8 oz	potatoes
		salt, pepper

Using butter
1 portion provides:

126 kcals/531 kJ
5.3 g fat of which 3.3 g saturated
16.7 g carbohydrate of which 6.3 g sugars
3.9 g protein
4.2 g fibre

1 Cut the white and light green of leek into ½ cm (¼ in) paysanne.
2 Slowly cook in the butter in a pan with a lid on until soft, but without colouring.
3 Add the stock, the bouquet garni, the potatoes cut into ½ cm (¼ in), paysanne, 2 mm (1/12 in) thick, season with salt and pepper.
4 Simmer until the leeks and potatoes are cooked, approx. 15 min.

4 portions

61 · **Potato and leek soup** *Potage bonne femme*

1 Prepare as for leek and potato soup.
2 Just before serving add 25–50 g (1–2 oz) of butter and 1/16 litre (⅛ pt) of cream and stir in.

62 · Mixed vegetable soup *Potage paysanne*

300 g	12 oz	mixed vegetables (onion, leek, carrots, turnips, cabbage, celery)
50 g	2 oz	butter or margarine
750 ml	1 ½ pt	white stock or water
		bouquet garni
		salt, pepper
25 g	1 oz	peas
25 g	1 oz	French beans (cut into diamonds)

Using hard margarine
1 portion provides:

112 kcals/472 kJ
10.3 g fat of which 4.4 g saturated
3.5 g carbohydrate of which 0.0 g sugars
1.7 g protein
2.8 g fibre

1 Cut the peeled, washed vegetables into paysanne. Thinly cut
   a) 1 cm-sided (½ in) triangles, or
   b) 1 cm-sided (½ in) squares, or
   c) approx. round small pieces.
2 Cook slowly in the butter in a pan with a lid on until tender. Do not colour.
3 Add the hot stock, bouquet garni, season and simmer approx. 20 min.
4 Add the peas and beans, simmer until all the vegetables are cooked.
5 Skim off all fat, correct the seasoning and serve.

4 portions

63 · Autumn vegetable soup

100 g	4 oz	courgettes	small dice
100 g	4 oz	red, green, yellow pepper	small dice
100 g	4 oz	potatoes (peeled weight)	small dice
100 g	4 oz	onion	small dice
100 g	4 oz	celery	small dice
50 g	2 oz	butter, margarine or oil	
¾ litre	1 ½ pts	vegetable stock or water	
		bouquet garni	
		salt and pepper	

1 Dice the washed vegetables and sweat without colour.
2 Add the stock, bouquet garni and seasoning.
3 Bring to the boil and simmer until the vegetables are just tender.
4 Correct the consistence and seasoning, remove the bouquet garni and serve.

Note Other vegetables may also be used to produce a colourful soup, e.g. carrots, pumpkin, sweetcorn etc.

4 portions

64 Minestroni *Minestrone*

300 g	12 oz	mixed vegetables (onion, leek, celery carrot, turnip, cabbage)
50 g	2 oz	butter, margarine or oil
¾ litre	1½ pt	white stock or water
		bouquet garni
		salt, pepper
25 g	1 oz	peas
25 g	1 oz	French beans
25 g	1 oz	spaghetti
50 g	2 oz	potatoes
		1 teaspn tomato purée
100 g	4 oz	tomatoes, skinned, deseeded, diced
50 g	2 oz	fat bacon
		chopped parsley
		1 clove garlic

Using sunflower oil
1 portion provides:

265 kcals/1115 kJ
22.9 g fat of which 5.8 g saturated
11.9 g carbohydrate of which 4.2 g sugars
3.8 g protein
4.1 g fibre

1 Cut the peeled and washed mixed vegetables into paysanne.
2 Cook slowly without colour in the oil or fat in the pan with a lid on.
3 Add stock, bouquet garni and seasoning, simmer for approx. 20 min.
4 Add the peas, beans cut in diamonds and simmer for 10 min.
5 Add the spaghetti in 2 cm (1 in) lengths, the potatoes cut in paysanne, the tomato purée and the tomatoes and simmer gently until all the vegetables are cooked.
6 Meanwhile finely chop the fat bacon, parsley and garlic and form into a paste.
7 Mould the paste into pellets the size of a pea and drop into the boiling soup.
8 Remove the bouquet garni, correct the seasoning.
9 Serve grated Parmesan cheese and thin toasted flutes separately.

4 portions

65 Beetroot soup

1 litre	2 pts	stock (meat or vegetable)
400 g	1 lb	beetroot (raw)
100 g	4 oz	onion
50 g	2 oz	butter, margarine or oil
50 g	2 oz	flour
		seasoning

1 Shred the peeled beetroot and onion.
2 Sweat in the butter, margarine or oil until cooked.
3 Add the flour and cook for a few minutes.
4 Bring to the boil, skim, season and simmer for approx. 30 mins.

If desired a little vinegar or lemon juice may be added. Correct the seasoning and consistency and serve. This soup may be finished with sour cream, yoghurt or cream.

4 portions

66 Lobster bisque *Bisque de homard*

400 g	1 lb	live lobster
100 g	4 oz	butter
50 g	2 oz	onion
50 g	2 oz	carrot
60 ml	⅛ pt	brandy
75 ml	3 oz	flour
50 g	2 oz	tomato purée
1 ¼ litres	2 ¼ pt	white stock (beef or veal or chicken or a combination of any 2 or 3)
120 ml	¼ pt	white wine (dry)
		bouquet garni
		salt, cayenne
120 ml	¼ pt	cream

1 portion provides:

438 kcals/1841 kJ
28.7 g fat of which 17.2 g saturated
18.8 g carbohydrate of which 4.2 g sugars
14.4 g protein
1.2 g fibre

1 Wash the live lobster
2 Cut in half lengthwise tail first, then the carapace.
3 Discard the sac from the carapace, clean the trail from the tail and wash all the pieces.
4 Crack the claws and the four claw joints.
5 Melt the butter in a thick-bottomed pan.
6 Add the lobster and the roughly cut onion and carrot.
7 Allow to cook steadily without colouring the butter for a few minutes stirring with a wooden spoon.
8 Add the brandy and allow it to ignite.
9 Remove from heat and mix in the flour and tomato purée.
10 Return to gentle heat and cook out the roux.
11 Cool slightly and gradually add the white stock and white wine.
12 Stir until smooth and until the bisque comes to the boil.
13 Add the bouquet garni and season lightly with salt.
14 Simmer for 15–20 min. Remove lobster pieces.
15 Remove lobster meat, crush the lobster shells, return them to the bisque and allow to continue simmering for further 15–20 min.
16 Cut lobster meat into large brunoise.
17 Remove bouquet garni and as much bulk from the bisque as possible.
18 Pass through a coarse and then fine strainer or liquidise, and then through a fine strainer again. Return the soup to a clean pan.
19 Re-boil, correct seasoning with a little cayenne, and add the cream.
20 Add the brunoise of lobster meat and serve. At this stage 25 g (1 oz) butter may be stirred into the bisque as a final enriching finish.

In order to produce a less expensive soup, cooked lobster shell (not shell from the claws) may be crushed and used in place of live lobster.

An alternative method of thickening is to omit the flour and, ten minutes before the final cooked stage is reached, to thicken by stirring in 75 g (3 oz) rice flour diluted in a little cold water.

4 portions

67 · Country style French vegetable soup *Soupe au pistou*

50 g	2 oz	dried haricot beans
		2 tablesp olive oil
100 g	4 oz	white of leek, finely shredded
100 g	4 oz	carrot
50 g	2 oz	turnip
50 g	2 oz	French beans, cut into 2.5 cm (1 in) lengths
100 g	4 oz	courgettes
100 g	4 oz	broad beans
		4 tomatoes skinned, deseeded and chopped
50 g	2 oz	tomato purée
50 g	2 oz	macaroni
1 litre	2 pts	vegetable stock
		seasoning
25 g	1 oz	basil } pistou
		1 clove garlic } pistou
50 g	2 oz	Gruyère cheese } pistou
		6 tablesp olive oil } pistou

1 Soak the haricot beans for appox. 8 hours.
2 Place the beans in a pan of cold water, bring to the boil and gently simmer for approx. 20 mins. Refresh and drain.
3 Heat 2 tablespoons of oil in a suitable pan, add the white of leek and sweat for 5 mins.
4 Add the carrot and turnip (both cut into brunoise) and cook for a further 2 mins.
5 Add the haricot beans. Cover with the vegetable stock and add the remaining ingredients. Cook until everything is tender.
6 Make the pistou by puréeing the basil, garlic and cheese in a food processor (if available). Gradually add the oil until well mixed and emulsified.
7 Correct the seasoning and consistency of the soup and serve with the pistou separately.

4 portions

Clockwise from left: jam omelette (p. 512); Spanish omelette (p. 190); tomato omelette (p. 188)

8

EGGS

General objectives
To be aware of the various methods of cooking and presenting egg dishes suitable for different meals.

Specific objectives
To explain the methods of preparation, cooking and the presentation of each dish. To demonstrate each dish paying particular attention to the details of cooking. To select suitable garnishes as appropriate and to state where and when egg dishes are served.

Eggs

Fried, scrambled, poached, boiled and omelettes are mainly served at breakfast. A variety of dishes may be served for lunch, high teas, supper and snacks. To reduce risk of Salmonella infection pasteurised eggs may be used where appropriate, eg omelettes, scrambled eggs.

Egg Dishes Les Oeufs

1 · **Scrambled eggs** (basic recipe) *Oeufs brouillés*

		6–8 eggs
		2 tablespns milk (optional)
		salt, pepper
50 g	2 oz	butter

Using hard margarine
1 portion provides:

263 kcals/1105 kJ
22.9 g fat of which 8.7 g saturated
0.5 g carbohydrate of which 0.5 g sugars
13.9 g protein
0.0 g fibre

1 Break the eggs in a basin, add milk (if using), season with salt and pepper and thoroughly mix with a whisk.
2 Melt 25 g (1 oz) butter in a thick-bottomed pan, add the eggs and cook over a gentle heat stirring continuously until the eggs are lightly cooked.
3 Remove from the heat, correct the seasoning and mix in the remaining 25 g (1 oz) butter. (A tablespoon of cream may also be added.)
4 Serve in individual egg dishes.

If scrambled eggs are cooked too quickly or for too long the protein will toughen, the eggs will discolour because of the iron and sulphur compounds being released and syneresis or separation of water from the eggs will occur. This means that they will be unpleasant to eat. The heat from the pan will continue to cook the eggs after it has been removed from the stove, therefore the pan should be removed from the heat just before the eggs are cooked.

4 portions

2 · **Scrambled eggs on toast**

As above, serving each portion on a slice of freshly-buttered toast with the crust removed.

3 · **Scrambled eggs with tomatoes** *Oeufs brouillés aux tomates*

400 g	1 lb	tomatoes
25 g	1 oz	chopped onion or shallot
25 g	1 oz	butter or margarine
		chopped parsley

1 Prepare, cook and serve the eggs as for the basic method.
2 Prepare a cooked tomato concassée (see page 431).
3 To serve, place a spoonful of tomato in the centre of each dish of egg and a little chopped parsley on the top of the tomato.

4 · **Scrambled eggs with mushrooms** *Oeufs brouillés aux champignons*

200 g	8 oz	button mushrooms
25 g	1 oz	butter
		chopped parsley

1 Prepare, cook and serve the eggs as for the basic method.
2 Peel, wash and slice the mushrooms.
3 Toss in the butter in a frying-pan until cooked, drain well.
4 Dress neatly on top of the eggs with a little parsley.

5 · Scrambled eggs with croûtons *Oeufs brouillés aux croûtons*

		2 slices stale bread
50 g	2 oz	butter

1 Prepare, cook and serve the eggs as for the basic recipe.
2 Remove the crusts from the bread and cut into neat ½ cm (¼ in) dice.
3 Melt the butter in a frying-pan, add the croûtons and fry to a golden brown.
4 Place a spoonful in the centre of each dish of eggs.

6 · Scrambled eggs with chopped herbs *Oeufs brouillés aux fines herbes*

1 teaspn chopped parsley
chervil, tarragon and chives

1 Prepare, cook and serve as for the basic recipe.
2 Add the herbs with the last 25 g (1 oz) of butter.

7 · Scrambled eggs with ham *Oeufs brouillés au jambon*

100 g	4 oz	thick-sliced lean ham

1 Prepare, cook and serve the eggs as for the basic recipe.
2 Trim off all fat from the ham and cut into ½ cm (¼ in) dice.
3 Add to the eggs with the last 25 g (1 oz) of butter.

There are many other foods served with scrambled eggs, e.g. shrimps, cheese, asparagus tips, kidneys, etc.

8 · Egg in cocotte (basic recipe) *Oeuf en cocotte*

25 g	1 oz	butter
		salt, pepper
		4 eggs

1 portion provides:

127 kcals/534 kJ
11.2 g fat of which 5.2 g saturated
0.0 g carbohydrate of which 0.0 g sugars
6.8 g protein
0.0 g fibre

1 Butter and season four egg cocottes.
2 Break an egg carefully into each.
3 Place the cocottes in a sauté pan containing 1 cm (½ in) water.
4 Cover with a tight-fitting lid, place on a fierce heat so that the water boils rapidly.
5 Cook for 2–3 min until the eggs are lightly set and serve.

9 Egg in cocotte with cream *Oeuf en cocotte à la crème*

1 Proceed as for the basic recipe.
2 Half a minute before the cooking is completed add 1 dessertspn of cream to each egg and complete the cooking.

10 Egg in cocotte with thickened gravy *Oeuf en cocotte au jus*

1 Proceed as for the basic recipe.
2 When cooked add 1 dessertspn jus-lié to each egg.

11 Egg in cocotte with creamed chicken *Oeuf en cocotte à la reine*

20 g	2 oz	diced cooked chicken
125 ml	¼ pt	sauce suprême (page 96)

1 Combine the chicken with half of the sauce and place in the bottom of the egg cocottes.
2 Break the eggs on top of the chicken and cook as for the basic recipe.
3 When serving, pour over the eggs 1 dessertspn of the remaining sauce or fresh cream.

12 Egg in cocotte with tomato *Oeuf en cocotte aux tomates*

200 g	8 oz	tomatoes (cooked concassée) (page 431)
125 ml	¼ pt	tomato sauce (page 106)

1 Place the tomato in the bottom of the egg cocottes.
2 Break the eggs on top and cook as for the basic method.
3 Add 1 dessertspn tomato sauce to the eggs before serving.

13 Boiled eggs *Oeufs à la coque*

Allow 1 or 2 eggs per portion.

Method I

Place the eggs in cold water, bring to the boil, simmer 2–2½ min, remove from the water and serve at once in an egg cup.

Method II

Plunge the eggs in boiling water, re-boil, simmer 3–5 min.

Note Boiled eggs are always served in the shell.

1 portion provides:

251 kcals/1052 kJ
18.9 g fat of which 8.7 g saturated
8.0 g carbohydrate of which 3.3 g sugars
12.5 g protein
1.2 g fibre

Using 1 egg per portion
1 portion provides:

81 kcals/340 kJ
6.0 g fat of which 1.9 g saturated
0.0 g carbohydrate of which 0.0 g sugars
6.8 g protein
0.0 g fibre

14 · Soft-boiled eggs *Oeufs mollets*

Plunge the eggs into boiling water, re-boil, simmer for 5½ min. Refresh immediately. Remove the shells carefully. Reheat when required for ½ min in hot salted water.

All the recipes given for poached eggs (recipes 22–27) can be applied to soft-boiled eggs.

15 · Hard-boiled eggs *Oeuf durs*

1 Plunge the eggs into a pan of boiling water.
2 Re-boil and simmer for 8–10 min.
3 Refresh until cold under running water.

If high temperatures or a long cooking time are used to cook eggs, iron in the yolk and sulphur compounds in the white are released to form an unsightly blackish ring around the yolk. Stale eggs will also show a black ring round the yolk.

16 · Hard-boiled eggs with mushroom and cheese sauce *Oeufs Chimay*

		4 hard-boiled eggs	
10 g	½ oz	chopped shallots	duxelle
10 g	½ oz	butter	duxelle
100 g	4 oz	mushrooms	duxelle
		chopped parsley	
		salt, pepper	
250 ml	½ pt	Mornay sauce, page 95	
		grated Parmesan cheese	

Using 2 eggs per portion
1 portion provides:

162 kcals/679 kJ
12.0 g fat of which 3.8 g saturated
0.0 g carbohydrate of which 0.0 g sugars
13.5 g protein
0.0 g fibre

1 Cut the eggs in halves lengthwise.
2 Remove the yolks and pass through a sieve.
3 Place the whites in an earthenware serving dish.
4 Prepare the duxelle by cooking the chopped shallot in the butter without colouring, add the well-washed and finely chopped mushroom or mushroom trimmings, cook for 3–4 min.
5 Mix the yolks with the duxelle and parsley and correct the seasoning.
6 Spoon or pipe the mixture into the egg white halves.
7 Cover the eggs with Mornay sauce, sprinkle with grated Parmesan cheese and brown slowly under a salamander or in the top of a moderate oven and serve.

17 · Hard-boiled eggs with cheese and tomato sauce *Oeufs aurore*

1 Proceed as for eggs Chimay using béchamel in place of Mornay.
2 Add a little tomato sauce or tomato purée to the béchamel to give it a pinkish colour.
3 Mask the eggs, sprinkle with grated cheese.
4 Gratinate under the salamander.

18 · Hard-boiled eggs with parsley and onion sauce *Oeuf à la tripe*

		4 sliced hard-boiled eggs
250 ml	½ pt	Soubise sauce, page 95
		chopped parsley

1 Place the sliced eggs in a buttered, earthenware dish.
2 Coat with boiling Soubise sauce (page 95).
3 Sprinkle with chopped parsley, and serve.

19 · Fried eggs *Oeufs frits*

1 Allow 1 or 2 eggs per portion.
2 Melt a little fat in a frying pan. Add the eggs, season lightly.
3 Cook gently until lightly set. Serve on a plate or flat dish.

To prepare an excellent fried egg it is essential to use a high quality egg, to maintain a controlled low heat and use a high quality fat (butter or oil, e.g. sunflower oil).

Preparation for fried eggs

Fried in olive oil
1 portion provides:

128 kcals/536 kJ
10.7 g fat of which 2.6 g saturated
0.0 g carbohydrate of which 0.0 g sugars
7.6 g protein
0.0 g fibre

Fried in sunflower oil
1 portion provides:

360 kcals/1512 kJ
31.0 g fat of which 9.8 g saturated
0.0 g carbohydrate of which 0.0 g sugars
20.2 g protein
0.0 g fibre

20 · Fried eggs and bacon *Oeufs au lard*

1 Allow 2–3 rashers per portion. Remove the rind and bone.
2 Fry in a little fat or grill on a flat tray under the salamander on both sides. Dress neatly around the fried egg.

Fried in butter
1 portion provides:

128 kcals/536 kJ
10.7 g fat of which 4.1 g saturated
0.0 g carbohydrate of which 0.0 g sugars
7.6 g protein
0.0 g fibre

Fried eggs, may also be served with grilled or fried tomatoes, mushrooms, sauté potatoes, etc., as ordered by the customer.

21 · French fried eggs *Oeufs frits à la française*

1 Fry two eggs separately in a frying-pan in a fairly deep hot oil.
2 Shape each egg with a spoon so as to enclose the yolk in crisply fried white.
3 Drain well and serve.

22 · Poached eggs *Oeufs pochés*

High quality eggs should be used for poaching because they have a large amount of thick white and consequently have less tendency to spread in the simmering water. Low quality eggs are difficult to manage because the large quantity of thin white spreads in the simmering water.

A well-prepared poached egg has a firm tender white surrounding the slightly thickened unbroken yolk. The use of a little vinegar (an acid) helps to set the egg white so preventing it from spreading; it also makes the white more tender and whiter. Too much malt vinegar will discolour and give the eggs a strong vinegar flavour; white vinegar may be used.

1 Carefully break the eggs one by one into a shallow pan containg at least 8 cm (3 in) gently boiling water to which a little vinegar has been added (1 litre (1 qt) water to 1 tablespn vinegar).
2 Simmer until lightly set, approx. 2½–3 min.
3 Remove carefully with a perforated spoon into a bowl of cold water.
4 Trim the white of egg if necessary.
5 Reheat, when required, by placing into hot salted water for approx. ½–1 min.
6 Remove carefully from the water using a perforated spoon.
7 Drain on a cloth and use as required.

Stages involved in poaching an egg

1 portion provides:

85 kcals/358 kJ
6.4 g fat of which 2.0 g saturated
0.0 g carbohydrate of which 0.0 g sugars
6.8 g protein
0.0 g fibre

23 Poached eggs with cheese sauce *Oeufs pochés Mornay*

		4 eggs
		4 short paste tartlets or
		4 half slices of buttered toast
250 ml	½ pt	Mornay sauce (page 95)

1 portion provides:
280 kcals/1 177 kJ
19.1 g fat of which 8.7 g saturated
15.2 g carbohydrate of which 3.4 g sugars
12.8 g protein
0.8 g fibre

1 Cook eggs as for poached eggs.
2 Place tartlets or toast in an earthenware dish (the slices of toast may be halved, cut in rounds with a cutter, crust removed).
3 Add the hot well-drained eggs.
4 Completely cover with sauce, sprinkle with grated Parmesan cheese, brown under the salamander and serve.

24 Poached eggs with cheese sauce and spinach *Oeufs pochés florentine*

¾ kg	1 lb 8 oz	spinach
		4 eggs
250 ml	½ pt	Mornay sauce (page 95)

1 Remove the stems from the spinach.
2 Wash very carefully in plenty of water several times if necessary.
3 Cook in boiling salted water until tender, approx. 5 min.
4 Refresh under cold water, squeeze dry into a ball.
5 When required for service, place into a pan containing 25–50 g (1–2 oz) butter, loosen with a fork and reheat quickly without colouring, season lightly.
6 Place in an earthenware dish.
7 Place the eggs on top and finish as for eggs Mornay.

25 Poached eggs with curry sauce *Oeufs pochés Bombay*

		4 eggs
50 g	2 oz	plain boiled rice
250 ml	½ pt	curry sauce (page 104)

Poached eggs are placed on a bed of rice, coated with strained curry sauce.

26 Poached eggs with minced chicken *Oeufs pochés à la reine*

100 g	4 oz	minced chicken
250 ml	½ pt	sauce suprême (page 96)
		4 short pastry tartlets
		4 poached eggs

1 Mix the chicken with half the sauce suprême, correct the seasoning.
2 Place the tartlets in an earthenware dish.
3 Add a spoonful of chicken in each tartlet.
4 Place a hot poached egg on top.
5 Coat with sauce suprême and serve.

27 Poached eggs with sweet corn *Oeufs pochés Washington*

250 ml	½ pt	sauce suprême (page 96)
100 g	4 oz	prepared sweet corn
		4 poached eggs

1 Boil half the sauce suprême with the sweet corn, correct the seasoning.
2 Place in an earthenware dish with the poached eggs on top.
3 Coat with sauce suprême.

Note Poached eggs with sweet corn may also be served in pastry tartlets.

28 Egg croquette *Croquette d'oeuf*

250 ml	½ pt	thick béchamel
		4 hard-boiled eggs
		salt, pepper
		1 egg yolk
25 g	1 oz	flour
		1 beaten egg
50 g	2 oz	white breadcrumbs

1 portion provides:

411 kcals/1726 kJ
31.8 g fat of which 8.6 g saturated
18.8 g carbohydrate of which 3.5 g sugars
13.6 g protein
0.9 g fibre

1 Boil the béchamel in a thick-bottomed pan.
2 Add the eggs cut into ½ cm (¼ in) dice.
3 Re-boil, season, mix in the egg yolk, and remove from the heat.
4 Pour on to a greased tray and leave until cold.
5 Mould into 4 or 8 even sized croquette shapes.
6 Pass through flour, beaten egg, and crumbs (twice if necessary).
7 Shake off surplus crumbs and reshape with a palette knife.
8 Deep fry to a golden brown in hot fat, drain well.
9 Garnish with fried or sprig parsley and serve with a suitable sauce, e.g. tomato (page 106).

29 Egg mayonnaise *Oeuf mayonnaise*

See page 130, Hors-d'oeuvre.

30 · Curried eggs

50 g	2 oz	rice (long grain)
		4 hard-boiled eggs
250 ml	½ pt	curry sauce (page 104)

1 Pick and wash the rice.
2 Add to plenty of boiling, salt water.
3 Stir to the boil and allow to simmer gently till tender, approx. 12–15 min.
4 Wash well under running water, drain and place on a sieve and cover with a cloth.
5 Place on a tray in a moderate oven or on a hot plate until hot.
6 Place the rice in an earthenware dish.
7 Reheat the eggs in hot salt water, cut in halves and dress neatly on the rice.
8 Coat the eggs with sauce and serve.

31 · Scotch eggs

		4 hard-boiled eggs
300 g	12 oz	sausage meat
25 g	1 oz	flour
		1 beaten egg
50 g	2 oz	breadcrumbs

1 portion provides:

499 kcals/2094 kJ
39.9 g fat of which 11.4 g saturated
18.4 g carbohydrate of which 0.6 g sugars
18.0 g protein
1.0 g fibre

1 Completely cover each egg with sausage meat.
2 Pass through flour, egg and breadcrumbs.
3 Shake off surplus crumbs.
4 Deep fry to a golden brown in a moderately hot fat.
5 Drain well, cut in halves and serve hot or cold.
6 *Hot:* garnish with fried or sprig parsley, and a sauceboat of suitable sauce, e.g. tomato (page 106).
Cold: garnish with salad in season and a sauceboat of salad dressing (page 119).

32 **Omelette** (basic recipe) *Omelette nature*

Using 2 eggs per portion
1 portion provides:

236 kcals/990 kJ
20.2 g fat of which 9.1 g saturated
0.0 g carbohydrate of which 0.0 g sugars
13.6 g protein
0.0 g fibre

Using 3 eggs per portion
1 portion provides:

317 kcals/1330 kJ
26.2 g fat of which 11.0 g saturated
0.0 g carbohydrate of which 0.0 g sugars
20.3 g protein
0.0 g fibre

1 Allow 2–3 eggs per portion.
2 Break the eggs into a basin, season with salt and pepper.
3 Beat well with a fork or whisk until the yolks and whites are thoroughly combined and no streaks of white can be seen.
4 Heat the omelette pan.
5 Wipe thoroughly clean with a dry cloth.
6 Add 10 g (½ oz) butter.
7 Heat until foaming but not brown.
8 Add the eggs and cook quickly, moving the mixture continuously with a fork until lightly set.
9 Remove from the heat.
10 Half fold the mixture over at right-angles to the handle.
11 Tap the bottom of the pan to bring up the edge of the omelette.
12 Tilt the pan completely over so as to allow the omelette to fall carefully into the centre of the dish or plate.
13 Neaten the shape if necessary and serve immediately.

Stages involved in making an omelette

33 · **Savoury herb omelette** *Omelette fines herbes*

Add a pinch of chopped parsley, chervil and chives to the mixture and proceed as for basic omelette (recipe 32).

34 · **Mushroom omelette** *Omelette aux champignons*

1 25–50 g (1–2 oz) button mushrooms per portion.
2 Wash and slice the mushrooms and cook in a frying-pan in a little butter, seasoning with salt and pepper. Drain well.
3 Add to the butter in the hot cleaned pan and proceed as for basic omelette (recipe 32).

35 · **Cheese omelette** *Omelette au fromage*

1 Allow 25 g (1 oz) grated cheese per portion.
2 Proceed as for basic omelette (recipe 32).
3 Before folding, add the cheese.
4 Fold and serve as for basic omelette.

36 · **Tomato omelette** *Omelette aux tomates* or *portugaise*

25 g	1 oz	butter	tomato concassée (page 429)
25 g	1 oz	chopped shallots or onion	tomato concassée (page 429)
400 g	1 lb	tomatoes	tomato concassée (page 429)
125 ml	¼ pt	tomato sauce (page 106)	
		chopped parsley	

1 Prepare a plain omelette (recipe 32).
2 Make an incision down the centre.
3 Fill with hot tomato concassée.
4 Sprinkle the tomato with a little chopped parsley.
5 Serve tomato sauce separately.

(The service of this dish is illustrated on page 175.) *4 portions*

37 · **Omelette with chicken livers** *Omelette aux foies de volaille*

100 g	4 oz	chicken livers (trimmed)
25 g	1 oz	butter
125 ml	¼ pt	jus-lié or demi-glace
		salt and pepper
		chopped parsley

1 Prepare as for basic omelette (recipe 32).
2 Make an incision down the centre.
3 Cut the livers into neat scallops.
4 Season with salt and pepper.
5 Fry quickly in the hot butter.
6 Drain and place in the hot jus-lié or demi-glace, correct the seasoning.
7 Place a spoonful of the mixture in the incision of each omelette, sprinkle a little chopped parsley on the liver.

4 portions

38 · **Kidney omelette** *Omelette aux rognons*

		2 sheep's kidneys
		salt and papper
25 g	1 oz	butter
125 ml	¼ pt	jus-lié or demi-glace
		chopped parsley

1 Skin the kidneys, remove the gristle and cut into 1 cm (½ in) dice.
2 Season with salt and pepper.

3 Quickly fry in the hot butter for 2–3 min, drain and discard liquid.
4 Add to the hot jus-lié or demi-glace, correct the seasoning.
5 Do not reboil or the kidneys will become tough.
6 Prepare the basic omelette (recipe 32).
7 Make an incision down the centre and fill with kidneys.
8 Sprinkle with chopped parsley on the kidney.

4 portions

39 · **Shrimp omelette** *Omelette aux crevettes*

250 ml	½ pt	picked shrimps
125 ml	¼ pt	béchamel

1 Prepare a plain omelette (recipe 32). Make an incision down the centre.
2 Place a spoonful of the shrimps, bound with béchamel in the centre.

4 portions

40 · **Ham omelette** *Omelette au jambon*

1 Allow 25–50 g (1–2 oz) lean diced cooked ham per portion.
2 Add to the beaten eggs.
3 Proceed as for basic omelette (recipe 32).

41 · **Bacon omelette** *Omelette au lard*

1 Allow 1–2 rashers of bacon per portion.
2 Cut the bacon into ½ cm (¼ in) thick strips.
3 Fry in a little dripping or butter in a frying-pan.
4 Add to the beaten eggs.
5 Proceed as for basic omelette (recipe 32).

42 · **Onion omelette** *Omelette lyonnaise*

1 Allow 50 g (2 oz) onion per portion.
2 Peel, then thinly slice the onion and cook in a little butter, colouring slightly.
3 Mix with the beaten eggs. Proceed as for basic omelette (recipe 32).

43 · **Potato omelette** *Omelette Parmentier*

1 Allow 50 g (2 oz) peeled potatoes per portion.
2 Cut the potatoes in neat 3 mm (⅛ in) dice.
3 Wash well and drain.
4 Quickly fry in a little fat in a frying-pan until golden brown, drain in a colander.
5 When making omelettes place potatoes in the pan with the butter before adding the eggs.
6 Proceed as for basic omelette (recipe 32).

44 · Potato, onion and bacon omelette *Omelette paysanne*

For 4 omelettes allow 50 g (2 oz) peeled potatoes, 50 g (2 oz) onion and 2 rashers of bacon. Prepare as in the three previous recipes.

1 Proceed as for basic omelette (recipe 32).
2 Sharply tap the pan on the stove to loosen the omelette.
3 Toss as for a pancake. Turn out on a plate, serve flat.

45 · Ham and parsley omelette *Omelette fermière*

As for ham omelette with chopped parsley. Prepared and served flat.

46 · Spanish omelette *Omelette espagnole*

For 4 portions allow 200 g (8 oz) tomatoes (concassé), 100 g (4 oz) onions (cooked as for onion omelette) and 50 g (2 oz) diced red pimento.

Cook and serve flat. (Illustrated on page 175.)

47 · Eggs on the dish *Oeufs sur le plat* (basic recipe)

1 Butter and season an egg dish.
2 Add 1–2 eggs and season with salt and pepper.
3 Allow to cook gently on the side of the stove and finish under the salamander or in a hot oven. The yolks should be soft.

48 · Eggs on the dish with bacon *Oeuf sur le plat au lard*

1 Allow 1–2 rashers of bacon per portion.
2 Grill or fry the bacon. Cut each rasher in half.
3 Place in the bottom of a buttered, seasoned egg dish.
4 Break the eggs on top of the bacon.
5 Cook and serve as for the previous recipe.

49 · Eggs on the dish with chipolata and tomato sauce *Oeuf sur le plat Bercy*

1 As for the basic recipe (recipe 47).
2 Serve a grilled chipolata on each portion and a thread of hot tomato sauce, page 106.

50 · Eggs on the dish with cream *Oeuf sur le plat à crème*

1 As for the basic recipe (recipe 47).
2 When almost cooked add a tablespoon of cream over each egg.
3 Complete the cooking and serve.

Clockwise from top left: spaghetti bolognaise (p. 194); tagliatelli with tomato sauce (p. 193); riccioli with cheese (p. 193)

9

FARINACEOUS DISHES

General objectives	*Specific objectives*
To understand the terms farinaceous and pasta and to know where, when and how they are served.	To list the points to be observed when cooking pasta and to explain why they should be followed. To list the ingredients and state how pasta is made. To produce a selection of pasta dishes, using ready-prepared and self-prepared pastes.

Farinaceous Dishes Les Farineuses

Farinaceous dishes are commonly referred to as pasta. There are at least 56 varieties of pasta each of which can be made into dishes with numerous regional variations. Pasta may be served for lunch, dinner, supper or as a snack meal and also used as garnish to other dishes. Pasta is traditionally cooked *al dente* which means 'firm to the bite'. Certain rice dishes, e.g. pilaff and risotto are included in this section.

1 · General points on pasta

1. Always cook in plenty of gently boiling salted water.
2. Stir to the boil. Do not over cook.
3. It not to be used immediately, refresh and reheat carefully in hot salted water when required. Drain well in a colander.
4. With most pasta, grated cheese (preferably Parmesan) should be served separately.
   Allow 10 g (½ oz) pasta per portion as a garnish.
   Allow 25–50 g (1–2 oz) pasta per portion for a main course.

2 · Spaghetti with cheese *Spaghetti italienne*

100 g	4 oz	spaghetti
25 g	1 oz	butter
25–50 g	1–2 oz	grated cheese (preferably Parmesan)
		salt, mill pepper

Using 28 g/1 oz cheese
This recipe provides:

628 kcals/2640 kJ
30.8 g fat of which 18.4 g saturated
74.2 g carbohydrate of which 3.4 g sugars
18.6 g protein
5.2 g fibre

Using 52 g/2 oz cheese
This recipe provides:

730 kcals/3066 kJ
39.0 g fat of which 23.8 g saturated
74.2 g carbohydrate of which 3.4 g sugars
25.2 g protein
5.2 g fibre

1. Plunge spaghetti into a saucepan containing plenty of boiling salted water. Allow to boil gently.
2. Stir occasionally with a wooden spoon. Cook 12–15 min approx.
3. Drain well in a colander. Return to a clean, dry pan.
4. Mix in the butter and cheese. Correct the seasoning and serve.

(The service of this dish, using riccioli instead of spaghetti, is illustrated on page 191.)

3 · Spaghetti with tomato sauce *Spaghetti napolitaine*

100 g	4 oz	spaghetti
25 g	1 oz	butter (optional)
250 ml	½ pt	tomato sauce (page 106)
		salt, mill pepper
100 g	4 oz	tomato concassée (page 431)

Using hard margarine
This recipe provides:

400 kcals/1672 kJ
17.2 g fat of which 9.4 g saturated
50.0 g carbohydrate of which 10.2 g sugars
11.8 g protein
4.0 g fibre

1. Plunge spaghetti into a saucepan containing boiling salted water. Allow to boil gently.
2. Stir occasionally with a wooden spoon. Cook 12–15 min approx.
3. Drain well in a colander. Return to a clean, dry pan.
4. Mix in the butter and add the tomato sauce. Correct the seasoning.
5. Add the tomato concassée and serve with grated cheese.

(The service of this dish, using tagliatelli instead of spaghetti, is illustrated on page 191.)

4 · Spaghetti milanaise *Spaghetti milanaise*

100 g	4 oz	spaghetti
25 g	1 oz	butter (optional)
125 ml	¼ pt	tomato sauce (page 106)
25 g	1 oz	ham, tongue and cooked mushroom in julienne
		salt, mill pepper

1 Plunge the spaghetti into plenty of boiling salted water.
2 Allow to boil gently. Stir occasionally with a wooden spoon.
3 Cook for approximately 12–15 min. Drain well in a colander.
4 Return to a clean pan containing the butter. Add tomato sauce.
5 Correct the seasoning. Add the julienne of ham, tongue, and mushroom and mix in carefully, then serve with grated cheese.

(An example of the service of this dish is illustrated on page 319.)

5 · Spaghetti bolognaise *Spaghetti bolonaise*

25 g	1 oz	butter or oil
50 g	2 oz	chopped onion
		1 clove garlic, chopped
100 g	4 oz	lean minced beef or tail end fillet, cut in ⅛ in dice
125 ml	¼ pt	jus-lié or demi-glace
	4 oz	1 tablespn tomato purée
		marjoram or oregano
100 g	4 oz	diced mushrooms
		salt, mill pepper
100g	4 oz	spaghetti

Spaghetti bolognaise

Prepare sauce as follows:

1 Place 10 g (½ oz) butter or oil in a sauteuse.
2 Add the chopped onion and garlic and cook for 4–5 min without colour.

Using sunflower oil
This recipe provides:

760 kcals/3188 kJ
32.2 g fat of which 5.6 g saturated
83.4 g carbohydrate of which 10.4 g sugars
39.0 g protein
9.6 g fibre

3 Add the beef and cook, colouring lightly.
4 Add the jus-lié or demi-glace, the tomato purée and the herbs.
5 Simmer till tender.
6 Add the mushrooms and simmer for 5 minutes then correct the seasoning.
7 Meanwhile cook the spaghetti in plenty of boiling salted water.
8 Allow to boil gently and stir occasionally with a wooden spoon.
9 Cook for approximately 12–15 min. Drain well in a colander.
10 Return to a clean pan containing 10 g (½ oz) butter (optional).
11 Correct the seasoning.
12 Serve with the sauce in centre of the spaghetti.
13 Serve grated cheese separately.

6 · **Macaroni cheese** *Macaroni au gratin*

100 g	4 oz	macaroni
25 g	1 oz	butter (optional)
100 g	4 oz	grated cheese
500 ml	1 pt	thin béchamel
		½ teaspn diluted English or Continental mustard
		salt, mill pepper

This recipe provides:

1808 kcals/7596 kJ
116.6 g fat of which 64.2 g saturated
138.6 g carbohydrate of which 26.6 g sugars
60.0 g protein
6.8 g fibre

1 Plunge the macaroni into a saucepan containing plenty of boiling salted water.
2 Allow to boil gently and stir occasionally with a wooden spoon.
3 Cook for approximately 15 min. and drain well in a colander.
4 Return to a clean pan containing the butter.
5 Mix with half the cheese and add the béchamel and mustard.
6 Place in an earthenware dish and sprinkle with the remainder of the cheese.
7 Brown lightly under the salamander and serve.

Macaroni may also be prepared and served as for any of the spaghetti dishes.

Macaroni cheese

7 · **Noodles** *Nouilles*

100 g	4 oz	flour
		salt
		1 teaspn olive or other vegetable oil
		1 egg and 1 egg yolk

Using white flour, olive oil
This recipe provides:

534 kcals/2246 kJ
18.4 g fat of which 4.8 g saturated
77.8 g carbohydrate of which 1.6 g sugars
19.4 g protein
3.6 g fibre

Using wholemeal flour, olive oil
This recipe provides:

504 kcals/2116 kJ
19.2 g fat of which 4.8 g saturated
65.8 g carbohydrate of which 2.2 g sugars
22.6 g protein
8.6 g fibre

Noodles are usually bought ready prepared but may be made as follows:

1 Sieve the flour and salt. Make a well.
2 Add oil and eggs. Mix to a dough.
3 Knead well till smooth. Leave to rest.
4 Roll out to a thin rectangle 45 cm×15 cm (18 in×6 in).
5 Cut into ½ cm (¼ in) strips. Leave to dry.

Note For wholemeal noodles use 50 g (2 oz) wholemeal flour and 50 g (2 oz) strong flour.

Semolina is a good dusting agent to use when handling this paste.

The noodles are cooked in the same way as spaghetti and may be served as for any of the spaghetti recipes. The most popular method of serving them is Nouilles au beurre (recipe 8).

8 · **Noodles with butter** *Nouilles au beurre*

100 g	4 oz	noodles
		salt, mill pepper
		a little grated nutmeg
50 g	2 oz	butter or margarine

1 Cook noodles in plenty of gently boiling salted water.
2 Drain well in a colander and return to the pan.
3 Add the seasoning and butter and toss carefully until mixed.
4 Correct the seasoning and serve.

Noodles may also be used as a garnish, e.g. with braised beef (see illustration on page 291).

9 · **Ravioli** *Ravioli*

Ravioli are small envelopes of a noodle-type paste filled with a variety of stuffings, e.g. beef, chicken, veal, spinach, etc.

10 Ravioli paste

200 g	8 oz	flour
		salt
35 ml	1 ½ fl oz	olive oil
105 ml	4 fl oz	water

1 Sieve flour and salt. Make a well. Add the liquid.
2 Knead to a smooth dough. Rest for at least ½ hr in a cool place.
3 Roll out to a very thin oblong 30 cm×45 cm (12 in×18 in).
4 Cut in half and egg wash.
5 Place the stuffing in a piping bag with a large plain tube.
6 Pipe out the filling in small pieces about the size of a cherry approx. 4 cm (1½ in) apart on to one-half of the paste.
7 Carefully cover with the other half of the paste, seal, taking care to avoid air pockets.
8 Mark each with the back of a plain cutter.
9 Cut in between each line of filling, down and across with a serrated pastry wheel.
10 Separate on a well-floured tray.
11 Poach in gently boiling salted water approx. 10 min. Drain well.
12 Place in an earthenware serving dish.
13 Cover with 250 ml (½ pt) jus-lié, demi-glace or tomato sauce.
14 Sprinkle with 50 g (2 oz) grated cheese.
15 Brown under the salamander and serve.

Note For wholemeal ravioli use 100 g (4 oz) wholemeal flour and 100 g (4 oz) strong flour.

8 portions approx.

11 Ravioli filling

200 g	8 oz	braised or boiled beef or veal
400 g	1 lb	spinach
50 g	2 oz	chopped onion or shallot
		1 clove garlic, chopped
10 g	½ oz	oil or butter
		salt, mill pepper
		marjoram or oregano
		little demi-glace to bind

1 Mince the beef or veal.
2 Cook and mince the spinach.
3 Cook the onion and garlic in the fat without colouring.
4 Mix the meat, spinach and onion
5 Season and add a little demi-glace to bind the mixture if necessary, but keep the mixture firm.

12 · **Cannelloni** *Cannelloni*

These are poached rolls of ravioli paste filled with a variety of stuffings as for ravioli.

Paste and fillings as for ravioli.

1 Roll out the paste as for ravioli.
2 Cut into squares approx. 6 cm×6 cm (2½ in×2½ in).
3 Cook in gently boiling salted water approx. 10 min. Refresh in cold water.
4 Drain well and lay out singly on the table.
5 Pipe out the filling across each.
6 Roll up like a sausage-roll.
7 Place in a greased earthenware dish.
8 Add 250 ml (½ pt) demi-glace, jus-lié or tomato sauce.
9 Sprinkle with 25–50 g (1–2 oz) grated cheese.
10 Brown slowly under the salamander or in the oven and serve.

13 · **Lasagne** *Lasagne*

200 g	8 oz	lasagne
		1 tablespn oil
50 g	2 oz	thin strips of streaky bacon
100 g	4 oz	chopped onion
50 g	2 oz	chopped carrot
50 g	2 oz	chopped celery
200 g	8 oz	minced beef
50 g	2 oz	tomato purée
375 ml	¾ pt	jus-lié or demi-glace
		1 clove garlic
		salt, pepper
		½ level teaspn marjoram
100 g	4 oz	sliced mushrooms
250 ml	½ pt	béchamel sauce
25 g	2 oz	grated Parmesan or Cheddar cheese

1 portion provides:

575 kcals/2416 kJ
28.7 g fat of which 11.4 g saturated
56.1 g carbohydrate of which 10.0 g sugars
26.7 g protein
5.8 g fibre

1 This recipe can be made using 200 g (8 oz) ready bought lasagne or preparing it fresh using 8 oz flour noodle paste recipe 7. Wholemeal lasagne can be made using noodle paste made with 100 g (4 oz) wholemeal flour and 100 g (4 oz) strong flour.
2 Prepare noodle paste and roll out 1 mm (1/16 in) thick.
3 Cut into 6 cm (2½ in) squares.
4 Allow to rest in a cool place and dry slightly on a cloth dusted with flour.
5 Whether using fresh or ready bought lasagne, cook in gently simmering salted water for approx. 10 mins.
6 Refresh in cold water, drain on a cloth.
7 Gently heat the oil in a thick-bottomed pan, add bacon and cook 2–3 mins.

8 Add onion, carrot, celery and cover pan with lid and cook 5 mins.
9 Add the minced beef, increase heat and stir until lightly brown.
10 Remove from heat and mix in the tomato purée.
11 Return to heat, mix in jus-lié or demi-glace, stir to boil.
12 Add garlic, salt, pepper and marjoram and simmer for 15 mins. Remove garlic.
13 Mix in mushrooms, reboil for 2 mins, remove from the heat.
14 Butter an ovenproof dish and cover bottom with a layer of the meat sauce.
15 Add layer of lasagne and cover with meat sauce.
16 Add another layer of lasagne and cover with remainder of the meat sauce.
17 Cover with the béchamel.
18 Sprinkle with cheese, cover with lid and place in moderately hot oven 190 °C (Reg. 5), approx 20 mins.
19 Remove lid cook further 15 mins approx and serve in the cleaned ovenproof dish.

14 · **Gnocchi parisienne** *Gnocchi parisienne*

125 ml	¼ pt	water	choux paste
50 g	2 oz	margarine or butter	choux paste
		salt	choux paste
60 g	2½ oz	flour, white or wholemeal	choux paste
		2 eggs	choux paste
50 g	2 oz	grated cheese	
250 ml	½ pt	béchamel (thin)	

Using hard margarine
1 portion provides:

341 kcals/1433 kJ
25.0 g fat of which 11.8 g saturated
19.5 g carbohydrate of which 3.3 g sugars
10.7 g protein
0.8 g fibre

1 Boil water, margarine or butter, and salt in a saucepan.
2 Remove from the heat.
3 Mix in flour with a wooden spoon. Return to a gentle heat.
4 Stir continuously until mixture leaves sides of pan.
5 Cool slightly. Gradually add the eggs, beating well.
6 Add half the cheese.
7 Place in a piping bag with ½ cm (¼ in) plain tube.
8 Pipe out in 1 cm (½ in) lengths into a shallow pan of gently simmering salted water. Do not allow to boil.
9 Cook approx. 10 min. Drain well in a colander.
10 Combine carefully with béchamel. Correct the seasoning.
11 Pour into an earthenware dish.
12 Sprinkle with the remainder of the cheese.
13 Brown lightly under salamander and serve.

4 portions

15 Gnocchi romaine *Gnocchi romaine*

500 ml	1 pt	milk
100 g	4 oz	semolina
		salt, pepper
		grated nutmeg
		1 egg yolk
25 g	1 oz	grated cheese
25 g	1 oz	butter or margarine
250 ml	½ pt	tomato sauce (page 106)

1. Boil milk in a thick-bottomed pan.
2. Sprinkle in the semolina, stirring continuously.
3. Stir to the boil.
4. Season, simmer till cooked 5–10 min.
5. Remove from heat.
6. Mix in egg yolk, cheese and butter.
7. Pour into a buttered tray 1 cm (½ in) deep.
8. When cold cut into rounds with 5 cm (2 in) round cutter.
9. Place the debris in a buttered earthenware dish.
10. Neatly arrange the rounds on top.
11. Sprinkle with melted butter and cheese.
12. Lightly brown in the oven or under the salamander.
13. Serve with a thread of tomato sauce round the gnocchi.

4 portions

16 Gnocchi piemontaise *Gnocchi piémontaise*

300 g	12 oz	mashed potato
100 g	4 oz	flour, white or wholemeal
		1 egg and 1 egg yolk
25 g	1 oz	butter
		salt, pepper
		grated nutmeg
250 ml	½ pt	tomato sauce (page 106)

1. Bake or boil potatoes in jackets.
2. Remove from skins and mash with a fork or pass through a sieve.
3. Mix with flour, egg, butter and seasoning while hot.
4. Mould into balls the size of a walnut.
5. Dust well with flour and flatten slightly with a fork.
6. Poach in gently boiling water approx. 5 min. Drain carefully.
7. Dress in a buttered earthenware dish, cover with tomato sauce.
8. Sprinkle with grated cheese and brown lightly under the salamander and serve.

4 portions

17 · Braised rice *Riz pilaff*

50 g	2 oz	butter
25 g	1 oz	chopped onion
100 g	4 oz	rice (long grain), white or brown
200 ml	appox. ⅜ pt	white stock (preferably chicken)
		salt, mill pepper

Using white rice and hard marg
1 portion provides:

184 kcals/774 kJ
10.4 g fat of which 4.5 g saturated
22.1 g carbohydrate of which 0.3 g sugars
1.9 g protein
0.6 g fibre

Using brown rice and hard marg
1 portion provides:

183 kcals/769 kJ
10.9 g fat of which 4.6 g saturated
20.7 g carbohydrate of which 0.7 g sugars
1.9 g protein
1.0 g fibre

1 Place 25 g (1 oz) butter in a small sauteuse. Add the onion.
2 Cook gently without colouring 2–3 min. Add the rice.
3 Cook gently without colouring 2–3 min.
4 Add twice the amount of stock to rice.
5 Season, cover with a buttered paper, bring to the boil.
6 Place in a hot oven 230–250 °C approx. 15 min until cooked.
7 Remove immediately into a cool sauteuse.
8 Carefully mix in the remaining butter with a two-pronged fork.
9 Correct the seasoning and serve.

It is usual to use long-grain rice for pilaff because the grains are firm, and there is less likelihood of them breaking up and becoming mushy. During cooking the long-grain rice absorbs more liquid, loses less starch and retains its shape as it swells, the short or medium grains may split at the ends and become less distinct in outline.

(An example of the service of braised wild rice is illustrated on page 379.)

4 portions

18 · Braised rice with mushrooms *Riz pilaff aux champignons*

As for braised rice with the addition of 50–100 g (2–4 oz) button mushrooms.

1 Place 25 g (1 oz) butter in a small sauteuse. Add the onion.
2 Cook gently without colour 2–3 min.
3 Add the rice and well-washed sliced mushrooms.
4 Complete as for braised rice from point 4 (recipe 17).

19 · Braised rice with peas and pimento *Riz à l'orientale*

As for braised rice (recipe 17) plus 25 g (1 oz) cooked peas and 25 g (1 oz) 1 cm (½ in) diced pimento carefully mixed in when finishing with butter.

Many other variations of pilaff may be made with the addition of such ingredients as tomate concassée, diced ham, prawns, etc.

20 · **Braised rice with cheese** *Riz pilaff au fromage*

As recipe 17 with 50–100 g (2–4 oz) grated cheese added with the butter, before serving.

21 · **Risotto** *Risotto*

50 g	2 oz	butter or oil
25 g	1 oz	chopped onion
100 g	4 oz	rice (short grain or brown)
185 ml	approx. ⅜ pt	white stock (preferably chicken)
		salt, mill pepper
25 g	1 oz	grated Parmesan cheese

Using white rice, hard marg
1 portion provides:

210 kcals/881 kJ
12.3 g fat of which 5.7 g saturated
22.1 g carbohydrate of which 0.3 g sugars
4.1 g protein
0.6 g fibre

Using brown rice, hard marg
1 portion provides:

210 kcals/881 kJ
12.3 g fat of which 5.7 g saturated
22.1 g carbohydrate of which 0.3 g sugars
4.1 g protein
1.0 g fibre

1 Melt the butter or oil in a small sauteuse. Add the chopped onion.
2 Cook gently without colour for 2–3 min. Add the rice.
3 Cook without colour 2–3 min. Add the stock, season lightly.
4 Cover with a lid. Allow to simmer on the side of the stove.
5 Stir frequently and if necessary add more stock until the rice is cooked.
6 When cooked all the stock should have been absorbed into the rice and evaporated: a risotto should be more moist than a pilaff.
7 Finally mix in the cheese with a two pronged fork, correct the seasoning and serve.

Any variations given for braised rice may be prepared as a risotto.

Clockwise from top left: fillets of fish coated in – flour, egg and crumbs (p. 221), batter (p. 220), milk and flour (p. 221); with tartare sauce (p. 111) and tomato sauce (p. 106); marinating for à l'Orly (p. 222)

10

FISH

General objectives
To know the classification of fish, to understand the principles of purchase, preparation, cooking and service as appropriate for different catering establishments.

Specific objectives
To classify fish and to list the purchasing and storage points. To identify types of fish and to describe the cuts of fish. To state ingredients required and demonstrate the cooking and presentation of fish dishes using various methods of cooking and using suitable sauces and garnishes.

Fish Poisson

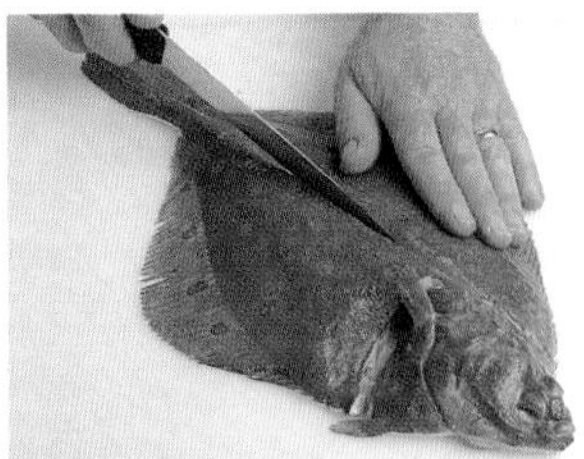

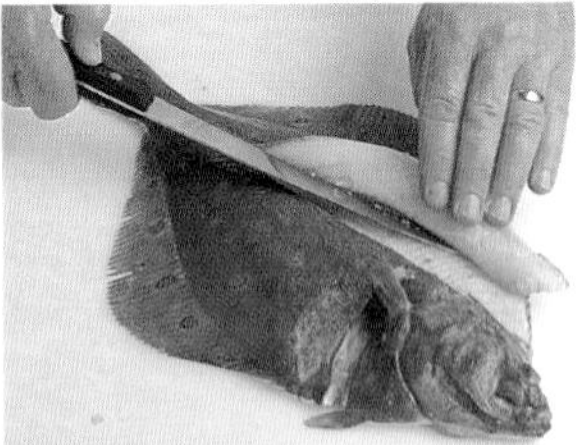

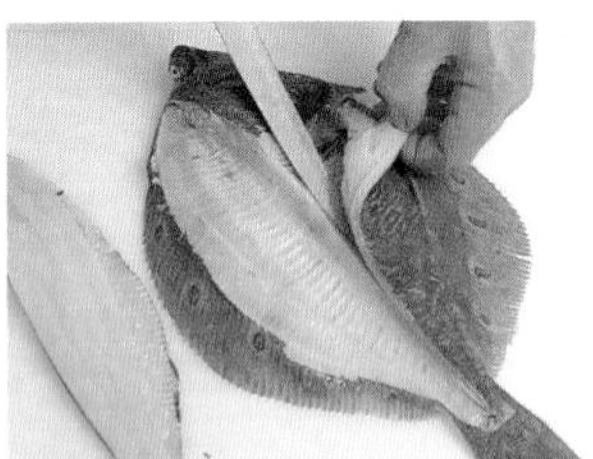

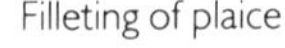

Filleting of plaice

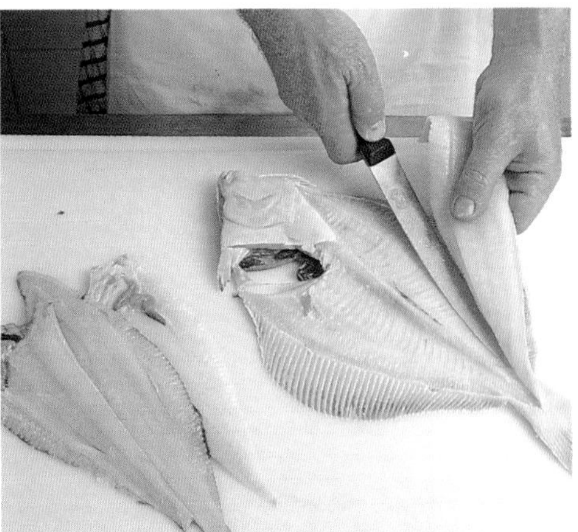

Skinning of plaice

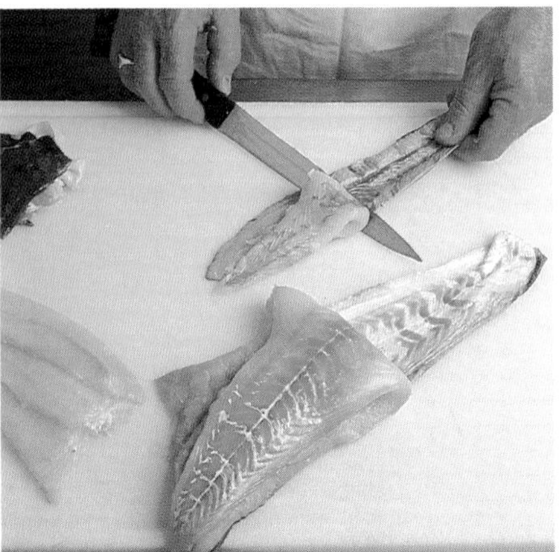

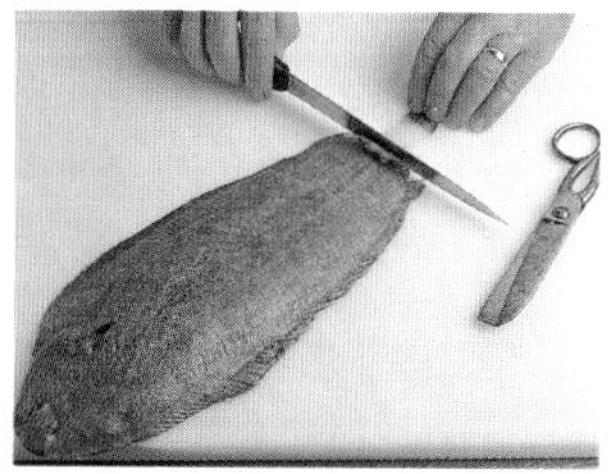

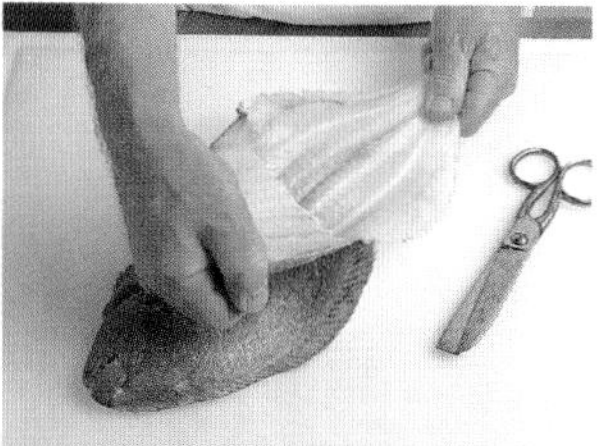

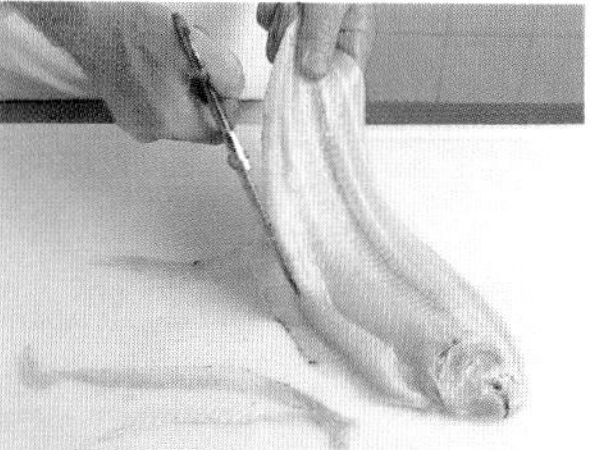

Preparation of whole Dover sole

Preparation of turbot

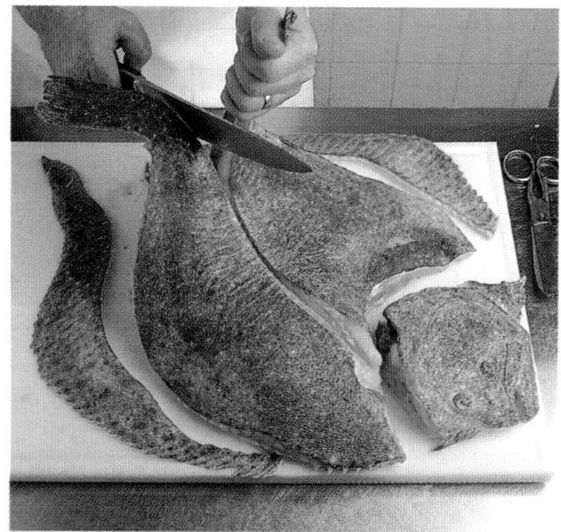

Filleting of trout

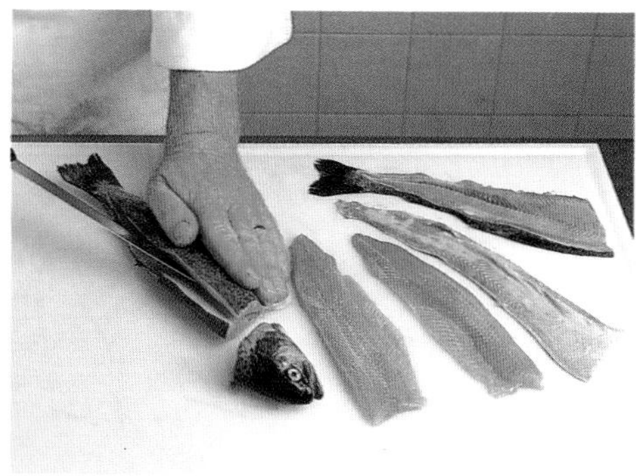

Fish may be divided into two main groups:

A *White* – which may be flat, e.g. sole, plaice or turbot, or round, e.g. whiting or cod.

B *Oily* – these are round, e.g. salmon, herring, mackerel, etc.

1 · Indications of quality

1 The eyes are bright and full, not sunken.
2 The gills are bright red in colour.
3 The flesh should be firm.
4 Scales, if any, should be plentiful.
5 There should be no unpleasant smell.

Certain fish are cured by either salting or smoking, e.g. haddock, herring, salmon, etc.

2 · Shellfish

These are also divided into two main groups:

a) *Crustacea* – e.g. lobster, crab, crawfish, crayfish, prawns and shrimps.
b) *Mollusca* – e.g. oysters, mussels, scallops.

3 · Basic fish preparation

Unless otherwise stated, as a guide, allow 100 g (4 oz) fish off the bone and 150 g (6 oz) on the bone for a portion.

Filleting of flat fish with the exception of Dover sole (see page 206)

1 Using a filleting knife make an incision from the head to tail down the line of the backbone.
2 Remove each fillet, holding the knife almost parallel to the work surface and keeping the knife close to the bone.

Skinning of flat fish with the exception of Dover sole (see page 206)

1 Hold the fillet firmly at the tail end.
2 Cut the flesh as close to the tail as possible, as far as the skin.
3 Keep the knife parallel to the work surface, grip the skin firmly and move the knife from side to side to remove the skin.

Preparation of whole Dover sole (see page 207)

1 Hold the tail firmly, then cut and scrap the skin until sufficient is lifted to be gripped.
2 Pull the skin away from the tail to the head.
3 Both black and white skins may be removed in this way.
4 Trim the tail and side fins with fish scissors, remove the eyes and clean and wash the fish thoroughly.

Preparation of turbot (see page 207)

Allow approximately 300 g (12 oz) per portion on the bone.

1 Remove the head with a large chopping knife.
2 Cut off the side bones.
3 Commencing at the tail end, chop down the centre of the backbone, dividing the fish into two halves.
4 Divide each half into portions (tronçons) as required.

Note A 3½ kg (7 lb) fish will yield approx 10 portions.

Filleting of round fish (see page 207)

1 Remove head and clean thoroughly.
2 Remove first fillet by cutting along the backbone from head to tail.
3 Keeping the knife close to the bone, remove the fillet.
4 Reverse the fish and remove the second fillet in the same way, this time cutting from tail to head.

4 · Methods of cooking fish

Boiling, poaching, steaming, grilling, shallow frying, deep frying and baking.

Boiling

This method is suitable for whole fish, e.g. salmon, turbot, trout and certain cuts of fish, e.g. salmon, cod, turbot, halibut, brill, etc. In either case the fish should be completely immersed in the cooking liquid which can be water, water and milk, milk, fish stock (for white fish) or a court bouillon (water, vinegar, thyme, bay leaf, parsley stalks, onion, carrot, peppercorns) for oily fish.

Whole fish are covered with a cold liquid and brought to the boil, cut fish are usually placed in a simmering liquid.

Poaching

This is suitable for small whole fish, cuts or fillets. Barely cover the fish with fish stock, cover with a buttered paper, bring to the boil and cook in the oven without allowing the liquid to boil. The cooking liquor is usually used for the sauce which masks the fish.

Steaming

Any fish which can be poached or boiled may be cooked by steaming.

Grilling

This method is suitable for small whole fish, cuts and fillets. With the exception of fish cooked Saint-Germain (recipe 27), it is passed through seasoned flour, brushed with oil and grilled on both sides. When grilling fish under the salamander, grill bar marks may be made with a red-hot poker before cooking.

Shallow frying

Shallow fried fish is termed meunière and is suitable for small whole fish, cuts and fillets. The fish is passed through seasoned flour, shallow fried on both sides, presentation side first, in clarified fat in a frying-pan. It is placed on a serving dish and masked with nut-brown butter, lemon juice, slice of lemon and chopped parsley.

Deep frying

This is suitable for small whole fish, cuts and fillets. The fish must be coated by one of the following:

a) flour, egg and crumb (pané) — à l'anglaise
b) milk and flour — à la française
c) batter

The coating forms a surface to prevent penetration of the fat into the fish. Deep-fried fish is served with a quarter of lemon and/or a suitable sauce and fried parsley.

Baking

Many fish, whole, portioned or filletted, may be baked. A savoury stuffing, e.g. with a duxelle base is often used, the fish cooked on a bed of roots with sprigs of fresh herbs, e.g. fennel, parsley, in a buttered ovenproof dish with a lid.

5 · The cuts of fish

La darne	A slice of round fish cut on the bone, e.g. darne de saumon (salmon), darne de cabillaud (cod).
Le tronçon	A slice of flat fish cut on the bone, e.g. tronçon de turbot (turbot), tronçon de barbue (brill).
Le filet	A cut of fish free from bone. A round fish yields two fillets and a flat fish four fillets.

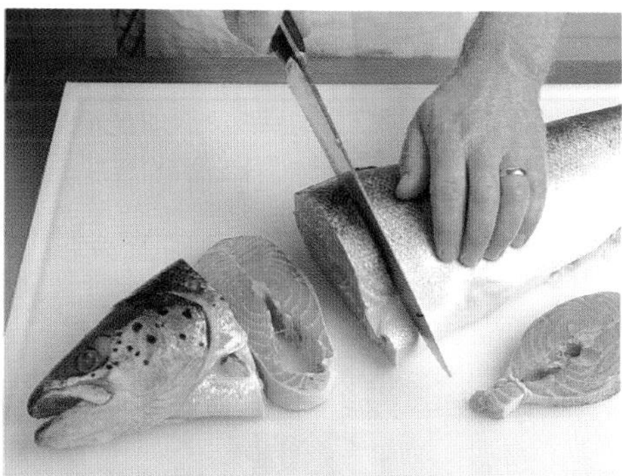

Darne of salmon

Tronçon of turbot

Suprême of salmon

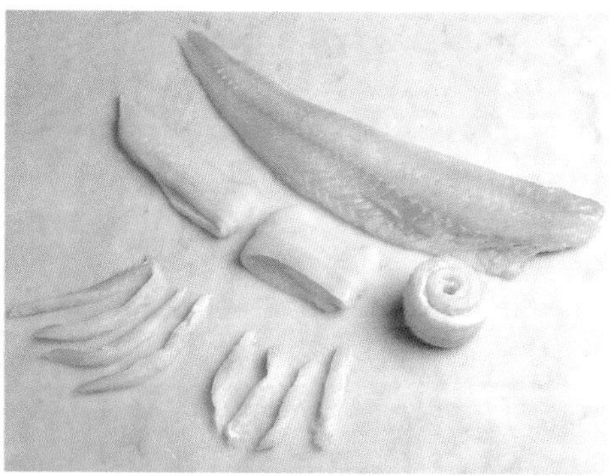

Cuts of fish: (back row) fillet; (middle row) suprême, délice, paupiette; (front row) goujons, goujonettes

Le suprême	Usually applied to fillets of large fish cut on the slant, e.g. suprême de turbot.
Le délice	A term usually applied to a trimmed and neatly folded fillet of fish, e.g. délice de sole.
Les goujons (f)	This term is applied to fillet of fish cut into strips approx. 8 cm × ½ cm (3 in × ¼ in).
Les goujonnettes (f)	As for goujons but smaller, 5 cm × ½ cm (2 in × ¼ in).
La paupiette	Fillet of fish, usually sole, spread with stuffing and rolled.

Fish Recipes

6 · **Fish stock** *Fond or fumet de poisson*

50 g	2 oz	margarine or butter
200 g	8 oz	onions
2 kg	4 lb	white fish bones (preferably sole, whiting, or turbot)
		juice of ½ lemon
		6 peppercorns
		1 bay leaf
		parsley stalks
5 litres	1 gal	water

Using hard margarine
This recipe provides:

366 kcals/1536 kJ
40.1 g fat of which 17.6 g saturated
0.2 g carbohydrate of which 0.2 g sugars
0.1 g protein
0.0 g fibre

1 Melt the margarine or butter in a thick-bottomed pan.
2 Add the sliced onions, the well-washed fish bones and remainder of the ingredients except the water.
3 Cover with greaseproof paper and a lid and sweat (cook gently without colouring) for 5 min.
4 Add the water, bring to the boil, skim and simmer for 20 min then strain.

5 litres (1 gallon)

7 · **Fish glaze** *Glace de poisson*

This is fish stock reduced by boiling to a gelatinous consistency. It is used for increasing the flavour of fish sauces. When cold it may be kept in jars and stored in a refrigerator. See also page 92.

8 · **Fish velouté** *Velouté de poisson*

100 g	4 oz	margarine or butter
100 g	4 oz	flour
1 litre	1 qt	fish stock

This is the basic fish sauce made from fish stock and a blond roux.

This recipe provides:

1144 kcals/4805 kJ
90.4 g fat of which 39.0 g saturated
77.8 g carbohydrate of which 1.6 g sugars
9.5 g protein
3.6 g fibre

1 Prepare a blond roux using the margarine or butter and flour.
2 Gradually add the stock, stirring continuously until boiling point is reached.
3 Simmer for 1 hr approx.
4 Pass through a fine conical strainer.

This will give a thick sauce which can be thinned down with the cooking liquor from the fish for which the sauce is intended.

1 litre (1 quart)

9 · Sabayon *Sabayon*

This is a mixture of egg yolks and a little water whisked to the ribbon stage over gentle heat. The mixture should be the consistency of thick cream. It is added to sauces to assist their glazing.

10 · White wine sauce *Sauce vin blanc*

250 ml	½ pt	fish velouté
		2 tablespns dry white wine
50 g	2 oz	butter
		2 tablespns cream
		salt, cayenne
		few drops of lemon juice

This recipe provides:

775 kcals/3255 kJ
73.7 g fat of which 42.2 g saturated
21.0 g carbohydrate of which 2.0 g sugars
3.3 g protein
1.1 g fibre

1 Boil the fish velouté. Whisk in the wine.
2 Remove from the heat.
3 Gradually add the butter. Stir in the cream.
4 Correct the seasoning and consistency, add the lemon juice.
5 Pass through a tammy cloth or fine strainer.

¼ litre (½ pint)

11 · White wine sauce (to be glazed) *Sauce vin blanc glacé*

If the sauce is to be used for a glazed fish dish then 1 egg yolk or 1 tablespn sabayon should be added as soon as the sauce is removed from the heat. (Trade practice could be to whisk in 1 tablespn Hollandaise to the sauce.)

12 · Mushroom sauce *Sauce aux champignons*

250 ml	½ pt	fish velouté
		fish stock, or cream as necessary
		salt, cayenne
100 g	4 oz	white button mushrooms
10 g	½ oz	butter or margarine
		lemon juice

1 Boil the fish velouté.
2 Adjust the consistency with fish stock or cream.
3 Correct the seasoning and strain.
4 Peel, wash and slice the mushrooms.
5 Cook the mushrooms in the butter and lemon juice in a covered pan.
6 Drain well and add to the sauce.

May be served with boiled halibut, e.g. Flétan poché, sauce aux champignons.

¼ litre (½ pint)

13 · Shrimp sauce *Sauce aux crevettes*

250 ml	½ pt	fish velouté or béchamel
		salt, cayenne
60 ml	⅛ pt	picked shrimps

1 Boil the fish velouté or béchamel.
2 Correct the seasoning and consistency using fish stock or cream.
3 Pass through a tammy or fine strainer. Mix in the shrimps.

¼ litre (½ pint)

14 · Lobster sauce *Sauce de homard*

¾–1 kg	1½–2 lb	live hen lobster	
75 g	3 oz	butter or oil	
100 g	4 oz	onion	roughly cut (mirepoix)
100 g	4 oz	carrot	roughly cut (mirepoix)
50 g	2 oz	celery	roughly cut (mirepoix)
60 ml	⅛ pt	brandy	
75 g	3 oz	flour	
100 g	4 oz	tomato purée	
1¼ litres	2½ pt	fish stock	
120 ml	¼ pt	dry white wine	
		bouquet garni	
		½ crushed clove garlic	
		salt	

1 Well wash the lobster.
2 Cut in half lengthwise tail first, then the carapace.
3 Discard the sac from the carapace, clean the trail from the tail, remove any spawn into a basin.
4 Wash the lobster pieces.
5 Crack the claws and the four claw joints.
6 Melt the butter or oil in a thick-bottomed pan.
7 Add the lobster pieces and the onion, carrot and celery.
8 Allow to cook steadily without colouring the butter for a few minutes, stirring continuously with a wooden spoon.
9 Add the brandy and allow it to ignite.
10 Remove from the heat, mix in the flour and tomato purée.
11 Return to a gentle heat and cook out the roux.
12 Cool slightly, gradually add the fish stock and white wine.
13 Stir to the boil.
14 Add bouquet garni, garlic and season lightly with salt.
15 Simmer for 15–20 min.
16 Remove the lobster pieces.
17 Remove the lobster meat from the pieces.
18 Crush the lobster shells, return them to the sauce and continue simmering for ¼–¾ hour.

19 Crush the lobster spawn, stir in to the sauce, reboil and pass through a coarse strainer.

This sauce may be made in a less expensive way by substituting cooked lobster shell (not shell from the claws) which should be well crushed in place of the live lobster.

1 litre (2 pints)

Shallow Fried Fish

15 **Fish meunière** *Poisson meunière*

Many fish, whole or filleted, may be cooked by this method, e.g. sole, fillets of plaice, trout, brill, cod, turbot, herring, scampi, etc.

1. Prepare and clean the fish, wash and drain.
2. Pass through seasoned flour, shake off all surplus flour.
3. Shallow fry on both sides, presentation side first, in hot clarified butter, margarine or oil.
4. Dress neatly on an oval flat dish.
5. Peel a lemon, removing the peel, white pith and pips.
6. Cut the lemon into slices and place one slice on each portion.
7. Squeeze some lemon juice on the fish.
8. Allow 10–25 g (½–1 oz) butter per portion and colour in a clean frying-pan to the nut-brown stage (beurre noisette).
9. Pour over the fish.
10. Sprinkle with chopped parsley and serve, e.g. Filets de plie meunière.

Fillets of fish meunière, with accompaniments for Doria (p. 216) and Grenobloise (p. 216)

1 portion (125 g white fish) provides:
313 kcals/1314 kJ
24.1 g fat of which 10.3 g saturated
3.1 g carbohydrate of which 0.0 g sugars
21.2 g protein
0.1 g fibre

16 · **Fish meunière with almonds** *Poisson meunière aux amandes*

As for fish meunière (recipe 15) adding 10 g (½ oz) of almonds cut in short julienne or coarsely chopped to the meunière butter just before it begins to turn brown. This method is usually applied to trout, e.g. Truite meunière aux amandes.

17 · **Fish belle meunière** *Poisson belle meunière*

As for recipe 15 with the addition of a grilled mushroom, a slice of peeled tomato and a soft herring roe (passed through flour and shallow fried), all neatly dressed on each portion of fish, e.g. Sole belle meunière.

18 · **Fish Doria**

As for fish meunière (recipe 15) with a sprinkling of small turned pieces of cucumber carefully cooked in 25 g (1 oz) of butter in a small covered pan, or blanched in boiling salted water, e.g. Filet d'aigrefin Doria.

19 · **Grenobloise**

As for fish meunière (recipe 15), the peeled lemon being cut into segments, neatly dressed on the fish with a few capers sprinkled over, e.g. Truite grenobloise.

20 · **Bretonne**

As for fish meunière (recipe 15), with a few picked shrimps and cooked sliced mushroom sprinkled over the fish, e.g. Suprême de turbot bretonne.

Grilled Fish

21 · **Grilled cod steaks** *Darne de cabillaud grillée*

Fried in sunflower oil
1 portion provides:

216 kcals/907 kJ
7.3 g fat of which 1.1 g saturated
0.0 g carbohydrate of which 0.0 g sugars
37.4 g protein
0.0 g fibre

1. Wash the steaks well and drain.
2. Pass through seasoned flour and brush with melted butter, margarine or oil.
3. Place on a greased baking tray.
4. Cook on both sides under a salamander, brushing occasionally with fat.
5. To test if cooked, carefully remove the centre bone.
6. Serve garnished with a slice or quarter of lemon, picked parsley and a suitable sauce or butter separately (e.g. parsley butter), e.g. Darne de cabillaud grillée maître d'hôtel.

22 · Grilled herring *Hareng grillé*

1 portion provides:
239 kcals/1003 kJ
15.6 g fat of which 3.3 g saturated
0.0 g carbohydrate of which 0.0 g sugars
24.5 g protein
0.0 g fibre

1 Remove the scales from the fish with the back of a knife.
2 Remove the head, clean out the intestines, trim off all fins, take care not to damage the roe, and trim the tail.
3 Wash and drain well.
4 Make three light incisions 2 mm (½ in) deep on either side of the fish.
5 Pass through seasoned flour.
6 Brush with melted butter, margarine or oil, place on a greased baking tray.
7 Grill on both sides taking care not to burn the tails.
8 Garnish with a slice or quarter of lemon and picked parsley.
9 Serve with a sauceboat of mustard sauce, e.g. Hareng grillé, sauce moutarde (page 95).

23 · Grilled mackerel *Maquereau grillé*

1 Remove the head and intestines and clean the fish.
2 Cut down both sides of the backbone and remove the bone carefully.
3 Trim off all fins and excess rib bones, trim the tail.
4 Wash well and drain.
5 Pass through seasoned flour, shake off all surplus flour.
6 Place on a greased baking tray, cut side down.
7 Brush with melted butter, margarine or oil.
8 Grill on both sides under salamander.
9 Serve garnished with slice or quarter of lemon, picked parsley and a suitable sauce separately, e.g. Maquereau grillé, beurre d'anchois.

24 · Fillets of grilled plaice *Filets de plie grillés*

1 Fillet the plaice, remove the black skin.
2 Wash well and drain.
3 Pass through seasoned flour, shake off all surplus flour.
4 Place on a greased baking tray, skinned side down.
5 Brush with melted butter, margarine or oil.
6 Grill on both sides under the salamander.
7 Serve with a slice or quarter of lemon, picked parsley and suitable sauce or butter, e.g. Filet de plie grillé, beurre maître d'hôtel.

25 · Grilled whiting *Merlan grillé*

Prepare, grill and serve as for mackerel (recipe 23).

26 · Grilled sole or plaice *Sole grillée ou plie grillée*

1 Remove the black skin, and scales from soles.
2 Remove the head and side bones, clean well.
3 Wash well and drain.
4 Pass through seasoned flour and shake off surplus flour.
5 Place on a greased baking tray white skin down.
6 Brush with melted butter, margarine or oil.
7 Grill on both sides under salamander.
8 Serve with a slice or quarter of lemon, picked parsley, and a suitable sauce or butter, e.g. Sole grillée, sauce anchois.

Brushed with sunflower oil
1 portion provides:

167 kcals/703 kJ
6.9 g fat of which 0.9 g saturated
3.9 g carbohydrate of which 0.1 g sugars
22.7 g protein
0.2 g fibre

Preparation of lemon for fish meunière Grenobloise

Grilled sole, whole and fillets

27 Grilled fillets of sole *Filets de sole grillés*

Proceed as for fillets of plaice (recipe 24), e.g. Filets de sole grillés, sauce diable.

28 · Grilled fish St Germain *Poisson grillé St Germain*

1 Clean and prepare the fish (usually filleted).
2 Pass through seasoned flour, melted butter or margarine and fresh white breadcrumbs.
3 Neaten with a palette knife.
4 Place on a greased baking tray, brush with melted butter, margarine or oil.

5 Grill on both sides under salamander.
6 Serve with a sauceboat of sauce béarnaise (page 109), e.g. Filet de sole St Germain.

29 · Fish caprice *Poisson caprice*

1 As for recipe 28, points 1–5.
2 Peel and halve a banana, pass through flour and shallow fry in butter.
3 Place half a banana on each portion of fish and serve a sauceboat of sauce Robert (page 102) separately, e.g. Filet de plie caprice.

30 · Grilled salmon *Darne de saumon grillée*

1 Pass darnes of salmon through seasoned flour, shake off all surplus.
2 Place on a greased baking sheet or grill bars and brush with oil.
3 Grill on both sides, brush frequently with oil, for approx. 10 min.
4 Remove the centre bone and garnish with picked parsley.
5 Accompany with sliced cucumber and a suitable sauce, e.g. sauce verte (page 111), e.g. Darne de saumon grillée, sauce verte.

Brushed with sunflower oil
1 portion provides:

280 kcals/1178 kJ
19.5 g fat of which 3.6 g saturated
3.9 g carbohydrate of which 0.1 g sugars
22.6 g protein
0.2 g fibre

Fried Fish

Right: (clockwise from top left) fillets of fish coated in – flour, egg and crumbs; batter; milk and flour; with tartare sauce (p. 111) and tomato sauce (p. 106);

Below: Preparation of fried fish

Points on deep frying

1 Use a suitable recommended fat or oil (see *The Theory of Catering*, pages 146–147).
2 When fat or oil smokes at about 177 °C (350 °F), foams, tastes or smells bad, it should be discarded.
3 Refer to page 67 on deep frying.

31 Frying batters *Pâtes à frire*

Recipe 1

200 g	8 oz	flour
		salt
10 g	⅜ oz	yeast
250 ml	½ pt	water or milk

1 Sift the flour and salt into a basin.
2 Dissolve the yeast in a little of the water.
3 Make a well in the flour.
4 Add the yeast and the liquid.
5 Gradually incorporate the flour and beat to a smooth mixture.
6 Allow to rest for at least 1 hr before using.

Recipe 2

200 g	8 oz	flour
		salt
		1 egg
250 ml	½ pt	water or milk
		2 tablespns oil

1 Sift the flour and salt into a basin.
2 Make a well.
3 Add the egg and the liquid.
4 Gradually incorporate the flour, beat to a smooth mixture.
5 Mix in the oil.
6 Allow to rest before using.

Recipe 3

200 g	8 oz	flour
		salt
250 ml	½ pt	water or milk
		2 tablespns oil
		2 stiffly-beaten egg whites

1 As for previous method.
2 Fold in the whites just before using.

approx. 6–8 portions

32 · **Fried whiting** *Merlan frit*

Fried in peanut oil
1 portion provides:

346 kcals/1453 kJ
18.6 g fat of which 3.6 g saturated
12.6 g carbohydrate of which 0.4 g sugars
32.6 g protein
0.6 g fibre

1 Skin the fish and remove intestines, clean out the head by removing the gills and the eyes.
2 Wash well and drain.
3 Pass through seasoned flour, beaten egg and white breadcrumbs (pané).
4 Shake off all surplus crumbs.
5 Deep fry to a golden brown in moderately hot fat 175 °C approx. 5–6 min.
6 Drain well.
7 Serve garnished with fried or picked parsley, quarter of lemon and a suitable sauce, e.g. Merlan frit, sauce tartare.

33 · **Fried fillets of whiting** *Filets de merlan frits*

1 Fillet, wash well and drain.
2 Pané, or pass through batter. Deep fry at 185 °C, drain well and serve as for fried whiting with a suitable sauce.

34 · **Fried fillets of plaice** *Filets de plie frits*

1 Fillet the fish, remove the black skin.
2 Wash well and drain.
3 Pass through flour and batter or flour, egg and crumb.
4 Deep fry at 185 °C, drain well and serve as for fried whiting, e.g. Fried fillets of plaice and lemon.

35 · **Goujons of sole** *Filets de sole en goujons*

1 Fillet the sole.
2 Cut each fillet into strips approx. 8 cm × ½ cm (3 in × ¼ in).
3 Pané, deep fry at 185 °C, drain well and serve as above, e.g. Filets de sole en goujons, sauce tartare.

All filleted white fish may be prepared, cooked and served by this method.

36 · **Fried sole** *Sole frite*

For fish courses use 200–250 g (8–10 oz) sole per portion, for main course 300–400 g (12–16 oz) sole per portion.

1 Remove the black and white skin. Remove the side fins.
2 Remove the head. Clean well.
3 Wash well and drain. Pané and deep fry at 175 °C.
4 Serve on a dish paper with picked or fried parsley and quarter of lemon on a flat dish, and with a suitable sauce, e.g. Sole frite, sauce anchois.

37 · **Sole Colbert** *Sole Colbert*

1 Remove the black and white skins.
2 Remove the head and side fins. Clean well and wash.
3 Make an incision down the backbone on one side and proceed as though filleting, to within an inch of the sides.
4 Break the backbone in two or three places.
5 Curl the opened fillets back.
6 Pané, deep fry at 175 °C and drain.
7 Carefully remove the backbone.
8 Serve as for fried fish with one or two slices of parsley butter at the last moment in the opened part of the fish.

38 · **Fried fish in batter** *Poisson frit à l'Orly*

This is usually applied to fillets of white fish, e.g. plaice, sole, haddock, etc. or rock fish (a term used for catfish, coley, conger eel, dogfish etc.), when cleaned and skinned.

Fried in peanut oil
1 portion (200 g plaice) provides:

558 kcals/2344 kJ
36.0 g fat of which 6.6 g saturated
28.8 g carbohydrate of which 1.2 g sugars
31.6 g protein
1.2 g fibre

1 Marinate the fillets in a little oil, lemon juice and chopped parsley for a few minutes (see photograph on page 219).
2 Pass through seasoned flour and batter.
3 Deep fry at 175 °C, drain well and serve with fried or pickled parsley.
4 Serve with a sauceboat of tomato sauce (page 106).

Lemons are a suitable accompaniment to many fish dishes

39 · **Whitebait** *Blanchailles*

1 Pick over the whitebait.
2 Wash carefully and drain well.
3 Pass through milk and seasoned flour.
4 Shake off all surplus flour in a wide mesh sieve and place the fish into a frying-basket.
5 Plunge into very hot fat, just smoking (195 °C).
6 Cook till brown and crisp, approx. 1 min.
7 Drain well.
8 Season with salt and cayenne pepper.
9 Serve garnished with fried or pickled parsley and quarters of lemon.

(100 g (4 oz) per portion)

40 · **Fried scampi** *Scampi frits*

375–500 g	¾–1 lb	shelled scampi
50 g	2 oz	flour
		1 egg
50 g	2 oz	fresh white breadcrumbs
		1 lemon
		parsley

Fried in peanut oil
1 portion provides:

316 kcals/1327 kJ
17.6 g fat of which 3.1 g saturated
28.9 g carbohydrate of which 1.1 g sugars
12.2 g protein
1.2 g fibre

1 Pass the scampi through flour, egg-wash and roll in fresh white breadcrumbs.
2 Shake off all surplus crumbs and lightly roll each piece of scampi to firm the surface.
3 Deep fry at 185 °C.
4 Drain well and serve.
5 Garnish with quarters of lemon and sprigs of fried or fresh parsley.
6 Accompany with a suitable sauce, e.g. sauce tartare.

4 portions

Boiled Fish

41 · **Boiled turbot** *Tronçon de turbot poché*

1 portion provides:

236 kcals/990 kJ
7.2 g fat of which 0.8 g saturated
0.0 g carbohydrate of which 0.0 g sugars
42.8 g protein
0.0 g fibre

1 Place the prepared turbot into a shallow pan of simmering salted water, containing lemon juice. The citric acid in the lemon juice helps to make the fish firm and white.
2 Allow to simmer gently until cooked, the time depends very much on the thickness of the fish.
3 Remove with a fish slice from the pan.
4 Remove the black skin, drain and serve.
5 When served in an earthenware dish add a little of the cooking liquor.
6 Garnish with picked parsley and a plain boiled potato.
7 Serve with a suitable sauce separately, e.g. Turbot poché, sauce hollandaise.

42 · **Boiled brill** *Tronçon de barbue poché*

Proceed as for Turbot, recipe 41.

43 · **Boiled halibut** *Tronçon de flétan poché*

Proceed as for Turbot, recipe 41.

44 · **Boiled cod** *Cabillaud poché*

1 When using whole cod cut into 1–2 cm (½–1 in) slices on the bone (darne). Where required, tie with string.
2 Cook as for turbot (recipe 41) and serve in the same way.
3 Remove the centre bone and string before serving.
4 A suitable sauce should be served separately, e.g. parsley, egg, anchovy.

45 · **Boiled salmon** *Saumon poché*

½ kg (1 lb) uncleaned salmon yields 2–3 portions

Salmon may be obtained in varying weights from 3½–15 kg (7–30 lb). Size is an important consideration, depending on whether the salmon is to be cooked whole or cut into darnes. A salmon of any size may be cooked whole. When required for darnes, a medium-sized salmon will be more suitable. See recipes 47 and 48.

46 · **Fish cooking liquid** *Court bouillon*

1 litre	1 qt	water
10 g	½ oz	salt
50 g	2 oz	carrots (sliced)
		1 bay leaf
		2–3 parsley stalks
60 ml	⅛ pt	vinegar
		6 peppercorns
50 g	2 oz	onions (sliced)
		sprig of thyme

Simmer all the ingredients for 30–40 min. Pass through a strainer, use as required.

47 · **Cooking of a whole salmon**

1 Scrape off all scales with the back of a knife.
2 Remove all gills and clean out the head.
3 Remove the intestines and clear the blood from the backbone.
4 Trim off all fins. Wash well.
5 Place in a salmon kettle, cover with cold court bouillon.
6 Bring slowly to the boil, skim, then simmer gently.
7 Allow the following approx. simmering times:

3½ kg (7 lb)	15 min
7 kg (14 lb)	20 min
10½ kg (21 lb)	25 min
14 kg (28 lb)	30 min

Always allow the salmon to remain in the court bouillon until cold.

48 · **Boiled cut salmon** *Darne de saumon pochée*

Cooking salmon in darnes. When cooking:

1. Place in a simmering court bouillon and simmer gently for approx. 5 min. Drain well, remove the centre bone.
2. When served in an earthenware dish add a little of the cooking liquor. Garnish with picked parsley, and a plain boiled potato.
3. Accompany with sliced cucumber and a suitable sauce, e.g. Sauce hollandaise, beurre fondu.

49 · **Cold salmon** *Saumon froid*

1¼ kg	2½ lb	cleaned salmon
1 litre	1 qt	court bouillon (recipe 46)
		½ cucumber
		1 large lettuce
200 g	8 oz	tomatoes
250 ml	½ pt	mayonnaise or green sauce

1 portion provides:

427 kcals/1794 kJ
33.6 g fat of which 6.0 g saturated
1.3 g carbohydrate of which 1.2 g sugars
29.9 g protein
0.7 g fibre

1. Cook the salmon in the court bouillon (a) whole; (b) cut into 8 darnes; (c) cut into 4 darnes.
2. Allow to cool thoroughly in the cooking liquid to keep it moist, then for
   a) divide into eight even portions;
   b) remove centre bone and
   c) cut each darne in half.
3. Except when whole, remove the centre bone, also the skin and brown surface and dress neatly on a flat dish.
4. Peel and slice the cucumber and neatly arrange a few slices on each portion.
5. Garnish with quarters of lettuce and quarters of tomatoes.
6. Serve the sauce in a sauceboat separately.

8 portions

Poached Fish

Although recipes 50–60 are given for fillets of sole, any white fish may be prepared and served in the following manner. Always place a little sauce under the fish before masking; this is to keep the fish moist, to prevent it overcooking and sticking to the dish, thus facilitating the service. Shallots must be finely chopped and may need to be sweated in a little butter before use.

50 · Fillets of sole Dugléré *Filets de sole Dugléré*

500–600 g	1–1¼ lb	2 soles
10 g	½ oz	finely chopped shallot
200 g	8 oz	tomatoes concassée
		pinch chopped parsley
		salt, pepper
60 ml	⅛ pt	fish stock
60 ml	⅛ pt	dry white wine
		juice of ¼ lemon
250 ml	½ pt	fish velouté
50 g	2 oz	butter

1 portion provides:

167 kcals/699 kJ
11.6 g fat of which 6.8 g saturated
1.9 g carbohydrate of which 1.9 g sugars
11.5 g protein
0.9 g fibre

1 Remove the black and white skins and fillet the soles.
2 Wash and drain well.
3 Butter and season an earthenware dish or sauté pan.
4 Sprinkle in the sweated chopped shallots.
5 Add the fillets which may be folded in two, add the tomatoes and chopped parsley.
6 Season with salt and pepper.
7 Add the fish stock, wine and the lemon juice.
8 Cover with a buttered greaseproof paper.
9 Poach gently in a moderate oven (150–200 °C) for 5–10 min.
10 Remove the fillets and the garnish, place on a flat dish, or in a clean earthenware dish, keep warm.
11 Pass and reduce the cooking liquor in a small sauteuse, add the fish velouté, then incorporate the butter.
12 Correct the seasoning and consistency.
13 Coat the fillets with the sauce and serve.

4 portions

Fillets of sole Dugléré

51 · Fillets of sole with white wine sauce *Filets de sole vin blanc*

500–600 g	1–1¼ lb	2 soles
10 g	½ oz	finely chopped shallot
60 ml	⅛ pt	fish stock
60 ml	⅛ pt	dry white wine
		juice of ¼ lemon
250 ml	½ pt	fish velouté
50 g	2 oz	butter
		2 tablespns cream, lightly whipped

1 Skin and fillet soles, trim and wash.
2 Butter and season an earthenware dish.
3 Sprinkle with the sweated chopped shallot and add the fillets of sole.
4 Season, add the fish stock, wine and lemon juice.
5 Cover with a buttered greaseproof paper.
6 Poach in a moderate oven (150–200 °C, Reg. 2–6) for 5–10 min.
7 Drain the fish well, dress neatly on a flat dish or earthenware dish.
8 Bring the cooking liquor to the boil with the velouté.
9 Correct the seasoning and consistency and pass through a tammy cloth or a fine strainer.
10 Mix in the butter, finally add the cream.
11 Coat the fillets with the sauce. Garnish with fleurons (puff paste crescents).

4 portions

52 · Fillets of sole Véronique *Filets de sole Véronique*

500–600 g	1–1 ¼ lb	2 soles
		salt, pepper
60 ml	⅛ pt	fish stock
60 ml	⅛ pt	dry white wine
		juice ¼ lemon
250 ml	½ pt	fish velouté
50 g	2 oz	butter
		2 tablespns cream, lightly whipped
50 g	2 oz	white grapes (blanched, skinned and pipped)

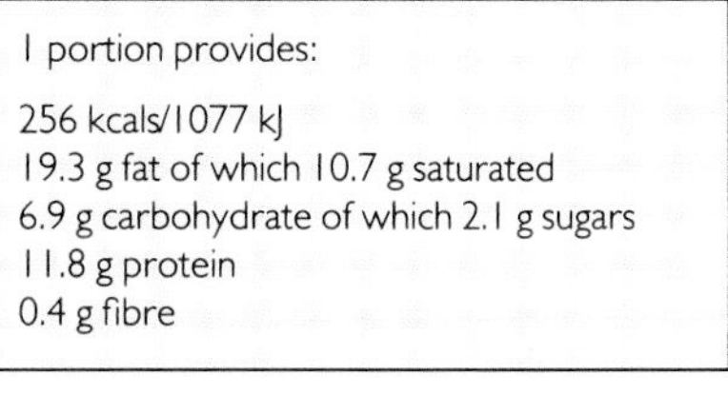
1 portion provides:

256 kcals/1077 kJ
19.3 g fat of which 10.7 g saturated
6.9 g carbohydrate of which 2.1 g sugars
11.8 g protein
0.4 g fibre

1 Prepare and cook as for filet de sole vin blanc (recipe 52), adding an egg yolk or spoonful of sabayon to the sauce.
2 Glaze under the salamander.
3 Arrange the grapes neatly on the dish.

4 portions

Sole Véronique

53 · Whole soles

These may be prepared and served as for any recipe for fillets of sole. A sole weighing 200–300 g (8–12 oz) is usually served, allowing one sole per portion.

Preparation of whole soles

Remove the black and white skin, cut off the head, remove the side bones. Clean and wash thoroughly.

Preparation of soles after cooking

Before coating with sauce: place the fish on a flat surface and using a palette knife, remove all the side bones. Carefully fold back two of the fillets and remove approx. 2–5 cm (1–2 in) of backbone.

54 · Fillets of sole Bercy *Filets de sole Bercy*

500–600 g	1–1 ¼ lb	2 soles
25 g	1 oz	chopped shallot
		chopped parsley
60 ml	⅛ pt	fish stock
	⅛ pt	dry white wine
		juice of ¼ lemon
250 ml	¼ pt	fish velouté
50 g	2 oz	butter
		2 tablespns cream, lightly whipped
		1 egg yolk or sabayon

1. Skin, fillet, trim and wash the fish.
2. Season and butter an earthenware dish.
3. Sprinkle with sweated, chopped shallots and chopped parsley.
4. Add the fillets of sole, season.
5. Add the stock, wine and lemon juice.
6. Cover with a buttered paper.
7. Poach in a moderate oven (150–200 °C, Reg. 2–6) approx. 5–10 min.
8. Remove the fillets, place in a clean earthenware or flat dish. Keep warm.
9. Place the cooking liquor and velouté in a small sauteuse.
10. Correct the consistency and seasoning and pass through a strainer.
11. Finish with the butter and then the cream and sabayon.
12. Mask the fish and glaze under the salamander.

4 portions

55 · Fillets of sole bonne femme *Filets de sole bonne femme*

As for fillets of sole Bercy with the addition of 100 g (4 oz) sliced button mushrooms which are placed in the earthenware dish with raw fish. Finish as for Bercy (recipe 54).

56 · Fillets of sole Bréval or d'Antin

Filets de sole Bréval Filets de sole d'Antin

As for bonne femme (recipe 55) with the addition of 100 g (4 oz) tomatoes which are added with the mushrooms. The tomatoes are cut concassée. Finish as for Bercy.

57 · Fillets of sole Marguery *Filets de sole Marguery*

As for fillets of sole Bercy (recipe 54). Garnish the fillets of sole with 75 g (3 oz) cooked prawns and twelve cooked mussels before coating with the sauce. Finish the dish by glazing under the salamander and garnish with fleurons.

4 portions

58 · Fillets of sole Mornay *Filets de sole Mornay*

500–600 g	1–1½ lb	2 soles
125 ml	¼ pt	fish stock
250 ml	½ pt	béchamel sauce
		1 egg yolk or sabayon
50 g	2 oz	grated cheese, preferably Gruyère or Parmesan
		salt, cayenne
25 g	1 oz	butter
		2 tablespns cream, lightly whipped

1 Prepare fillets, place in a buttered, seasoned earthenware dish or shallow pan, such as a sauté pan.
2 Add the fish stock, cover with a buttered paper.
3 Cook in a moderate oven (150–200 °C, Reg. 2–6) approx. 5–10 min.
4 Drain the fish well, place in a clean earthenware or flat dish.
5 Bring the béchamel to the boil, add the reduced cooking liquor, whisk in the yolk and remove from the heat. Add the cheese and correct the consistency. Do not reboil otherwise the egg will curdle.
6 Correct the seasoning and pass through a fine strainer.
7 Mix in the butter and cream, check the consistency.
8 Mask the fish, sprinkle with grated cheese and gratinate under the salamander.

4 portions

59 · Fillets of sole florentine *Filets de sole florentine*

Ingredients as for
Fillet of sole Mornay, recipe 58
½ kg (1 lb) leaf spinach

1 Remove the stems from the spinach.
2 Wash very carefully in plenty of water several times if necessary.
3 Cook in boiling salted water until tender, approx. 5 min.
4 Refresh under cold water, squeeze dry into a ball.
5 When required for service, place into a pan containing 25–50 g (1–2 oz) butter, loosen with a fork and reheat quickly without colouring, season lightly with salt and mill pepper.
6 Place in the serving dish.
7 Proceed as for fillet of sole Mornay.
8 Dress the fillets on the spinach. Coat with Mornay sauce, sprinkle with grated cheese and gratinate under the salamander.

60 · Fillets of sole Walewska *Filets de sole Walewska*

Prepare as for fillet sole Mornay (recipe 58) placing a slice of cooked lobster on each fish fillet before coating with the sauce. After the dish is browned decorate each fillet with a slice of truffle.

61 · Fish in the shell with cheese sauce *Coquille de poisson Mornay*

The fish to be used should be named, e.g. Coquille de cabillaud Mornay.

1 Prepare ½ kg (1 lb) duchess potato mixture (page 439).
2 Using a piping bag and a large star tube pipe a neat border around the serving shells or dishes.
3 Dry in the oven or under the salamander for two or three minutes.
4 Brush with eggwash.
5 Prepare and cook the fish and sauce as for filet de sole Mornay (recipe 58).
6 Place a little sauce in the bottom of each serving shell or dish.
7 Add the well-drained fish, which is usually flaked.
8 Coat with sauce, taking care not to splash the potato.
9 Sprinkle with grated cheese, brown under the salamander and serve.

62 · Fish kedgeree *Cadgery de poisson*

400 g	1 lb	fish (usually smoked haddock or fresh salmon)
200 g	8 oz	rice pilaff (page 201)
		2 hard-boiled eggs
50 g	2 oz	butter
250 ml	½ pt	curry sauce (page 104)

The fish to be used should be named, e.g. cadgery de saumon.

1 Poach the fish. Remove all skin and bone. Flake.
2 Cook the rice pilaff. Cut the eggs in dice.
3 Combine the eggs, fish, rice and heat in the butter. Correct the seasoning.
4 Serve hot with a sauceboat of curry sauce.

4 portions

63 · Poached smoked haddock *Haddock fumé poché*

400–600 g	1–1½ lb	smoked haddock
250 ml	½ pt	milk
250 ml	½ pt	water

1 Trim off all fins from the fish. Cut into four even pieces.
2 Simmer gently in the milk and water.
3 When cooked, the backbone should be easy to remove.
4 Remove the backbone and serve.

4 portions

64 Haddock Monte Carlo *Haddock Monte Carlo*

As for poached haddock garnished with slices of peeled tomato or tomato concassée, poached egg and cream or cream sauce.

65 · Skate with black butter *Raie au beurre noir*

400–600 g	1–1½ lb	skate wings
		court bouillon
50 g	2 oz	butter
		1 teaspn vinegar
		chopped parsley
10 g	½ oz	capers

1 Cut the skate into four even pieces.
2 Simmer in a court bouillon (page 224) till cooked, approx. 10 min.
3 Drain well, place on a serving dish or plates.
4 Heat the butter in a frying-pan until well browned, almost black, add the vinegar, pour over the fish, sprinkle with chopped parsley and a few capers and serve.

4 portions

66 · Fish cakes

200g	8 oz	cooked fish (free from skin and bone)
200 g	8 oz	mashed potatoes
		1 egg
		salt, pepper
25 g	1 oz	flour } coating
		1 egg } coating
50 g	2 oz	breadcrumbs } coating

1 Combine the fish, potatoes and egg and season.
2 Divide into four or eight pieces. Mould into balls.
3 Pass through flour, egg and breadcrumbs.
4 Flatten slightly, neaten with a palette knife.
5 Deep fry in hot fat (185 °C) for 2–3 min.
6 Serve with fried or picked parsley.
7 Serve with a suitable sauce, e.g. Tomato sauce (page 106). *4 portions*

67 · Salmon cutlets

Method A

Prepare a fish-cake mixture using cooked salmon. Shape into cutlets, insert a piece of macaroni, deep fry and serve as for fish cakes.

Method B

Boil ¼ litre (¼ pt) very thick béchamel (page 94), add 300 g (12 oz) cooked flaked salmon free from skin and bone. Season, add 1–2 egg yolks, mix in and remove from the heat. Place on a greased tray.

When cold mould into four even-sized cutlet-shaped pieces. Flour egg and crumb and insert a piece of macaroni into each.

Deep fry (185 °C) and serve with fried or pickled parsley. Serve a suitable sauce separate, e.g. anchovy sauce (page 95).

68 · Fish pie

250 ml	½ pt	béchamel (thin) (page 94)
200 g	8 oz	fish cooked free from skin and bone
50 g	2 oz	cooked diced mushrooms
		1 chopped hard-boiled egg
		chopped parsley
		salt, pepper
200 g	8 oz	mashed or duchess potatoes

1 portion provides:

209 kcals/879 kJ
12.0 g fat of which 5.3 g saturated
11.9 g carbohydrate of which 3.2 g sugars
14.1 g protein
0.9 g fibre

1 Bring the béchamel to the boil.
2 Add the fish, mushrooms, egg and parsley. Correct the seasoning.
3 Place in a buttered pie-dish.
4 Place or pipe the potato on top. Brush with eggwash or milk.
5 Brown in a hot oven or under the salamander and serve. *4 portions*

69 Seafood in puff pastry *Bouchées de fruits de mer*

50 g	2 oz	button mushrooms
25 g	1 oz	butter
		juice ¼ lemon
200 g	8 oz	cooked lobster, prawns, shrimps, mussels, scallops
125 ml	¼ pt	white wine sauce (page 213)
		chopped parsley
		4 bouchée cases (page 490)

1 Peel and wash the mushrooms, cut in neat dice.
2 Cook in butter with the lemon juice.
3 Add the shellfish (mussels, prawns, shrimps left whole, the scallops and lobster cut in dice).
4 Cover the pan with a lid and heat through slowly 3–4 min.
5 Add the white wine sauce, chopped parsley and season.
6 Meanwhile warm the bouchées in the oven or hot plate.
7 Fill the bouchées with the mixture and place the lids on top.
8 Serve garnished with picked parsley.

70 Vol-au-vent with sea food *Vol-au-vent de fruits de mer*

1 Prepare and cook the puff pastry cases (page 490).
2 Prepare the filling as for recipe 69.
3 Dress and serve as for recipe 69.

71 Salmon mayonnaise *Mayonnaise de saumon*

		1 lettuce
300 g	12 oz	cooked salmon
125 ml	¼ pt	mayonnaise (page 110)
200 g	8 oz	tomatoes
		1 hard-boiled egg
		¼ cucumber
5 g	¼ oz	anchovies
5 g	¼ oz	capers
		4 stoned olives
		chopped parsley

1 Shred the washed and drained lettuce, place in a salad bowl.
2 Add the flaked salmon, free from skin and bone.
3 Coat with mayonnaise sauce.
4 Decorate with quarters of tomato, egg, slices of cucumber, thin fillets of anchovies, capers, olives and chopped parsley.

4 portions

72 · **Salmon salad** *Salade de saumon*

Ingredients as for salmon mayonnaise (recipe 71).

Dress and serve in the same way without coating the fish. Mayonnaise sauce should be served separately.

73 · **Cold salmon, mayonnaise sauce** *Saumon froid, Sauce mayonnaise*

Portions of cold salmon garnished with quarters of lettuce, quarters of tomato, slices of cucumber, quarters of egg.

Mayonnaise sauce separate.

74 · **Lobster mayonnaise** *Mayonnaise de homard*

As for salmon mayonnaise, using 1 kg (2 lb) lobster cut in escalopes, in place of salmon.

Decorate with the lobster's head, tail, legs and chopped coral.

Clockwise from left: salmon salad; cold salmon with mayonnaise sauce; salmon mayonnaise

75 · **Lobster salad** *Salade de homard*

As for salmon salad using one 1 kg (2 lb) cooked lobster, cut in escalopes in place of the salmon.

Decorate as for lobster mayonnaise (recipe 72).

76 · **Cold lobster, mayonnaise sauce** *Homard froid, Sauce mayonnaise*

Half a ½ kg (1 lb) cooked lobster per portion.

Clean the halves, remove the trail and sac, remove the meat from the claws and place in the sac aperture. Serve garnished with quarters of lettuce and quarters of tomato accompanied by a sauceboat of sauce mayonnaise.

77 · Cooking a lobster

Lobsters are usually bought in sizes from ¼–1 kg (½–2 lb). They should be bought alive to ensure freshness. They should be washed, then plunged into a pan of boiling salted water contaning 60 ml (⅛ pt) vinegar to 1 litre (1 qt) water. Cover with a lid, bring to the boil and allow to simmer 15–25 min according to size. Do not over-cook otherwise the tail-flesh can become tough and the claws hard and fibrous. When possible allow to cool in the cooking liquor.

78 · Cleaning of cooked lobster

1 Remove the claws and the pincers.
2 Crack the claws and joints and remove the meat in one piece.
3 Cut the lobster in half with a large knife, by inserting the point of the knife 2 cm (1 in) above the tail on the natural centre line.
4 Cut through the centre of the tail firmly.
5 Turn the lobster round the other way and cut through the carapace.
6 Remove the halves of the sac from each half (this is situated at the top of the head).
7 With a small knife remove the trail. Wash if necessary.

79 · Lobster Mornay *Homard Mornay*

350–450 g	¾–1 lb	2 cooked lobsters
25 g	1 oz	butter
		salt, cayenne
250 ml	½ pt	Mornay sauce (page 95)
		grated cheese (Parmesan)

1 Remove lobsters' claws and legs.
2 Cut lobsters carefully in half lengthwise.
3 Remove all meat. Discard the sac and trail.
4 Wash, shell and drain on a baking sheet upside down.
5 Cut the lobster meat into escalopes.
6 Heat the butter in a thick-bottomed pan, add the lobster and season.
7 Turn two or three times; overcooking will toughen the meat.
8 Meanwhile, finish the Mornay sauce.
9 Place a little sauce in the bottom of each shell.
10 Add the lobster, press down to make a flat surface.
11 Mask completely with sauce, sprinkle with grated cheese, and brown under the salamander and serve garnished with picked parsley.

4 portions

80 · Lobster Thermidor *Homard Thermidor*

350–450 g	¾–1 lb	2 cooked lobsters
25 g	1 oz	butter
12 g	½ oz	finely chopped shallot
60 ml	⅛ pt	dry white wine
		½ teaspn diluted English mustard
		chopped parsley
¼ litre	½ pt	Mornay sauce (page 95)
25 g	1 oz	grated Parmesan cheese

1 Remove lobsters' claws and legs.
2 Cut lobsters carefully in halves lengthwise. Remove the meat.
3 Discard the sac and remove the trail from the tail.
4 Wash the halves of shell and drain on a baking sheet.
5 Cut the lobster meat into thick escalopes.
6 Melt the butter in a sauteuse, add the chopped shallot and cook until tender without colour.
7 Add the white wine to the shallot and allow to reduce to a quarter of its original volume.
8 Mix in the mustard and chopped parsley.
9 Add the lobster slices, season lightly with salt, mix carefully and allow to heat slowly for 2–3 min. If this part of the process is overdone the lobster will become tough and chewy.
10 Meanwhile spoon a little of the warm Mornay sauce into the bottom of each lobster half-shell.
11 Neatly add the warmed lobster pieces and the juice in which they were re-heated. If there should be an excess of liquid it should be reduced and incorporated into the Mornay sauce.
12 Coat the half lobsters with the remaining Mornay sauce, sprinkle with Parmesan cheese and place under a salamander until a golden brown, and serve garnished with picked parsley. *4 portions*

81 · Lobster American style *Homard americaine*

1 kg	2 lb	live hen lobster
100 g	4 oz	butter
60 ml	⅛ pt	oil
50 g	2 oz	finely chopped shallot
		1 chopped clove garlic
60 ml	⅛ pt	brandy
125 ml	¼ pt	dry white wine
250 ml	½ pt	fish stock
200 g	8 oz	tomatoes, skinned, deseeded, diced
25 g	1 oz	tomato purée
		coarsely chopped parsley
		salt, cayenne pepper

1 Wash the lobster
2 Remove the legs and claws. Crack the claws.
3 Cut the lobster in halves crosswise between the tail and carapace.

4 Cut the carapace in two lengthwise.
5 Discard the sac but retain the coral and place in a basin.
6 Cut the tail across in thick slices through the shell.
7 Remove the trail. Wash the lobster pieces.
8 Heat 50 g (2 oz) of the butter with the oil, in a sauté-pan.
9 Add the pieces of lobster, season with salt and fry off rapidly until a red colour on all sides. Pour off all the butter.
10 Add the shallot and garlic, cover the pan with a lid and allow to sweat for a few seconds.
11 Add the brandy and allow it to ignite.
12 Add the white wine, fish stock, tomatoes, tomato purée and a little of the chopped parsley. Allow to simmer 20 min.
13 Remove the lobster, pick the meat from the shells and place in a covered serving dish and keep warm.
14 Reduce the cooking liquor by a half.
15 Pound lobster coral, mix in the other 50 g (2 oz) butter until smooth.
16 Add this lobster butter to the sauce, mix in well until the sauce thickens then remove it from the heat.
17 Add a little cayenne and correct the seasoning.
18 Pass the sauce through a coarse strainer, mix in a little fresh coarsely chopped parsley and pour over the lobster.
19 Decorate with the head and tail of the lobster and serve.
20 Serve accompanied with a pilaff of rice (page 201). *4 portions*

82 **Mussels** *Moules*

When mussels are fresh the shells should be tightly closed. If the shells are open there is the possibility of danger from food poisoning therefore the mussels should be discarded.

Preparation for cooking

Scrape the shells to remove any barnacles, etc.

Wash well and drain in a colander.

To cook

1 Take a thick-bottomed pan with a tight-fitting lid.
2 For 1 litre (1 qt) mussels place in the pan 25 g (1 oz) chopped shallot or onion.
3 Add the mussels, cover with a lid and cook on a fierce heat 4–5 min until the shells open completely.

Preparation for use

1 Remove mussels from shells, checking carefully for sand, weed, etc.
2 Retain the liquid.

83 · **Mussels with white wine sauce** *Moules marinière*

50 g	2 oz	fine chopped shallot
		chopped parsley
60 ml	⅛ pt	dry white wine
2 litres	2 qts	mussels
		fish stock if necessary
25 g	1 oz	beurre manié (butter/flour)
		salt, pepper

1 portion provides:

133 kcals/559 kJ
3.0 g fat of which 0.5 g saturated
0.7 g carbohydrate of which 0.7 g sugars
26.1 g protein
0.2 g fibre

1. Take a thick-bottomed pan.
2. Add chopped shallot, parsley, wine and the well-cleaned and washed mussels.
3. Cover with a tight-fitting lid.
4. Cook over fierce heat till shells open, approx. 4–5 min.
5. Drain off all cooking liquor into a basin, allow to stand in order to allow any sand to sink to the bottom.
6. Carefully check the mussels for sand, etc. If in doubt, discard.
7. Place mussels in an earthenware casserole, cover with a lid and keep warm.
8. Carefully pour the cooking liquor into a small sauteuse.
9. If necessary make up to ¼ litre (½ pt) with fish stock.
10. Bring to the boil, whisk in the beurre manié.
11. Correct the seasoning, add a little chopped parsley.
12. Pour over the mussels and serve.

4 portions

84 · **Scallops** *Coquille St Jacques*

To remove from shells

If fresh, the shells should be tightly closed. Place the shells on top of the stove or in the oven for a few seconds, they will then open, the scallop may be cut away with a small knife.

Wash well, clean and remove the trail leaving only the white scallop and the orange curved roe. All other parts should be discarded.

Poach the scallops gently in dry white wine with a little onion, carrot, thyme, bay leaf and parsley for 2–3 minutes. When lightly cooked cut the white and orange parts into slices and use as required. Scallops may be used in a variety of ways, e.g. bercy, bonne femme (page 228). They may also be cut into escallops raw, coated in batter or egg and crumbled and deep fried.

Roast best-end of lamb (p. 248) with roast gravy (p. 104) and mint sauce (p. 112)

11

LAMB AND MUTTON

General objectives	*Specific objectives*
To know the uses of lamb and mutton in the kitchen and to understand their use on the menu.	To state the quality points and list the joints and cuts with approx weights. To describe and demonstrate the correct butchery of lamb and mutton; methods of cookery and presentation of dishes with suitable accompaniments and garnishes, paying due attention to details of standards and economy.

Lamb and mutton Agneau et mouton

As a guide when ordering, allow approximately 100 g (4 oz) meat off the bone per portion, and 150 g (6 oz) on the bone per portion.

It must be clearly understood that the weights given can only be approximate. They must vary according to the quality of the meat and also for the purpose for which the meat is being butchered. For example, a chef will often cut differently from a shop butcher, i.e. a chef frequently needs to consider the presentation of the particular joint whilst the butcher is more often concerned with economical cutting. We have given simple orders of dissection for each carcass. In general, bones need to be removed only when preparing joints, so as to facilitate carving. The bones are used for stock and the excess fat can be rendered down for second-class dripping.

1 · Clarification of fat

All fat trimmings can be chopped or minced and placed in a pan with a little water, then allowed to cook until there is no movement, and the fat is golden in colour. When cool, pass through a clean cloth, then use as required.

2 · Joints, uses and weights

			Approx. weight	
			Lamb	Mutton
Joint	French	Uses	kg (lb)	kg (lb)
Whole carcass				25 (50)
1 Shoulder (two)	l'épaule (f)	roasting, stewing	16 (32)	4½ (9)
2 Leg (two)	le gigot	roasting	3 (6)	5½ (11)
		(mutton boiled)	3½ (7)	2½ (5)
3 Breast (two)	la poitrine	roasting, stewing		3 (6)
4 Middle neck		stewing	1½ (3)	1 (2)
5 Scrag end	le cou	stewing, broth	2 (4)	3 (6)
6 Best-end (two)	le carré	roasting,	½ (1)	
		grilling, frying	2 (4)	5½ (11)
7 Saddle	la selle	roasting,		
		grilling, frying	3½ (7)	
Kidneys	les rognons (m)	grilling, sauté		
Heart	le coeur	braising		
Liver	le foie	frying		
Sweetbreads	le ris	braising, frying		
Tongue	la langue	braising, boiling		

3 · Quality of lamb and mutton

(Lamb is under 1 year old)

1 A good quality animal should be compact and evenly fleshed.
2 The lean flesh should be firm, of a pleasing dull red colour and of a fine texture or grain.
3 There should be an even distribution of surface fat which should be hard, brittle and flaky in structure and a clear white colour.
4 In a young animal the bones should be pink and porous, so that, when cut, a degree of blood is shown in their structure. As age progresses the bones become hard, dense, white and inclined to splinter when chopped.

4 · Order of dissection of a carcass

1. Remove the shoulders.
2. Remove the breasts.
3. Remove the middle neck and scrag.
4. Remove the legs.
5. Divide the saddle from the best-end.

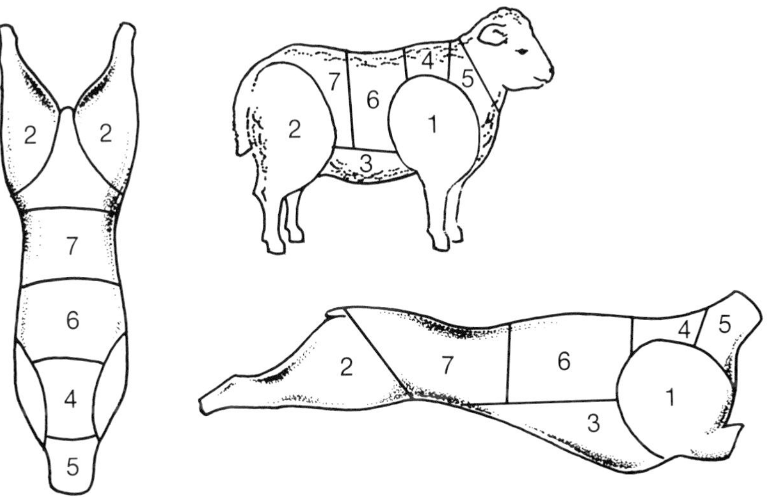

5 · Preparation of the joints and cuts

Clockwise from top left: pair of best-ends; chump; full saddle; loin; middle neck

Clockwise from top left: loin chop; chump chop; Barnsley chop (double loin chop); fillet; loin – fillet removed

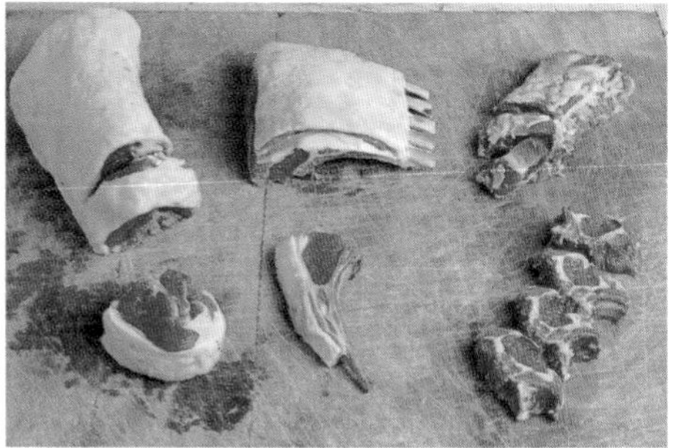

Left to right: loin chop; cutlet; uncovered cutlets

Left: rosettes; right: noisettes

Shoulder

Roasting Clean and trim knucklebone so as to leave approximately 3 cm (1½ in) of clean bone.
Boning Remove the blade bone and upper arm bone (see below), tie with string. The shoulder may be stuffed (page 249) before tying.
Cutting for Stews Bone out, cut into even 25–50 g (1–2 oz) pieces.

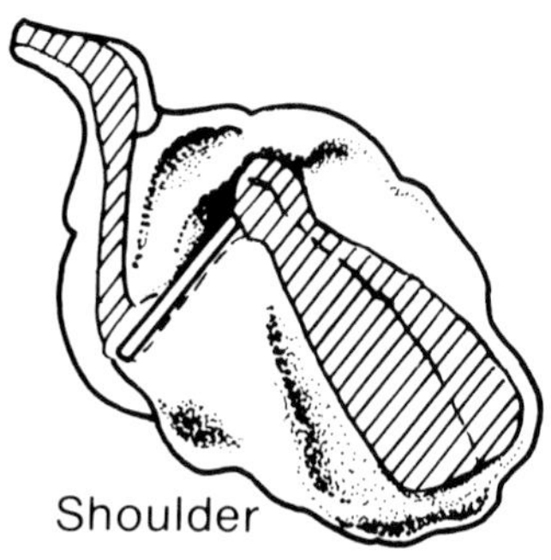

Roasting Remove the pelvic or aitchbone. Trim the knuckle cleaning 3 cm (1½ in) bone. Trim off excess fat and tie with string if necessary.

Breasts

Remove excess fat and skin.
Roasting Bone, stuff and roll, tie with string.
Stewing Cut into even 25–50 g (1–2 oz) pieces.

Middle neck

Stewing Remove excess fat, excess bone and the gristle. Cut into even 50 g (2 oz) pieces. This joint, when correctly butchered, can give good uncovered second-class cutlets.

Scrag-end

Stewing This can be chopped down the centre, the excess bone, fat and gristle removed and cut into even 50 g (2 oz) pieces, or boned out and cut into pieces.

Saddle

A full saddle is illustrated in (a) including the chumps and the tail.
For large banquets it is sometimes found better to remove the chumps and use short saddles. Saddles may also be boned and stuffed.

Saddle	la selle	roasting, pot roasting (poêlé)
Loin	la longe	roasting
Fillet	le filet mignon	grilling, frying
Loin chop	chop	grilling, frying, stewing
Chump chop	chump chop	grilling, frying, stewing
Kidney	le rognon	grilling, sauté

The saddle may be divided as follows:

Remove skin, starting from head to tail and from breast to back, split down the centre of the backbone to produce two loins. Each loin can be roasted whole, boned and stuffed, or cut into loin and chump chops.

Saddle for roasting

1 Skin and remove the kidney.
2 Trim the excess fat and sinew.
3 Cut off the flaps leaving about 15 cm (6 in) each side so as to meet in the middle under the saddle.
4 Remove the aitch or pelvic bone.
5 Score neatly and tie with string.
6 For presentation the tail may be left on, protected with paper and tied back.
7 The saddle can also be completely boned, stuffed and tied.

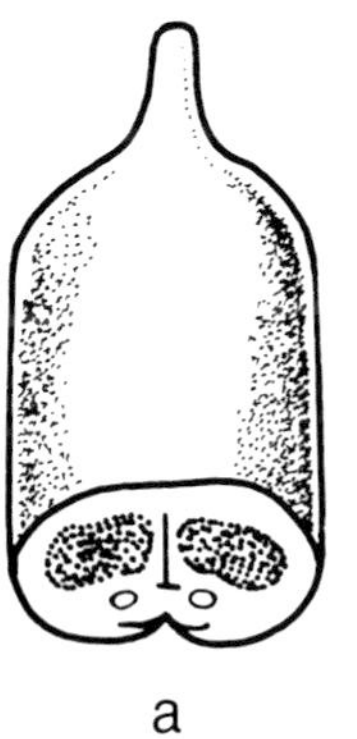

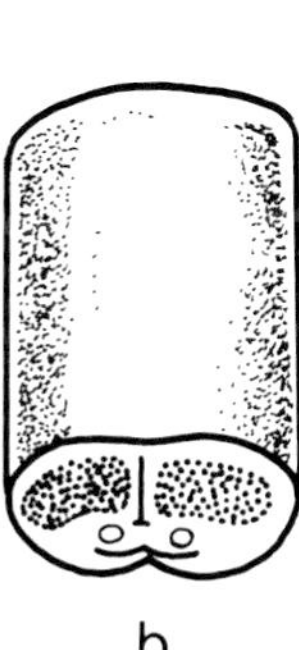

Loin for roasting

Skin, remove excess fat and sinew, remove pelvic bone, tie with string.

Loin boned and stuffed

Remove the skin, excess fat and sinew. Bone out, replace the fillet and tie with string. When stuffed, bone out, season, stuff and tie.

Chops

Loin chops

Skin the loin, remove the excess fat and sinew, then cut into chops approx. 100–150 g (4–6 oz) in weight. A first-class loin chop should have a piece of kidney skewered in the centre.

Double loin chop

Also known as a Barnsley chop. These are cut approx. 2 cm (1 in) across a saddle on the bone. When trimmed they are secured with a skewer and may include a piece of kidney in the centre of each chop.

Chump chops

These are cut from the chump end of the loin. Cut into approx. 150 g (6 oz) chops, trim where necessary.

Noisette

This is a cut from a boned-out loin. Cut slantwise into approx. 2 cm (1 in) thick slices, bat out slightly, trim cutlet shape.

Rosette

This is a cut from a boned out loin approx. 2 cm (1 in) thick. It is shaped round and tied with string.

Best-end

Best-end preparation

1 Remove the skin from head to tail and from breast to back.
2 Remove the sinew and the tip of the blade bone.
3 Complete the preparation of the rib bones as indicated in the diagram.
4 Clean the sinew from between the rib bones and trim the bones.
5 Score the fat neatly to approx. 2 mm (1/12 in) deep as shown.

The overall length of the rib bones to be trimmed to two and a half times the length of the nut of meat.

Roasting – prepare as above.

Cutlets (*Côtelettes*) – prepare as for roasting, excluding the scoring and divide evenly between the bones, or the cutlets can be cut from the best-end and prepared separately. A double cutlet (*côtelette double*) consists of two bones; therefore a six bone best-end yields six single or three double cutlets.

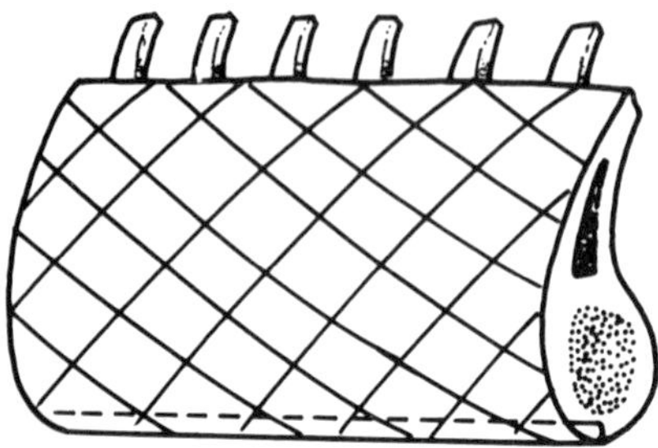

Ingredients for preparing roast best-end

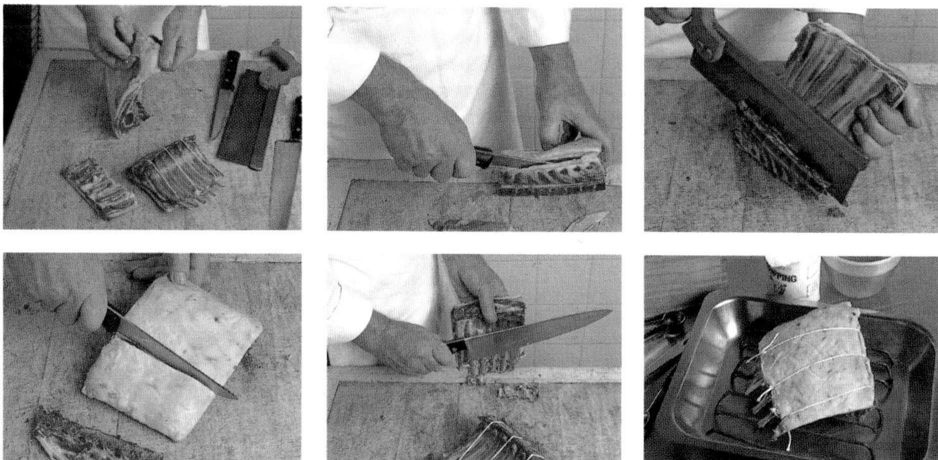

Preparation of best-end

6 · Preparation of offal

Kidney

Grilling Skin and split three-quarters the way through lengthwise and skewer.

Sauté Skin and remove the gristle. Cut slantways into 6–8 pieces.

Hearts

Braising Remove the tubes and excess fat.

Liver

Skin, remove gristle and cut into thin slices on the slant.

Sweetbreads

Wash well, blanch and trim.

Tongue

Remove bone and gristle from the throat end.

7 Roasting of lamb and mutton

Allow approx. 150 g (6 oz) meat on the bone per portion (legs, shoulders, saddle or loin, best-end and breast.)

> Using leg of lamb
> 1 portion (113 g/4 oz lamb) provides:
>
> 301 kcals/1262 kJ
> 20.2 g fat of which 10.5 g saturated
> 0.0 g carbohydrate of which 0.0 g sugars
> 29.5 g protein
> 0.0 g fibre

1 The joints are seasoned with salt and placed on a trivet, or bones, in a roasting tray.
2 Place a little vegetable oil or dripping on top and cook in a hot oven (230–250 °C, Reg. 8–9).
3 Baste frequently and reduce the heat gradually when necessary, as for example in the case of large joints.
4 Roasting time approx. 20 min per ½ kilo (1 lb) and 20 min over.
5 To test if cooked, place on a tray and press firmly in order to see if the juices released contain any blood.
6 In general, all joints should be cooked through. If joints are required pink reduce cooking time by a quarter.
7 Allow to stand for approx. 10–15 min before carving; if this is not done the meat will tend to shrink and curl.

Roast gravy Jus rôti

1 Place the roasting tray on the stove over a gentle heat to allow the sediment to settle.
2 Carefully strain off the fat, leaving the sediment in the tray.
3 Return to the stove and brown carefully, deglaze with brown stock.
4 Allow to simmer for a few minutes.
5 Correct the seasoning and colour, then strain and skim.

In some establishments the gravy served with stuffed joints and also pork and veal is slightly thickened with diluted cornflour, fécule or arrowroot.

Carving

Roast leg Gigot d'agneau rôti or Gigot de mouton rôti

Holding the bone, carve with a sharp knife at an angle of 45° and take off each slice as it is cut. Continue in this manner along the joint, turning it from side to side as the slices get wider.

Shoulder Epaule d'agneau rôtie

To obtain reasonable sized slices of meat, carve the flesh side not the skin side of the joint. Having obtained the slices it is then necessary to carve round the bones. Due to the awkward shape of the bone structure, the shoulder may be boned out, rolled and tied before cooking to facilitate carving.

Roast saddle Selle d'agneau rôtie

Carving on the bone. There are two usual ways of carving the saddle, one is by carving lengthways either side of the backbone, the other by making a deep cut lengthwise either side of the backbone and then slicing across each loin. It is usual to carve the saddle in thick slices.

Carving off the bone. For economical kitchen carving it is often found best to bone the loins out whole, carve into slices, then reform on the saddle bone.

The filet mignon may be left on the saddle or removed; in either case it is carved and served with the rest of the meat.

Roast loin Longe d'agneau rôtie

On the bone. Proceed as for the saddle.
Boned-out, cut in slices across the joint. When stuffed cut slightly thicker.

Roast best-end Carré d'agneau rôti

Divide into cutlets by cutting between bones.

Service

All roast joints are served garnished with watercress and a sauceboat of roast gravy separately.

When carved, serve a little gravy over the slices as well as a sauce-boat of gravy. Mint sauce should be served with roast lamb and redcurrant jelly should be available. For roast mutton, redcurrant jelly and/or onion sauce should be served, with mint sauce available.

8 Stuffing for lamb

This is used for stuffing joints, e.g. loin, shoulder, breast.

50 g	2 oz	chopped suet
50 g	2 oz	chopped onions cooked in a little butter or margarine without colour
		1 egg yolk or small egg
100 g	4 oz	white breadcrumbs
		pinch powdered thyme
		pinch chopped parsley
		salt, pepper
		grated zest of lemon

Combine all the ingredients together.

Mint sauce – See Sauce section, page 112.

Best-end of lamb recipes

9 · Best-end of lamb with breadcrumbs and parsley *Carré d'agneau persillé*

Roast the best-end and 10 min before the cooking is completed cover the fat surface of the meat with a mixture of 25–50 g (1–2 oz) of fresh white breadcrumbs mixed with plenty of chopped parsley, an egg and 25–50 g (1–2 oz) melted butter or margarine. Return to the oven to complete the cooking, browning carefully.

10 · Best-end of lamb boulanger *Carré d'agneau boulanger*

Any roast lamb joint may be served in this manner.

1 Prepare a dish of pommes boulangère (savoury potatoes) (page 445).
2 Roast the joint.
3 Remove from the tray 15 min before completion of cooking.
4 Place on top of the cooked potatoes.
5 Return to the oven to complete the cooking.
6 Serve the joint whole or carved as required on the potatoes.
7 Garnish with watercress and serve with a sauceboat of gravy separately.

Roast best-end of lamb

Cutlets

11 · Grilled cutlets *Côtelettes d'agneau grillées*

1 Season the cutlets lightly with salt and mill pepper.
2 Brush with oil or fat.
3 When cooked on the bars of the grill, place the prepared cutlet on the pre-heated bars which have been greased.
4 Cook for approx. 5 min, turn and complete the cooking.

5 When cooked under the salamander place on a greased tray, cook for approx. 5 min, turn and complete the cooking.
6 Serve dressed garnished with a deep-fried potato and watercress. Parsley butter may also be served.
7 Each cutlet bone may be capped with a cutlet frill.

1 portion (2 cutlets) provides

488 kcals/2050 kJ
40.8 g fat of which 19.3 g saturated
0.0 g carbohydrate of which 0.0 g sugars
30.4 g protein
0.0 g fibre

With straw potatoes, parsley, watercress
1 portion provides:

726 kcals/3050 kJ
59.2 g fat of which 26.6 g saturated
20.2 g carbohydrate of which 2.5 g sugars
29.5 g protein
4.9 g fibre

12 · Mixed grill

4 sausages	4 rashers streaky bacon
4 cutlets	watercress
4 kidneys	straw potatoes
4 tomatoes	parsley butter (page 109)
4 mushrooms	

These are the usually accepted items for a mixed grill, but it will be found that there are many variations to this list, e.g. steaks, liver. In economical catering a Welsh rarebit and fried egg may be used in place of more expensive items.

Grill in the order given and dress neatly on an oval flat dish. Garnish with deep-fried potato, watercress and a slice of parsley butter on each kidney.

Right: preparation of mixed grill; Above: service

13 · Fried cutlets

Season and carefully cook in a sauté pan. Garnish as required. For some typical garnishes see page 255.

14 Breadcrumbed cutlets *Côtelettes d'agneau panées*

1 Pass prepared cutlets through seasoned flour, eggwash and fresh white breadcrumbs. Pat firmly, then shake off surplus crumbs.
2 Shallow fry in hot clarified fat for the first few minutes; then allow to cook gently.
3 Turn, and continue cooking until a golden brown.
4 To test if cooked, press firmly, no signs of blood should appear. Approx. time 5 min each side.

In the following recipes prepare cutlets as recipe 14 and garnish with the appropriate prepared spaghetti. Finish with a cordon of jus-lié around the dish. Beurre noisette may be served over the cutlets.

15 Breadcrumbed cutlets with spaghetti (3 variations)

(a) Cutlets with spaghetti italienne *Côtelettes d'agneau italienne*

Garnish with recipe 2 page 193.

(b) Cutlets with spaghetti napolitaine *Côtelettes d'agneau napolitaine*

Garnish with recipe 3 page 193.

(c) Cutlets with spaghetti milanaise *Côtelettes d'agneau milanaise*

Garnish with recipe 4 page 194.

16 Lamb cutlets Reform *Côtelettes d'agneau Reforme*

1 Pass the prepared cutlets through seasoned flour, eggwash and breadcrumbs containing chopped ham and chopped parsley.
2 Cook as for crumbed cutlet.
3 Serve garnished with Reform sauce (page 103) and a sauceboat of Reform sauce separately.

17 Boiled leg of mutton or lamb, caper sauce

1 Place the prepared leg into boiling salted water.
2 Re-boil, skim and simmer.
3 Add 2–3 whole carrots and onions, a whole leek, 2–3 sticks of celery and a bouquet garni.
4 Allow to cook for 20 min ½ kg (1 lb) and 20 min over.

5 Serve whole or carved as required with a little of the cooking liquor, accompanied with a sauceboat of caper sauce.

Caper sauce Sauce aux câpres

50 g	2 oz	margarine or butter
50 g	2 oz	flour
½ litre	1 pt	cooking liquor in which the leg has been cooked
		1 tablespn capers

Make a velouté and cook out. Correct the seasoning and consistency, strain and add the capers.

18 · **Brochette of lamb** *Shish kebab*

Prime tender meat must be used, the ideal cuts being the nut of the lean meat of the loin and best-end.

1 Cut the meat into thin slices, season and place on a skewer with peeled washed mushrooms and two halves of bay leaf per skewer. Pieces of onion and red or green pepper may also be included on the skewer.
2 Season, brush with melted fat and grill gently, turning and brushing with fat. Brochettes are usually served on a riz pilaff (page 201).

Variations

Other items that may be used are tender cuts of beef, pork and liver, also kidney, bacon, ham, sausage, chicken, tomato, pineapple and apple.

Different flavours may be introduced by marinading the skewered meats in wine, oil, lemon juice, spices and herbs for 1–2 hours before cooking.

19 · **Grilled loin chop** *Chop d'agneau grillée*

1 Season chops with salt and pepper mill.
2 Brush with fat and place on hot greased grill bars or place on a greased baking tray.
3 Cook quickly for the first 2–3 min on each side, in order to seal the pores of the meat.
4 Continue cooking steadily allowing approx. 12–15 min in all.

Parsley butter may also be served and a deep fried potato such as pommes frites, pommes allumettes, pommes mignonettes or straw potatoes.

20 · Braised loin chops or Braised chump chop
Chops d'agneau braisées

		4 chops
25 g	1 oz	dripping or oil
100 g	4 oz	onion
100 g	4 oz	carrot
25 g	1 oz	flour, white or wholemeal
		level teaspn tomato purée
500 ml	1 pt	brown stock
		bouquet garni
		1 clove garlic (optional)
		seasoning
		chopped parsley

1 Fry seasoned chops in a sauté pan quickly on both sides in hot fat.
2 When turning the chops add the mirepoix.
3 Draw aside, drain off the surplus fat.
4 Add the flour and mix in, singe in the oven or on top of the stove. (Alternatively, use flour which has been browned in the oven.)
5 Add the tomato purée and the hot stock.
6 Stir with a wooden spoon till thoroughly mixed.
7 Add the bouquet garni and garlic, season, skim and allow to simmer and cover with a lid.
8 Cook preferably in the oven, skimming off all fat and scum.
9 When cooked transfer chops to a clean pan.
10 Correct the seasoning and consistency of the sauce.
11 Skim off any fat and pass through a fine chinois on to the chops. Serve, sprinkled with chopped parsley. *4 portions*

21 · Chops Champvallon *Chops d'agneau Champvallon*

		4 chops
25 g	1 oz	flour
25 g	1 oz	dripping or oil
100 g	4 oz	onions
		1 clove garlic (optional)
250 ml	½ pt	brown stock
400 g	1 lb	potatoes

1 Pass chops through seasoned flour.
2 Fry quickly on both sides in hot fat or oil.
3 Shred onions finely and toss lightly in butter, with garlic if using, and place in a shallow earthenware dish.
4 Place the chops on top, cover with brown stock.
5 Add ¼ cm (⅛ in) sliced potatoes neatly arranged with a knob or two of good dripping on top or brush with oil.
6 Cook in a hot oven (230–250 °C, Reg. 8–9) till the potatoes are cooked and a golden brown, approx. 1½–2 hrs.
7 Serve sprinkled with chopped parsley, in the cleaned earthenware dish.

4 portions

22 · Grilled chump chop

As for loin chop, recipe 19.

23 · Noisettes of lamb grilled *Noisettes d'agneau grillées*

These may be grilled as for lamb chops, recipe 19.

24 · Noisettes of lamb sauté *Noisettes d'agneau sautées*

Season and shallow fry on both sides in a sauté pan and serve with the appropriate garnish and sauce. Unless specifically stated a jus-lié or demi-glace sauce should be served.

Suitable garnishes

Fleuriste	Tomatoes filled with jardinière of vegetables and château potatoes.
Dubarry	Balls of cauliflower Mornay and château potatoes.
Montmorency	Artichoke bottoms filled with carrot balls and noisette potatoes.
Princess	Artichoke bottoms filled with asparagus heads and noisette potatoes.
Parisienne	Braised lettuce and parisienne potatoes.
Clamart	Artichoke bottoms filled with peas and cocotte potatoes.

25 · Fillet of lamb *Filet mignon*

Trim off all excess fat and sinew then proceed as for noisettes d'agneau, recipe 24.

26 · Valentine of lamb

1 Prepare short saddle with all bones, kidneys and internal fat removed.
2 Split into two loins.
3 Trim off excess fat and sinew.
4 Cut across the muscle grain into thick boneless chops.
5 Slice three parts through the lean meat and open to give a double sized cut surface (butterfly cut).
6 Valentines are cooked in the same way as noisettes and rosettes. They may also be grilled or braised.

Best-end may be used in place of the loin.

27 · Brown lamb or mutton stew *Navarin d'agneau*

500 g	1 lb 4 oz	stewing lamb
		2 tablespns oil
		salt, pepper
100 g	4 oz	onion } mirepoix
100 g	4 oz	carrot } mirepoix
		clove of garlic (if desired)
25 g	1 oz	flour, white or wholemeal
		level tablespn tomato purée
500 g	1 pt	brown stock (mutton stock or water) (approx.)
		bouquet garni

Using sunflower oil
1 portion provides:

314 kcals/1320 kJ
18.7 g fat of which 6.2 g saturated
9.4 g carbohydrate of which 3.2 g sugars
27.9 g protein
1.3 g fibre

1. Trim the meat and cut into even pieces.
2. Partly fry off the seasoned meat, then add the mirepoix and garlic and continue frying.
3. Drain off the surplus fat, add the flour and mix.
4. Singe in the oven or brown on top of the stove for a few minutes or add previously browned flour.
5. Add the tomato purée and stir with a wooden spoon.
6. Add the stock and season.
7. Add the bouquet garni, bring to the boil, skim, cover with a lid.
8. Simmer gently till cooked, preferably in the oven, approx. 1–2 hr.
9. When cooked, place the meat in a clean pan.
10. Correct the sauce and pass the sauce on to the meat.
11. Serve sprinkled with chopped parsley. *4 portions*

28 · Brown stew of lamb or mutton garnished with vegetables *Navarin printanier*

As above, with a garnish of vegetables, i.e. turned glacé carrots and turnips, glacé button onions; potatoes, peas and diamonds of French beans, which may be cooked separately or in the stew (glacé vegetables, page 281).

29 · Curried lamb *Kari d'agneau* or *Currie d'agneau*

500 g	1 lb 4 oz	stewing lamb
		3 tablespns oil
200 g	8 oz	onions
		1 clove garlic
10 g	½ oz	curry powder
10 g	½ oz	flour, white or wholemeal
10 g	½ oz	tomato purée
½ litre	1 pt	stock or water
25 g	1 oz	chopped chutney
25 g	1 oz	desiccated coconut
25 g	1 oz	sultanas
50 g	2 oz	chopped apple
10 g	½ oz	grated root ginger

Using sunflower oil
1 portion provides:

405 kcals/1699 kJ
26.6 g fat of which 10.0 g saturated
14.8 g carbohydrate of which 11.6 g sugars
27.7 g protein
3.2 g fibre

1 Trim the meat and cut into even pieces.
2 Season and quickly colour in hot oil.
3 Add the chopped onion and chopped garlic, cover with a lid and sweat for a few minutes. Drain off the surplus fat.
4 Add the curry powder and flour, mix in and cook out.
5 Mix in the tomato purée, gradually add the hot stock, thoroughly stir, bring to the boil, season with salt and skim.
6 Allow to simmer and add the rest of the ingredients.
7 Cover with a lid and simmer in the oven or on top of the stove till cooked.
8 Correct the seasoning and consistency, skim off all fat. At this stage a little cream or yoghurt may be added.
9 Serve accompanied with rice which may be plain boiled, pilaff or pilaff with saffron.

4 portions

Plain boiled rice

100 g	4 oz	rice (long-grain)
1½ litres	3 pt	water
		salt

1 Pick and wash the long-grain rice.
2 Add to plenty of boiling salted water.
3 Stir to the boil and simmer gently till tender, approx. 12–15 min.
4 Wash well under running water, drain and place on a sieve and cover with a cloth.
5 Place on a tray in a moderate oven or in the hot plate until hot.
6 Serve in vegetable dish separately.

4 portions

Other accompaniments to curry

There are many other accompaniments to curry, for example grilled Bombay duck (dried fish fillets) and poppadums (thin vegetable wafers) which are grilled or deep fried. Also:

chopped chutney
sultanas
desiccated coconut
slices of lemon
chopped apple
segments of lime
chow-chow
quarters of orange
sliced banana
chopped onions
diced cucumber in natural yoghurt

30 Irish stew

500 g	1 lb 4 oz	stewing lamb
		bouquet garni
400 g	1 lb	potatoes
100 g	4 oz	onions
100 g	4 oz	celery
100 g	4 oz	Savoy cabbage
100 g	4 oz	leeks
100 g	4 oz	button onions
		chopped parsley

1 portion provides:

319 kcals/1339 kJ
11.2 g fat of which 5.2 g saturated
26.1 g carbohydrate of which 5.7 g sugars
30.2 g protein
5.0 g fibre

1. Trim the meat and cut into even pieces. Blanch and refresh.
2. Place in a sauteuse or shallow saucepan, cover with water, bring to the boil, season with salt and skim.
   If tough meat is being used, allow ½–1 hr stewing before adding any vegetables.
3. Add the bouquet garni. Turn the potatoes into barrel shapes.
4. Cut the potato trimmings, onions, celery, cabbage and leeks into small neat pieces and add to the meat, simmer for 30 min.
5. Add the button onions and simmer for a further 30 min.
6. Add the potatoes and simmer gently, with a lid on the pan till cooked.
7. Correct the seasoning and skim off all fat.
8. Serve sprinkled with chopped parsley.
9. Optional accompaniments: Worcester sauce or pickled red cabbage.

4 portions

Irish stew

31 · White lamb stew *Blanquette d'agneau*

500 g	1 lb 4 oz	stewing lamb	
750 ml	1½ pts	(approx.) white stock	
50 g	2 oz	onion piqué	
50 g	2 oz	carrot	
		bouquet garni	
25 g	1 oz	butter or margarine	blond roux
25 g	1 oz	flour	blond roux
		2–3 tablespns cream, yoghurt or quark	
		chopped parsley	

1 Trim the meat and cut into even pieces. Blanch and refresh.
2 Place in a saucepan and cover with cold water.
3 Bring to the boil then place under running cold water until all the scum has been washed away.
4 Drain and place in a clean saucepan and cover with stock, bring to the boil and skim.
5 Add whole onion and carrot, bouquet garni, season lightly with salt and simmer until tender, approx. 1–1½ hr.
6 Meanwhile prepare the roux and make into a velouté with the cooking liquor. Cook out for approx. 20 min.
7 Correct the seasoning and consistency and pass through a fine strainer on to the meat, which has been placed in a clean pan.
8 Reheat, mix in the cream and serve, finished with chopped parsley.
9 To enrich this dish a liaison of yolks and cream is sometimes added at the last moment to the boiling sauce, which must not be allowed to re-boil otherwise the eggs will scramble.

4 portions

32 · Cornish pasties

200 g	½ lb	short paste	
100 g	4 oz	finely diced potato (raw)	filling
100 g	4 oz	raw lamb or beef (cut in thin pieces)	filling
50 g	2 oz	chopped onion	filling
50 g	2 oz	finely diced swede (raw) (optional)	filling

1 portion provides:

290 kcals/1217 kJ
16.2 g fat of which 6.0 g saturated
29.3 g carbohydrate of which 1.2 g sugars
8.7 g protein
1.8 g fibre

1 Roll out the short paste 3 mm (⅛ in) thick and cut into rounds 12 cm (5 in) diameter.
2 Mix the filling together, moisten with a little water and place in the rounds in piles. Eggwash the edges.
3 Fold in half and seal, flute the edge and brush with eggwash.
4 Cook in moderate oven (150–200 °C, Reg. 2–6) for ¾–1 hr.
5 Serve with a suitable sauce separately, e.g. demi-glace.
6 A variety of cooked fillings and seasonings may be used.

4 portions

33 Hot pot of lamb or mutton

500 g	1 lb 4 oz	stewing lamb
		salt and pepper
100 g	4 oz	onions
400 g	1 lb	potatoes
1 litre	2 pt	brown stock
25 g	1 oz	dripping or oil
		chopped parsley

Using sunflower oil
1 portion provides:

360 kcals/1505 kJ
17.0 g fat of which 6.4 g saturated
22.0 g carbohydrate of which 1.8 g sugars
29.0 g protein
2.5 g fibre

1. Trim the meat and cut into even pieces.
2. Place in a deep earthenware dish. Season with salt and pepper.
3. Mix the shredded onion and thinly sliced potatoes together.
4. Season and place on top of the meat.
5. Three parts cover with stock.
6. Neatly arrange an overlapping layer of 2 mm thick (1/12 in) sliced potatoes on top.
7. Add the dripping in small pieces.
8. Thoroughly clean the edges of the dish and place to cook in a hot oven (230–250 °C, Reg. 8–9) till lightly coloured.
9. Reduce heat and simmer gently till cooked, approx. 1½–2 hr.
10. Press the potatoes down occasionally during cooking.
11. Serve with the potatoes brushed with butter or margarine and sprinkle with chopped parsley.

There are many accepted regional variations to this dish.

4 portions

34 Haricot mutton *Haricot mouton*

500 g	1 lb 4 oz	stewing lamb
25 g	1 oz	lard or oil
50 g	2 oz	lean bacon
		8 button onions
		small clove of garlic
25 g	1 oz	flour, white or wholemeal
25 g	1 oz	tomato purée
750 ml	1½ pt	brown stock or water
		bouquet garni
200 g	8 oz	haricot beans ¾ cooked
		chopped parsley

Using sunflower oil
1 portion provides:

447 kcals/1878 kJ
19.1 g fat of which 6.5 g saturated
29.8 g carbohydrate of which 3.3 g sugars
40.9 g protein
13.2 g fibre

1. Trim the meat and cut into even pieces.
2. Heat the lard or oil in a sauté pan.
3. Add the diced bacon, and the button onions, colour lightly and remove from the pan.
4. In the same fat fry the meat and colour on all sides.
5. Drain off half of the fat.
6. Add the crushed garlic and flour.

7 Singe in the oven or cook out on top of the stove.
8 Mix in the tomato purée.
9 Add the hot water or stock.
10 Bring to the boil, season with salt, skim, add the bouquet garni.
11 Cover with a lid and simmer for 30 min.
12 Transfer the meat to clean pan, add the bacon and onions and the previously three-quarter cooked haricot beans.
13 Strain the sauce over and cover with a lid.
14 Complete the cooking, allowing a further 1–2 hr.
15 Correct the seasoning and consistency and skim off all fat.
16 Serve sprinkled with chopped parsley.

4 portions

35 Shepherd's pie

100 g	4 oz	chopped onion
35 g	1½ oz	fat or oil
400 g	1 lb	cooked lamb or mutton (minced)
		salt and pepper
		2–3 drops Worcester sauce
125 250 ml	¼–½ pt	jus-lié or demi-glace
400 g	1 lb	cooked potato
25 g	1 oz	butter or margarine
		milk

Using sunflower oil, hard marg in topping
1 portion provides:

415 kcals/1744 kJ
25.3 g fat of which 9.1 g saturated
22.1 g carbohydrate of which 2.5 g sugars
26.3 g protein
1.6 g fibre

1 Cook the onion in the fat or oil without colouring.
2 Add the cooked meat from which all fat and gristle has been removed.
3 Season, add Worcester sauce and add sufficient sauce to bind.
4 Bring to the boil, simmer 10–15 mins.
5 Place in a pie or earthenware dish.
6 Prepare the mashed potatoes and pipe or arrange neatly on top.
7 Brush with milk or eggwash.
8 Colour lightly under the salamander or in a hot oven.
9 Serve accompanied with a sauceboat of jus-lié.

Note This dish prepared with cooked beef is known as cottage pie. When using reheated meats care must be taken to heat thoroughly and quickly.

4 portions

36 Minced lamb or mutton *Hachis d'agneau ou de mouton*

Prepare the meat for shepherd's pie (recipe 36). Then place on a dish which has been previously piped with a border of duchess potatoes dried for a few minutes in the oven, egg-washed and lightly browned.

37 · Moussaka

50 g	2 oz	onions
		1 small clove garlic
25 g	1 oz	butter, margarine or oil
25 g	1 oz	tomato purée
400–600 g	1–1½ lb	cooked mutton (diced or minced)
125 ml	¼ pt	demi-glace
200 g	½ lb	aubergine
200 g	½ lb	tomatoes
		flour, white or wholemeal
60 ml	⅛ pt	oil
25 g	1 oz	breadcrumbs
25 g	1 oz	grated Parmesan cheese
		melted butter, margarine or oil, as necessary

Using hard marg, sunflower oil
1 portion provides:

455 kcals/1909 kJ
33.3 g fat of which 11.1 g saturated
10.5 g carbohydrate of which 5.1 g sugars
28.9 g protein
2.8 g fibre

1 Finely chop the onions and garlic.
2 Cook in the butter, margarine or oil without colour.
3 Mix in the tomato purée and the cooked mutton.
4 Add the demi-glace and bring to the boil.
5 Correct the seasoning and allow to simmer 10–15 min. The mixture should be fairly dry.
6 Peel the aubergines and cut into ½ cm (¼ in) slices.
7 Pass the slices of aubergine through the flour.
8 Fry the slices of aubergine in shallow hot oil on both sides and drain.
9 Peel the tomatoes and cut into ½ cm ¼ in) slices.
10 Place the mixture of mutton into an earthenware dish.
11 Cover the mixture with the slices of tomato, and then neatly with the slices of aubergine.
12 Season with salt and pepper.
13 Sprinkle with breadcrumbs, cheese and melted butter.
14 Gratinate in a hot oven (230–250 °C, Reg. 8–9).
15 Sprinkle with chopped parsley and serve. Minced beef may be used in place of mutton.

This is a dish of Greek origin. It may also be seasoned with a little cinnamon and oregano. Moussaka may also be finished by masking the dish when all the ingredients have been added with 250 ml (½ pt) of thin béchamel sauce to which 2 beaten eggs have been added. If this method is being adopted then the breadcrumbs, cheese and melted butter should be added after the béchamel.

4 portions

38 Lamb cutlets in pastry *Côtelettes d'agneau en croûte*

		8 prepared lamb cutlets, trimmed of almost all fat	
25 g	1 oz	butter, margarine or oil	stuffing
100 g	4 oz	chopped onion	stuffing
25 g	1 oz	chopped mint	stuffing
25 g	1 oz	fresh breadcrumbs	stuffing
		1 egg	stuffing
		salt and pepper	stuffing
		few drops lemon juice	stuffing
300 g	12 oz	puff pastry	

1. Prepare stuffing by sweating onion in butter without colouring.
2. Remove from heat and mix in breadcrumbs, seasoning, mint, lemon juice and beaten egg.
3. Quickly grill or fry the cutlets on both sides for 2–3 minutes. Allow to cool.
4. Thinly roll out pastry and cut into eight squares.
5. Place a cutlet in the centre of each square, with the bone protruding to the edge of the pastry.
6. Press a portion of stuffing onto each cutlet.
7. Egg-wash the pastry edges, neatly fold over and seal.
8. Place on a dampened baking sheet, folded sides underneath. The tops may be decorated using cutouts from the pastry trimmings.
9. Allow to rest in the refrigerator for 30 mins.
10. Egg-wash and bake at 200 °C (Reg. 7) for 15–20 mins. until the pastry is golden brown.

Alternative stuffings

(a) Replace the mint with ½ teaspoon of chopped rosemary, oregano or thyme and parsley.
(b) Delete the mint and add 100 g (4 oz) dried apricots (soaked, cooked, squeezed dry and chopped).
(c) As in (b), but use prunes instead of apricots.
(d) 25 g (1 oz) chopped mixed nuts may be added to any of the stuffings mentioned above.

4 portions

39 Grilled kidneys *Rognons grillés*

1. Season the prepared skewered kidneys.
2. Brush with melted butter, margarine or oil.
3. Place on pre-heated greased grill bars or on a greased baking tray.
4. Grill fairly quickly on both sides, approx. 5–10 min depending on size.
5. Serve with parsley butter, pickled watercress and straw potatoes.

40 Kidney sauté *Rognons sautés*

		8 sheep's kidneys
50 g	2 oz	butter, fat or oil
250 ml	½ pt	demi-glace

Using sunflower oil
1 portion provides:

400 kcals/1680 kJ
28.3 g fat of which 4.3 g saturated
15.5 g carbohydrate of which 3.7 g sugars
21.8 g protein
1.8 g fibre

1 Skin and halve the kidneys.
2 Remove the sinews.
3 Cut each half into three or five pieces and season.
4 Fry quickly in a frying-pan using the butter for approx. 4–5 min.
5 Place in a colander to drain and discard the drained liquid.
6 Deglaze pan with demi-glace, correct the seasoning and add the kidneys.
7 Do not reboil before serving as kidneys will toughen.
8 After draining the kidneys the pan may be deglazed with white wine, sherry or port.
9 As an alternative, a sauce suprême page 96 may be used in place of demi-glace.

4 portions

41 Kidney sauté Turbigo *Rognons sautés Turbigo*

As for kidney sauté then add 100 g (4 oz) small button mushrooms cooked in a little butter, margarine or oil and 8 small 2 cm (1 in) long grilled or fried chipolatas. Serve with the kidneys in an entrée dish, garnished with heart-shaped croûtons. *4 portions*

42 Braised lambs' hearts *Coeurs d'agneau braisés*

		4 lambs' hearts
		salt and pepper
25 g	1 oz	fat or oil
100 g	4 oz	onions
100 g	4 oz	carrots
500 ml	1 pt	brown stock (approx.)
		bouquet garni
10 g	½ oz	tomato purée
250 ml	½ pt	espagnole or demi-glace

Using sunflower oil
1 portion provides:

354 kcals/1489 kJ
19.0 g fat of which 5.6 g saturated
5.0 g carbohydrate of which 4.3 g sugars
41.2 g protein
1.7 g fibre

1 Remove tubes and excess fat from the hearts.
2 Season and colour quickly on all sides in hot fat to seal the pores.
3 Place into a small braising pan (any pan with a tight-fitting lid which may be placed in the oven) or in a casserole.
4 Place the hearts on the lightly fried, sliced vegetables.

5 Add the stock, which should be two-thirds of the way up the meat, season lightly.
6 Add the bouquet garni and tomato purée and if available add a few mushroom trimmings.
7 Bring to the boil, skim and cover with a lid and cook in a moderate oven (150–200 °C, Reg. 2–6).
8 After 1½ hr cooking add the espagnole, re-boil, skim and strain.
9 Continue cooking till tender.
10 Remove hearts and correct the seasoning, colour and consistency of the sauce.
11 Pass the sauce on to the sliced hearts and serve.

One per portion

43 · **Stuffed braised lambs' hearts** *Coeurs d'agneau braisés farcis*

50 g	2 oz	chopped suet
50 g	2 oz	chopped onions cooked in a little fat without colour
		1 egg yolk or small egg
100 g	4 oz	white breadcrumbs
		pinch powdered thyme
		pinch chopped parsley
		salt, pepper

Combine all the ingredients together for the stuffing.

Prepare as for braised hearts, then after removing the tubes fill the hearts with the stuffing. Place on a lightly fried bed of roots and continue as for braised hearts.

Cut in halves, coat with the corrected sauce and serve.

44 · **Fried lambs' liver and bacon** *Foie d'agneau au lard*

300 g	12 oz	liver
50 g	2 oz	fat for frying
50 g	2 oz	streaky bacon (4 rashers)
125 ml	¼ pt	jus-lié

1 Skin the liver and remove the gristle.
2 Cut in thin slices on the slant.
3 Pass the slices of liver through seasoned flour.
4 Shake off the excess flour.
5 Quickly fry on both sides in hot fat.
6 Remove the rind and bone from the bacon and grill on both sides.
7 Serve the liver and bacon with a cordon of jus-lié and a sauceboat of jus-lié separately.

45 · **Lamb sweetbreads** *Ris d'agneau*

The recipes for veal sweetbreads, pages 316–317, may all be used.

Grilled T-bone steak (p. 282)

12

BEEF

General objectives	*Specific objectives*
To know the use of beef in the kitchen and to understand its use on the menu.	To state the quality points and list the joints and cuts with approximate weights. To describe and demonstrate the correct butchery of beef; methods of cookery and presentation of dishes with suitable accompaniments and garnishes, paying due attention to details of standards and economy.

Butchery

1 · **Beef** *Boeuf*

Side of beef, approx. weight 180 kg (360 lb).

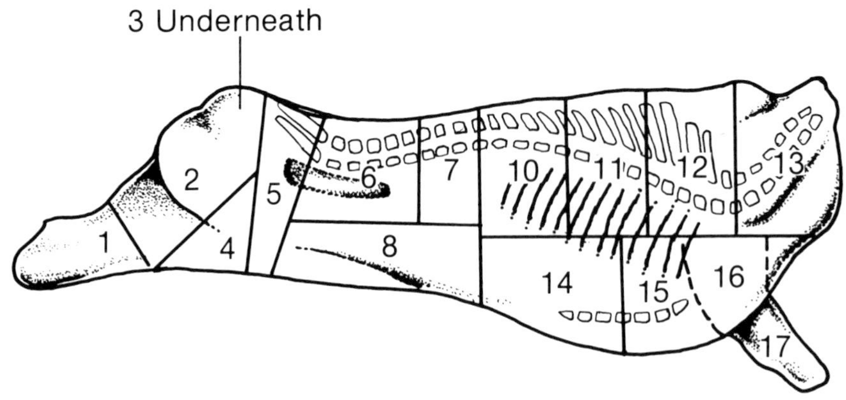

2 · **Hindquarter of Beef**

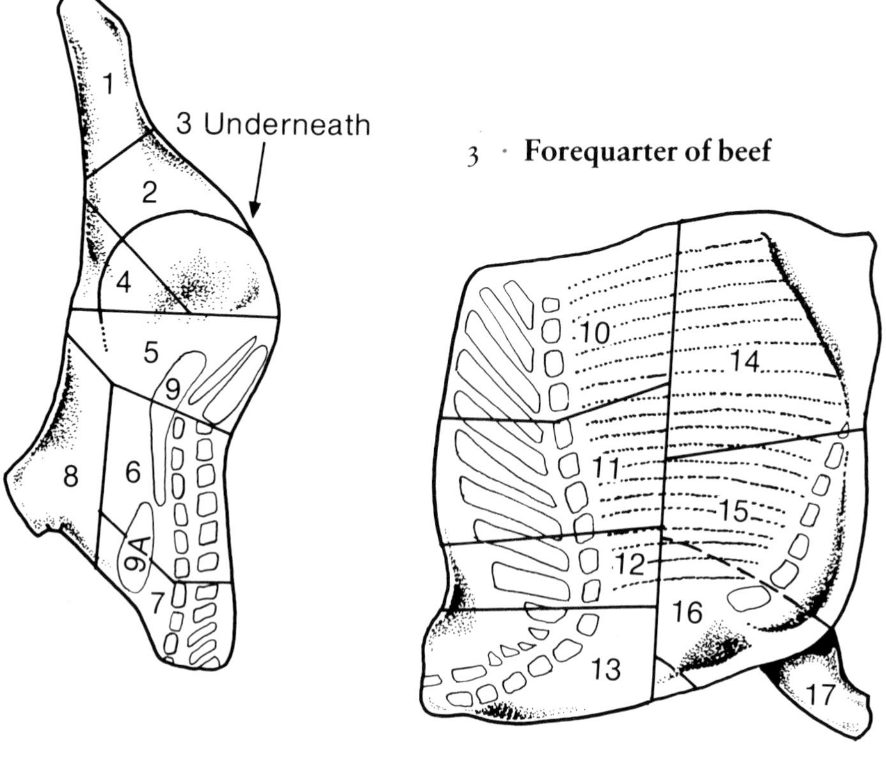

3 · **Forequarter of beef**

4 · Hindquarter: joints, uses and weights

Joint	Uses	Approx. Weight (kilo)	(lb)
1 Shin	Consommé, beef tea, stewing	7	14
2 Topside	Braising, stewing, second-class roasting	10	20
3 Silverside	Pickled in brine then boiled	14	28
4 Thick flank	Braising and stewing	12	24
5 Rump	Grilling and frying as steaks, braised in the piece	10	20
6 Sirloin	Roasting, grilling and frying in steaks	9	18
7 Wing ribs	Roasting, grilling and frying in steaks	5	10
8 Thin flank	Stewing, boiling, sausages	10	20
9 Fillet	Roasting, grilling and frying in steaks	3	6
Fat and kidney		10	20
	Total weight	90	180

5 · Forequarter: joints, uses and weights

Joint	Uses	Approx. Weight (kilo)	(lb)
10 Fore rib	Roasting and braising	8	16
11 Middle rib	Roasting and braising	10	20
12 Chuck rib	Stewing and braising	15	30
13 Sticking piece	Stewing and sausages	9	18
14 Plate	Stewing and sausages	10	20
15 Brisket	Pickled in brine and boiled, pressed beef	19	38
16 Leg of Mutton cut	Braising and stewing	11	22
17 Shank	Consommé, beef tea	6	12
	Total weight	88	176

6 · Beef offal

Offal	French	Uses
Tongue	la langue	Pickled in brine, boiling, braising
Heart	le coeur	Braising
Liver	le foie	Braising, frying
Kidney	le rognon	Stewing, soup
Sweetbread	le ris	Braising, frying
Tripe	la tripe	Boiling, braising
Tail	la queue	Braising, soup
Suet	la graisse de rognon	Suet paste and stuffing or rendered down for first-class dripping
Bones	les os (m.)	Beef stocks
Marrow	la moelle	Savouries and sauces

7 · Quality of beef

1 The lean meat should be bright red, with small flecks of white fat (marbled).
2 The fat should be firm, brittle in texture, creamy white in colour and odourless.

Older animals and dairy breeds have fat which is usually a deeper yellow colour.

8 · Order of dissection

A whole side is divided between the wing ribs and the fore ribs.

Dissection of the hindquarter

1 Remove the rump suet and kidney.
2 Remove the thin flank.
3 Divide the loin and rump from the leg (topside, silverside, thick flank and shin).
4 Remove the fillet.
5 Divide rump from the sirloin.
6 Remove the wing ribs.
7 Remove the shin.
8 Bone-out the aitchbone.
9 Divide the leg into the three remaining joints (silverside, topside and thick flank).

Dissection of the forequarter

1 Remove the shank.
2 Divide in half down the centre.
3 Take off the fore ribs.
4 Divide into joints.

9 **Brine** *Saumure*

2½ litres	4 qt	cold water
15 g	¾ oz	saltpetre
½–1 kg	1–2 lb	salt
		1 bayleaf
		6 juniper berries
50 g	2 oz	brown sugar
		6 peppercorns

Boil the ingredients together for 10 minutes, skimming frequently. Strain into a china, wooden or earthenware container. When the brine is cold, add the meat. Immerse the meat for up to 10 days under refrigeration.

10 **Hindquarter: preparation of joints and cuts**

Shin

Bone-out, remove excess sinew. Cut or chop as required.

Topside

Roasting – remove excess fat, cut into joints and tie with string.
Braising – as for roasting.
Stewing – cut into dice or steaks as required.

Silverside

Remove the thigh bone. This joint is usually kept whole and pickled in brine prior to boning.

Thick flank

As for Topside.

Rump

Bone-out. Cut off the first outside slice for pies and puddings. Cut into approx. 1½ cm (¾ in) slices for steaks. The point steak, considered the tenderest, is cut from the pointed end of the slice.

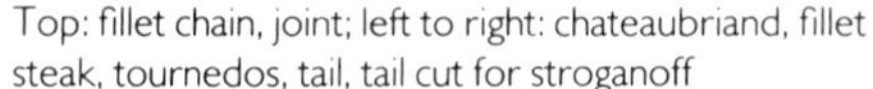

Top: fillet chain, joint; left to right: chateaubriand, fillet steak, tournedos, tail, tail cut for stroganoff

T-bone steak; rump cut into steaks

11 Sirloin: preparation of joints and steaks

Roasting

Method I: Whole on the bone Aloyau de boeuf

Saw through the chine bone, lift back the covering fat in one piece for approx. 10 cm (4 in). Trim off the sinew and replace the covering fat. String if necessary. Ensure that the fillet has been removed.

Method II: Boned-out Contrefilet de boeuf

The fillet is removed and the sirloin boned-out and the sinew is removed as before. Remove the excess fat and sinew from the boned side. This joint may be roasted open, or rolled and tied with string.

Grilling and Frying

Prepare as for Method II above and cut into steaks as required.

Minute steaks Entrecôte minute

Cut into 1 cm (½ in) slices, flatten with a cutlet bat dipped in water, making as thin as possible, then trim.

Sirloin steaks Entrecôte

Cut into 1 cm (½ in) slices and trim. Approx. weight 150 g (6 oz).

Double sirloin steaks Entrecôte double

Cut into 2 cm (1 in) thick slices and trim. Approx. weight 250–300 g (10–12 oz).

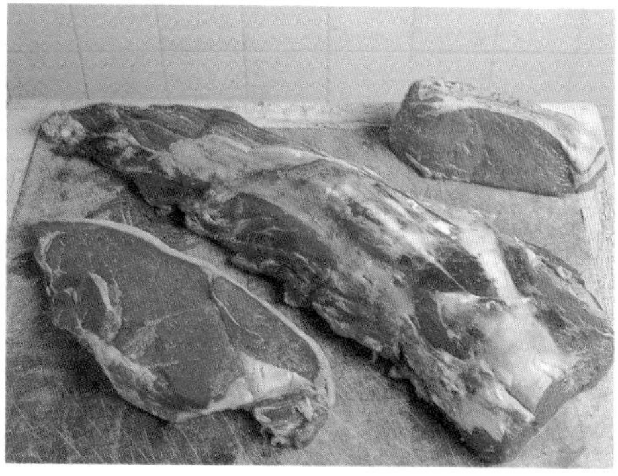

Left to right: slice of rump; whole fillet; piece of sirloin

Left to right: minute steak; sirloin steak; double sirloin steak

Porterhouse and T-bone steak

Porterhouse steaks are cut including the bone from the rib end of the sirloin.

T-bone steaks are cut from the rump end of the sirloin, including the bone and fillet.

12 · **Fillet: preparation of cuts** *Filet de boeuf*

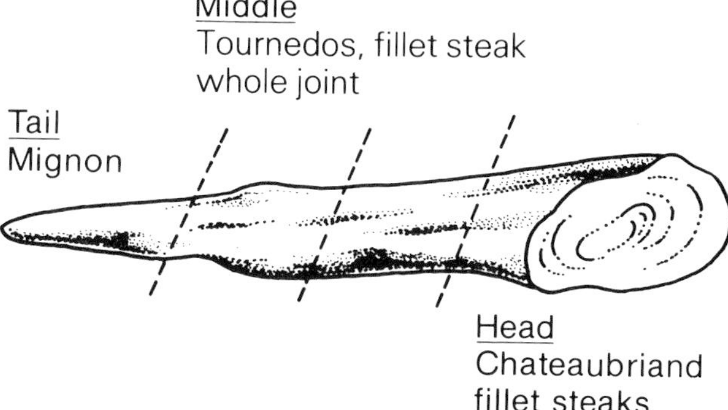

As a fillet of beef can vary from 2½–4½ kg (5–9 lb) it follows that there must be considerable variation in the number of steaks obtained from it. A typical breakdown of a 3 kg (6 lb) fillet would be as above.

Chateaubriand

Double fillet steak 3–10 cm (1½–4 in) thick 2–4 portions. Average weight 300 g–1 kilo (¾–2 lb).

Cut from the head of the fillet, trim off all nerve and leave a little fat on the steak.

Fillet steaks

Approx. 4 steaks of 100–150 g (4–6 oz) each 1½–2 cm (¾–1 in) thick.
These are cut as shown in the diagram and trimmed as for chateaubriand.

Tournedos

Approx. 6–8 at 100 g (4 oz) each, 2–4 cm (1–1½ in) thick.
Continue cutting down the fillet. Remove all the nerve and all the fat and tie each tournedos with string.

Tail of fillet (mignon)

Approx. ½ kg (1 lb).
Remove all fat and sinew and slice or mince as required.

Whole fillet

Preparation for roasting and pot roasting (poêlé).
Remove the head and tail of the fillet leaving an even centre piece from which all nerve and fat is removed. This may be larded by inserting pieces of fat bacon cut into long strips, with a larding needle.

13 **Wing rib: preparation** *Côte de boeuf*

This joint usually consists of the last three rib bones which, because of their curved shape, act as a natural trivet and because of its prime quality make it a first-class roasting joint, for hot or cold, particularly when it is to be carved in front of the customer.
To prepare, cut seven-eighths of the way through the spine or chine bone, remove the nerve, saw through the rib bones on the underside 5–10 cm (2–4 in) from the end. Tie firmly with string. When the joint is cooked the chine bone is removed to facilitate carving.

Thin flank Bavette

Trim off excessive fat and cut or roll as required.

14 **Forequarter: preparation of joints**

Fore ribs and middle ribs – prepare as for wing ribs.

Chuck ribs
Sticking piece
Brisket
Plate
Leg of mutton cut
Shank } bone-out, remove excess fat and sinew, use as required.

15 Beef offal: preparation

Tongue	Remove bone and gristle from the throat end.
Hearts	Remove arterial tubes and excess fat.
Liver	Skin, remove the gristle and cut in thin slices on the slant.
Kidney	Skin, remove the gristle and cut as required.
Sweetbreads	Wash well, trim, blanch and refresh.
Tripe	Wash well and soak in cold water, then cut into even pieces.
Tail	Cut between the natural joints, trim off excess fat. The large pieces may be split in two.

Recipes

16 Horseradish sauce *Sauce raifort*

25–30 g	1–1½ oz	grated horseradish
120 ml	¼ pt	lightly whipped cream
		1 tablespn vinegar (approx.)
		pepper, salt

Wash, peel and re-wash the horseradish and grate finely then mix all the ingredients together.

8 portions

17 Yorkshire pudding

100 g	4 oz	flour
		salt
		1 egg
250 ml	½ pt	milk or milk and water
25 g	1 oz	dripping or oil

Sieve flour and salt into a basin, make a well in the centre. Break in the egg, add half the liquid and whisk to a smooth mixture, gradually adding the rest of the liquid and allow to rest.

Select a shallow pan 15 cm (6 in) in diameter, preferably a plat à sauté. Add 25 g (1 oz) dripping from the joint and heat in the oven, pour in the mixture and cook in a hot oven (230–250 °C) for approx. 15 min.

4–6 portions

18 · **Roasting of beef** *Boeuf rôti*

(a) · **Roast sirloin of beef (on the bone)** *Aloyau de boeuf rôti*

(b) · **Roast boned sirloin of beef** *Contrefilet de boeuf rôti*

(c) · **Roast rib of beef** *Côte de boeuf rôtie*

(d) · **Roast fillet of beef** *Filet de boeuf rôti*

Suitable Joints

First class – Sirloin, wing ribs, fore ribs, fillet.
Second class – Topside, middle ribs.

1 portion provides:

217 kcals/911 kJ
10.3 g fat of which 4.7 g saturated
0.0 g carbohydrate of which 0.0 g sugars
31.2 g protein
0.0 g fibre

1 Season joints with salt, place on a trivet, or bones, in a roasting tray.
2 Place a little dripping or oil on top and cook in a hot oven (230–250 °C).
3 Baste frequently and reduce the heat gradually when necessary, as for example in the case of large joints.
4 Roasting time approx. 15 min per ½ kilo (1 lb) and 15 min over.
5 To test if cooked, place on a tray and press firmly in order to see if the juices released contain any blood.
6 Beef is normally cooked underdone and a little blood should show in the juice which issues when the meat if pressed.
7 On removing the joint from the oven, rest for 15 min to allow the meat to set and facilitate carving, then carve against the grain.

Serve the slices moistened with a little gravy. Garnish with Yorkshire pudding (recipe 17) (allowing 25 g (1 oz) flour per portion) and watercress. Serve separately sauceboats of gravy and horseradish sauce.

Roast gravy Jus rôti

1 Place the roasting tray on the stove over a gentle heat to allow the sediment to settle.
2 Carefully strain off the fat, leaving the sediment in the tray.
3 Return to stove and brown carefully, deglaze with brown stock.
4 Allow to simmer for a few minutes.
5 Correct the seasoning and colour, then strain and skim off all fat.

19 · Boiled silverside, carrots and dumplings

400 g	1 lb	silverside
200 g	8 oz	onions
200 g	8 oz	carrots
100 g	4 oz	suet paste (page 461)

1 portion provides:

254 kcals/1068 kJ
10.1 g fat of which 4.6 g saturated
15.5 g carbohydrate of which 5.5 g sugars
26.3 g protein
2.6 g fibre

1 Soak the meat in cold water to remove excess brine for 1–2 hr.
2 Place in a saucepan and cover with cold water, bring to the boil, skim and simmer 45 mins.
3 Add whole prepared onions and carrots and simmer until cooked.
4 Divide the suet paste into 8 even pieces, lightly mould into balls.
5 Add the dumplings and simmer for a further 15–20 min.
6 Serve by carving the meat across the grain, garnish with carrots, onions and dumplings and moisten with a little of the cooking liquor.

Note It is usual to cook a large joint of silverside (approx. 6 kg (12 lb)), in which case it is necessary to soak it overnight and to allow 25 min per ½ kg (1 lb) plus 25 min.

4 portions

Left: (background) boiled beef French style; (foreground) boiled silverside with carrots, onions and dumplings
Below: (top) boiled beef French style ingredients; (bottom) boiled silverside ingredients

20 · Boiled beef – French style *Boeuf bouilli à la française*

600 g	1 lb 8 oz	thin flank or brisket
		salt, pepper
		1 head celery
200 g	8 oz	leek
		small cabbage
200 g	8 oz	onions
100 g	4 oz	turnips
200 g	8 oz	carrots

This recipe provides:

995 kcals/4178 kJ
28.3 g fat of which 12.5 g saturated
50.4 g carbohydrate of which 49.9 g sugars
137.1 g protein
29.6 g fibre

1 Blanch and refresh the meat.
2 Place in a clean pan and cover with cold water.
3 Bring to the boil and skim, season and allow to simmer.
4 Prepare all the vegetables by tying the celery and leek into bundles and by tying the cabbage to keep it in one piece, and leaving the rest of the vegetables whole.
5 After the meat has simmered for 30 min, add the celery, onions and carrots and continue cooking for 30 min.
6 Add the leek, cabbage and turnips and continue cooking till all is tender, approx. 2–2½ hr in all.
7 Serve by carving the meat in slices against the grain, garnish with the vegetables and a little liquor over the meat.

This dish may be accompanied by pickled gherkins and coarse salt.

4 portions

21 · Brown beef stew *Ragoût de boeuf*

400 g	1 lb	prepared stewing beef
25 g	1 oz	dripping or oil
75 g	3 oz	onions
75 g	3 oz	carrots
25 g	1 oz	flour, white or wholemeal
		1 tablespn tomato purée
750 ml	1½ pt	brown stock
		bouquet garni
		clove of garlic (if desired)
		seasoning

Using sunflower oil
1 portion provides:

216 kcals/907 kJ
11.0 g fat of which 2.9 g saturated
7.7 g carbohydrate of which 2.5 g sugars
21.9 g protein
1.0 g fibre

1 Remove excess sinew and fat from the beef.
2 Cut into 2 cm (1 in) pieces.
3 Fry quickly in hot fat till lightly browned.
4 Add the mirepoix (roughly cut onion and carrot) and continue frying to a golden colour.
5 Add the flour and mix in and singe in the oven or brown on top of the stove for a few minutes, or use previously browned flour.
6 Add the tomato purée and stir in with a wooden spoon.
7 Mix in the stock, bring to the boil and skim.

8 Add the bouquet garni and garlic, season and cover with a lid and simmer gently till cooked, preferably in the oven, approx. 1½–2 hr.
9 When cooked place the meat into a clean pan.
10 Correct the sauce and pass on to the meat.
11 Serve with chopped parsley sprinkled on top of the meat.

22 · **Brown beef stew with vegetables** *Ragoût de boeuf aux légumes*

As above with a garnish of vegetables, that is, turned glazed carrots, turnips and button onions; peas and diamonds of French beans. Mushrooms may also be used. The vegetables are cooked separately and they may be mixed in, arranged in groups or sprinkled on top of the stew.

To cook carrots and turnips glacé (glazed), turn or cut into even shapes, barely cover with water in separate thick-bottomed pans and add 25–50 g (1–2 oz) butter or margarine per ½ kg (1 lb) of vegetables. Season very lightly and allow to cook fairly quickly so as to evaporate the water. Check that the vegetables are cooked, if not add a little more water, then toss over a quick fire to give a glossy appearance and a little colour. Care should be taken with turnips as they may break up easily. This also applies to button onions which may be cooked as above or they may be coloured first in the oil, butter or margarine and then allowed to cook slowly with a little stock or water, in a saucepan with a lid.

Button mushrooms should be used for this purpose, and if of good quality, need not be peeled, but a slice should be removed from the base of the stalk. Wash well, then use whole, halved, quartered or turned, depending on size. Cook in a little stock and butter and season lightly, cover with a lid and cook for a few minutes only.

23 · **Beef stew with red wine sauce** *Ragoût de boeuf au vin rouge*

As for brown stew (recipe 21) using 125–150 ml (¼–½ pt) of red wine in place of the same amount of stock. It may be necessary to add a few drops of cochineal or extra tomato purée to give a typical red wine appearance.

Noodles are often served with beef stew.

24 · **Beef Burgundy style** *Boeuf Bourguignonne*

As brown beef stew (recipe 21) using red wine in place of stock and garnishing with glazed button onions, sautéd button mushrooms and lardons of bacon and heart-shaped croûtons.

Illustrated on page 286.

25 · Beef grills

Approximate weight per portion 100–150 g (4–6 oz); in many establishments these weights will be exceeded.

Rump steak	—
Point steak	—
Double fillet steak	chateaubriand
Fillet steak	filet grillé
Tournedos	tournedos grillé
Porterhouse or T-bone steak	—
Sirloin steak	entrecôte grillée
Double sirloin steak	entrecôte double
Minute steak	entrecôte minute

All steaks are lightly seasoned with salt and pepper and brushed on both sides with oil. Place on hot pre-heated greased grill bars. Turn half-way through the cooking and brush occasionally with oil and cook to the degree ordered by the customer.

Stages involved in grilling steak

Degrees of cooking grilled meats

Rare	au bleu	Just done	à point
Underdone	saignant	Well done	bien cuit

Test with finger pressure and the springiness or resilience of the meat together with the amount of blood issuing from the meat indicates the degree to which the steak is cooked. This calls for experience, but if the meat is placed on a plate and tested, then the more underdone the steak the greater the springiness and the more blood will be shown on the plate.

Serve garnished with watercress, deep-fried potato, e.g. straw potatoes (pommes pailles) and offer a suitable sauce, e.g. parsley butter or sauce béarnaise.

Garnishes for grills

Henry IV	watercress and pommes Pont Neuf
Vert Pré	watercress and pommes pailles

1 portion 100 g cooked weight per portion provides:
168 kcals/706 kJ 6.0 g fat of which 2.7 g saturated 0.0 g carbohydrate of which 0.0 g sugars 28.6 g protein 0.0 g fibre

Grilled T-bone steak

26 · Sirloin steak with mushroom, tomato, tarragon and white wine sauce *Entrecôte chasseur*

Fried sirloin steak with French fried onions (p. 427) sauté potatoes (p. 442) French beans (p. 424) and uncooked and cooked stir-fry (p. 383)

50 g	2 oz	butter or oil
150–200 g	6–8 oz	4 × sirloin steaks
60 ml	⅛ pt	dry white wine
¼ litre	½ pt	chasseur sauce (page 99)
		chopped parsley

1 Heat the butter in a sauté pan
2 Season the steaks on both sides with salt and pepper.
3 Fry the steaks quickly on both sides, keep them underdone.
4 Dress the steaks on a serving dish.
5 Pour off the fat from the pan.
6 Deglaze with the white wine. Reduce by half and strain.
7 Add the chasseur sauce, reboil, correct seasoning.
8 Coat the steaks with the sauce.
9 Sprinkle with chopped parsley and serve.

4 portions

27 · Sirloin steak with red wine sauce *Entrecôte bordelaise*

50 g	2 oz	butter or oil
150–200 g	6–8 oz	4 × sirloin steaks
60 ml	⅛ pt	red wine
¼ litre	½ pt	bordelaise sauce (page 99)
100 g	4 oz	beef bone marrow
		chopped parsley

Using sunflower oil
1 portion (150 g raw steak) provides:

717 kcals/3013 kJ
62.2 g fat of which 21.6 g saturated
6.0 g carbohydrate of which 3.0 g sugars
26.1 g protein
1.4 g fibre

Using sunflower oil
1 portion (200 g raw steak) provides:

853 kcals/3584 kJ
73.6 g fat of which 26.2 g saturated
6.0 g carbohydrate of which 3.0 g sugars
34.4 g protein
1.4 g fibre

1. Heat the butter in a sauté pan.
2. Lightly season the steaks on both sides with salt and pepper.
3. Fry the steaks quickly on both sides, keep them underdone.
4. Dress the steaks on a serving dish
5. Pour off the fat from the pan.
6. Deglaze with the red wine. Reduce by a half and strain.
7. Add the bordelaise sauce, reboil and correct seasoning.
8. Cut the marrow into ½ cm (¼ in) slices.
9. Poach the marrow in a little stock for 1–2 min.
10. Dress two slices of marrow on each steak.
11. Coat the steaks with the sauce.
12. Sprinkle with chopped parsley and serve.

4 portions

28 · Tournedos

Lightly season and shallow fry on both sides in a sauté pan and serve with the appropriate garnish or sauce. It is usual to serve the tournedos cooked underdone on a round croûte of bread fried in butter.

29 · Tournedos *Tournedos bordelaise*

Cook as above and serve bordelaise sauce (page 99).

30 · Tournedos *Tournedos chasseur*

Cook as above and sauce over with chasseur sauce (page 99).

31 · Tournedos *Tournedos aux champignons*

Cook as recipe 28 and sauce over with a mushroom sauce made from ¼ litre (½ pt) demi-glace sauce to which has been added 100 g (4 oz) of sliced button mushrooms cooked in butter.

32 · Tournedos *Tournedos Parmentier*

Cook as recipe 28 and garnish with Parmentier potatoes (page 448) and finish with noisette butter.

33 · Curried beef *Currie ou Kari de boeuf*

Proceed as for Curried lamb on page 256 using 500 g (1 lb 4 oz) stewing beef.

34 · Steak pudding

200 g	8 oz	suet paste (page 461)
400 g	1 lb	prepared stewing beef (chuck rib)
		Worcester sauce
		teaspn chopped parsley
		salt, pepper
50–100 g	2–4 oz	onion (optional)
125 ml	¼ pt	water (approx.)

1 portion provides:

326 kcals/1369 kJ
17.3 g fat of which 7.8 g saturated
20.6 g carbohydrate of which 1.0 g sugars
23.0 g protein
1.1 g fibre

1. Line a greased ¾ litre (1½ pt) basin with three-quarters of the suet paste and retain one-quarter for the top.
2. Mix all the other ingredients together.
3. Place in the basin with the water to within 1 cm (½ in) of top.
4. Moisten the edge of the suet paste, cover with the top and seal firmly.
5. Cover with greased greaseproof paper and also, if possible, a pudding cloth securely tied with string, or foil.
6. Cook in a steamer for at least 3½ hr.
7. Serve with the paper and cloth removed, clean the basin, place on a round flat dish and fasten a serviette round the basin.

Extra gravy should be served separately.

This may also be made with a cooked filling in which case simmer the meat until cooked in brown stock with onions, parsley, Worcester sauce and seasoning. Cool quickly and proceed as before, steaming for 1–1½ hours.

4 portions

35 · Steak and kidney pudding

As for steak pudding with the addition of 50–100 g (2–4 oz) ox kidney, or 1 or 2 sheep's kidneys with the skin and gristle removed and then cut into neat pieces.

36 · Steak, kidney and mushroom pudding

As steak and kidney pudding with the addition of 50–100 g (2–4 oz) washed, sliced or quartered button mushrooms.

37 · Sauté of beef
Sauté de boeuf

Beef Burgundy style (p. 281)

This term is often applied to a brown beef stew, and it will be found that the word 'sauté' in this case is used instead of the word 'ragoût'. Alternatively, a sauté may be made using first-quality meat, e.g. fillet. The meat is then sautéd quickly and served in a finished sauce, this would be a typical à la carte dish.

See Method of Cookery, page 65.

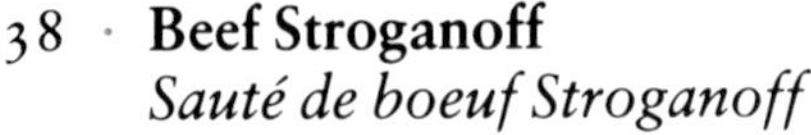

38 · Beef Stroganoff
Sauté de boeuf Stroganoff

400 g	1 lb	fillet of beef (tail end)
50 g	2 oz	butter, margarine or oil
25 g	1 oz	finely chopped shallots
125 ml	¼ pt	dry white wine
125 ml	¼ pt	cream
		juice of ¼ lemon
		chopped parsley

1. Cut the meat into strips approx 1 cm × 5 cm (½ in × 2 in).
2. Place the butter in a sauteuse over a fierce heat.
3. Add the beef strips, season with salt and pepper and allow to cook rapidly for a few seconds. The beef should be brown but underdone.
4. Drain the beef into a colander.
5. Pour the butter back into the pan.
6. Add the shallots, cover with a lid and allow to cook gently until tender.
7. Drain off the fat, add the wine and reduce to one-third.
8. Add the cream and reduce by a quarter.
9. Add the lemon juice and the beef strips – do not re-boil.
10. Correct the seasoning.

> Using sunflower oil
> 1 portion provides:
>
> 325 kcals/1364 kJ
> 23.7 g fat of which 7.9 g saturated
> 1.7 g carbohydrate of which 1.7 g sugars
> 21.2 g protein
> 0.3 g fibre

11 Place in serving dish and sprinkle with chopped parsley.
12 Accompany with rice pilaff (page 201). *4 portions*

39 **Goulash of beef** *Goulash de boeuf*

400 g	1 lb	prepared stewing beef
35 g	1½ oz	lard or oil
100 g	4 oz	onions, chopped
25 g	1 oz	flour
10–25 g	½–1 oz	paprika
25 g	1 oz	tomato purée
750 ml	1½ pt	stock or water (approx.)
		8 turned potatoes or small new potatoes
125 ml	¼ pt	choux paste

1 Remove excess fat from the beef.
2 Cut into 2 cm (1 in) square pieces.
3 Season and fry in the hot fat till slightly coloured.
4 Add the chopped onion.
5 Cover with a lid and sweat gently for 3 or 4 min.
6 Add the flour and paprika and mix in with a wooden spoon.
7 Cook out in the oven or on top of the stove.
8 Add the tomato purée, mix in.
9 Gradually add the stock, stir to the boil, skim, season and cover.
10 Allow to simmer preferably in the oven approx. 1½–2 hr, till the meat is tender.
11 Add the potatoes and check that they are covered with the sauce. (Add more stock if required.)
12 Re-cover with the lid and cook gently till the potatoes are cooked.
13 Skim and correct the seasoning and consistency. A little cream or yoghurt may be added at the last moment.
14 Serve sprinkled with a few gnocchis, reheated in hot salted water or lightly tossed in butter or margarine.

In Hungary this traditional dish is called *gulyas*. *4 portions*

Choux paste for gnocchi (as a garnish, sufficient for 8 portions)

1 Prepare the choux paste following the recipe on page 462 omitting the sugar.
2 Place the mixture into a piping bag with a ½ cm (¼ in) or 1 cm (½ in) plain tube.
3 Pipe into a shallow pan of gently simmering salted water, cutting the mixture into 2 cm (1 in) lengths with a small knife, dipping the knife into the water frequently to prevent sticking.
4 Poach very gently for approx. 10 min. If not required at once lift out carefully into cold water and when required reheat in hot salted water.

40 Steak pie

Method I: with raw filling

400 g	1 lb	prepared stewing beef (chuck rib)
		salt, pepper
		few drops Worcester sauce
		1 teaspn chopped parsley
50–100 g	2–4 oz	chopped onion (optional)
125 ml	¼ pt	water or stock
100 g	4 oz	puff paste or rough puff (page 458, 460)

Using puff paste
1 portion provides:

234 kcals/981 kJ
12.9 g fat of which 5.6 g saturated
8.5 g carbohydrate of which 0.8 g sugars
21.4 g protein
0.6 g fibre

1. Cut the meat into 2 cm square (1 in) strips.
2. Cut into thin slices or into small squares.
3. Mix with the remainder of the ingredients.
4. Place in a ½ litre (1 pt) pie dish with a pie funnel in the centre if the level of the meat is below that of the rim of the dish. The amount of liquid should barely cover the meat.
5. Roll out the pastry, eggwash the rim of the pie dish and line with a 1 cm (½ cm) strip of pastry, press down firmly and eggwash.
6. Without stretching the pastry, cover the pie and seal firmly.
7. Trim off the excess paste with a sharp knife, notch the edge neatly, eggwash and decorate.
8. Allow to rest in a cool place for as long as possible.
9. Place in a hot oven (approx. 220 °C, Reg. 7) for 10–15 min till the paste is set and lightly coloured.
10. Cover with foil and reduce to 190 °C, Reg. 5 for 15 min, then to 160 °C, Reg. 3 for a further 15 min, then to 140 °C, Reg. 1 for 15 min.
11. Complete the cooking at this heat, ensuring that the liquid is simmering in the pie.
12. Allow 2–2½ hr cooking in all.
13. Serve with the pie dish thoroughly cleaned, place on an oval flat dish and surround the pie dish with a pie collar.

Method II: With cooked filling

Prepare the filling as follows:

1. Seal the meat in hot oil in a frying pan.
2. Drain meat in a colander and place in a thick-bottomed pan.
3. Mix in 25 g (1 oz) browned flour, onion, Worcester sauce, parsley, brown stock or water and season.
4. Simmer until cooked, skim and cool.
5. Cover with short, puff or rough pastry.

6 Bake at 200 °C, Reg. 6 for approximately 30–40 minutes.
7 25–50% wholemeal flour may be used in place of plain flour if using short pastry.

4 portions

41 Steak and kidney pie

As for steak pie with the addition of 50–100 g (2–4 oz) ox kidney or 1 or 2 sheep's kidneys with skin and gristle removed and cut into neat pieces.

42 Steak, kidney and mushroom pie

As for steak and kidney pie with the addition of 50–100 g (2–4 oz) washed sliced or quartered button mushrooms.

43 Carbonnade of beef *Carbonnade de boeuf*

400 g	1 lb	lean beef (e.g. topside)
25 g	1 oz	flour, white or wholemeal
25 g	1 oz	dripping or oil
200 g	8 oz	sliced onions
250 ml	½ pt	beer
10 g	½ oz	castor sugar
25 g	1 oz	tomato purée
500 ml	1 pt	brown stock (approx.)

1 Cut meat into thin slices.
2 Season with salt and pepper and pass through flour.
3 Quickly colour on both sides in hot fat and place in a casserole.
4 Fry the onions to a light brown colour. Add to the meat.
5 Add the beer, sugar and tomato purée and sufficient brown stock to cover the meat.
6 Cover with a tight-fitting lid and simmer gently in a moderate oven (150–200 °C, Reg. 2–6) till the meat is tender. Approx. 2 hr.
7 Skim, correct the seasoning and serve.

44 · Braised steaks

400 g	1 lb	stewing beef
25 g	1 oz	fat or oil
75 g	3 oz	onions
75 g	3 oz	carrots
25 g	1 oz	flour, browned in the oven
25 g	1 oz	tomato purée
750 ml	1½ pt	brown stock
		bouquet garni
		clove of garlic (if desired)
		seasoning

1 Remove excess sinew and fat from the beef.
2 Cut into ½–1 cm (¼–½ in) thick steaks.
3 Fry quickly in hot fat till lightly browned.
4 Add the mirepoix (roughly cut onion and carrot) and continue frying to a golden colour. Mix in the flour.
5 Add the tomato purée and stir in with a wooden spoon.
6 Mix in the stock, bring to the boil and skim.
7 Add the bouquet garni and garlic, season and cover with a lid and simmer gently till cooked, preferably in the oven, approx. 1½–2 hr.
8 When cooked place the meat into a clean pan.
9 Correct the sauce and pass on to the meat.
10 Serve in an entrée dish with chopped parsley.
11 Braised steaks may be garnished with vegetables cut in macédoine or jardinière, or turned or cut in neat, even pieces.

45 · Braised beef *Boeuf braisé*

400 g	1 lb	lean beef (topside or thick flank)
25 g	1 oz	fat or oil
100 g	4 oz	onions
100 g	4 oz	carrots
500 ml	1 pt	brown stock
		bouquet garni
25 g	1 oz	tomato purée
250 ml	½ pt	espagnole

Using sunflower oil
1 portion provides:

329 kcals/1380 kJ
14.3 g fat of which 3.3 g saturated
26.8 g carbohydrate of which 4.7 g sugars
24.7 g protein
2.4 g fibre

Method I

1 Trim and tie the joint securely.
2 Season and colour quickly on all sides in hot fat to seal the pores.
3 Place into a small braising pan (any pan with a tight-fitting lid which may be placed in the oven) or in a casserole.
4 Place the joint on the lightly fried, sliced vegetables.
5 Add the stock, which should be two-thirds of the way up the meat, season lightly.

Above: ingredients for braised beef;
Below: larding in preparation for braising

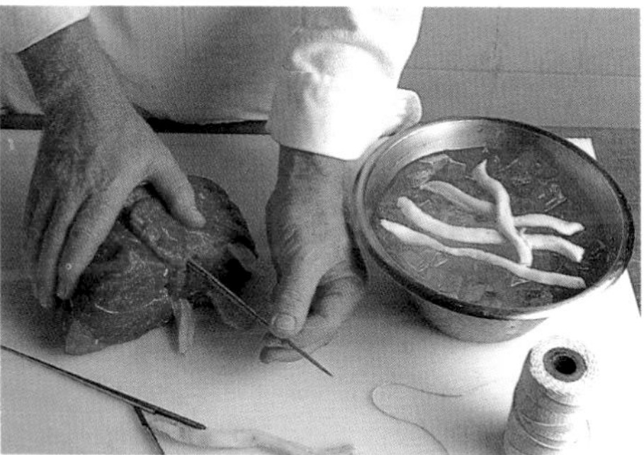

Plated service of braised beef with noodles (p. 196) and courgettes (p. 421); top: ratatouille (p. 411) and joint of braised beef

6 Add the bouquet garni and tomato purée and if available add a few mushroom trimmings.
7 Bring to the boil, skim and cover with a lid and cook in a moderate oven (150–200 °C, Reg. 2–6).
8 After approx. 1½ hr cooking remove the meat.
9 Add the espagnole, re-boil, skim and strain.
10 Replace the meat, do not cover, but baste frequently and continue cooking approx. 2–2½ hr in all. Braised beef should be well cooked and approx. 35 min per ½ kg (1 lb) plus 35 min may be allowed. To test if cooked, pierce with a trussing needle, which should penetrate the meat easily and there should be no sign of blood.
11 Remove the joint and correct the colour, seasoning and consistency of the sauce.
12 To serve: remove the string and carve slices across the grain.

Pour some of the sauce over the slices and serve the remainder of the sauce in a sauceboat.

Suitable garnishes, spring vegetables (see page 281, recipe 22), or noodles (page 196).

Method II

As for Method I, but use for cooking liquor either

a) jus-lié or
b) half brown stock and half demi-glace or espagnole.

Method III

As for Method I, but when the joint and vegetables are browned sprinkle with 25 g (1 oz) flour and singe in the oven, add the tomato purée and stock, bouquet garni, season and complete the recipe.

4 portions

46 Braised steak and dumplings

1 Cut the beef into ½–1 cm (¼–½ in) thick steaks and proceed as for brown beef stew, page 280.
2 Prepare 100 g (4 oz) suet paste (page 461) and make 8 dumplings.
3 After the meat has cooked for 1½ hr pick out the meat and place into a clean pan.
4 Strain the sauce on to the meat.
5 Re-boil and correct the seasoning and consistency, which should be fairly thin and sufficient to cover the dumplings.
6 When boiling add the dumplings, cover with a lid.
7 Complete cooking, preferably in the oven ¾–1 hr (150–200 °C, Reg. 2–6). Alternatively, the dumplings can be cooked gently in simmering salted water, approx. 20 min., drained and served with the braised steak.
8 Skim off all fat and serve.

4 portions

47 Beef olives *Paupiettes de boeuf*

50 g	2 oz	stuffing
400 g	1 lb	lean beef
35 g	1½ oz	fat or oil
100 g	4 oz	carrot
100 g	4 oz	onion
25 g	1 oz	flour (browned in the oven)
25 g	1 oz	tomato purée
500–750 ml	1–1½ pt	brown stock
		bouquet garni

1 Prepare the stuffing (page 293).
2 Cut the meat into thin slices across the grain and bat out.
3 Trim to approx. 10×8 cm (4×3 in), chop the trimmings finely and add to the stuffing.

4 Season the slices of meat lightly with salt and pepper and spread a quarter of the stuffing down the centre of each slice.
5 Roll up neatly and secure with string.
6 Fry off the meat to a light brown colour add the mirepoix and continue cooking to a golden colour.
7 Drain off the fat into a clean pan and make up to 25 g (1 oz) fat if there is not enough. Mix in the flour.
8 Mix in the tomato purée, cool, and mix in the boiling stock.
9 Bring to the boil, skim, season and pour on to the meat.
10 Add the bouquet garni.
11 Cover and simmer gently, preferably in the oven, approx. 1½–2 hr.
12 Remove the string from the meat.
13 Skim and correct the sauce and pass on to the meat.

4 portions

Stuffing

50 g	2 oz	white or wholemeal breadcrumbs
		1 teaspn chopped parsley
		pinch of thyme
		approx ½ egg to bind
5 g	¼ oz	prepared chopped suet
25 g	1 oz	finely chopped sweated onion
		salt, pepper

Mix all the ingredients together with the chopped meat trimmings. Other stuffings may be used, for example, sausage meat.

4 portions

48 **Minced beef** *Hachis de boeuf*

50–100 g	2–4 oz	chopped onion
25 g	1 oz	butter, margarine or oil
300 g	12 oz	lean minced beef
		jus-lié or stock
250 ml	½ pt	demi-glace
		seasoning

Method I: Using raw minced beef

1 Sweat the onion in the fat or oil.
2 Add the beef and cook to a light colour.
3 Add the liquid, season.
4 Bring to the boil, skim and simmer gently till cooked, approx. ½ hr.

If using stock, thickening may be added by either adding
a) 10 g (½ oz) flour after cooking the meat and before adding the stock or
b) by finishing with approx. 5 g (¼ oz) of diluted cornflour or fécule.

Method II: Using cooked beef

Sweat the onion in the dripping and add the minced cooked beef, add the demi-glace or jus-lié, bring to the boil and skim, season and boil for 10 min.

To aid presentation, minced beef may be served with a border of piped duchess potatoes. Additions to this recipe may include cooked sweetcorn, peas, tomatoes and herbs.

4 portions

49 · Hamburg or Vienna steak *Bitok*

25 g	1 oz	finely chopped onion
10 g	½ oz	butter, margarine or oil
200 g	½ lb	lean minced beef
		1 small egg
100 g	4 oz	breadcrumbs
		2 tablespns cold water or milk (approx.)
		salt and pepper

1 portion provides:

162 kcals/681 kJ
6.7 g fat of which 1.9 g saturated
12.7 g carbohydrate of which 1.0 g sugars
13.8 g protein
1.0 g fibre

1. Cook the onion in the fat without colour then allow to cool.
2. Add to the rest of the ingredients and mix in well.
3. Divide into four even pieces and using a little flour make into balls, flatten and shape round.
4. Shallow fry in hot fat on both sides, reducing the heat after the first few minutes, making certain they are cooked right through.
5. Serve with a demi-glace based sauce, e.g. sauce piquante (page 102). The steaks may be garnished with French fried onions (page 427) and sometimes with a fried egg.

4 portions

50 · Hamburger American style

The hamburger was originally made using 200 g (8 oz) of minced beef per portion, moulded into a round flat shape and cooked on both sides on a lightly greased hot griddle grill or pan. The hamburger should not be pricked whilst cooking as the juices would seep out leaving a dry product. In its simplest form when cooked it is placed between two halves of a freshly toasted round flat bun.

There are many variations to the seasonings and ingredients which may be added to the minced beef, and many garnishes and sauces may accompany the hamburger. The bun may be plain or seeded (sesame seed).

51 · Croquettes of beef *Croquettes de boeuf*

50 g	2 oz	butter or margarine
50 g	2 oz	flour
250 ml	½ pt	stock
200 g	8 oz	minced cooked meat
		seasoning
		1 yolk
		flour
		eggwash
		breadcrumbs

1. Make a thick sauce with the butter or margarine, flour and stock (or use demi-glace).
2. Add the meat and bring to the boil.
3. Season, add the yolk and bring back to boiling point, stirring continuously.
4. Spread on a greased tray and cover with greased paper and allow to cool.
5. Divide into even pieces (four or eight).
6. Roll into approx. 5 cm (2 in) lengths.
7. Flour, egg and crumb and reshape and deep fry (180 °C).
8. Serve with a suitable sauce, e.g. tomato (page 106), piquant (page 102).

Note It may be necessary to egg and crumb twice to ensure that the filling is well enclosed.

4 portions

52 · Tripe and onions

400 g	1 lb	tripe
500 ml	1 pt	milk and water
200 g	8 oz	onions
		salt, pepper
25 g	1 oz	flour or cornflour

1. Wash the tripe well. Cut into neat 5 cm (2 in) squares.
2. Blanch and refresh.
3. Cook the tripe in the milk and water with the sliced onions.
4. Season and simmer 1½–2 hr.
5. Gradually add the diluted flour or cornflour, stir with a wooden spoon to the boil.
6. Simmer for 5–10 min, correct the seasoning and serve.

An alternative thickening is 125 ml (¼ pt) of béchamel in place of the cornflour and milk.

4 portions

53 · **Miroton of beef** *Emincé de boeuf en miroton*

200 g	8 oz	piece of cooked beef
50 g	2 oz	onion
25 g	1 oz	butter or margarine
		dessertspn vinegar
		2 tablespns dry white wine
250 ml	½ pt	demi-glace

1. Cut the beef into thin slices.
2. Place in a shallow earthenware dish.
3. Fry the shredded onion in the butter or margarine till cooked and a golden colour.
4. Drain off the fat.
5. Add the vinegar and wine and reduce by half.
6. Add the demi-glace, bring to the boil.
7. Skim and season.
8. Correct the consistency and pour over the meat.
9. Allow to heat through for a few minutes on top of the stove or in the oven.
10. Do not allow to boil as this will toughen the fibres, hardening the protein and making the meat difficult to digest.
11. Sprinkle with chopped parsley and serve.

4 portions

54 · **Ox tongue** *Langue de boeuf*

Ox tongues are usually pickled in brine. Wash and place in cold water, bring to the boil, skim and simmer 3–4 hr. Cool slightly and peel off the skin and trim off the root. Secure into a neat shape either on a board or in a wooden frame. Unsalted ox tongues may also be braised whole.

55 · **Braised ox tongue with Madeira sauce** *Langue de boeuf braisée au Madère*

Cut the cooked tongue in 3 mm (⅛ in) thick slices and arrange neatly in an entrée dish. Sauce over with Madeira sauce (page 101) and allow to heat through slowly and thoroughly.

56 · **Braised ox liver and onions** *Foie de boeuf lyonnaise*

300 g	12 oz	liver
25 g	1 oz	flour, white or wholemeal
50 g	2 oz	fat or oil
200 g	½ lb	onions
500 ml	1 pt	brown stock
25 g	1 oz	tomato purée
		bouquet garni
		1 clove garlic

1. Prepare the liver by removing the skin and tubes then cut into slices.
2. Pass the sliced liver through seasoned flour.
3. Fry on both sides in hot fat.
4. Place in a braising pan or casserole.
5. Fry the sliced onion to a golden brown, drain and add to the liver.
6. Just cover with the stock and add the tomato purée, bouquet garni and garlic.
7. Season and cover with a lid.
8. Simmer gently in the oven till tender approx. 1½–2 hr.
9. Correct the sauce and serve.

4 portions

57 · **Stewed ox kidney**

400 g	1 lb	ox kidney
25 g	1 oz	fat or oil
75 g	3 oz	onions
75 g	3 oz	carrots
25 g	1 oz	flour, browned in the oven
25 g	1 oz	tomato purée
750 ml	1½ pt	brown stock
		bouquet garni
		clove of garlic (if desired)
		seasoning

1. Remove excess sinew and fat from the kidney.
2. Cut into 2 cm (1 in) pieces.
3. Fry quickly in hot fat till lightly browned.
4. Add the mirepoix (roughly cut onion and carrot) and continue frying to a golden colour. Mix in the flour.
5. Add the tomato purée and stir in with a wooden spoon.
6. Add the stock, bring to the boil and skim.
7. Add the bouquet garni and garlic, season and cover with a lid and simmer gently till cooked, preferably in the oven, approx. 1½–2 hr.
8. When cooked place the kidney into a clean pan.
9. Correct the sauce and pass on to the kidney.
10. Serve with chopped parsley sprinkled on top of the kidney.

58 · **Stewed oxtail** *Ragoût de queue de boeuf*

1 kg	2 lb	oxtail
50 g	2 oz	fat or oil
100 g	4 oz	onion
100 g	4 oz	carrot
35 g	1½ oz	flour, browned in the oven
25 g	25 g	tomato purée
1 litre	2 pt	brown stock
		bouquet garni
		1 clove garlic
		salt and pepper

1. Cut the oxtail into sections. Remove excess fat.
2. Fry on all sides in hot fat.
3. Place in a braising pan or casserole.
4. Add the fried mirepoix (roughly cut onion and carrot).
5. Mix in the flour.
6. Add tomato purée, brown stock, bouquet garni, garlic, and season.
7. Bring to the boil, skim.
8. Cover with a lid and simmer in the oven till tender, approx. 3 hr.
9. Remove the meat from the sauce, place in a clean pan.
10. Correct the sauce and pass on to the meat and re-boil.
11. Serve sprinkled with chopped parsley.

This dish, also known as braised oxtail, is usually garnished with glazed turned or neatly cut carrots and turnips, button onions, peas and diamonds of beans. Oxtail must be very well cooked so that the meat comes away easily from the bone.

4 portions

59 · **Haricot oxtail** *Ragoût de queue de boeuf aux haricots blancs*

As for previous recipe with the addition of 100 g (4 oz) cooked haricot beans, added approx. ½ hr before the oxtail has completed cooking.

Escalopes of veal Viennoise (p. 310) showing two methods of serving

13

TENUTA DI
POMINO
1987
POMINO
Marchesi de' FRESCOBALDI
ITALIA
FLAT FILLETS OF ANCHOVIES

VEAL

General objectives	*Specific objectives*
To know the use of veal in the kitchen and to understand its use on the menu.	To state the quality points and list the joints and cuts with approximate weights. To describe and demonstrate the correct butchery of veal, methods of cookery and presentation of dishes with suitable accompaniments and garnishes paying due attention to details of standards and economy.

Butchery

1 · **Veal** *Veau*

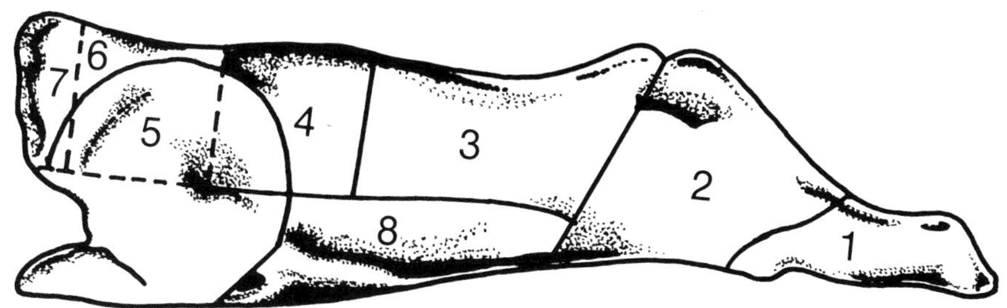

2 Joints, uses and weights

Joint	French	Uses	Approx. Weight (kilo)	(lb)
1 Knuckle	le jarret	Osso buco, sauté, stock	2	4
2 Leg	le cuissot	Roasting, braising, escalopes, sauté	5	10
3 Loin	la longe	Roasting, frying, grilling	3½	7
4 Best-end	le carré	Roasting, frying, grilling	3	6
5 Shoulder	l'épaule (f.)	Braising, stewing	5	10
6 Neck-end	—	Stewing, sauté	2½	5
7 Scrag	le cou	Stewing stock	1½	3
8 Breast	la poitrine	Stewing, roasting	2½	5
Kidneys	les rognons (m.)	Stewing (pies and puddings), sauté	—	—
Liver	le foie	Frying	—	—
Sweetbreads	le ris	Braising, frying	—	—
Head	la tête	Boiling, soup	4	8
Brains	la cervelle	Boiling, frying	—	—
Bones	les os (m.)	Used for stock	—	—

3 Joints of the leg

Average weight of English or Dutch milk fed – 18 kg (36 lb).

Cuts – English	French	Weight	Proportion of leg	Uses
Cushion or nut	noix	2.75 kg (5½ lb)	15%	Escalopes, roasting, braising, sauté
Under cushion or under nut	soux-noix	3 kg (6 lb)	17%	Escalopes, roasting, braising, sauté
Thick flank	gîte à la noix	2.5 kg (5 lb)	14%	Escalopes, roasting, braising, sauté
Knuckle (whole)	jarret	2.5 kg (5 lb)	14%	Osso buco, sauté
Bones (thigh and aitch)		2.5 kg (5 lb)	14%	Stock, jus-lié
Usable trimmings		2 kg (4 lb)	11%	Pies, stewing, Pojarski
Skin and fat		2.75 kg (5½ lb)	15%	

Corresponding joints in beef

Cushion = topside
Under cushion = silverside
Thick flank = thick flank

Dissection of leg of veal

1 Remove knuckle by dividing knee joint (A) and cut through the meat away from the cushion-line A–B.
2 Remove aitch bone (C) at thick end of leg separating it at the ball and socket joint.
3 Remove all outside skin and fat thus exposing the natural seams. It will now be seen that the thigh bone divides the meat into 2/3 and 1/3 (thick flank).

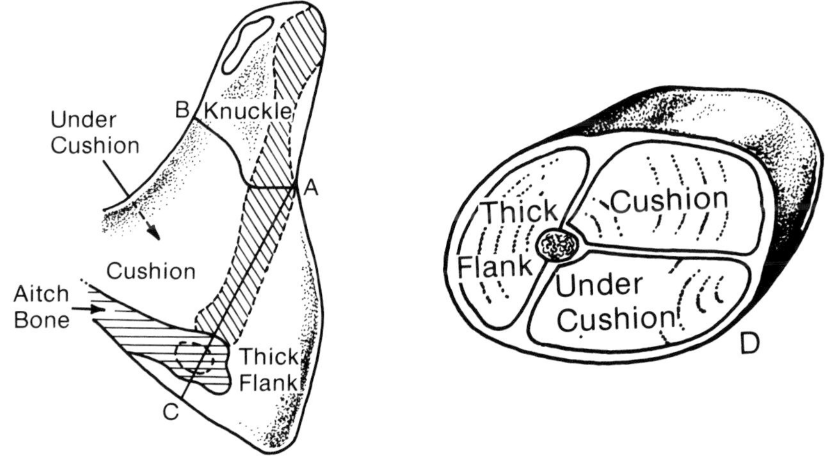

4 Stand the leg on the thick flank with point D uppermost. Divide the cushion from the under-cushion, following the natural seam, using the hand and the point of a knife. Having reached the thigh bone, remove it completely.
5 Allowing the boned leg to fall open the 3 joints can easily be seen joined only by membrane. Separate and trim the cushion removing the loose flap of meat.
6 Trim the undercushion removing the layer of thick gristle. Separate into 3 small joints through the natural seams. It will be seen that one of these will correspond with the round in silverside of beef.
7 Trim the thick flank by laying it on its round side and making a cut along the length about 1 in deep. A seam is reached and the two trimmings can be removed.

The anticipated yield of escalopes from this size leg would be 220 ounces, i.e. 55×4 oz or 73×3 oz.

4 · Quality of veal

1. Veal is available all the year round, but is best from May to September.
2. The flesh should be pale pink in colour.
3. The flesh should be firm in structure, not soft or flabby.
4. Cut surfaces should be slightly moist, not dry.
5. Bones, in young animals, should be pinkish white, porous and with a degree of blood in their structure.
6. The fat should be firm and pinkish white.
7. The kidney should be hard and well covered with fat.

5 · Order of dissection

1. Remove the shoulders.
2. Remove the breast.
3. Take off the leg.
4. Divide the loin and best-end from the scrag and neck-end.
5. Divide the loin from the best-end.

6 · Preparation of the joints and cuts of veal

Shin

Stewing (on the bone) – osso buco Cut and saw into 2–4 cm (1–1½ in) thick slices through the knuckle.
Sauté Bone-out and trim and cut into even 25 g (1 oz) pieces.

Leg

Braising or roasting whole Remove the aitch bone, clean and trim 4 cm (1½ in) off the knuckle bone. Trim off excess sinew.
Braising or roasting the noix, sous-noix or quasi Remove the sinew and if there is insufficient fat on the joint then bard thinly and secure with string.
Escalopes Remove all sinew and cut into large 50–75 g (2–3 oz) slices against the grain and bat out thinly.
Sauté Remove all sinew and cut into 25 g (1 oz) pieces.

Loin *and* Best-end

Roasting Bone-out and trim the flap, roll out and secure with string. This joint may be stuffed before rolling.
Frying Trim and cut into cutlets (côte de veau).

Shoulder

Braising Boned-out as for lamb and usually stuffed (page 313).
Stewing Bone-out, remove all sinew and cut into 25 g (1 oz) pieces.

Neck-end *and* Scrag

Stewing and sauté Bone-out and remove all sinew and cut into approx. 25 g (1 oz) pieces.

Breast

Stewing As for neck-end.
Roasting Bone-out, season, stuff and roll up then tie with string.

Kidneys

Remove the fat and skin and cut down the middle lengthwise. Remove sinew and cut into thin slices or neat dice.

Liver

Skin if possible, remove gristle and cut into thin slices on the slant.

Sweetbreads

Wash well, blanch and trim.

Head

1 Bone-out by making a deep incision down the middle of the head to the nostrils.
2 Follow the bone carefully and remove all the flesh in one piece.
3 Lastly remove the tongue.
4 Wash the flesh well and keep covered in acidulated water.
5 Wash off, blanch and refresh.
6 Cut into 2–5 cm (1–2 in) squares.
7 Cut off the ears and trim the inside of the cheek.

Brains

Using a chopper or saw, remove the top of the skull, making certain that the opening is large enough to remove the brain undamaged. Soak the brains in running cold water, then remove the membrane, or skin and wash well to remove all blood. Keep in cold salted water till required.

Recipes

7 · **Brown veal stew** *Ragoût de veau, Sauté de veau*

Proceed as for Brown beef stew recipe, page 280, using veal in place of beef and allowing 1–1½ hours cooking time.

8 · **White stew of veal** *Blanquette de veau*

Proceed as for White lamb stew recipe, page 259, using 400 g (1 lb) prepared stewing veal.

9 · **Fricassée of veal** *Fricassée de veau*

400 g	1 lb	boned stewing veal (shoulder or breast)
35 g	1½ oz	margarine or butter
25 g	1 oz	flour
500 ml	1 pt	white veal stock
		salt, pepper
		1 egg yolk
		2–3 tablespns cream (dairy or vegetable)
		few drops of lemon juice

Using butter
1 portion provides:

236 kcals/992 kJ
13.6 g fat of which 7.5 g saturated
5.3 g carbohydrate of which 0.4 g sugars
23.3 g protein
0.2 g fibre

1. Trim the meat. Cut into even 25 g (1 oz) pieces.
2. Set the meat gently in the butter without colour in a sauté pan.
3. Mix in the flour with a wooden spoon and cook out without colour.
4. Allow to cool.
5. Gradually add boiling stock just to cover the meat, stir till smooth.
6. Season, bring to the boil, skim.
7. Cover and simmer gently on the stove till tender, 1½–2 hr.
8. Pick out the meat into a clean pan.
9. Correct the sauce.
10. Pass on to the meat and re-boil.
11. Mix the yolk and cream in a basin.
12. Add a little of the boiling sauce, mix in and pour back on to the meat, shaking the pan till thoroughly mixed; do not re-boil.
13. Add the lemon juice.
14. Serve in an entrée dish, finished with chopped parsley and heart-shaped croûtons fried in butter or oil.

10 · **White veal stew with button onion and mushrooms** *Fricassée de veau à l'ancienne*

Proceed as in recipe 9, after one hour's cooking pick out the meat, strain the sauce back on to the meat, add 8 small button onions, simmer for 15 min, add 8 small white button mushrooms, washed and peeled if necessary, then complete the cooking. Finish and serve as in recipe 9.

11 · Braised veal *Noix de veau braisée*

100 g	4 oz	carrots
100 g	4 oz	onions
25 g	1 oz	fat or oil
400 g	1 lb	cushion or nut of veal
25 g	1 oz	tomato purée
		bouquet garni
250 ml	½ pt	brown veal stock
250 ml	½ pt	jus-lié

1. Slice carrots and onions thickly.
2. Fry lightly and place in a braising pan.
3. Trim and tie the joint with string and fry quickly on all sides.
4. Place on the bed of roots.
5. Add the tomato purée, bouquet garni, stock, jus-lié, mushroom trimmings if available. Season lightly.
6. Bring to the boil, skim, cover with a lid and cook gently in a moderate oven (150–200 °C, Reg. 2–6) for 1 hr.
7. Remove the lid and continue cooking with the lid off for a further 30 min basting frequently.
8. Remove the joint from the sauce, take off the strings.
9. Correct the colour, consistency and seasoning of the sauce.
10. Pass through a fine chinois.
11. Carve in slices against the grain.
12. Pour some of the sauce over the slices and serve a sauceboat of sauce separately.

For larger joints allow 30–35 min per ½ kg (1 lb) plus 35 min (approx.) cooking time. 125 ml (¼ pt) red wine may replace the same amount of jus-lié. Noodles are often served with this dish. *4 portions*

12 · Hot veal and ham pie

100 g	4 oz	bacon rashers
400 g	1 lb	stewing veal without bone
		1 chopped or quartered hard-boiled egg
		1 teaspn chopped parsley
50 g	2 oz	chopped onion
		salt, pepper
250 ml	½ pt	stock (white)
100 g	4 oz	rough puff or puff paste (pages 456–8)

1 portion provides:

332 kcals/1394 kJ
20.7 g fat of which 8.1 g saturated
8.9 g carbohydrate of which 0.8 g sugars
27.9 g protein
0.7 g fibre

1. Bat out bacon thinly and line the bottom and sides of a ½ litre (1 pt) pie dish, leaving two or three pieces for the top.
2. Trim the veal, cut into small pieces and mix with the egg, parsley and onion. Season and place in the pie dish.
3. Just cover with stock. Add the rest of the bacon.
4. Cover and cook as for steak pie (page 288) allowing approx. 1½ hr cooking. *4 portions*

13 · Veal olives *Paupiettes de veau*

50 g	2 oz	stuffing
400 g	1 lb	lean veal
35 g	1 ½ oz	fat or oil
100 g	4 oz	onion } mirepoix
100 g	4 oz	carrot } mirepoix
25 g	1 oz	flour, white or wholemeal
25 g	1 oz	tomato purée
500–750 ml	1–1 ½ pt	brown veal stock
		bouquet garni
		1 clove garlic (optional)

1. Prepare the stuffing as on page 313.
2. Cut the meat into thin slices across the grain and bat out.
3. Trim to approx. 10×8 cm (4×3 in), chop the trimmings finely and add to the stuffing.
4. Season the slices of meat with salt and pepper and spread a quarter of the stuffing down the centre of each slice.
5. Roll up neatly and secure with string.
6. Fry off the meat to a light brown colour, add the mirepoix and continue cooking to a golden colour.
7. Drain off the fat into a clean pan and make up to 25 g (1 oz) fat if there is not enough.
8. Add the flour and cook to a brown roux, or use pre-browned flour.
9. Mix in the tomato purée, cool, and mix in the boiling stock.
10. Bring to the boil, skim, season and pour on to the meat and vegetables. Add the bouquet garni and the garlic.
11. Cover with a lid and allow to simmer gently, preferably in the oven, approx. 1½–2 hr. Remove the string from the meat.
12. Skim and correct the sauce, pass on to the meat and serve.
13. Suitable garnishes – noodles or rice pilaff (page 201).

14 · Grilled veal cutlet *Côte de veau grillée*

1. Season the prepared chop with salt and mill pepper.
2. Brush with oil. Place on previously heated grill bars.
3. Cook on both sides for 8–10 min in all.
4. Brush occasionally to prevent the meat from drying up.
5. Serve with watercress, a deep-fried potato and a suitable sauce or butter, e.g. béarnaise or parsley butter.

> Using sunflower oil
> 1 portion provides:
>
> 236 kcals/990 kJ
> 9.7 g fat of which 2.6 g saturated
> 0.0 g carbohydrate of which 0.0 g sugars
> 36.9 g protein
> 0.0 g fibre

15 Fried veal cutlet *Côte de veau sautée*

Season and cook in a sauté pan, in clarified butter or oil and butter, on both sides for 8–10 min in all. Chops must be started in hot fat, the heat reduced to allow the meat to cook through.

Serve with a suitable garnish, e.g. jardinière or braised celery and finish with a cordon of jus-lié.

16 Crumbed veal cutlet *Côte de veau panée*

Cook as for previous recipe and finish with beurre noisette, a cordon of jus-lié and a suitable garnish, e.g. napolitaine, fleuriste.

17 Braised stuffed shoulder of veal *Epaule de veau farcie*

100 g	4 oz	onion
100 g	4 oz	carrot
25 g	1 oz	fat or oil
400 g	1 lb	shoulder of veal (boned)
50 g	2 oz	tomato purée
250 ml	½ pt	brown veal stock
		bouquet garni
250 ml	½ pt	jus-lié or demi-glace
		1 clove garlic, crushed

Using sunflower oil
1 portion provides:

196 kcals/824 kJ
9.0 g fat of which 1.9 g saturated
5.0 g carbohydrate of which 4.1 g sugars
24.0 g protein
1.1 g fibre

1 Bone-out the shoulder, season, stuff (recipe 29) and secure with string. Cook and serve as for braised veal (recipe 11).
2 For larger joints allow 30–35 min per ½ kg (1 lb) plus 35 min (approx.) cooking time.

Note A whole shoulder may serve from 8 portions depending on size.

4 portions

18 Braised stuffed breast of veal *Poitrine de veau farcie*

Prepare and cook as for stuffed shoulder.

19 Roast leg of veal *Cuissot de veau rôti*

Whole or in joints.

In order to increase the flavour it is usual to roast on a bed of root vegetables with a sprig of thyme or rosemary. Baste frequently and allow approx. 25 min per ½ kilo (1 lb) plus 25 min over. There should be no sign of blood when cooked. Prepare the roast gravy from the sediment and thicken slightly with a little arrowroot or cornflour diluted with water.

Serve the slices, carved against the grain, dress neatly with thin slices of ham and veal stuffing (recipe 29). Lightly cover with gravy and garnish with watercress and a sauceboat of gravy separately.

20 · **Escalope of veal** *Escalope de veau*

400 g	1 lb	nut or cushion of veal
25 g	1 oz	seasoned flour
		1 egg
50 g	2 oz	breadcrumbs
50 g	2 oz	oil } for frying
50 g	2 oz	butter } for frying
50 g	2 oz	beurre noisette

Fried in sunflower oil, butter to finish
1 portion provides:

495 kcals/2079 kJ
39.8 g fat of which 11.4 g saturated
10.3 g carbohydrate of which 0.5 g sugars
24.7 g protein
1.0 g fibre

1 Trim and remove all sinew from the veal.
2 Cut into four even slices and bat out thinly using a little water.
3 Flour, egg and crumb. Shake off surplus crumbs.
4 Mark with a palette knife.
5 Place the escalopes into shallow hot fat and cook quickly for a few minutes on each side.
6 Dress on a serving dish or plate.
7 Pour over 50 g (2 oz) beurre noisette (nut-brown butter).
8 Finish with a cordon of jus-lié (page 105).

4 portions

21 · **Escalope of veal viennoise** *Escalope de veau viennoise*

As recipe 20.

Garnish the dish with chopped yolk, white of egg and chopped parsley. On top of each escalope place a slice of peeled lemon decorated with chopped egg yolk, egg white and parsley, an anchovy fillet and a stoned olive. Finish with a little lemon juice and beurre noisette.

Two methods of serving escalopes of veal Viennoise

22 · **Veal esclalope Holstein** *Escalope de veau Holstein*

1 Prepare and cook the escalopes as for recipe 20.
2 Each escalope should then have added an egg fried in butter or oil.
3 Place two neat fillets of anchovy criss-crossed on each egg and serve.

23 Escalope of veal with spaghetti and tomato sauce *Escalope de veau napolitaine*

Cook and serve the escalopes as for recipe 20, and garnish with spaghetti napolitaine (page 193) allowing 10 g (½ oz) spaghetti per portion. (Wholemeal spaghetti may be used.)

24 Veal escalope cordon bleu *Escalope de veau cordon bleu*

400 g	1 lb	nut or cushion of veal
		4 slices of cooked ham
		4 slices of Gruyère cheese
25 g	1 oz	seasoned flour
		1 egg
50 g	2 oz	breadcrumbs
50 g	2 oz	oil } for frying
50 g	2 oz	butter } for frying
50 g	2 oz	butter } for finishing
60 ml	⅛ pt	jus-lié (page 105) } for finishing

Fried in sunflower oil, butter to finish
1 portion provides:

627 kcals/2632 kJ
48.1 g fat of which 16.3 g saturated
12.0 g carbohydrate of which 1.3 g sugars
37.1 g protein
0.7 g fibre

1 Trim and remove all sinew from the veal.
2 Cut into eight even slices and bat out thinly using a little water.
3 Place a slice of ham and a slice of cheese on to four of the veal slices, cover with the remaining four slices and press firmly together.
4 Flour, egg and crumb. Shake off all surplus crumbs.
5 Mark on one side with a palette knife.
6 Place the escalopes marked side down into shallow hot fat and cook quickly for a few minutes on each side, until golden brown.
7 Serve coated with nut-brown butter (beurre noisette) and a cordon of jus-lié.

4 portions

Note Veal escalopes may be cooked plain (not crumbed) in which case they are only slightly battened.

25 Veal escalope with Madeira *Escalope de veau au Madère*

50 g	2 oz	butter or margarine
25 g	1 oz	seasoned flour
		4 veal escalopes (slightly battened)
30 ml	1/16 pt	Madeira
125 ml	¼ pt	demi-glace

1 Heat the butter in a sauté pan.
2 Lightly flour the escalopes. Fry to a light brown on both sides.
3 Drain off the fat from the pan. Deglaze with the Madeira.
4 Add the demi-glace and bring to the boil.
5 Correct the seasoning and consistency.
6 Pass through a fine chinois on to the escalopes and serve.

Note In place of Madeira, sherry or Marsala may be used.

4 portions

26 · Veal escalope with cream *Escalope de veau à la crème*

50 g	2 oz	butter or margarine
25 g	1 oz	seasoned flour
		4 veal escalopes (slightly battened)
30 ml	1/16 pt	sherry or white wine
125 ml	1/4 pt	double cream
		salt, cayenne

1 Heat the butter in a sauté pan.
2 Lightly flour the escalopes.
3 Cook the escalopes gently on both sides with the minimum of colour. They should be a delicate light brown.
4 Place the escalopes in an earthenware serving dish, cover and keep warm.
5 Drain off all fat from the pan.
6 Deglaze the pan with the sherry.
7 Add the cream, bring to the boil and season.
8 Allow to reduce to a lightly thickened consistency, correct the seasoning.
9 Pass through a fine chinois over the escalopes and serve.

An alternative method of preparing the sauce is to use half the amount of cream and an equal amount of chicken velouté (page 96).

4 portions

27 · Veal escalope with cream and mushrooms *Escalope de veau à la crème et champignons*

50 g	2 oz	butter or margarine
25 g	1 oz	seasoned flour
		4 veal escalopes (slightly battened)
100 g	4 oz	button mushrooms
30 ml	1/16 pt	sherry or white wine
125 ml	1/4 pt	double cream
		salt, cayenne

1 Heat the butter in a sauté pan.
2 Lightly flour the escalopes.
3 Cook the escalopes on both sides with the minimum of colour. They should be a delicate light brown.
4 Place the escalopes in a serving dish, cover and keep warm.
5 Peel, wash and slice the mushrooms.
6 Gently sauté the mushrooms in the same butter and pan as the escalopes and add them to the escalopes.
7 Drain off all the fat from the pan.
8 Deglaze the pan with the sherry.
9 Add the cream bring to the boil and season.

10 Reduce to a lightly thickened consistency. Correct the seasoning.
11 Pass through a fine chinois over the escalopes and mushrooms.

An alternative method of preparing the sauce is to use half the amount of cream and an equal amount of chicken velouté (page 96).

4 portions

28 · Veal escalopes with Parma ham and Mozzarella cheese *Involtini di vitello*

400 g	1 lb	small, thin veal escalopes (8 in total)
100 g	4 oz	Parma ham, thinly sliced
200 g	8 oz	Mozzarella cheese, thinly sliced
		8 fresh leaves of sage or
		1 teasp dried sage
		seasoning
50 g	2 oz	butter, margarine or oil
		grated Parmesan cheese

1 Sprinkle each slice of veal lightly with flour and flatten.
2 Place a slice of Parma ham on each escalope.
3 Add several slices of Mozzarella cheese to each.
4 Add a sage leaf or a light sprinkling of dried sage.
5 Season, roll up each escalope and secure with a toothpick or cocktail stick.
6 Melt the butter in a sauté pan, add the escalopes and brown on all sides.
7 Transfer the escalopes and butter to a suitably sized ovenproof dish.
8 Sprinkle generously with grated Parmesan cheese and bake in a moderately hot oven (190 °C, Reg. 5) for 10 mins.
9 Clean the edges of the dish and serve.

4 portions

29 · Veal stuffing

100 g	4 oz	white or wholemeal breadcrumbs
50 g	2 oz	onion cooked in oil, butter or margarine without colour
		pinch of chopped parsley
50 g	2 oz	chopped suet
		good pinch of powdered thyme or rosemary
		grated zest and juice of ½ lemon
		salt, pepper

Combine all the ingredients.

This may be used for stuffing joints or may be cooked separately in buttered paper or in a basin in the steamer for approx. 1 hr.

4 portions

30 · Roast stuffed breast of veal *Poitrine de veau farcie*

Bone, trim, season and stuff (page 313). Tie with string and cook and serve as for roast leg of veal.

31 · Veal and ham pie

150 g	6 oz	ham or bacon
		salt, pepper
		1 hard-boiled egg
250 g	10 oz	lean veal
		½ teaspn parsley and thyme
		grated zest of 1 lemon
		2 tablespns stock or water
50 g	2 oz	bread soaked in milk
		hot-water paste

Proceed as for raised pork pie (page 329). Place the shelled egg in the centre of the mixture. Serve when cold garnished with picked watercress and offer a suitable salad.

32 · Pojarski of veal *Pojarski de veau*

200 g	8 oz	trimmed veal
40 g	1½ oz	white or wholemeal breadcrumbs soaked in milk
60 ml	⅛ pt	single cream or non-dairy unsweetened creamer
		1 egg
		seasoning

1 Mince the veal finely twice or chop finely in a food processor.
2 Remove into a clean basin, add the breadcrumbs, cream and egg.
3 Season thoroughly and mix.
4 Form into cutlet shape and breadcrumb with white or wholemeal breadcrumbs.
5 Shallow fry in hot butter, margarine or oil gently on both sides, presentation side down first, until cooked and golden brown.
6 Serve with a cordon of jus-lié and a sauceboat of jus-lié.

4 portions

33 · Grenadin of veal *Grenadin de veau*

1 Prepare slices of veal, cutting a little thicker than for escalopes.
2 Lard with fat bacon strips. Sauté in oil and butter.
3 Serve with a suitable garnish, e.g. bouquetière, clamart, florentine.

34 Braised shin of veal *Osso buco*

1½ kg	3 lb	meaty knuckle of veal
25 g	1 oz	flour
50 g	2 oz	butter or margarine
60 ml	⅛ pt	oil
50 g	2 oz	onion
		1 small clove garlic
50 g	2 oz	carrot
25 g	1 oz	leek
25 g	1 oz	celery
60 ml	⅛ pt	dry white wine
60 ml	⅛ pt	white stock
25 g	1 oz	tomato purée
		bouquet garni
200 g	½ lb	tomatoes
		grated zest and juice of ½ lemon or orange
		chopped parsley

Using hard marg, sunflower oil
1 portion provides:

416 kcals/1748 kJ
28.6 g fat of which 7.8 g saturated
9.3 g carbohydrate of which 4.1 g sugars
28.5 g protein
1.9 g fibre

1. Prepare the veal knuckle by cutting and sawing through the bone in 5 cm (2 in) thick pieces.
2. Season the veal pieces with salt and pepper and pass through flour on both sides.
3. Melt the butter and oil in a sauté pan.
4. Add the veal slices and cook on both sides, colouring slightly.
5. Add the finely chopped onion and garlic, cover with a lid and allow to sweat gently for 2–3 min.
6. Add the carrot, leek and celery cut in brunoise, cover with a lid and allow to sweat for 3–4 min. Pour off the fat.
7. Deglaze with the white wine and stock. Add tomato purée.
8. Add the bouquet garni, replace the lid and allow the dish to simmer gently, preferably in an oven, for 1 hour.
9. Add the concasséed tomatoes, correct the seasoning.
10. Replace the lid, return to the oven and allow to continue simmering until the meat is so tender that it can be pulled away from the bone easily with a fork.
11. Remove bouquet garni, add lemon juice, correct seasoning and serve sprinkled with a mixture of chopped fresh basil, parsley and grated orange and lemon zest.

A risotto with saffron may be served separately (page 202).
Osso buco is an Italian regional dish which has many variations.

4 portions

35 · **Calf's liver and bacon** *Foie de veau au lard*

300 g	12 oz	calf's liver
50 g	2 oz	oil for frying
50 g	2 oz	streaky bacon
125 ml	¼ pt	jus-lié

I portion provides:

238 kcals/998 kJ
13.4 g fat of which 5.0 g saturated
2.8 g carbohydrate of which 2.7 g sugars
26.9 g protein
1.1 g fibre

1 Skin the liver and remove the gristle.
2 Cut in slices on the slant.
3 Pass the slices of liver through seasoned flour.
4 Shake off the excess flour.
5 Quickly fry on both sides in hot fat.
6 Remove the rind and bone from the bacon and grill on both sides.
7 Serve the liver and bacon with a cordon of jus-lié and a sauceboat of jus-lié separately.

4 portions

36 · **Veal sweetbreads** *Ris de veau*

Sweetbreads are glands, and two types are used for cooking. The thymus (throat) are usually long in shape and are of inferior quality. The pancreas (stomach) are heart-shaped and of superior quality.

37 · **Braised veal sweetbreads (white)** *Ris de veau braisé (à blanc)*

		8 heart-shaped sweetbreads
		salt, pepper
100 g	4 oz	onion
100 g	4 oz	carrot
		bouquet garni
250 ml	½ pt	veal stock

Using hard marg, sunflower oil
I portion provides:

263 kcals/1103 kJ
20.7 g fat of which 4.4 g saturated
1.7 g carbohydrate of which 0.0 g sugars
17.6 g protein
0.0 g fibre

1 Wash, blanch, refresh and trim the sweetbreads.
2 Season and place in a casserole or sauté pan on a bed of roots.
3 Add the bouquet garni and stock.
4 Cover with buttered greaseproof paper and a lid.
5 Cook in a moderate oven (150–200 °C, Reg. 2–6) approx. 45 mins.
6 Remove lid, baste occasionally with cooking liquor to glaze.
7 Serve with some of the cooking liquor, thickened with diluted arrowroot if necessary, and passed on to the sweetbreads.

4 portions

38 · Braised veal sweetbreads (brown)
Ris de veau braisé (à brun)

Prepare as in previous recipe and place on a lightly browned bed of roots. Barely cover with brown veal stock, or half-brown veal stock and half jus-lié. Cook in a moderate oven (150–200 °C, Reg. 2–6) without a lid, basting frequently (approx. 1 hr). Cover with the corrected, strained sauce to serve. (If veal stock is used thicken with arrowroot.)

39 · Braised veal sweetbreads with vegetables
Ris de veau bonne maman

Braise white (recipe 37) with a julienne of vegetables in place of the bed of roots, the julienne served in the sauce.

40 · Sweetbread escalope
Escalope de ris de veau

Braise sweetbreads white, press slightly between two trays and allow to cool. Cut into thick slices, ½–1 cm (¼–½ in) thick and shallow fry.

Serve with the garnish and sauce as indicated, e.g. florentine – on a bed of leaf spinach, coat with Mornay sauce and glaze.

41 · Sweetbread escalope (crumbed)
Escalope de ris de veau

Braise the sweetbreads white, press slightly and allow to cool. Cut into thick slices. Then flour, egg and crumb and shallow fry. Serve with a suitable garnish, e.g. asparagus tips and a cordon of jus-lié. Finish with nut-brown butter.

42 · Grilled veal sweetbreads
Ris de veau grillé

Blanch, braise, cool and press. Cut in halves crosswise, pass through melted butter and grill gently on both sides. Serve with a sauce and garnish as indicated.

In some recipes they may be passed through butter and crumbs before being grilled, e.g. Saint-Germain – garnished with noisette potatoes, buttered carrots, purée of peas and béarnaise sauce.

Pork escalope (p. 327) with spaghetti milanaise (p. 194)

14

PORK AND BACON

General objectives
To know the use of pork and bacon in the kitchen and to understand its use on the menu.

Specific objectives
To state the quality points and list the joints and cuts with approximate weights. To describe the correct butchery and be able to demonstrate the correct preparation, methods of cookery and presentation of pork and bacon dishes with suitable accompaniments and garnishes, paying due attention to details of standards and economy.

Bacon Butchery

Bacon Recipes

Butchery

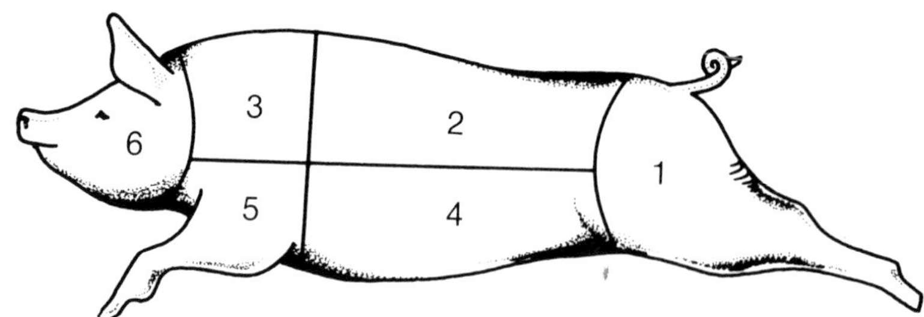

2 · Cuts, uses and weights

English	French	Uses	Approx. Weight (kilo)	(lb)
1 Leg	le cuissot	Roasting and boiling	5	10
2 Loin	la longe	Roasting, frying, grilling	6	12
3 Spare rib	la basse côte	Roasting, pies	1½	3
4 Belly	la poitrine	Pickling, boiling Stuffed, rolled and roasted	2	4
5 Shoulder	l'epaule (f.)	Roasting, sausages, pies	3	6
6 Head (whole)	la tête	Brawn	4	8
7 Trotters	le pied	Grilling, boiling		
Kidneys	les rognons (m.)	Sauté, grilling		
Liver	le foie	Frying, pâté		

When 5–6 weeks old a piglet is known as a sucking or suckling pig. The weight is then between 5–10 kg (10–20 lb) (recipe in *Contemporary Cookery*.)

3 · Signs of quality

1 Lean flesh should be pale pink, firm and of a fine texture.
2 The fat should be white, firm, smooth and not excessive.
3 Bones should be small, fine and pinkish.
4 The skin or rind should be smooth.

4 · Order of Dissection

1 Remove the head.
2 Remove the trotters.
3 Remove the leg.
4 Remove shoulder.
5 Remove spare ribs.
6 Divide loin from the belly.

5 · Preparation of joints and cuts

Leg

Roasting

Remove the pelvic or aitch bone, trim and score the rind neatly. That is to say with a sharp-pointed knife, make a series of 3 mm (1/8 in) deep incisions approx. 2 cm (1 in) apart all over the skin of the joint. Trim and clean the knuckle bone.

Boiling

It is usual to pickle the joint either by rubbing dry salt and saltpetre into the meat or by soaking in a brine solution (page 273). Then remove the pelvic bone, trim and secure with string if necessary.

Loin

Roasting (on the bone)

Saw down the chine bone in order to facilitate carving; trim excess fat and sinew and score the rind in the direction that the joint will be carved. Season and secure with string.

Roasting (boned-out)

Remove the filet mignon and bone-out carefully. Trim off excess fat and sinew, score the rind and neaten the flap, season, replace the filet mignon, roll up and secure with string.

This joint is sometimes stuffed (recipe 10, page 325.)

Grilling or frying chops

Remove the skin, excess fat and sinew, then cut and saw or chop through the loin in approx. 1 cm (1/2 in) slices, remove excess bone and trim neatly.

Spare rib

Roasting

Remove excess fat, bone and sinew and trim neatly.

Pies

Remove excess fat and sinew, bone-out and cut as required.

Belly

Remove all the small rib bones, season with salt, pepper and chopped sage, roll and secure with string. This joint may be stuffed.

Shoulder

Roasting

The shoulder is usually boned-out, excess fat and sinew removed, seasoned, scored and rolled with string. It may be stuffed and can also be divided into two smaller joints.

Sausages and pies

Skin, bone-out, remove the excess fat and sinew and cut into even pieces or mince.

Head

Brawn

a) Bone-out as for calf's head (page 305) and keep in acidulated water till required.
b) Split down the centre and remove the brain and tongue.

Trotters

Boil in water for a few minutes, scrape with the back of a knife to remove the hairs, wash off in cold water and split in half.

Kidneys

Remove the fat and skin, cut down the middle lengthwise. Remove the sinew and cut into slices or neat dice.

Liver

Skin if possible, remove the gristle and cut into thin slices on the slant.

Pork Recipes

6 Roast leg of pork *Cuissot de porc rôti*

4 oz (113 g) portion (with lean, fat) 1 portion provides:
323 kcals/1357 kJ
22.4 g fat of which 8.9 g saturated
0.0 g carbohydrate of which 0.0 g sugars
30.4 g protein
0.0 g fibre

1 Season the prepared leg of pork.
2 Lightly brush the skin with oil in order to make the crackling crisp.
3 Place on a trivet in a roasting tin with a little oil or dripping on top.
4 Start to cook in a hot oven (230–250 °C, Reg. 7–9) basting frequently.
5 Gradually reduce the heat, allowing approx. 25 min per ½ kg (1 lb) and 25 min over. Pork must always be well cooked.
6 When cooked, remove from the pan and prepare a roast gravy from the sediment, see page 104.
7 Serve the joint garnished with picked watercress and accompanied by roast gravy, apple sauce and sage and onion stuffing. If to be carved, proceed as for roast lamb, page 248.

7 Roast loin of pork *Longe de porc rôtie*

8 Roast shoulder of pork *Epaule de porc rôtie*

9 Roast spare rib of pork *Basse côte de porc rôtie*

(7–9: As for roast leg of pork)

10 Sage and onion stuffing for pork

100 g	4 oz	white breadcrumbs
50 g	2 oz	pork dripping
		pinch chopped parsley
50 g	2 oz	chopped onion
		good pinch powdered sage
		salt, pepper

1 Cook the onion in the dripping without colour.
2 Combine all the ingredients. Stuffing is usually served separately.

4 portions

11 Boiled leg of pork *Cuissot de porc bouilli*

1 Place the leg in cold water. Bring to the boil and skim.
2 Add bouquet garni and a garnish of vegetables as for boiled beef (page 280), onions, carrots, leeks and celery.
3 Simmer gently for approx. 25 min per ½ kg (1 lb) and 25 min over.
4 Serve garnished with the vegetables.
5 A sauceboat of cooking liquor and a dish of pease pudding (purée of peas) may be served separately (page 432).

12 · Pork chop charcutière *Côte de porc à la charcutière*

1 Season the chop on both sides with salt and mill pepper.
2 Brush with melted fat and either grill on both sides with moderate heat for approx. 10 min or cook in a little fat in a plat à sauté.
3 Serve accompanied by a sauceboat of charcutière sauce (page 102).

13 · Pork chop flamande *Côte de porc à la flamande*

		4 pork chops
300 g	12 oz	dessert apples

1 Season the chops with salt and mill pepper.
2 Half cook on both sides in a little fat or oil in a sauté pan.
3 Peel, core and slice the apples and place in an earthenware dish.
4 Put the chops on the apples. Sprinkle with a little fat.
5 Complete the cooking in a moderate oven (180–200 °C, Reg. 4–6) approx. 10–15 min. Clean the dish and serve.

14 · Grilled pork chop *Côte de porc grillée*

Season and grill in the usual way (page 253) and serve with picked watercress and a deep fried potato, and offer a suitable sauce separately, e.g. apple sauce (page 106).

Using 150 g chop (with bone, lean, fat)
1 portion provides:

387 kcals/1625 kJ
28.2 g fat of which 11.3 g saturated
0.0 g carbohydrate of which 0.0 g sugars
33.3 g protein
0.0 g fibre

15 · Barbecued spare ribs of pork

100 g	4 oz	finely chopped onion
		1 clove of garlic (chopped)
60 ml	⅛ pt	oil
60 ml	⅛ pt	vinegar
150 g	6 oz	tomato purée
60 ml	⅛ pt	honey
250 ml	½ pt	brown stock
		4 tablespns Worcester sauce
		1 teaspn dry mustard
		pinch thyme
		salt
2 kg	4 lb	spare ribs of pork

Using sunflower oil
1 portion provides:

1465 kcals/6151 kJ
126 g fat of which 37.3 g saturated
20.3 g carbohydrate of which 17.1 g sugars
63.5 g protein
0.3 g fibre

1 Sweat the onion and garlic in the oil without colour.
2 Mix in the vinegar, tomato purée, honey, stock, Worcester sauce, mustard, thyme and season with salt.
3 Allow the barbecue sauce to simmer 10–15 min.
4 Place the prepared spare ribs fat side up on a trivet in a roasting tin.
5 Brush the spare ribs liberally with the barbecue sauce.
6 Place in a moderately hot oven (180–200 °C, Reg. 4–6).
7 Cook for ¾–1 hour.

8 Baste generously with the barbecue sauce every 10–15 min.
9 The cooked spare ribs should be brown and crisp.
10 Cut the spare ribs into individual portions and serve.

4 portions

16 · Pork escalopes *Escalopes de porc*

Pork escalopes are usually cut from the prime cuts of meat in the leg and can be dealt with in the same way as a leg of veal (page 304). They may be cut into 75–100 g (3–4 oz) slices, flattened with a meat bat. They may be used plain or crumbed and served with vegetables or noodles or as with veal escalope recipes page 310.

17 · Pork escalopes with Calvados sauce

4× 100 g	4 oz	4 pork escalopes (see recipe 16)
50 g	2 oz	shallot or onion finely chopped
50 g	2 oz	butter, margarine or oil
30 ml	1/16 pt	Calvados
125 ml	1/4 pt	double cream or natural yoghurt
		chopped basil, sage or rosemary
		salt, cayenne pepper
		2 crisp eating apples (eg russet)
		cinnamon
		lemon juice
		brown sugar
		butter, melted

1 Core and peel the apples.
2 Cut into ½ cm (¼ in) thick rings and sprinkle with a little cinnamon and a few drops of lemon juice.
3 Place onto a baking sheet, sprinkle with brown sugar, a little melted butter and caramelise under the salamander or in the top of a hot oven.
4 *Lightly* sauté the escalopes on both sides in the butter.
5 Remove from the pan and keep warm.
6 Add the chopped shallots to the same pan, cover with a lid and cook gently without colouring (use a little more butter if necessary).
7 Strain off the fat leaving the shallots in the pan and deglaze with the Calvados.
8 Reduce by a half, add the cream or yoghurt, seasoning and herbs.
9 Reboil, correct the seasoning and consistency and pass through a fine strainer onto the meat.
10 Garnish with slices of caramelised apples.

Alternative: replace Calvados with twice the amount of cider and reduce by ¾. Add a crushed clove of garlic and 1 tablespoon of continental mustard.

4 portions

18 · Toad in the hole

8 sausages
Yorkshire pudding, made with 100 g (4 oz) flour, page 277

1 Place sausages in a roasting tray or ovenproof dish with a little oil.
2 Place in a hot oven (230–250 °C, Reg. 8–9) for 5–10 minutes.
3 Remove, add Yorkshire pudding and return to hot oven until sausages and Yorkshire pudding are cooked, approx. 15–20 minutes.
4 Cut into portions and serve with a thickened gravy or sauce.

4 portions

19 · Fried pork meat balls *Frikadeller* (Danish)

400 g	1 lb	lean pork
100 g	4 oz	onion, peeled and sliced
		salt and pepper
		flour
		1 egg beaten
		milk
		oil for frying

1 Finely mince the pork and onion together.
2 Mix in the seasoning, flour, egg and milk (if required) to give a soft mixture that will hold its shape.
3 Roll into 24–28 balls.
4 Deep fry at 185 °C until the meat balls are cooked and a golden brown.
5 Drain well and serve with tomato sauce (page 106).

4 portions

20 · Forcemeat

This is a term given to numerous mixtures of meats (usually veal and pork); meat and poultry; poultry; game; fish; vegetables and bread.

Forcemeats range from a simple sausagemeat to the finer mixtures used in the making of hot mousses (e.g. ham, chicken, fish) and soufflés. Also included are mixtures of bread, vegetables and herbs which alternatively are referred to as stuffings.

Forcemeats are used for galantines, raised pies, terrines, meat balls and a wide variety of other dishes.

Further information: Contemporary Cookery by Ceserani, Kinton and Foskett; *The Larder Chef* by Leto and Bode.

21 Raised pork pie

Hot water paste

125 g	5 oz	lard or margarine (alternatively use 100 g (4 oz) lard and 25 g (1 oz) butter or margarine)
250 g	10 oz	strong plain flour
125 ml	¼ pt	water
		salt

1 portion provides:

683 kcals/2867 kJ
41.8 g fat of which 17.1 g saturated
54.1 g carbohydrate of which 1.5 g sugars
26.1 g protein
3.2 g fibre

1 Sift the flour and salt into a basin.
2 Make a well in the centre.
3 Boil the fat with the water and pour immediately into the flour.
4 Mix with a wooden spoon until cool.
5 Mix to a smooth paste and use while still warm.

300 g	12 oz	shoulder of pork (without bone)
100 g	4 oz	bacon
		½ teaspn allspice, or mixed spice, and chopped sage
		salt and pepper
50 g	2 oz	bread soaked in milk
		2 tablespns stock or water

1 Cut the pork and bacon into small even pieces and combine with the rest of the ingredients.
2 Keep one-quarter of the paste warm and covered.
3 Roll out the remaining three-quarters and carefully line a well-greased raised pie mould.
4 Add the filling and press down firmly.
5 Roll out the remaining pastry for the lid.
6 Eggwash the edges of the pie.
7 Add the lid, seal firmly, neaten the edges, cut off any surplus paste.
8 Decorate if desired.
9 Make a hole 1 cm (½ in) in diameter in the centre of the pie.
10 Brush all over with eggwash.
11 Bake in a hot oven (230–250 °C, Reg. 8–9) approx. 20 min.
12 Reduce the heat to moderate (150–200 °C, Reg. 2–6) and cook for 1½–2 hr in all.
13 If the pie colours too quickly, cover with greaseproof paper. Remove from the oven and carefully remove tin, eggwash the pie all over and return to the oven for a few minutes.
14 Remove from the oven and fill with approx. 125 ml (¼ pt) of good hot stock in which 5 g (¼ oz) of gelatine has been dissolved.
15 Serve when cold, garnished with picked watercress and offer a suitable salad.

22 · Sweet and sour pork

250 g	10 oz	loin of pork
12 g	½ oz	sugar
70 ml	⅛ pt	dry sherry
70 ml	⅛ pt	soy sauce
70 ml	⅛ pt	vegetable oil
50 g	2 oz	cornflour
		2 tablespns oil
		1 clove garlic
50 g	2 oz	fresh root ginger
75 g	3 oz	onion, chopped
		1 green pepper in 1 cm (½ in) dice
		2 chillies, chopped
210 ml	⅜ pt	sweet and sour sauce
		2 pineapple rings (fresh or canned)
		2 spring onions

Using sunflower oil
1 portion provides:

730 kcals/3067 kJ
43.9 g fat of which 9.2 g saturated
69.7 g carbohydrate of which 54.7 g sugars
13.4 g protein
1.6 g fibre

1 Cut the boned loin of pork into ¾ in. pieces.
2 Marinade the pork for 30 mins. in the sugar, sherry and soy sauce.
3 Pass the pork through cornflour, pressing the cornflour in well.
4 Deep fry the pork pieces in oil 190 °C/375 °F until golden brown, drain. Add the 2 tablespoons of oil to a sauté pan.
5 Add the garlic and ginger, fry until fragrant.
6 Add the onion, pepper and chillies, sauté for a few minutes.
7 Stir in sweet and sour sauce, bring to boil.
8 Add the pineapple cut into small chunks, thicken slightly with diluted cornflour. Simmer for 2 mins.
9 Deep fry the pork again until crisp. Drain, mix into vegetables and sauce or serve separately.
10 Serve garnished with rings of spring onions or button onions.

Sweet and sour sauce

375 ml	¾ pt	white vinegar
150 g	6 oz	brown sugar
125 ml	¼ pt	tomato ketchup
		1 tablespn Worcester sauce
		seasoning

1 Boil vinegar and sugar in a suitable pan.
2 Add the tomato ketchup, Worcester sauce and seasoning.
3 Simmer for a few minutes then use as required. This sauce may also be lightly thickened with cornflour.

Butchery

23 · Bacon *Lard*

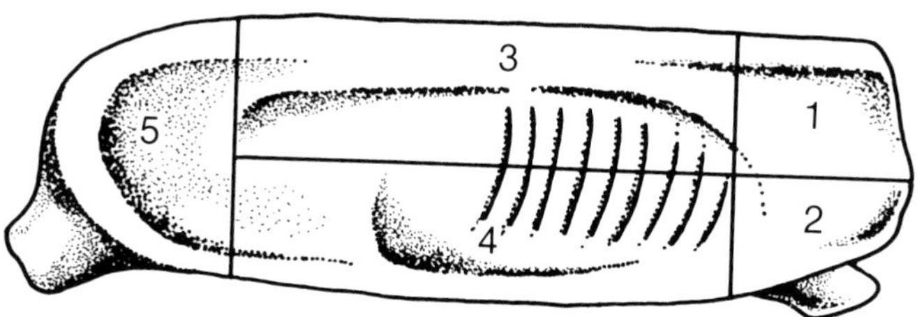

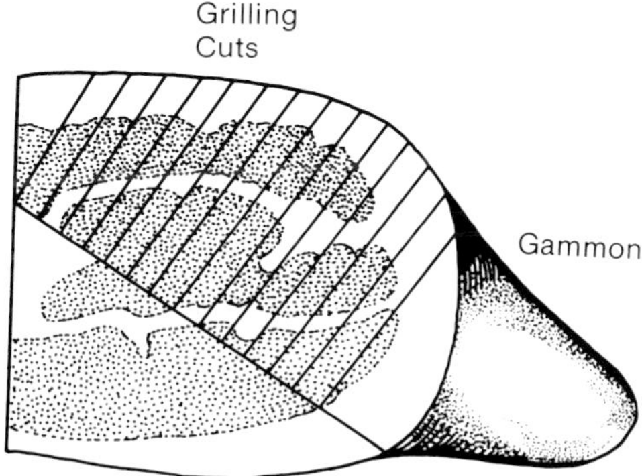

24 · Cuts, uses and weights

Side of bacon	Uses	Approx. Weight (kilo)	(lb)
1 Collar	Boiling, grilling	4½	9
2 Hock	Boiling, grilling	4½	9
3 Back	Grilling, frying	9	18
4 Streaky	Grilling, frying	4½	9
5 Gammon	Boiling, grilling, frying	7½	15

25 · Quality

1 There should be no sign of stickiness.
2 There should be a pleasant smell.
3 The rind should be thin, smooth and free from wrinkles.
4 The fat should be white, smooth and not excessive in proportion to the lean.
5 The lean should be a deep pink colour and firm.

26 Preparation of joints and cuts

Collar

Boiling	Remove bone (if any) and tie with string.
Grilling	Remove the rind and trim off outside surface and cut into thin slices (rashers), across the joint.

Hock

Boiling	Leave whole or bone-out and secure with string.

Back

Grilling	Remove all bones and rind and cut into thin rashers.
Frying	Remove the rind, trim off outside surface and cut into rashers or chops of the required thickness.

Streaky

As for back.

Gammon

Grilling	Fairly thick slices are cut from the middle of the gammon. They are then trimmed and the rind removed.
Frying	As for grilling.

Note Where possible, check the salt content of bacon joints before soaking. For example, Danish bacon does not require soaking as it contains the correct degree of salt.

Bacon Recipes

27 **Boiled bacon** (hock, collar or gammon)

1 Soak the bacon in cold water for 24 hr before cooking.
2 Change the water.
3 Bring to the boil, skim and simmer gently, approx. 25 min per ½ kg (1 lb) and 25 min over. Allow to cool in the liquid.
4 Remove the rind and brown skin and carve.
5 Serve with a little of the cooking liquor.

Boiled bacon may be served with pease pudding (page 432) and a suitable sauce such as parsley sauce (page 95).

Using 4 oz (113 g) per portion
1 portion provides:

367 kcals/1543 kJ
30.5 g fat of which 12.2 g saturated
0.0 g carbohydrate of which 0.0 g sugars
23.1 g protein
0:0 g fibre

28 **Grilled back or streaky rashers**

Arrange on a baking tray and grill on both sides under the salamander.

29 **Fried bacon**

Fry on both sides in a frying-pan in very little fat.

Using sunflower oil
1 portion (50 g) provides:

233 kcals/977 kJ
20.3 g fat of which 7.2 g saturated
0.0 g carbohydrate of which 0.0 g sugars
12.5 g protein
0.0 g fibre

Mixed grill (p. 251) comprising lamb cutlets, kidneys with parsley butter, sausages, streaky bacon, tomatoes, mushrooms, straw potatoes and watercress

30 · Bacon with pineapple

1. Hock, collar or gammon may be used.
2. Soak the bacon joint in cold water for approx. 24 hrs (if necessary).
3. Change the water.
4. Cover with water, bring to the boil, skim, simmer gently for half the required cooking time (30 mins per ½ kg (per pound) and 30 mins over).
5. Allow to cool. Remove rind and brown skin.
6. Cover the fat surface of the joint with demerara sugar and press well into surface. Stud with 12–24 cloves.
7. Arrange a layer of tinned pineapple rings down the centre of the joint (secure with cocktail sticks if necessary).
8. Place joint in a baking tin for second half of the cooking time.
9. Bake in a moderate oven (200 °C, Reg. 6) basting frequently with pineapple juice until well cooked.
10. Remove the cloves and pineapple.
11. Carve in thickish slices and serve garnished with the pineapple.

31 · Bacon chops with honey and orange sauce

4× 100 g	4 oz	4 bacon chops (trimmed weight)
50 g	2 oz	butter, margarine or oil
		2 oranges
		1 dessertsp honey
		½ lemon, juice of
		arrowroot

1. Ensure that the chops are well trimmed of fat.
2. Lightly fry the chops on both sides in the butter, margarine or oil without colouring.
3. Remove from the pan and keep warm.
4. Thinly remove zest from one orange so that no white pith remains; cut into very fine julienne; blanch and refresh.
5. Peel and segment both oranges ensuring that all the white pith and pips are removed. Retain all the juice.
6. Boil the orange and lemon juice and honey and lightly thicken with diluted arrowroot.
7. Strain the sauce, add the julienne of orange and pour over the chops.
8. Garnish with the segments of orange.

Variations include: (a) using 1 orange and 1 pink grapefruit instead of 2 oranges; (b) using a small tin of peaches or apricots or pineapple in place of the oranges.

4 portions

32 Sauerkraut with frankfurters and garlic sausage *Choucroûte garni*

50 g	2 oz	lard or margarine
400 g	1 lb	sauerkraut
300 g	12 oz	streaky bacon
		2 whole peeled carrots
		1 onion clouté
		bouquet garni
		10 juniper berries } tied in a muslin bag
		5 peppercorns } tied in a muslin bag
		seasoning
125 ml	¼ pt	white wine
100 g	4 oz	bacon rind
200 g	8 oz	garlic sausage
		8 frankfurter sausages
		8 boiled potatoes

1. Well grease a braising pan with the lard or margarine.
2. Place a layer of sauerkraut in the bottom of the pan.
3. Place the piece of streaky bacon on top with the carrots, onion, bouquet garni, juniper berries and peppercorns.
4. Cover with remainder of sauerkraut, season and add white wine.
5. Cover with bacon rind and a tight-fitting lid.
6. Place in a moderate oven at 180 °C and braise gently for 1 hour.
7. Remove the streaky bacon and replace with the garlic sausage. Continue braising for another hour until the sauerkraut is tender.
8. Reheat the frankfurters if canned or poach in water if fresh.
9. Remove the sauerkraut from the oven and discard the bacon rind.
10. Slice the streaky bacon, garlic sausage, carrots and frankfurters.
11. Dress the sauerkraut in an earthenware dish with the sliced items.
12. Serve plain boiled potatoes separately.

Other sauerkraut recipes are given on pages 417–8.

Note Sauerkraut is a pickled white cabbage and a traditional German dish.

33 Grilled gammon rashers

Brush the rashers with fat on both sides and cook on greased, pre-heated grill bars on both sides for approx. 5–10 min in all. Serve with watercress and any other food as indicated, e.g. tomatoes, mushrooms, eggs. If a sauce is required, serve any sharp demi-glace sauce, e.g. diable.

Using 100 g per portion
1 portion provides:

228 kcals/958 kJ
12.2 g fat of which 4.8 g saturated
0.0 g carbohydrate of which 0.0 g sugars
29.5 g protein
0.0 g fibre

34 **Ham** *Jambon*

Ham should not be confused with gammon. A gammon is the hind leg of a baconer pig, and is cut from a side of bacon. A ham is the hind leg of a porker pig, and is cut round from the side of pork with the aitch bone and usually cured by dry salting. Ham is boiled and can be served hot or cold. Certain imported hams, e.g. Parma ham, may be sliced thinly and eaten raw, generally as an hors-d'oeuvre. In order to carve the ham efficiently it is necessary to remove the aitch bone after cooking.

Clockwise from top left: ballottines of chicken chasseur (p. 354); crumbed breast of chicken with asparagus and truffle (p. 359); chicken sauté with potatoes (p. 358)

15

POULTRY AND GAME

General objectives	*Specific objectives*
To know what comprises poultry and game and to understand their culinary use.	To recognise types of poultry and game available and to specify the use of different birds and animals. To list the points of quality, to describe and demonstrate the cleaning, trussing and other preparations including the handling of frozen birds. To produce suitable dishes to the required standard with appropriate sauces and garnishes.

Duck Recipes

Game Recipes

Poultry Volaille

1 · **Poultry** *Volaille*

The term in its general sense is applied to all domestic fowl bred for food and means turkeys, geese, ducks, fowls and pigeons.

When the word *volaille* appears on the menu it applies only to fowls (chicken). Originally fowl were classified according to size and feeding by specific names as follows:

Chickens

	Weight (kilo)	(lb)	Number of portions	
Single baby chicken	3/10–1/2	3/4–1	1	Single poussin
Double baby chicken	1/2–3/4	1–1 1/2	2	Double poussin
Small roasting chicken	3/4–1	1 1/2–2	3–4	Poulet de grain
Medium roasting chicken	1–2	2–4	4–6	Poulet de grain
Large roasting or boiling chicken	2–3	4–6	6–8	Poularde
Capon	3–4 1/2	6–9	8–12	Chapon
Old boiling fowl	2 1/2–4	5–8		Poule

There is approximately 15–20% bone in poultry.

Poussin

4–6 weeks old.
Uses – roasting and grilling.

Poulet de grain

A young fattened bird 3–4 months old. Sometimes termed a broiler.
Uses – roasting, grilling, en casserole.

Poulet reine

Fully-grown, tender, prime bird. Sometimes termed a broiler.
Uses – roasting, grilling, sauté, en casserole, suprêmes, pies.

Poularde

Large fully-grown prime bird.
Uses – roasting, boiling, en casserole, galantine.

Chapon

A cock bird specially fed and fattened. See *Theory of Catering* page 173.
Uses – roasting.

Poule

An old hen.
Uses – stocks and soups.

2 Signs of quality

1 Plump breast.
2 Pliable breast bone.
3 Flesh firm.
4 Skin white, unbroken and with a faint bluish tint.

Old birds have coarse scales and large spurs on the legs and long hairs on the skin.

3 Cleaning

1 Pick out any pens or down, using a small knife.
2 Singe in order to remove any hairs, take care not to scorch the skin.
3 Split the neck skin by gripping firmly and make and lengthwise incision on the underside, cut off the neck as close to the body as possible.
4 Cut off the head.
5 Remove the crop and loosen intestines and lungs with forefinger.
6 Cut out vent and wipe clean.
7 Loosen intestines with forefinger.
8 Draw out the innards being careful not to break the gall bladder.
9 Wipe vent end if necessary.
10 Split and clean the gizzard.
11 Cut off the gall bladder from the liver and discard.
12 Keep the neck and heart for stock.

4 Trussing for roasting (see page 346)

1 Clean the legs by dipping in boiling water for a few seconds then remove the scales with a cloth.
2 Cut off the outside claws leaving the centre ones, trim these to half their length.
3 To facilitate carving remove the wish-bone.
4 Place the bird on its back.
5 Hold the legs back firmly.
6 Insert the trussing needle through the bird, midway between the leg joints.
7 Turn on to its side.
8 Pierce the winglet, the skin of the neck, the skin of the carcass and the other winglet.
9 Tie ends of string securely.
10 Secure the legs by inserting the needle through the carcass and over the legs, take care not to pierce the breast.

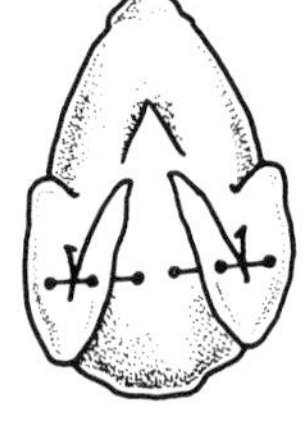

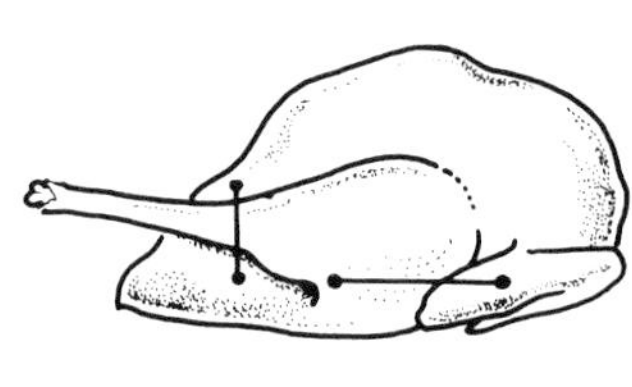

5 Trussing for boiling and entrées

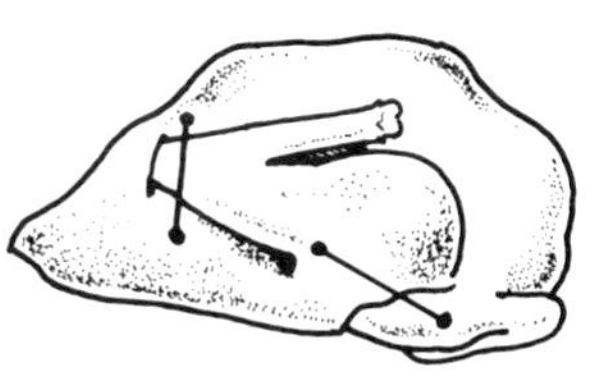

1 Proceed as for roasting.
2 Cut the leg sinew just below the joint.
3 Either:

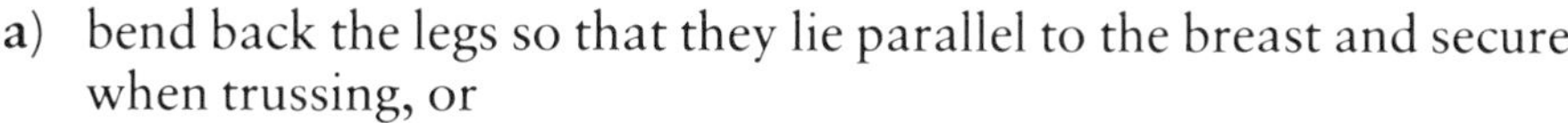

a) bend back the legs so that they lie parallel to the breast and secure when trussing, or

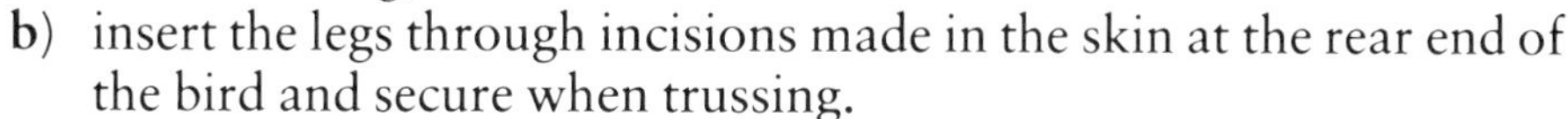

b) insert the legs through incisions made in the skin at the rear end of the bird and secure when trussing.

6 Cuts of chicken

The pieces of cut chicken are named as follows:

English		**French**	
Leg	4 drumstick 3 thigh	*Cuisse*	pilon de cuisse gras de cuisse
1 Wing		*Aile*	
2 Breast		*Blanc*	
5 Winglet		*Aileron*	
6 Carcass		*Carcasse*	

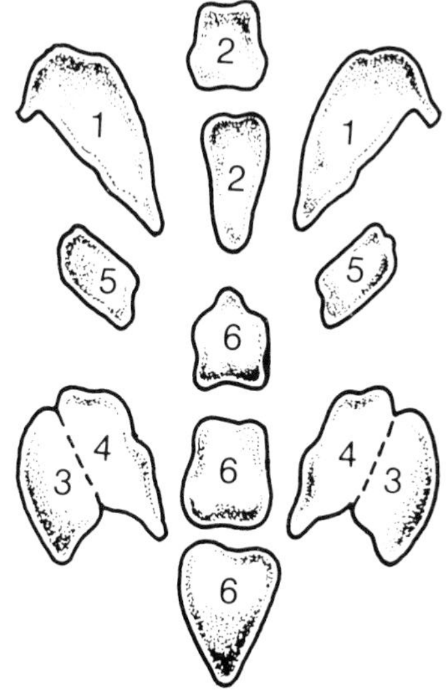

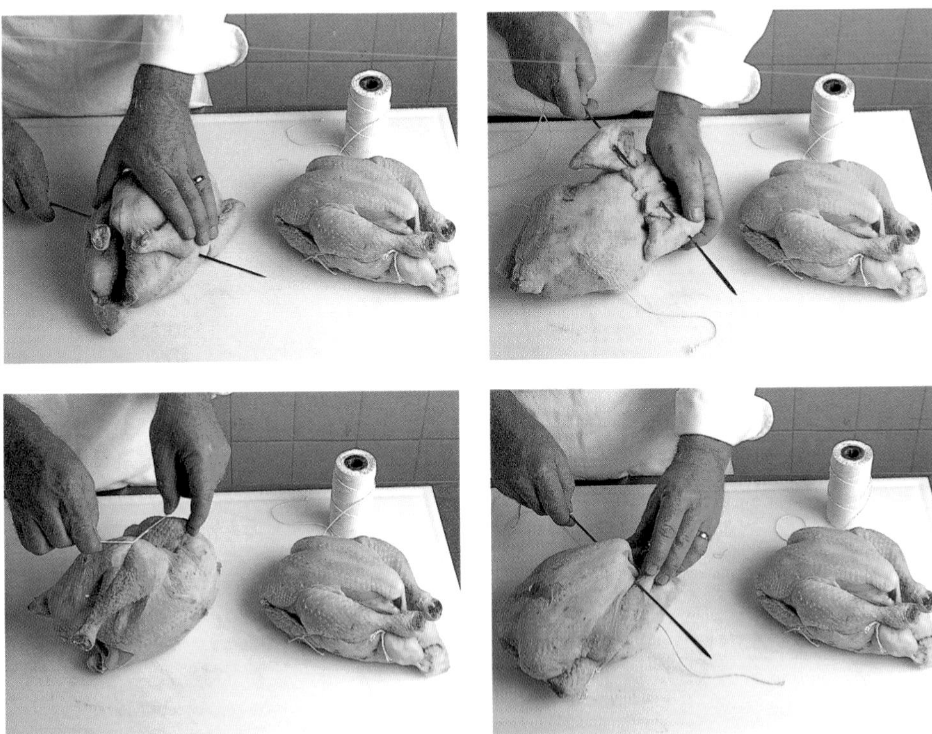

Trussing of chicken for roasting (p. 344)

7 · Cutting for sauté, fricassée, pies, etc.

1 Remove the feet at the first joint.
2 Remove the legs from the carcass.
3 Cut each leg in two at the joint.

Preparation of chicken for sauté

4 Remove the wish-bone. Remove winglets and trim.
5 Remove the wings carefully, leaving two equal portions on the breast.
6 Remove the breast and cut in two.
7 Trim the carcass and cut into three pieces.

8 · Preparation for grilling

1 Remove the wish-bone.
2 Cut off the claws at the first joint.
3 Place bird on its back.
4 Insert a large knife through the neck-end and out of the vent.
5 Cut through the backbone.
6 Open out.
7 Remove back and rib bones.

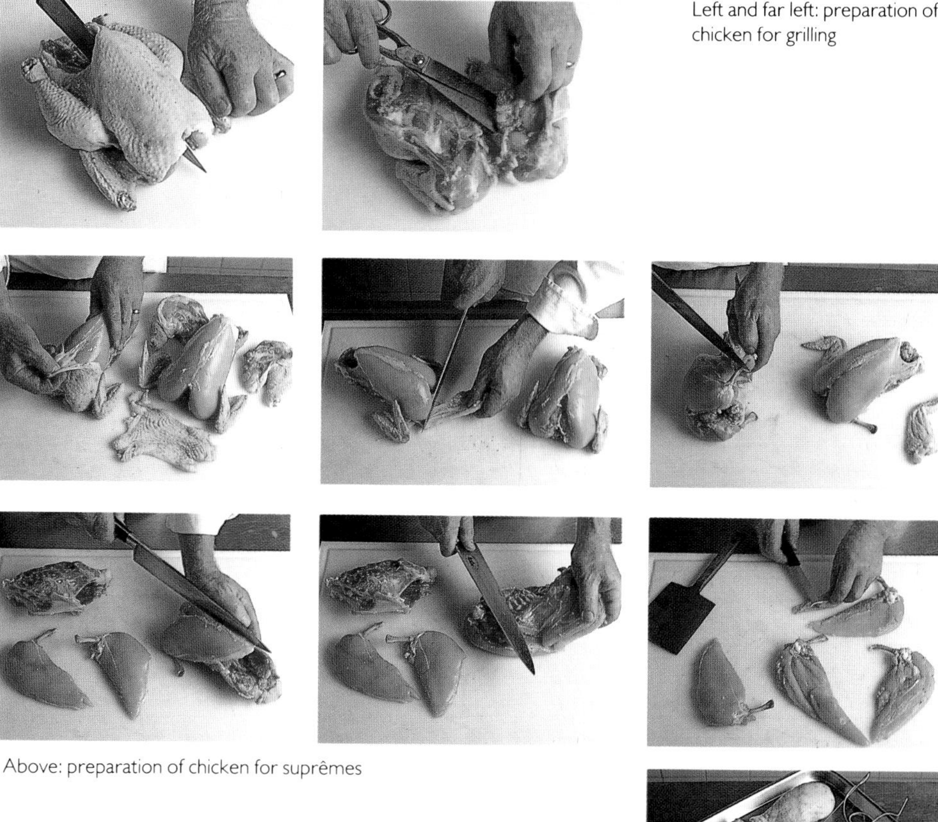

Left and far left: preparation of chicken for grilling

Above: preparation of chicken for suprêmes

Preparation of chicken for ballottines

9 Preparation for suprêmes (see page 347)

Suprême – this is the wing and half the breast of a chicken with the trimmed wing bone attached, i.e. the white meat of one chicken yields two suprêmes.

1. Use chicken weighing 1¼–1½ kg (2½–3 lb).
2. Cut off both legs from the chicken.
3. Remove the skin from the breasts.
4. Remove the wishbone.
5. Scrape the wing bone bare adjoining the breasts.
6. Cut off the winglets near the joints leaving 1½–2 cm (½–¾ in) of bare bone attached to the breasts.
7. Cut the breasts close to the breastbone and follow the bone down to the wing joint.
8. Cut through the joint.
9. Lay the chicken on its side and pull the suprêmes off assisting with the knife.
10. Lift the fillets from the suprêmes and remove the sinew from each.
11. Make an incision lengthways, along the thick side of the suprêmes, open and place the fillets inside.
12. Close, lightly flatten with a bat moistened with water and trim if necessary.

10 Preparation for ballottines (see page 347)

Ballottine – this is a boned stuffed leg of bird.

1. Using a small sharp knife remove the thigh bone.
2. Scrape the flesh off the bone of the drumstick towards the claw joint.
3. Sever the drumstick bone leaving approx. 2–3 cm (¾–1 in) at the claw joint end.
4. Fill the cavities in both the drumstick and thigh with a savoury stuffing.
5. Neaten the shape and secure with string using a trussing needle.

Ballottines of chicken may be cooked and served using any of the recipes for chicken sauté pages 353–4, 358.

11 Cutting of cooked chicken (roasted or boiled)

1. Remove the legs and cut in two (drumstick and thigh).
2. Remove the wings.
3. Separate breast from the carcass and divide in two.
4. Serve a drumstick with a wing and the thigh with the breast.

4 portions

12 **Duck** *Canard*

Approx. 2–3 kilo (4–6 lb).

Duckling Caneton

Approx. 1½–2 kilo (3–4 lb).

Signs of quality

1 Plump breast.
2 Lower back bends easily.
3 Webbed feet tear fairly easily.
4 The feet and bill should be yellow.

The preparation of duck for roasting is the same as for roast chicken, page 344. The gizzard is not split but trimmed off with a knife.

13 **Goose** *Oie*

Approx. 6 kilo (12 lb).

Gosling Oison

Signs of Quality

As for duck.

Preparation for roasting goose is the same as for roast chicken, page 344.

14 **Turkey** *Dinde*

Young Turkey Dindonneau

Turkeys can vary in weight from 3½–20 kilo (7–40 lb).

They are cleaned and trussed in the same way as chicken. The wish-bone should always be removed before trussing. The sinews should be drawn out of the legs. Allow 200 g (½ lb) per portion raw weight.

Note When cooking a large turkey the legs may be removed, boned, rolled, tied and roasted separately from the remainder of the bird. This will reduce the cooking time and enable the legs and breast to cook more evenly.

Stuffings may be rolled in foil, steamed or baked and thickly sliced. If a firmer stuffing is required, mix in one or two raw eggs before cooking.

15 · Roast Turkey *Dinde rôti*

200 g	½ lb	chestnuts	chestnut stuffing
600 g	1½ lb	sausage meat	
50 g	2 oz	chopped onion	
50 g	2 oz	chopped onion	parsley and thyme stuffing
100 g	4 oz	oil, butter or margarine	
		salt, pepper	
100 g	4 oz	white or wholemeal breadcrumbs	
		pinch powdered thyme	
		pinch chopped parsley	
		chopped turkey liver (raw)	
5 kilo	10 lb	turkey	
100 g	4 oz	fat bacon	
375 ml	¾ pt	brown stock	
		bread sauce (page 135)	

No accompaniments
1 portion (200 g raw with skin, bone):

200 kcals/836 kJ
11.75 g fat of which 4.0 g saturated
0.0 g carbohydrate of which 0.0 g sugars
29.0 g protein
0.0 g fibre

With stuffing, roast gravy, bread sauce
1 portion (200 g raw, with skin, bone):

380 kcals/1589 kJ
24.0 g fat of which 8.4 g saturated
8.6 g carbohydrate of which 1.6 g sugars
34.0 g protein
0.9 g fibre

1. Slit the chestnuts on both sides using a small knife.
2. Boil chestnuts in water for 5–10 min.
3. Drain and remove outer and inner skins whilst warm.
4. Cook the chestnuts in a little stock for 5 min approx.
5. When cold, dice and mix into the sausage meat and onion.
6. For the parsley and thyme stuffing, cook the onion in oil, butter or margarine without colour.
7. Remove from the heat, add the seasoning, crumbs and herbs.
8. Mix in the raw chopped liver.
9. Truss the bird firmly (removing wish-bone first).
10. Season with salt and pepper.
11. Cover the breast with fat bacon.
12. Place the bird in a roasting tray on its side and coat with 200 g (4 oz) dripping or oil.
13. Roast in a moderate oven (200–230 °C, Reg. 6–8).
14. Allow to cook on both legs and complete the cooking with the breast upright for the last 30 min.
15. Baste frequently and allow 15–20 min per lb.
16. Bake the two stuffings separately in greased trays until well cooked.
17. When cooked prepare the gravy from the sediment and the brown stock. Correct the seasoning and remove the fat.
18. Remove the string and serve with stuffings, roast gravy, bread sauce and/or hot cranberry sauce.
19. The turkey may be garnished with chipolata sausages and bacon rolls.

Chicken Recipes

16 · Roast chicken *Poulet rôti*

1¼–1½ kg	2½–3 lb	1 chicken
50 g	2 oz	oil, butter or margarine
125 ml	¼ pt	brown stock
25 g	1 oz	game chips
		1 bunch watercress
125 ml	¼ pt	bread sauce (page 135)

Without accompaniments
1 portion (200 g raw with skin, bone):

270 kcals/1134 kJ
16.0 g fat of which 5.3 g saturated
0.0 g carbohydrate of which 0.0 g sugars
28.3 g protein
0.0 g fibre

With game chips, bread sauce,
1 portion (200 g raw with skin, bone):

598 kcals/2513 kJ
46.8 g fat of which 17.3 g saturated
6.9 g carbohydrate of which 2.4 g sugars
37.8 g protein
1.1 g fibre

1 Season the chicken inside and out with salt.
2 Place on its side in a roasting tin.
3 Cover with the oil, butter or margarine.
4 Place in hot oven approx. 20–25 min.
5 Turn on to the other leg.
6 Cook for further 20–25 min approx. Baste frequently.
7 To test if cooked pierce with a fork between the drumstick and thigh and hold over a plate. The juice issuing from the chicken should not show any signs of blood.
8 Make roast gravy with the stock and sediment in the roasting tray.
9 Serve on a flat dish with game chips in front and the watercress at the back of the bird.

Roast gravy and bread sauce are served separately. Always remove the trussing string from the bird before serving.

4 portions

17 · Roast chicken and bacon *Poulet rôti au lard*

As for roast chicken with four grilled rashers of streaky bacon which may be rolled (after cooking).

1 portion provides:

683 kcals/2867 kJ
54.0 g fat of which 20.2 g saturated
6.9 g carbohydrate of which 2.4 g sugars
42.7 g protein
1.1 g fibre

Portioning of roast chicken (showing piece of white and piece of dark meat making one portion)

18 Roast chicken with stuffing *Poulet rôti à l'anglaise*

As for roast chicken, but served with stuffing.

25 g	1 oz	chopped onion
50 g	2 oz	oil, butter or margarine
		salt, pepper
		pinch chopped parsley
		pinch powdered thyme
50 g	2 oz	white or wholemeal breadcrumbs
		the chopped chicken liver (raw)

1 Gently cook the onion in the oil, butter or margarine without colour.
2 Add the seasoning, herbs and crumbs.
3 Mix in the liver.
4 Correct seasoning and bake or steam separately, approx. 20 min.

19 Roast stuffed spring chicken *Poussin polonaise*

100 g	¼ lb	bacon	stuffing
50 g	2 oz	butter or oil	stuffing
		½ bay leaf	stuffing
		small sprig of thyme	stuffing
25 g	1 oz	onion (chopped)	
200 g	½ lb	chicken livers (raw)	
		4 single or 2 double spring chickens	
¼ litre	½ pt	brown stock	
100 g	4 oz	butter	
25 g	1 oz	white or wholemeal breadcrumbs	
		juice of ½ lemon	
		chopped parsley	

1 Prepare the stuffing by cutting the bacon in small pieces.
2 Fry off quickly in a frying pan with the 50 g (2 oz) butter or oil, herbs and chopped onion for a few seconds.
3 Add the trimmed chicken livers.
4 Season with salt and pepper. Fry quickly until brown.
5 Pass all the mixture through a fine sieve.
6 Clean, prepare, season and truss the spring chicken as for entrée (page 345).
7 Fill the chicks with the prepared stuffing.
8 Roast or pot-roast the chicks.
9 Remove the lid half way through to obtain a golden brown colour.
10 When cooked, remove the string and place the chicks on a flat serving dish and keep warm.
11 Remove the fat from the cooking dish, deglaze with brown stock and lightly thicken with a little diluted arrowroot. Pass through a fine chinois and serve separately.
12 Cook the 100 g (4 oz) butter in a frying pan to a beurre noisette.
13 Mix in the breadcrumbs and the lemon juice and pour over the chicks. Sprinkle with chopped parsley and serve. *4 portions*

20 Sauté of chicken *Poulet sauté*

1¼–1½ kg	2½–3 lb	1 chicken
50 g	2 oz	butter, margarine or oil
		salt, pepper
250 ml	½ pt	jus-lié or demi-glace
		chopped parsley

1 To prepare the chicken for sauté remove the feet at the first joint.
2 Remove the legs from the carcass.
3 Cut each leg in two at the joint.
4 Remove the wish-bone. Remove winglets and trim.
5 Remove the wings, leaving two equal portions on the breast.
6 Remove the breast and cut in two.
7 Trim the carcass and cut into three pieces.
8 Place the butter, margarine or oil in a sauté pan on a fairly hot stove.
9 Season the pieces of chicken and place in the pan in the following order: drumsticks, thighs, carcass, wings, winglets and breast (tougher pieces first as they take longer to cook).
10 Cook to a golden brown on both sides.
11 Cover with a lid and cook on the stove or in the oven until tender.
12 Dress the chicken pieces neatly in an entrée dish.
13 Drain off all fat from the sauté pan.
14 Return to the heat and add the jus-lié or demi-glace.
15 Simmer for 3–4 min.
16 Correct the seasoning and skim.
17 Pass through a fine strainer on to the chicken.
18 Sprinkle with chopped parsley and serve.

Note The chicken giblets should always be used in the making of the jus-lié or demi-glace.

4 portions

21 Chicken sauté with mushrooms *Poulet sauté aux champignons*

50 g	2 oz	butter, margarine or oil
1¼–1½ kg	2½–3 lb	1 chicken cut for sauté
10 g	½ oz	chopped shallot
100 g	4 oz	button mushrooms
60 ml	⅛ pt	dry white wine
250 ml	½ pt	demi-glace or jus-lié
		salt, pepper
		chopped parsley

Proceed as for recipe 22 points 1–6.
7 Pour off the fat, add the white wine and reduce by half.
8 Add the demi-glace, simmer for 5 min and correct the seasoning.
9 Pour over the pieces of chicken, sprinkle with chopped parsley.

4 portions

22 · Chicken sauté chasseur
Poulet sauté chasseur

50 g	2 oz	butter, margarine or oil
1¼–1½ kg	2½–3 lb	1 chicken cut for sauté
10 g	½ oz	chopped shallot
100 g	4 oz	button mushrooms
		3 tablespns dry white wine
250 ml	½ pt	jus-lié or demi-glace
200 g	8 oz	tomatoes
		chopped parsley and tarragon

Using butter
1 portion provides:

579 kcals/2430 kJ
45.8 g fat of which 20.7 g saturated
2.1 g carbohydrate of which 1.6 g sugars
37.6 g protein
1.5 g fibre

1 Place the butter, margarine or oil in a sauté pan on a fairly hot stove.
2 Season the pieces of chicken and place in the pan in the following order: drumsticks, thighs, carcass, wings, winglets and breast.
3 Cook to a golden brown on both sides.
4 Cover with a lid and cook on the stove or in the oven until tender. Dress neatly in an entrée dish.
5 Add the shallot to the sauté pan, cover with a lid, cook on a gentle heat for 1–2 min without colour.
6 Add washed sliced mushrooms, cover with a lid, cook gently 3–4 min without colour.
7 Drain off fat.
8 Add white wine and reduce by half.
9 Add the demi-glace or jus-lié.
10 Add the tomate concassée, simmer for 5 minutes.
11 Correct the seasoning and pour over the chicken.
12 Sprinkle with chopped parsley and tarragon and serve.

Ballottines of chicken chasseur

4 portions

23 · Chicken spatchcock
Poulet grillé à la crapaudine

1¼–1½ kg	2½–3 lb	1 chicken

1 portion provides:

372 kcals/1560 kJ
24.1 g fat of which 8.0 g saturated
0.0 g carbohydrate of which 0.0 g sugars
38.9 g protein
0.0 g fibre

1 Prepare chicken as recipe 5 (page 345) but do not tie with string.
2 Cut horizontally from below the point of the breast over the top of the legs down to the wing joints without

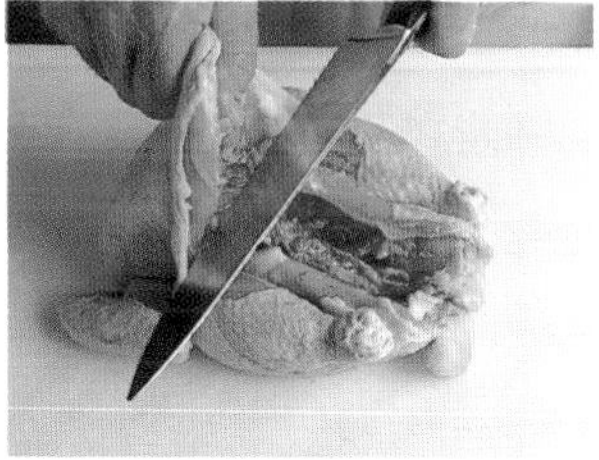
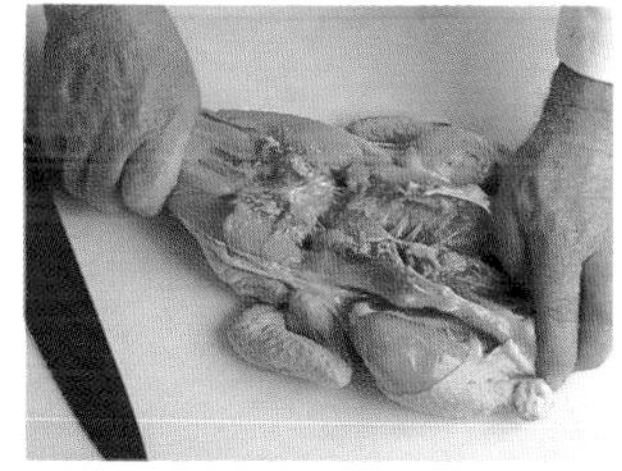
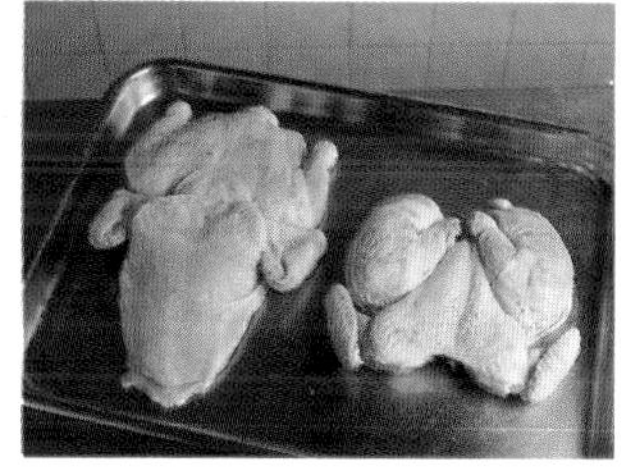

Preparation of chicken for spatchcock and grilling (far right)

removing the breasts. Fold back the breasts.

4 Snap and reverse the backbone into the opposite direction so that the point of the breast now extends forward to resemble the nose and face of a toad.
5 Flatten slightly. Remove any small bones.
6 Skewer wings and legs in position.
7 Season with salt and mill pepper.
8 Brush with oil or melted butter.
9 Place on pre-heated grill bars or on a flat tray under a salamander.
10 Brush frequently with melted fat or oil during cooking and allow approx. 15–20 min on each side.
11 Test if cooked by piercing the drumstick with a needle or skewer – there should be no sign of blood.

Top: grilled chicken; foreground: chicken spatchcock

12 When serving, two eyes for the 'toad' may be made from slices of hard boiled white of egg with a pupil of truffle or gherkin.
13 Serve garnished with picked watercress and offer a suitable sauce separately, e.g. sauce diable, beurre maître d'hôtel. *4 portions*

24 Grilled chicken *Poulet grillé*

1 Season the chicken prepared for grilling (see page 347) with salt and mill pepper.
2 Brush with oil or melted butter or margarine and place on pre-heated greased grill bars or on a flat baking tray under a salamander.
3 Brush frequently with melted fat during cooking and allow approx. 15–20 min each side.
4 Test if cooked by piercing the drumstick with a skewer or trussing needle; there should be no sign of blood issuing from the leg.
5 Serve garnished with picked watercress and offer a suitable sauce separately, e.g. poulet grillé, sauce diable.

Grilled chicken is frequently served garnished with streaky bacon, tomatoes and mushrooms.

See page 355 for illustrations of the preparation and service of this dish.

25 Grilled devilled chicken *Poulet grillé diablé*

		1 tablespn English or continental mustard
		cayenne pepper
		1 teaspn Worcester sauce
		2 tablespns water or vinegar
25 g	1 oz	white breadcrumbs

1 Combine all the ingredients, except for crumbs.
2 Proceed as for grilled chicken.
3 Approx. 5 min before each side of chicken is cooked brush liberally with the devil mixture, sprinkle with crumbs and complete the grilling.
4 Serve as for grilled chicken.

26 Wing and breast of chicken in cream sauce *Suprême de volaille à la crème*

50 g	2 oz	butter or margarine
25 g	1 oz	seasoned flour
		4 suprêmes of chicken (page 347)
30 ml	1/16 pt	sherry or white wine
125 ml	1/4 pt	double cream or non-dairy cream
		salt, cayenne

1 Heat the butter or margarine in a sauté pan.
2 Lightly flour the suprêmes.
3 Cook the suprêmes gently on both sides (7–9 min) with the minimum of colour.

4 Place the suprêmes in an earthenware serving dish, cover to keep warm.
5 Drain off the fat from the pan.
6 Deglaze the pan with the sherry or white wine.
7 Add the cream, bring to the boil and season.
8 Allow to reduce to a lightly thickened consistency. Correct the seasoning.
9 Pass through a fine chinois on to the suprêmes and serve.

An alternative method of preparing the sauce is to use half the amount of cream (fresh or non-dairy) and an equal amount of chicken velouté (page 96).

4 portions

27 Wing and breast of chicken in cream sauce with mushrooms

Suprême de volaille aux champignons à la crème

50 g	2 oz	butter or margarine
25 g	1 oz	seasoned flour, white or wholemeal
		4 suprêmes of chicken (page 347)
100 g	4 oz	button mushrooms
30 ml	1/16 pt	sherry or white wine
125 ml	1/4 pt	double or non-dairy cream
		salt, cayenne

Proceed as for recipe 26 points 1–4.

5 Peel, wash and slice the mushrooms.
6 Gently sauté the mushrooms in the same butter and pan as the suprêmes and add them to the suprêmes.
7 Drain off all the fat from the pan.
8 Deglaze the pan with the sherry.
9 Add the cream, bring to the boil and season.
10 Reduce to a lightly thickened consistency. Correct seasoning.
11 Pass through a fine chinois on to the suprêmes and serve.

An alternative method of preparing the sauce is to use half the amount of cream and an equal amount of chicken velouté (page 96).

4 portions

28 · Chicken sauté with potatoes *Poulet sauté Parmentier*

1¼–1½ kg	2½–3 lb	1 chicken cut for sauté
50 g	2 oz	butter, margarine or oil
		3–4 tablespns dry white wine
250 ml	½ pt	demi-glace or jus-lié
200 g	8 oz	potatoes
		salt, pepper
		chopped parsley

Chicken sauté with potatoes

1 Cook and dress chicken as for sauté. Pour off the fat.
2 Add wine and reduce by half. Add the demi-glace or jus-lié.
3 Simmer for 5 min.
4 Pass through a fine strainer over the chicken.
5 Meanwhile peel and wash the potatoes.
6 Cut into 1 cm (½ in) dice.
7 Wash well, drain and shallow fry to a golden brown in hot fat in a frying-pan.
8 Drain, season and sprinkle over the chicken.
9 Sprinkle with chopped parsley and serve.

4 portions

29 · Crumbed breast of chicken with asparagus *Suprême de volaille aux pointes d'asperges*

		4 suprêmes of chicken (page 347)	
25 g	1 oz	seasoned flour	
		1 egg	
50 g	2 oz	breadcrumbs, white or wholemeal	
50 g	2 oz	oil	for frying
50 g	2 oz	butter or margarine	for frying
50 g	2 oz	butter	
60 ml	⅛ pt	jus-lié	
200 g	½ lb	asparagus	

Suprêmes with asparagus and truffle

1 Pané the chicken suprêmes. Shake off all surplus crumbs.
2 Neaten and mark on one side with a palette knife.
3 Heat the oil and fat in a sauté pan.
4 Gently fry the suprêmes to a golden brown on both sides (6–8 min).
5 Dress the suprêmes on a flat dish and keep warm.
6 Mask the suprêmes with the remaining 50 g (2 oz) butter cooked to the nut-brown stage.

7 Surround the suprêmes with a cordon of jus-lié.
8 Garnish each suprême with a neat bundle of asparagus points. (previously cooked, refreshed and reheated with a little butter).
9 Place a cutlet frill on to each wing bone and serve.

4 portions

30 · Crumbed breast of chicken with asparagus and truffle
Suprême de volaille maréchale

Proceed as for recipe 29 adding one or two slices of truffle on to each suprême.

31 · Boiled chicken with rice and suprême sauce
Poulet poché au riz, sauce suprême

2–2½ kg	4–5 lb	1 boiling fowl	
50 g	2 oz	studded onion	for chicken
		bouquet garni	
50 g	2 oz	carrot	
50 g	2 oz	celery	
		6 peppercorns	
50 g	2 oz	chopped onion	rice
50 g	2 oz	butter, margarine or oil	
200 g	8 oz	rice (long grain)	
500 ml	1 pt	chicken stock	
75 g	3 oz	butter or margarine	sauce
75 g	3 oz	flour (white or wholemeal	
1 litre	2 pt	chicken stock	
		4 tablespns cream (non-dairy cream)	
		few drops of lemon juice	

Using hard margarine
1 portion provides:

1252 kcals/5259 kJ
86.0 g fat of which 35.7 g saturated
59.6 g carbohydrate of which 1.5 g sugars
63.3 g protein
1.9 g fibre

1 Place the chicken in cold water. Bring to the boil and skim.
2 Add peeled, whole vegetables, bouquet garni, peppercorns and salt.
3 Simmer till cooked. To test, remove the chicken from the stock and hold over a plate to catch the juices from the inside of the bird. There should be no sign of blood. Also test the drumstick with a trussing needle, which should penetrate easily to the bone.
4 Prepare ½ litre (1 pt) of velouté from the cooking liquor, cook out, correct the seasoning and pass through a fine strainer.
5 Finish with cream. Prepare a pilaff of rice (see page 201).

To serve, cut into portions. Dress the rice neatly in an entrée dish, arrange the portions of chicken on top and coat with sauce.

Note Poulet poché au riz, sauce ivoire is the same, but the sauce suprême is finished with a little meat glaze.

4 portions

32 Chicken à la king *Emincé de volaille à la king*

100 g	4 oz	button mushrooms
25 g	1 oz	butter or margarine
50 g	2 oz	red pimento (skinned)
400 g	1 lb	cooked boiled chicken
30 ml	1/16 pt	sherry
125 ml	1/4 pt	chicken velouté
30 ml	1/16 pt	cream or non-dairy cream

Using butter, hard margarine
1 portion provides:

292 kcals/1226 kJ
16.7 g fat of which 7.8 g saturated
3.2 g carbohydrate of which 0.8 g sugars
30.4 g protein
0.9 g fibre

1 Wash, peel and slice the mushrooms.
2 Cook them without colour in the butter or margarine.
3 If using raw pimento, discard the seeds, cut the pimento in dice and cook with the mushrooms.
4 Cut the chicken in small, neat slices.
5 Add the chicken to the mushrooms and pimento.
6 Drain off the fat. Add the sherry.
7 Add the velouté, bring to the boil.
8 Finish with the cream and correct the seasoning.
9 Place into a serving dish and decorate with small strips of cooked pimento.

One or 2 egg yolks may be used to form a liaison with the cream mixed into the boiling mixture at the last possible moment and immediately removed from the heat. Chicken à la king may be served in a border of golden brown duchesse potato or a pilaff of rice (page 201) may be offered as an accompaniment.

4 portions

33 Chicken galantine *Galantine de volaille*

200 g	8 oz	chicken meat free from all sinew
100 g	4 oz	lean veal
100 g	4 oz	belly of pork
75 g	3 oz	bread soaked in 125 ml (1/4 pt) of milk
250 ml	1/2 pt	double cream
		1 egg
		salt, pepper and nutmeg to season
12 g	1/2 oz	blanched and skinned pistachio nuts
25 g	1 oz	ham } cut into 1/2 cm (1/4 in) batons
25 g	1 oz	tongue } cut into 1/2 cm (1/4 in) batons
25 g	1 oz	bacon } cut into 1/2 cm (1/4 in) batons
		Thin slices of fat bacon or lardons.

1 portion provides:

390 kcals/1636 kJ
33.3 g fat of which 16.6 g saturated
6.3 g carbohydrate of which 1.6 g sugars
16.6 g protein
0.4 g fibre

1 Clean and carefully skin a chicken, place the skin in cold water to remove blood spots.
2 Bone the chicken and save one suprême for garnish.
3 Pass the rest through a fine mincer with the veal, pork and squeezed soaked breadcrumbs.
4 Remove into a basin, mix in the egg and pass through a sieve.

5 If using a food processor, add the egg while the mixture is in the processor and continue to chop until very fine.
6 Place into a basin over a bowl of ice, add the cream slowly, mixing well between each addition.
7 Place a damp cloth on a table, arrange the chicken skin on the cloth. Cover with slices of fat bacon, to about 5 cm (2 in), from the edge.
8 Spread on one-third of the mixture.
9 Garnish with alternative strips of ham, tongue, bacon, pistachio nuts and the chicken suprême also cut in ½ cm (¼ in) batons.
10 Place another layer of mixture on top and repeat the process.
11 Finish with a one-third layer of the mixture.
12 Roll the galantine up carefully. Tie both ends tightly.
13 Poach in chicken stock for approx 1½ hours.
14 When thoroughly cold remove cloth.
15 Cut in slices, serve garnished with salad.

Galantines may be coated with a white chaud-froid sauce, decorated and then masked with aspic jelly and served with a suitable salad.

approx. 8 portions

34 Chicken vol-au-vent *Vol-au-vent de volaille*

400 g	1 lb	puff paste (page 458)
2 kg	4 lb	1 boiling chicken
½ litre	1 pt	chicken velouté
		4 tablespns cream

Using hard margarine
1 portion provides:

656 kcals/2754 kJ
50.7 g fat of which 21.2 g saturated
20.0 g carbohydrate of which 0.6 g sugars
31.0 g protein
0.9 g fibre

1 Prepare the puff pastry using ½ kg (1 lb) flour and ½ kg (1 lb) margarine and ¼ litre (½ pt) water.
2 Roll out sufficient to cut eight rounds 8 cm (3 in) diameter.
3 Turn upside down on a lightly greased, dampened baking sheet.
4 Using a smaller plain cutter dipped in hot oil, make incisions half-way through each leaving approx. ½ cm (¼ in) border.
5 Egg wash, rest for approx. 20 min and bake in a hot oven (230–250 °C, Reg. 8–9) approx. 15–20 min.
6 When cool remove the lids carefully with a small knife.
7 Empty out the raw pastry from the centre.
8 Cook the chicken as for boiled chicken (recipe 31).
9 Make a velouté and cook out, correct the seasoning and pass through a fine strainer, finish with cream.
10 Remove all skin and bone from the chicken.
11 Cut into neat pieces, mix with the sauce.
12 Fill the warm vol-au-vent to overflowing.
13 Add the lids, garnish with picked parsley and serve.

8 portions

35 · Chicken and mushroom vol-au-vent

As for chicken vol-au-vent with the addition of 100 g (4 oz) of washed button mushrooms cut into quarters and cooked in a little stock with a few drops of lemon juice and 5 g (¼ oz) butter.

36 · Chicken cutlets *Côtelettes de volaille*

200 g	½ lb	cooked chicken free from bone and skin
125 ml	¼ pt	thick béchamel or chicken velouté
		1 egg yolk
		salt, pepper
25 g	1 oz	flour } for coating
		1 egg } for coating
50 g	2 oz	white or wholemeal breadcrumbs

Using hard marg, fried in peanut oil
1 portion provides:

284 kcals/1194 kJ
18.5 g fat of which 4.9 g saturated
13.4 g carbohydrate of which 0.5 g sugars
16.9 g protein
0.8 g fibre

1. Cut the chicken into 2 mm (1/12 in) dice.
2. Boil béchamel in a thick-bottomed pan.
3. Add the chicken and mix with a wooden spoon.
4. Bring to the boil and season. Add the yolk, mix well.
5. Correct the seasoning, remove from fire.
6. Turn out on to a buttered tray.
7. Cover with a greased paper and allow to set cold.
8. Mould into four even-sized cones.
9. Pass through flour, egg and breadcrumbs (twice if necessary).
10. Flatten and shape like cutlets.
11. Insert a small piece of macaroni to resemble a cutlet bone.
12. Deep or shallow fry in hot fat (180 °C) until golden brown.
13. Drain and garnish with fried or picked parsley.

A suitable sauce should be served separately, e.g. Madeira, demi-glace, mushroom.

4 portions

37 · Chicken and mushroom cutlets

As for recipe 36, adding 50–100 g (2–4 oz) washed mushrooms, cut the same as the chicken and cooked in a tablespoonful stock and 10 g (½ oz) butter and lemon juice. Add to the sauce with the chicken.

38 · Chicken and ham cutlets

As for chicken cutlets (recipe 36) using 300 g (12 oz) chicken and 100 g (4 oz) lean cooked ham.

39 · **Chicken pancakes** *Crêpes de volaille*

100 g	4 oz	flour, white or wholemeal	pancake
		1 egg	
		salt, pepper	
		chopped parsley	
¼ litre	½ pt	milk, whole or skimmed	
10 g	½ oz	melted butter or margarine	
125 ml	¼ pt	thick béchamel or chicken velouté	filling
200 g	½ lb	cooked chicken free from bone and skin	
		salt, pepper	

1 portion provides:

339 kcals/1423 kJ
18.9 g fat of which 6.3 g saturated
24.7 g carbohydrate of which 3.4 g sugars
19.0 g protein
1.1 g fibre

1 Sieve flour into a bowl and make a well in the centre.
2 Add the egg, salt, pepper, parsley and milk.
3 Gradually incorporate the flour from the sides of the bowl and whisk to a smooth batter.
4 Mix in the melted butter.
5 Heat the pancake pan, clean thoroughly.
6 Add 5 g (¼ oz) lard or oil and heat until smoking.
7 Add sufficient mixture to thinly cover the bottom of the pan.
8 Cook for a few seconds until lightly brown.
9 Turn and cook on the other side. Turn onto a plate.
10 Wipe pan clean and make a total of 8 small or 4 large pancakes.
11 Meanwhile prepare the filling by boiling the sauce.
12 Cut the chicken in neat small pieces and add to the sauce.
13 Mix in and correct the seasoning.
14 Divide the mixture between the pancakes, roll up each one and place in an earthenware dish.
15 Reheat in a hot oven and serve.

4 portions

40 · **Chicken pancakes with cheese sauce** *Crêpes de volaille Mornay*

1 Proceed as for recipe 39.
2 Coat the pancakes with ¼ litre (½ pt) Mornay sauce (page 95).
3 Sprinkle with 10 g (½ oz) grated cheese.
4 Brown under the salamander and serve.

4 portions

41 · **Chicken pancakes with tomato, mushroom and white wine sauce** *Crêpes de volaille chasseur*

1 Proceed as for recipe 39.
2 Coat pancakes with ¼ litre (½ pt) chasseur sauce (page 99).

4 portions

42 Chicken and mushroom pancakes
Crêpes de volaille et champignons

Add 50–100 g (2–4 oz) washed sliced cooked mushrooms to the filling and proceed as for recipe 39.

4 portions

43 Chicken and mushroom pancakes with cheese sauce
Crêpes de volaille et champignons Mornay

1. Add 50–100 g (2–4 oz) cooked mushrooms to the filling as recipe 39.
2. Coat with ¼ litre (½ pt) Mornay sauce.
3. Sprinkle with grated cheese.
4. Brown under the salamander and serve.

4 portions

44 Chicken and ham pancakes *Crêpes de volaille et jambon*

Proceed as for recipe 39 using 100 g (¼ lb) chicken and 100 g (¼ lb) lean ham cut in neat pieces.

4 portions

45 Fricassée of chicken *Fricassée de volaille*

1¼–1½ kg	2½–3 lb	1 chicken
50 g	2 oz	butter or margarine
35 g	1½ oz	flour
½ litre	1 pt	chicken stock (approx.)
		1–2 yolks of eggs
		4 tablespns cream or non-dairy cream
		chopped parsley

Using butter
1 portion provides:

643 kcals/2699 kJ
51.3 g fat of which 23.3 g saturated
7.4 g carbohydrate of which 0.6 g sugars
38.2 g protein
0.4 g fibre

1. Cut the chicken as for sauté and season with salt and pepper.
2. Place the butter in a sauté pan. Heat gently.
3. Add pieces of chicken (see stage 9, recipe 23). Cover with a lid.
4. Cook gently on both sides without colouring. Mix in the flour.
5. Cook out carefully without colouring. Gradually mix in the stock.
6. Bring to the boil and skim.
7. Allow to simmer gently till cooked.
8. Mix yolks and cream in a basin (liaison).
9. Pick out the chicken into a clean pan.
10. Pour a little boiling sauce on to the yolks and cream and mix well.
11. Pour all back into the sauce, combine thoroughly but do not re-boil.
12. Correct the seasoning and pass through a strainer.
13. Pour over the chicken, reheat without boiling.
14. Serve sprinkled with chopped parsley.
15. May be garnished with heart-shaped croûtons, fried in butter.

4 portions

46 Fricassée of chicken with button onions and mushrooms
Fricassée de volaille à l'ancienne

As for fricassée of chicken with 50–100 g (2–4 oz) button onions and 50–100 g (2–4 oz) button mushrooms. They are peeled and the mushrooms left whole, turned or quartered depending on size and quality. The onions are added to the chicken as soon as it comes to the boil and the mushrooms 15 min later. Heart-shaped croûtons may be used to garnish.

47 Chicken in casserole or cocotte
Poulet poêlé en casserole ou en cocotte

A casserole is made of earthenware, a cocotte of porcelain.

Basic Method

1¼–1½ kg	2½–3 lb	1 chicken
50 g	2 oz	onion
50 g	2 oz	carrot
50 g	2 oz	celery
		bouquet garni
50 g	2 oz	butter, margarine or oil
¼ litre	½ pt	jus-lié
		chopped parsley

Using hard margarine
1 portion provides:

530 kcals/2224 kJ
41.5 g fat of which 16.7 g saturated
2.0 g carbohydrate of which 1.5 g sugars
37.0 g protein
0.9 g fibre

1. Prepare the chicken and truss for entrée (page 345).
2. Slice the onion, carrot and celery, place in the bottom of the casserole or cocotte with the bouquet garni.
3. Season the chicken and place on the bed of roots.
4. Spread the butter on the bird.
5. Cover with a lid and place in a hot oven (230–250 °C, Reg. 8–9).
6. Baste occasionally, allow approx. ¾–1 hr.
7. When cooked extract remove the chicken and remove the string.
8. Pour off the fat from the casserole, remove the bouquet garni.
9. Deglaze the casserole or cocotte with the demi-glace or jus-lié.
10. Pour the sauce into a sauteuse, boil, skim and correct the seasoning and consistency.
11. Clean the casserole, and place the bird in the casserole.
12. Pass the sauce through a fine strainer on to the bird.
13. Sprinkle with chopped parsley and serve.

Chicken casserole is usually served garnished, e.g.:

Bonne femme	cocotte potatoes, glazed button onions, lardons
Champeaux	as bonne femme with white wine in the sauce
Grandmère	dice of mushrooms and croûtons
Parmentier	Parmentier potatoes, white wine in the sauce
Paysanne	paysanne of vegetables

48 · Chicken pie

1¼–1½ kg	2½–3 lb	1 chicken
		salt, pepper
100 g	4 oz	streaky bacon
100 g	4 oz	button mushrooms
		1 chopped onion
¼ litre	½ pt	chicken stock
		pinch of chopped parsley
		1 hard-boiled egg (chopped)
200 g	8 oz	puff paste (page 458)

Using hard margarine in pastry
1 portion provides:

799 kcals/3357 kJ
62.6 g fat of which 25.1 g saturated
16.4 g carbohydrate of which 1.9 g sugars
43.3 g protein
1.8 g fibre

1 Cut the chicken as for sauté or bone-out completely and cut into pieces 4×1 cm (1½×½ in).
2 Season with salt and pepper.
3 Wrap each piece in very thin streaky bacon. Place in a pie dish.
4 Add the washed sliced mushrooms and remainder of the ingredients.
5 Add sufficient cold stock to barely cover the chicken.
6 Cover and cook as for steak pie (page 288), allow approx. 1–1½ hr cooking.
7 Serve. If pie is served whole use a pie collar.

4 portions

49 · Chicken salad *Salade de poulet*

		1 lettuce (washed)
400 g	1 lb	cooked chicken, free from skin and bone
		2 tomatoes
		1 hard-boiled egg
10 g	½ oz	anchovies
		4 or 8 olives
5 g	¼ oz	capers
		4 tablespns vinaigrette (page 119)

1 Remove heart from the lettuce.
2 Shred the remainder.
3 Place in a salad bowl.
4 Cut the chicken in neat pieces and place on the lettuce.
5 Decorate with quarters of tomato, hard-boiled egg, anchovies, olives, quartered heart of the lettuce and capers.
6 Serve accompanied with vinaigrette.

4 portions

50 · Chicken mayonnaise *Mayonnaise de poulet*

Proceed as in previous recipe using 60 ml (¼ pt) mayonnaise instead of vinaigrette. The chicken is dressed on the lettuce, then coated with mayonnaise and the garnish neatly dressed on top.

51 · Curried chicken *Kari de poulet or Currie de poulet*

1¼–1½ kg	2½–3 lb	1 chicken
50 g	2 oz	oil
200 g	8 oz	onion
		1 clove garlic
10 g	½ oz	flour
10 g	½ oz	curry powder
25 g	1 oz	tomato purée
½ litre	1 pt	chicken stock
25 g	1 oz	sultanas
25 g	1 oz	chopped chutney
10 g	½ oz	desiccated coconut
50 g	2 oz	chopped apple
10 g	½ oz	grated root ginger
		or
5 g	¼ oz	ground ginger

Using sunflower oil
1 portion provides:

656 kcals/2755 kJ
49.9 g fat of which 17.1 g saturated
15.1 g carbohydrate of which 11.8 g sugars
37.4 g protein
2.3 g fibre

1. Cut the chicken as for sauté, season with salt.
2. Heat the oil in a sauté pan, add the chicken.
3. Lightly brown on both sides.
4. Add the chopped onion and garlic.
5. Cover with lid, cook gently 3–4 min.
6. Mix in the flour and curry powder.
7. Mix in the tomato purée. Moisten with stock.
8. Bring to the boil, skim.
9. Add remainder of the ingredients. Simmer till cooked.
10. The sauce may be finished with 2 tablespoons cream or yoghurt.

Accompany with 100 g (4 oz) plain boiled rice, grilled poppadum and Bombay duck; see also page 257 for extra accompaniments.

4 portions

52 · Braised rice with chicken livers *Pilaff aux foies de volailles*

100 g	4 oz	chicken livers
		salt, mill pepper
25 g	1 oz	butter or margarine
60 ml	⅛ pt	demi-glace or jus-lié
200 g	½ lb	braised rice (page 201)

Using hard margarine
1 portion provides:

265 kcals/1115 kJ
17.0 g fat of which 7.2 g saturated
22.4 g carbohydrate of which 0.3 g sugars
7.0 g protein
0.6 g fibre

1. Trim the livers, cut into 1 cm (½ in) pieces.
2. Season with salt and pepper.
3. Fry quickly in the butter in a frying-pan. Drain well.
4. Mix with the demi-glace or the jus-lié, do not re-boil.
5. Correct the seasoning.
6. Make a well with the riz pilaff on the dish.
7. Serve the livers in the centre of the rice.

4 portions

53 Chicken in red wine *Coq au vin*

1½ kg	1×3 lb	roasting chicken
50 g	2 oz	lardons
		4 small chipolatas
50 g	2 oz	button mushrooms
		4 tablespns sunflower oil
50 g	2 oz	butter or margarine
		12 small button onions
125 ml	¼ pt	red wine } or 500 ml (1 pt) red wine
375 ml	¾ pt	brown stock }
25 g	1 oz	butter or margarine
25 g	1 oz	flour
		4 heart-shaped croûtons
		chopped parsley

Using sunflower oil, hard margarine
1 portion provides:

1141 kcals/4794 kJ
95.7 g fat of which 32.9 g saturated
16.6 g carbohydrate of which 2.3 g sugars
49.0 g protein
1.7 g fibre

1 Cut the chicken as for sauté.
2 Blanch the lardons.
3 If the chipolatas are large divide into two.
4 Wash and cut the mushrooms in quarters.
5 Sauté the lardons, mushrooms and chipolatas in a mixture of butter/margarine and oil. Remove when cooked.
6 Season the pieces of chicken and place in the pan in the correct order with button onions. Sauté until almost cooked. Drain off fat.
7 Just cover with red wine and brown stock, cover with a lid and finish cooking.
8 Remove chicken and onions, place into a clean pan.
9 Lightly thicken the liquor with a beurre manié from the 25 g (1 oz) butter/margarine and 25 g (1 oz) flour.
10 Pass sauce over the chicken and onions, add mushrooms, chipolatas and lardons. Correct seasoning and re-heat.
11 Serve garnished with heart-shaped croûtons with the points dipped in chopped parsley.

Duck Recipes

54 Braised duck with peas *Canard braisé aux petits pois*

50 g	2 oz	butter or oil
100 g	4 oz	thick cut streaky bacon
200 g	8 oz	button onions
2 kg	4 lb	duck
375 ml	¾ pt	demi-glace
375 ml	¾ pt	brown stock
200 g	8 oz	peas

1 Place the butter in a braising pan.
2 Cut the bacon into thick lardons.

3 Add the lardons and button onions to the pan.
4 Gently fry to a light brown colour.
5 Remove the lardons and onions taking care not to burn the butter.
6 Add the prepared seasoned and trussed duck to the pan.
7 Carefully brown the duck on all sides without burning the butter.
8 Drain off all the fat.
9 Add the demi-glace and brown stock (the duck should be ½–¾ covered). Bring to the boil and cover with a lid.
10 Place in a moderate oven (150–200 °C) and allow to simmer gently for approx. ¾–1 hour.
11 Add the lardons, butter onions and the peas (only add the peas at this stage if raw fresh peas are being used – if frozen peas are being used they should be added 10–15 min. later).
12 Replace the lid, return the dish to the oven.
13 Continue simmering gently until the duck and garnish is tender – approx. a further ½–¾ hour.
14 Remove the duck, cut out the string and keep warm.
15 Degrease the sauce and correct the seasoning and consistency.
16 Cut the duck into portions and neatly place on a serving dish.
17 Mask with the sauce and garnish and serve. *4 portions*

55 **Roast duck or duckling** *Canard ou caneton rôti*

		1 duck
		oil
		salt
¼ litre	½ pt	brown stock
		bunch watercress
125 ml	¼ pt	apple sauce (page 106)

With apple sauce, watercress
1 portion provides:

734 kcals/3083 kJ
60.5 g fat of which 16.9 g saturated
8.2 g carbohydrate of which 7.8 g sugars
40.0 g protein
1.4 g fibre

1 Lightly season the duck inside and out with salt.
2 Truss and brush lightly with oil.
3 Place on its side in a roasting tin, with a few drops of water.
4 Place in hot oven approx. 20–25 min.
5 Turn on to the other side.
6 Cook for a further 20–25 min approx. Baste frequently.
7 To test if cooked, pierce with a fork between the drumstick and thigh and hold over a plate. The juice issuing from the duck should not show any signs of blood.
8 Prepare roast gravy with the stock and the sediment in the roasting tray. Correct the seasoning, remove surface fat.
9 Serve garnished with picked watercress.
10 Accompany with a sauceboat of hot apple sauce and a sauceboat of gravy and game chips. Also serve sauceboat of sage and onion stuffing as prepared in the following recipe for roast stuffed duck.

56 · **Roast stuffed duck** *Canard rôti à l'anglaise*

		Stuffing
100 g	4 oz	chopped onion
100 g	4 oz	duck dripping or butter
50 g	2 oz	½ teaspn powdered sage
		chopped parsley
		salt, pepper
		white or wholemeal breadcrumbs
50 g	2 oz	chopped duck liver

1 Gently cook the onion in the dripping without colour.
2 Add the herbs and seasoning. Mix in the crumbs and liver. Stuff the neck end and cook remaining stuffing separately. Cook and serve as for roast duck.

57 · **Roast duckling and orange salad** *Caneton rôti salade d'orange*

Proceed as for roast duck and serve separately in a bowl 4 hearts of lettuce or good leaves of lettuce and on each heart place 3 segments of orange, free from pips and skin, and a little blanched fine julienne of orange zest sprinkled over.

Accompany with a sauceboat of cream lightly acidulated with lemon juice.

58 · **Duckling with orange sauce** *Caneton bigarade*

2 kg	4 lb	duckling	
50 g	2 oz	butter	
50 g	2 oz	carrots	mirepoix
50 g	2 oz	onions	mirepoix
25 g	1 oz	celery	mirepoix
		1 bay leaf	mirepoix
		1 small sprig thyme	mirepoix
250 ml	½ pt	brown stock	
10 g	½ oz	arrowroot	
		2 oranges	
		1 lemon	
		2 tablespns vinegar	
25 g	1 oz	sugar	

Using butter
1 portion provides:

744 kcals/3125 kJ
60.1 g fat of which 17.1 g saturated
11.8 g carbohydrate of which 9.3 g sugars
39.9 g protein
0.1 g fibre

1 Clean and truss the duck. Use 10 g (½ oz) butter to grease a deep pan. Add the mirepoix.
2 Season the duck. Place the duck on the mirepoix.
3 Coat the duck with the remaining butter.
4 Cover the pan with a tight fitting lid.
5 Place the pan in oven (200–230 °C, Reg. 6–8).
6 Baste occasionally, cook approx. 1 hr.
7 Remove the lid and continue cooking the duck basting frequently until tender (approx. a further ½ hr).
8 Remove the duck, cut out the string and keep the duck in a warm place. Drain off all the fat from the pan.

9 Deglaze with the stock, bring to the boil and allow to simmer for a few minutes.
10 Thicken by adding the arrowroot diluted in a little cold water.
11 Reboil, correct seasoning, degrease and pass through a fine chinois.
12 Thinly remove the zest from one orange and the lemon and cut into fine julienne.
13 Blanch the julienne of zest for 3–4 min, refresh.
14 Place the vinegar and sugar in a small sauteuse and cook to a light caramel stage.
15 Add the juice of the oranges and the lemon.
16 Add the sauce and bring to the boil.
17 Correct seasoning and pass through a fine chinois.
18 Add the julienne to the sauce, keep warm.
19 Remove the legs from the duck, bone out and cut in thin slices.
20 Carve the duck breasts into thin slices and neatly dress.
21 Coat with the sauce and serve.

Note An alternative method of service is to cut the duck into eight pieces which may then be either left on the bone or the bones removed.

4 portions

59 · Duckling with cherries *Canteon aux cerises*

2 kg	4 lb	duckling	
50 g	2 oz	butter	
50 g	2 oz	carrots	mirepoix
50 g	2 oz	onions	mirepoix
25 g	1 oz	celery	mirepoix
		1 bay leaf	mirepoix
		1 small sprig thyme	mirepoix
		2 tablespns sherry or Madeira	
250 ml	½ pt	brown stock	
10 g	½ oz	arrowroot	
		24 stoned cherries	

Proceed as for recipe 58 points 1–8.
9 Deglaze the pan with the sherry.
10 Add the stock, bring to the boil, simmer 4–5 min.
11 Thicken by gradually adding the arrowroot diluted in a little cold water.
12 Reboil, correct seasoning, degrease and pass through a fine chinois.
13 Add the stoned cherries to the sauce and simmer gently 3–4 min.
14 Remove the legs from the duck, bone out and cut into thin slices.
15 Cut the duck breasts into thin slices and neatly dress.
16 Coat with the sauce and cherries and serve.

Note An alternative method is to cut the duck into eight pieces which may then either be left on the bone or have the bones removed. *4 portions*

Game Gibier

60 · Game

Game may be divided into two groups:
a) furred – venison, hare;
b) feathered.

Furred game

61 · Venison *Venaison*

This name applies to the flesh of deer. It is by nature dry, tough meat. This is overcome by hanging the carcass for 12–21 days according to the temperature, and by well-marinading the joints.

The prime cuts are the haunch, saddle and chops which may be roasted in joints or cut into steaks and fried. Roast joints are usually accompanied by a piquante or peppery sauce, cold joints by an Oxford or Cumberland sauce. Recipes for these sauces are in the sauce section. The meat from the shoulder is usually stewed.

62 · Marinade for venison

125 ml	¼ pt	oil
200 g	8 oz	onions
200 g	8 oz	carrots
		sprig of thyme
		1 bay leaf
100 g	4 oz	celery
		12 peppercorns
		parsley stalks
		4 tablespns vinegar
		salt
		1 bottle of red wine
		2 cloves
		2 cloves garlic

The vegetables are washed, peeled and chopped, combined with the other ingredients and sprinkled over the joint. The joint is turned occasionally and left to marinade for several hours.

63 · Hare *Lièvre*

Young hare 2½–3 kg (5–6 lb) in weight should be used. To test a young hare it should be possible to take the ear between the fingers and tear it quite easily, also the hare lip which is clearly marked in old animals, should only be faintly defined.

A hare should be hung for about a week before cleaning it out. It may be prepared as a brown stew known as a civet.

64 Jugged hare *Civet de lièvre*

		1 young hare	
50 g	2 oz	oil	
25 g	1 oz	flour, white or wholemeal	
50 g	2 oz	tomato purée	
½ litre	1 pt	brown stock	
		1 clove garlic	
¼ litre	½ pt	red wine	
100 g	4 oz	button onions	garnish
100 g	4 oz	button mushrooms	garnish
100 g	4 oz	streaky bacon	garnish
100 g	4 oz	stale bread	garnish
		chopped parsley	garnish

Using sunflower oil
1 portion provides:

744 kcals/3125 kJ
39.2 g fat of which 11.9 g saturated
20.5 g carbohydrate of which 3.7 g sugars
68.3 g protein
2.3 g fibre

1 Skin hare carefully.
2 Make an incision along the belly. Clean out the intestines.
3 Clean out the forequarter end carefully collecting all the blood into a basin.
4 Cut as follows: each leg into two pieces, each foreleg into two pieces, the forequarter into two, the saddle into three or four pieces.
5 Soak in a marinade as for venison, for 5–6 hr, but omit the vinegar.
6 Drain well in a colander.
7 Quickly fry the pieces of hare until brown on all sides.
8 Place into a thick-bottomed pan, mix in the flour, cook out, browning slightly.
9 Mix in the tomato purée. Gradually add the stock.
10 Add all the juice and vegetables and herbs from the marinade.
11 Bring to the boil, skim, add the garlic and the wine.
12 Cover with a lid and allow to simmer till tender.
13 Pick out the hare into a clean pan.
14 Re-boil the sauce, correct the seasoning and thicken by gradually pouring in the blood (after which it must not be re-boiled).
15 Pass through a fine strainer on to the hare.
16 Meanwhile prepare the garnish by cooking the button onions glacé, cooking the mushrooms whole, turned or in quarters in a little stock and cutting the bacon into lardons, strips 2 × ½ × ½ cm (1 × ¼ × ¼ in), and lightly browning them in a little fat in a frying-pan. Cut the bread into heart-shaped croûtons and fry to a golden brown.
17 Mix the garnish with the civet, serve in an entrée dish, dip the point of the croûtons into the sauce, then into the chopped parsley and place on the edge of the dish.

Red-currant jelly may be spread on the heart-shaped croûtons.

65 · Preparation of rabbit

Preparation of rabbit

1 Skin the rabbit carefully.
2 Make an incision along the belly.
3 Clear out the intestines.
4 Clean out the forequarter end carefully.
5 Cut as follows: each leg in two pieces, each foreleg into two pieces if large, the forequarter into two, the saddle into three or four pieces.

Rabbit may be cooked as follows:

66 · Braised saddle of rabbit

		4 prepared saddles of rabbit
100 g	4 oz	carrots } mirepoix
100 g	4 oz	onions } mirepoix
		bouquet garni
25 g	1 oz	butter, margarine or oil
½ litre	1 pt	demi-glace

1 Colour saddles on both sides in the fat.
2 Remove saddles and colour mirepoix in the same pan.
3 Drain off fat.
4 Place saddles on the mirepoix.
5 Add demi-glace and season lightly.
6 Bring to the boil, add bouquet garni, cover with a lid, place in the oven and simmer till tender.
7 Remove saddles, correct seasoning and consistency.
8 Straining liquid through a fine strainer, pour over the saddles and serve.

Using hard margarine
1 portion provides:

247 kcals/1037 kJ
11.8 g fat of which 5.2 g saturated
6.6 g carbohydrate of which 1.7 g sugars
28.9 g protein
0.9 g fibre

In recipes 67–71 substitute rabbit for the main ingredient and follow the appropriate method.

67 · Rabbit pie

See chicken pie, page 366.

68 · White rabbit stew *Blanquet de lapin*

See white lamb stew, page 259.

69 · **Fricassée of rabbit** *Fricassée de lapin*

See fricassée of veal, page 306.

70 · **Brown rabbit stew** *Ragoût de lapin*

See brown beef stew, page 280.

71 · **Rabbit curry** *Currie de lapin*

See lamb curry, page 256.

Top: rabbit pie; foreground: braised saddle of rabbit with marquis potatoes (p. 440), peas (p. 428) and sweetcorn

Feathered Game

72 · **Feathered game**

The term includes all edible birds which live in freedom, but only the following are generally used in catering today:

pheasant	*faisan*
partridge	*perdreau*
woodcock	*bécasse*
snipe	*bécassine*
wild duck	*canard sauvage*
teal	*sarcelle*
grouse	*grouse*

The flavour of most game birds is improved by their being hung for a few days in a moderate draught before being plucked. Hanging is to some degree essential for all game. It drains the flesh of blood and begins a process of disintegration which is essential to make the flesh tender and develop flavour – this is due to the action of enzymes. Game birds should be hung with the feet down. Care should be taken with the water-birds: wild duck, teal, etc., not to allow them to get too high, because the oiliness of their flesh will quickly turn them rancid.

When game birds are roasted they should always be served on a croûte of fried bread, garnished with thick round pieces of toasted French bread spread with game farce (see below), game chips and picked watercress.

As game birds are deficient in fat, a thin slice of fat bacon (bard) should be tied over the breast during cooking to prevent it from drying; this is also placed on the breast when serving. Roast gravy, bread sauce and browned breadcrumbs (toasted or fried) are served separately.

73 Game farce *Farce de gibier*

50 g	2 oz	butter or margarine
100 g	4 oz	game livers
25 g	1 oz	chopped onion
		sprig of thyme
		1 bay leaf
		salt, pepper

1. Heat 25 g (1 oz) butter in a frying-pan.
2. Quickly toss the seasoned livers, onion and herbs, browning well but keeping underdone. Pass through a sieve or mincer.
3. Mix in the remaining 25 g (1 oz) butter. Correct the seasoning.

74 Pheasant *Faisan*

Young birds have a flexible beak, pliable breast bone, grey legs and underdeveloped spurs or none at all. The last large feather in the wing is pointed.

They may be roasted or braised or pot roasted.

Season – 1st October to 1st February.

They should be well hung.

Approx. 1½–2 kg (3–4 lb) *4 portions*

75 **Partridge** *Perdreau*

Young birds indicated as for pheasant, the legs should also be smooth.
May be roasted, braised, etc.
Season – 1st September to 1st February.
Three to five days' hanging is ample time.

Approx. ¼–½ kg (½–1 lb) *1–2 portions*

76 **Woodcock** *Bécasse*

A good quality bird should have soft supple feet, clean mouth and throat, fat and firm breast. It has a distinctive flavour which is accentuated by the entrails being left in during cooking. The vent must be carefully checked for cleanliness.
Usually roasted.
Season – October to November.
Hang for 3–4 days.

Approx. 200–300 g (8–12 oz) *1 per portion*

77 **Snipe** *Bécassine*

Snipe resemble woodcock but are smaller. Points of quality are the same as for woodcock. The flavour of the flesh can be accentuated in the same way as the woodcock.
May be roasted and are sometimes cooked in steak pudding or pies.
Season – October to November.
Hang for 3–4 days.
Snipe and woodcock are prepared with the head left on and the beak is used for trussing. The head is prepared by removing the skin and eyes.

Approx. 100 g (4 oz) *1 per portion*

78 **Wild duck** *Canard sauvage*

The most common is the mallard, which is the ancestor of the domestic duck. The beak and webbed feet should be soft and pliable.
They may be roasted, slightly underdone or braised.
Season – August to February.
It is particularly important that water-birds be eaten only in season; out of season the flesh becomes coarse and acquires a fishy flavour.

Approx. 1–1½ kg (2–3 lb) *2–4 portions*

79 · Teal *Sarcelle*

This is a smaller species of wild duck. Select as for wild duck.

May be roasted or braised.

Season – October to January.

Approx. ½–¾ kg (1–1½ lb) *1–2 portions*

80 · Grouse

This is one of the most popular game birds.

Young birds have soft downy plumes on the breast and under the wings. They also have pointed wings and a rounded, soft spur knob, the spur becomes hard and scaly in older birds.

Usually served roasted, left slightly underdone.

Grouse is equally popular hot or cold.

Season – 12th August to 10th December.

Approx. 300 g (12 oz) *1–2 portions*

81 · Salmis of game *Salmis de gibier*

This is usually prepared from partridge or pheasant.

		1 cooked pheasant or 2 cooked partridges
25 g	1 oz	butter or margarine
50 g	2 oz	onion
50 g	2 oz	carrot
25 g	1 oz	celery
		4 tablespns red wine
		bouquet garni
100 g	4 oz	mushrooms, quartered or turned
½ litre	1 pt	demi-glace

Using hard margarine
1 portion provides:

310 kcals/1300 kJ
15.2 g fat of which 5.6 g saturated
2.4 g carbohydrate of which 1.5 g sugars
38.1 g protein
1.3 g fibre

1. Cut the bird into portions. Chop the carcass.
2. Melt the butter in a thick-bottomed pan.
3. Add the carcass, sliced onion, carrot, celery and colour slightly.
4. Pour off the fat. Deglaze with the wine.
5. Add the bouquet garni and mushroom trimmings and demi-glace. Simmer for 1 hr. Correct the seasoning.
6. Pass the sauce through a fine strainer on to the bird and heat through in a sauté pan, together with the cooked mushrooms.

Serve garnished with heart-shaped croûtons spread with game farce.

4 portions

Clockwise from top left: bean goulash with ingredients (p. 387); braised wild rice (p. 201); mushroom, celery and walnut vol-au-vent (p. 390)

16

VEGETARIAN DISHES

General objectives
To be aware of the need to produce a variety of vegetarian dishes that may be introduced on to menus. To be able to appreciate the concept of vegetarian cookery in society.

Specific objectives
To describe and demonstrate the various techniques involved in vegetarian cookery. To be able to produce a number of vegetarian dishes as alternatives to fish and meat dishes. To be able to analyse and evaluate vegetarian dishes as a separate concept.

Introduction

Vegetarians and vegans do not eat fish, meat, poultry or game and vegans in addition do not consume milk, dairy products and eggs. Because there are many people who are vegetarians, and many others who choose to eat vegetarian foods occasionally, this section of recipes is included. Further recipes suitably adapted can be found in the soup, eggs, farinaceous dishes, hors-d'oeuvre, salads and vegetable chapters.

1 White vegetarian stock

100 g	4 oz	onion	roughly chopped
100 g	4 oz	carrots	roughly chopped
100 g	4 oz	celery	roughly chopped
100 g	4 oz	leek	roughly chopped
1 ½ litres	3 pt	water	

1 Place all ingredients into a saucepan, add the water, bring to the boil.
2 Allow to simmer for approx. 1 hour, skim if necessary. Strain and use.

1 litre, 2 pts

2 Brown vegetarian stock

100 g	4 oz	onions	roughly chopped
100 g	4 oz	carrots	roughly chopped
100 g	4 oz	celery	roughly chopped
100 g	4 oz	leeks	roughly chopped
60 ml	⅛ pt	sunflower oil	
50 g	2 oz	tomatoes	
50 g	2 oz	mushroom trimmings	
		6 peppercorns	
1 ½ litres	3 pts	water	
5 g	¼ oz	yeast extract	

1 Fry the onions, carrots, celery and leeks in the sunflower oil until golden brown.
2 Drain the vegetables, place into a suitable saucepan.
3 Add all the other ingredients except the yeast extract.
4 Cover with the water, bring to the boil.
5 Add the yeast extract, simmer gently for approx. 1 hour.
6 Skim if necessary and use.

1 litre, 2 pts

3 · Avocado and blue cheese puffs

		1 large ripe avocado pear
100 g	4 oz	blue cheese (Danish, Roquefort, Stilton, etc.)
200 g	8 oz	puff pastry made with 30% wholemeal flour (page 458)
		egg wash

1 portion provides:

405 kcals/1699 kJ
34.2 g fat of which 12.8 g saturated
14.9 g carbohydrate of which 1.2 g sugars
10.3 g protein
2.0 g fibre

1 Cut the avocado in half and remove the stone and skin.
2 Purée the avocado and cheese in a food processor, and season.
3 Roll out puff pastry ¼ cm (⅛ in) thick. Cut into 4 × 10 cm (4 in) squares.
4 Divide the purée into the four squares slightly off centre.
5 Egg wash the edges. Fold over to form a triangle. Press down firmly. Mark edges with the back of a small knife.
6 Brush with egg wash, place on to a lightly greased baking sheet.
7 Bake in a pre-heated oven, 200 °C for approx. 15 minutes.

Serve on individual plates with a mushroom, white wine and mustard sauce garnished with a little cooked tomato concassé.

4 · Mushroom, wine and mustard sauce

100 g	4 oz	firm white button mushrooms
25 g	1 oz	margarine
		juice of ½ lemon
250 ml	1 pt	velouté made with vegetable stock
12 g	½ oz	English or Continental mustard
60 ml	⅛ pt	white wine (dry)
60 ml	⅛ pt	single cream or unsweetened vegetable creamer

1 Sweat sliced mushroom in margarine and lemon juice for 1–2 mins.
2 Add the boiled and passed velouté.
3 Stir in the English mustard diluted in the wine.
4 Finish with cream.

5 Bean and nut burgers

200 g	8 oz	aduki beans
60 ml	⅛ pt	sunflower oil
50 g	2 oz	finely chopped onion
		1 clove of garlic
3 g	⅛ oz	dried rosemary
100 g	4 oz	button mushrooms
		2 small carrots (grated)
100 g	4 oz	chopped walnuts and hazelnuts
50 g	2 oz	tomato purée
		seasoning
		1–2 eggs
		flour
100 g	4 oz	rolled oats
		parsley

1 portion provides:

556 kcals/2343 kJ
32.1 g fat of which 4.4 g saturated
48.8 g carbohydrate of which 5.6 g sugars
21.4 g protein
17.3 g fibre

1 Soak beans in cold water for 24 hours, drain. Cover with cold water in a saucepan, bring to the boil, simmer gently until tender. Drain, purée in food processor.
2 Heat the oil and sweat the onion and crushed garlic without colouring for 2 mins., add the rosemary and sweat for a further 2 mins.
3 Add washed and finely chopped mushrooms, grated carrot and nuts.
4 Cook for 2–3 mins. Drain off any surplus liquid. Remove from heat.
5 Mix in bean purée. Add tomato purée. Season, bind with beaten egg.
6 Shape into burgers, pass through flour, beaten egg and rolled oats.
7 Place on a greased baking sheet, brush with oil. Bake in a pre-heated oven 180 °C (Reg. 4) for 10–15 mins., turning over at half-way stage.
8 Alternatively, carefully shallow fry burgers in hot sunflower oil, taking special care that they do not break up.
9 Serve garnished with picked parsley and a suitable sauce, e.g. tomato sauce made with vegetable stock and no bacon flavouring.

4 portions

6 Chinese-style stir fry vegetables

Preparation of Chinese-style stir fry vegetables

100 g	4 oz	beansprouts
100 g	4 oz	button mushrooms
100 g	4 oz	carrots
100 g	4 oz	celery
100 g	4 oz	cauliflower
100 g	4 oz	broccoli
50 g	2 oz	baby sweetcorn
50 g	2 oz	French beans
50 g	2 oz	red peppers
50 g	2 oz	green peppers
125 ml	¼ pt	sunflower oil
5 g	¼ oz	grated root ginger
60 ml	⅛ pt	soy sauce
		ground white or mill pepper to season

1 portion provides:

340 kcals/1429 kJ
31.9 g fat of which 4.2 g saturated
9.1 g carbohydrate of which 4.2 g sugars
4.7 g protein
4.5 g fibre

1 Wash the beansprouts, wash and slice mushrooms. Peel the carrots, cut into large batons. Trim celery, cut into large batons. Wash cauliflower and broccoli and cut into florets. Top and tail French beans, cut in halves. Wash and slice peppers. The green vegetables may be quickly blanched and refreshed to retain colour.
2 Heat the sunflower oil in a wok or frying pan and add all the vegetables. Fry and continuously stir for approx. 3 mins.
3 Add the grated ginger cook for 1 min. Add the soy sauce, stir well.
4 Correct seasoning, serve immediately.

4 portions

7 Caribbean fruit curry

		1 small pineapple
		2 small dessert pears
		2 dessert apples
		2 mangoes
		2 bananas
		1 paw paw
		1 guava
		grated rind and juice of 1 lime
50 g	2 oz	chopped onion
25 g	1 oz	sunflower margarine
60 mls	⅛ pt	sunflower oil
50 g	2 oz	Madras curry powder
25 g	1 oz	wholemeal flour
10 g	½ oz	fresh grated ginger
50 g	2 oz	desiccated coconut
100 g	4 oz	tomato, skinned, deseeded and diced
25 g	1 oz	tomato purée
50 g	2 oz	sultanas
½ litre	1 pt	fruit juice
5 g	¼ oz	yeast extract
50 g	2 oz	cashew nuts
60 ml	⅛ pt	single cream or smetana (page 86)

Using single cream
1 portion provides:

412 kcals/1729 kJ
19.6 g fat of which 6.1 g saturated
57.2 g carbohydrate of which 51.6 g sugars
5.4 g protein
8.3 g fibre

1. Skin, cut the pineapple in half, remove the tough centre. Cut in 1 cm (½ in) chunks. Peel the apples and pears, remove core, cut into 1 cm (½ in) pieces. Peel and slice mangoes. Skin and cut bananas into 1 cm (½ in) pieces. Cut guavas and paw paws in half, remove seeds, peel, dice into 1 cm (½ in) pieces. Marinade the fruit in lime juice.
2. Fry the onion in the sunflower margarine and oil until lightly brown, add the curry powder, sweat together, add the wholemeal flour and cook for 2 mins.
3. Add the ginger, coconut, tomato concassé, tomato purée and sultanas.
4. Gradually add sufficient boiling fruit juice to make a light sauce.
5. Add yeast extract, stir well. Simmer for 10 mins.
6. Add the fruit and cashew nuts, stir carefully, allow to heat through.
7. Finish with cream or smetana.
8. Serve in a suitable dish, separately serve poppadums, wholegrain pilaff rice and a green salad.

4 portions

8 Cornish vegetable feast bake pie

200 g	8 oz	wholemeal bread dough (recipe 10)
200 g	8 oz	steamed or boiled jacket potatoes
150 g	6 oz	French beans
60 ml	⅛ pt	sunflower oil
50 g	2 oz	finely chopped onion
50 g	2 oz	button mushrooms
400 g	1 lb	cooked leaf spinach
250 ml	½ pt	béchamel made with wholemeal flour and skimmed milk
10 g	½ oz	English or continental mustard
		seasoning, ground nutmeg

1 portion provides:

436 kcals/1832 kJ
26.4 g fat of which 3.9 g saturated
37.7 g carbohydrate of which 0.0 g sugars
15.0 g protein
11.3 g fibre

1 Make the wholemeal bread dough.
2 Peel and cut potatoes into 1 cm (½ in) dice.
3 Top and tail French beans, cut in halves, blanch and refresh.
4 Heat the sunflower oil and gently fry the onion without colour.
5 Add the sliced button mushrooms, cook for 2–3 mins.
6 Add potatoes, French beans and spinach, mix and heat through.
7 Boil the béchamel, mix in the English mustard.
8 Add to the vegetables, stir, season and add grated nutmeg.
9 Line a deep 18 cm (7 in) flan ring using two-thirds of the dough.
10 Fill with vegetable, béchamel mixture.
11 Egg wash the edges, cover with the remaining dough.
12 Bake in a pre-heated oven 180–190 °C (Reg. 4–5) for 20–25 mins.
13 Serve with tomato sauce made with vegetable stock and no bacon.

4 portions

9 Deep-fried corn rolls

400 g	1 lb	cooked sweetcorn
100 g	4 oz	desiccated coconut
10 g	½ oz	grated root ginger
		2 cloves of garlic
		finely chopped coriander leaves
		seasoning
		juice of ½ lemon
50 g	2 oz	semolina
		2 egg yolks
		flour, oil for frying

1 Purée sweetcorn, coconut, ginger, garlic, coriander leaves, seasoning and lemon juice in a food processor.
2 Remove into a basin, add semolina and egg yolks.
3 The mixture should be fairly stiff. Shape into croquettes.
4 Pass the croquettes through seasoned flour.
5 Deep fry in hot oil (180–190 °C) until golden brown.
6 Drain, serve in a suitable dish with chopped coriander leaves.
7 Separately serve a tomato sauce garnished with chopped chives.

4 portions

10 Wholemeal bread dough

75 ml	3 fl oz	skimmed milk
10 g	½ oz	fresh yeast
150 g	6 oz	wholemeal flour
25 g	1 oz	sunflower margarine
		pinch salt
		pinch sugar
3 g	⅛ oz	ascorbic acid powder
		1 egg

1 Warm the skimmed milk to 90 °F/36 °C.
2 Disperse the yeast in milk and add sufficient of the sieved flour to make a light batter. Sprinkle a little flour over the top, cover with a damp cloth allow to prove until the ferment breaks through the flour.
3 Place remainder of the sieved flour into a mixing bowl, add the ferment, melted sunflower margarine, salt, sugar, acid and beaten egg.
4 Mix well together to form a smooth dough, if the dough is too tight add a little warm water or skimmed milk.
5 Place back into the basin, allow to prove until double in size, cover with a damp cloth.
6 Knock back to equalise the dough and bring the yeast back into contact with the dough. Then use as required.

11 Curried nut roast

		2 tablespns sunflower oil
100 g	4 oz	finely chopped onion
		1 medium green pepper, finely chopped
200 g	8 oz	hazel, Brazil or walnuts, finely chopped
75 g	3 oz	wholemeal breadcrumbs
		1 clove garlic, crushed
3 g	⅛ oz	dried mixed herbs or
10 g	½ oz	fresh chopped herbs (parsley, tarragon, basil, sage, chives, chervil)
25 g	1 oz	mild curry powder
200 g	8 oz	skinned, deseeded, diced tomatoes
		salt and pepper
		1 egg

1 Heat oil in a sauteuse, add the onion and green pepper, lightly fry until tender.
2 Mix nuts and breadcrumbs, add garlic, herbs and curry powder.
3 Stir in the onion and pepper, add tomatoes, mix and season.
4 Add beaten egg to bind the mixture together.
5 Place mixture into a greased 18 cm (7 in) square cake tin. Bake at 190 °C (Reg. 5) for 30–40 minutes until golden brown. (Alternatively, it can be cooked in a bain-marie to give a different texture.)

This can be served hot with pilaff rice, yoghurt and mango chutney. Serve a tomato sauce made with vegetable stock separately.

4 portions

12 Bean goulash

200 g	8 oz	red kidney beans or haricot beans
60 ml	1/8 pt	sunflower oil
50 g	2 oz	finely chopped onion
		1 clove garlic, crushed
25 g	1 oz	paprika
		2 red peppers
		1 green pepper
		1 yellow pepper
200 g	8 oz	sliced button mushrooms
50 g	2 oz	tomato purée
750 ml	1 1/2 pt	vegetable stock
		bouquet garni
		seasoning
		8 small turned potatoes

1 portion provides:

411 kcals/1728 kJ
17.9 g fat of which 2.7 g saturated
50.0 g carbohydrate of which 7.3 g sugars
17.3 g protein
18.5 g fibre

1 Soak beans for 24 hours in cold water. Drain, place into a saucepan. Cover with cold water, bring to the boil and simmer until tender.
2 Heat oil in a sauté pan, sweat onion and garlic without colour for 2–3 mins, add paprika, sweat for a further 2–3 mins.
3 Add peppers, cut in halves, seeds removed and cut into 1 cm (1/2 in) dice. Add button mushrooms, sweat for a further 2 mins.
4 Add tomato purée, vegetable stock and bouquet garni. Bring to boil and simmer until pepper and mushrooms are cooked.
5 Remove bouquet garni. Add drained cooked beans, correct seasoning and stir.
6 Garnish with potatoes and chopped parsley.
7 Serve wholegrain pilaff or wholemeal noodles separately.

Bean goulash

4 portions

13 Broccoli sauce

200 g	8 oz	cooked broccoli
40 g	1 1/2 oz	sunflower seeds
125 ml	1/4 pt	smetana or silken tofu (page 86)
		juice of 1/2 lemon
		seasoning

1 Place the broccoli, sunflower seeds and approx. 1/2 pint of water into a liquidiser with the smetana and lemon juice. Liquidise until smooth.
2 Strain through a coarse strainer into a small saucepan. Correct seasoning and consistency.
3 Heat *very* gently before serving. *Do not boil.*

1/2 litre (1 pint) approx.

14 Gougère

250 ml	½ pt	water	choux pastry (page 462)
100 g	4 oz	sunflower margarine	
125 g	5 oz	strong flour	
		4 eggs (size 3)	
75 g	3 oz	diced Gruyère cheese	
		seasoning	

1 Make choux pastry, cool and add the finely diced gruyère cheese.
2 With a 1 cm (½ in) plain tube, pipe individual rings approx. 8 cm (3 in) diameter on to a very lightly greased baking sheet.
3 Brush lightly with egg wash and relax for approx. 15 mins.
4 Bake in a pre-heated oven at 190 °C (Reg. 5) for approx. 20 to 30 mins.
5 When cooked place on individual plates. Fill the centre with a suitable filling, e.g.:

   ratatouille
   stir-fry vegetables
   cauliflower cheese
   button mushrooms in a tomato and garlic sauce
   leaf spinach with chopped onions in a béchamel sauce
   button mushrooms and sweetcorn in a béchamel yoghurt sauce.

15 Lentil and cider loaf

150 g	6 oz	red split lentils
250 ml	½ pt	dry cider
100 g	4 oz	sunflower margarine
50 g	2 oz	dried breadcrumbs
100 g	4 oz	chopped onion
100 g	4 oz	carrots
		1 stick of celery
		1 clove of garlic, chopped
3 g	⅛ oz	dried thyme
50 g	2 oz	ground roasted hazelnuts
50 g	2 oz	grated Parmesan cheese
		chopped parsley
		1 egg
		seasoning

1 portion provides:

497 kcals/2086 kJ
30.6 g fat of which 6.7 g saturated
35.3 g carbohydrate of which 6.3 g sugars
18.0 g protein
7.2 g fibre

1 Place the lentils in a saucepan with the cider and sufficient water to cover. Bring to boil and allow to cook until almost tender and all the liquid has been absorbed.
2 Line a 400 g (1 lb) loaf tin with silicone paper, brush with melted sunflower margarine and sprinkle with the breadcrumbs.
3 With the rest of the margarine cook the onions, the carrots and celery cut into large brunoise. Cook until soft and lightly brown.
4 Add garlic and vegetables to the lentils, mix well.

5 Add the thyme, nuts, cheese, parsley and egg. Season.
6 Place into prepared tin, cover with greased aluminium foil.Bake in a pre-heated oven at 180 °C (Reg. 4) for approx. 1 hour.
7 10 mins before completion of cooking remove foil to brown top.
8 To serve turn out on to a warm dish. Garnish with picked parsley and serve a suitable sauce separately, e.g. broccoli sauce (recipe 13).

4 portions

16 Light savoury bread and butter pudding

		2 slices of wholemeal bread spread with sunflower margarine
150 g	6 oz	grated Cheddar cheese
500 ml	1 pt	skimmed milk (or half milk and half vegetable stock)
		3 eggs (size 3)
		seasoning
150 g	6 oz	tomatoes

1 portion provides:

321 kcals/1349 kJ
17.9 g fat of which 9.0 g saturated
16.7 g carbohydrate of which 7.7 g sugars
24.4 g protein
2.2 g fibre

1 Grease a pie dish with sunflower margarine.
2 Remove the crusts from the bread and cut in half diagonally.
3 Arrange the slices of bread neatly in the pie dish.
4 Sprinkle in the grated cheese.
5 Warm the milk to blood heat, mix the eggs together with the seasoning, whisk in the milk and strain through a fine strainer.
6 Pour this mixture onto the bread and cheese.
7 Arrange slices of blanched peeled tomato on top.
8 Stand the pie dish in a tray of warm water, bake in a pre-heated oven 160 °C (Reg. 3) for approx. 40–45 mins until set and serve.

4 portions

17 Piquant mushroom sauce

		4 tablespns sunflower oil
50 g	2 oz	finely chopped onions
200 g	8 oz	button mushrooms (sliced)
125 ml	¼ pt	apple juice
		4 tablespns red wine vinegar
10 g	½ oz	yeast extract
3 g	¼ oz	dried mixed herbs
5 g	¼ oz	arrowroot

1 Heat sunflower oil in suitable pan and fry onions lightly for 5 mins until just brown. Add mushrooms, sweat for 2 mins.
2 Stir in the remaining ingredients, except the arrowroot, mix well.
3 Bring to the boil, simmer for 15 mins. Correct seasoning.
4 Dilute arrowroot with a little water, stir into sauce, mix well.
5 Simmer for 2 mins, use as required.

18 Meatless shepherd's pie

100 g	4 oz	lentils
500 ml	1 pt	vegetable stock
100 g	4 oz	textured vegetable protein (T.V.P.) mince, natural flavour
100 g	4 oz	onions, finely chopped
3 g	⅛ oz	dried mixed herbs
50 g	2 oz	sunflower margarine
25 g	1 oz	wholemeal flour
50 g	2 oz	tomato purée
10 g	½ oz	yeast extract
		seasoning
		2–3 drops Worcester sauce
500 g	1 lb	duchess potatoes (page 439)
50 g	2 oz	grated Cheddar cheese

1 portion provides:

523 kcals/2198 kJ
22.3 g fat of which 6.0 g saturated
54.3 g carbohydrate of which 4.9 g sugars
29.9 g protein
7.5 g fibre

1. Cook the lentils in vegetable stock.
2. Reconstitute tvp by soaking in cold water for the recommended time according to the manufacturer's instructions.
3. Sweat the onion and mixed herbs in the margarine without colour.
4. Stir in wholemeal flour and cook out for 1–2 minutes.
5. Add tvp and vegetable stock from lentils, simmer for 10 mins.
6. Mix in lentils, tomato purée and yeast extract.
7. Correct seasoning, add 2–3 drops Worcester sauce to taste.
8. Place this mixture into a pie dish, allow to cool.
9. Pipe duchess potato on top using a star tube.
10. Sprinkle with grated Cheddar cheese.
11. Bake in a pre-heated oven at 180 °C (Reg. 4) for approx. 20 minutes until golden brown.

Note In place of the tvp a selection of freshly diced blanched vegetables may be used or twice the amount of lentils.

4 portions

19 Mushroom, celery and walnut vol-au-vent

200 g	8 oz	puff pastry made with 25% wholemeal flour (page 458)
150 g	6 oz	button mushrooms
		4 celery sticks
		2–3 drops lemon juice
50 g	2 oz	walnuts
500 ml	1 pt	béchamel sauce made with sunflower margarine and skimmed milk
125 ml	¼ pt	natural yoghurt
		seasoning
		chopped parsley

1. Roll out the puff pastry, cut out four 8 cm (3 in) diameter rounds.
2. Turn the rounds upside down on a lightly greased baking sheet.

3 Using a smaller plain cutter dipped in hot oil, make incisions half way through each leaving approx. ½ cm (¼ in) border.
4 Allow to relax for at least 20 mins.
5 Egg wash and bake in a hot oven, 200 °C (Reg. 6), for approx. 15–20 mins.
6 When cooked remove lids carefully with a small knife.
7 Empty out centre. Retain lids.
8 Cut mushrooms and celery into ½ cm (¼ in) dice.
9 Melt a knob of sunflower margarine in a sauté pan, add celery, gently sweat without colour until almost tender.
10 Add mushrooms and lemon juice, continue to sweat until mushrooms are cooked.
11 Add the coarsely chopped walnuts.
12 Stir in the béchamel, finish with natural yoghurt.
13 Correct seasoning and consistency.
14 Sprinkle with chopped parsley. Stir well.
15 Fill warm vol-au-vent with this mixture, serve decorated with walnuts and parsley.

4 portions

Mushroom, celery and walnut vol-au-vent

20 Mexican bean pot

300 g	12 oz	dry red beans or haricot beans
100 g	4 oz	finely chopped onions
100 g	4 oz	sliced carrots
200 g	8 oz	tomato skinned, deseeded and diced
		2 cloves crushed and chopped garlic
10 g	½ oz	paprika
3 g	⅛ oz	dried marjoram
		1 small fresh chilli finely chopped
		1 small red pepper – finely diced
5 g	¼ oz	yeast extract
		chopped chives
		seasoning

1 portion provides:

161 kcals/672 kJ
1.2 g fat of which 0.2 g saturated
27.0 g carbohydrate of which 4.6 g sugars
12.3 g protein
14.0 g fibre

1 Soak the beans in cold water for 24 hours, drain. Place into a saucepan cover with cold water, bring to the boil and simmer gently.
2 When three-quarters cooked, add all the other ingredients except the chopped chives.
3 Continue to simmer until all is completely cooked.
4 Serve sprinkled with chopped chives.

4 portions

21 Potato and nut cutlets

50 g	2 oz	finely chopped onion
60 ml	⅛ pt	sunflower oil
300 g	12 oz	duchess potato
100 g	4 oz	ground walnuts
50 g	2 oz	ground cashew nuts
3 g	⅛ oz	yeast extract
		pinch of dried mixed herbs
		flour
		beaten egg
		wholemeal breadcrumbs

> 1 portion provides:
>
> 623 kcals/2616 kJ
> 53.0 g fat of which 6.8 g saturated
> 28.7 g carbohydrate of which 2.1 g sugars
> 9.7 g protein
> 4.3 g fibre

1 Cook the onion in the sunflower oil without colouring.
2 Mix the duchess potato with the nuts, yeast extract and mixed herbs.
3 Season and add the onion.
4 Place onto a floured board, divide and shape into cutlets.
5 Flour, egg and crumb cutlets.
6 Shallow or deep fry in hot oil (190 °C) until golden brown.
7 Drain on kitchen paper and serve with a suitable sauce, e.g. asparagus.

4 portions

Asparagus sauce

300 g	12 oz	cooked asparagus
250 ml	½ pt	vegetable stock
125 ml	¼ pt	white wine
		4 tablespns smetana or double cream
		seasoning

1 Liquidise asparagus, stock and wine until a smooth sauce is obtained.
2 Gently bring to the boil.
3 Strain through a coarse strainer into a clean saucepan. Season, reheat.
4 Add smetana or double cream. *Do not boil.*
5 Correct seasoning and consistency, use as required.

22 Ratatouille wholemeal pancakes with a cheese sauce

100 g	4 oz	wholemeal flour	pancake batter method on page 504
250 ml	½ pt	skimmed milk	
		1 egg	
		pinch of salt	
10 g	½ oz	melted sunflower margarine	
200 g	8 oz	courgettes	ratatouille method on page 504
200g	8 oz	aubergines	
		1 red pepper	
		1 green pepper	
100 g	4 oz	tomatoes	
		1 yellow pepper	
50 g	2 oz	chopped onion	
		1 clove of garlic chopped	
		4 tablespns sunflower oil	
400 g	16 oz	tin plum tomatoes	
50 g	2 oz	tomato purée	

500 ml	1 pt	skimmed milk	cheese sauce method on page 95
50 g	2 oz	sunflower oil	
50 g	2 oz	flour	
		1 onion studded with clove	
25 g	1 oz	grated Parmesan	
		1 egg yolk	
		seasoning	

1 Prepare and make the pancakes.
2 Prepare the ratatouille and cheese sauce.
3 Season with salt and cayenne pepper.
4 Fill pancakes with ratatouille, roll up and serve on individual plates or on a service dish, coated with cheese sauce, sprinkled with grated Parmesan cheese and finished by gratinating under the salamander.

1 portion provides:

571 kcals/2398 kJ
35.8 g fat of which 6.5 g saturated
46.1 g carbohydrate of which 19.0 g sugars
19.6 g protein
6.5 g fibre

4 portions

23 Vegetable curry with wholegrain rice pilaff

600 g	1½ lb	mixed vegetables, e.g.: cauliflower, broccoli, peppers, carrots, courgettes, mushrooms, aubergines
100 g	4 oz	sunflower margarine
150 g	6 oz	onions, chopped finely
25 g	1 oz	garam masala (page 85)
25 g	1 oz	creamed coconut or 2 oz (50 g) desiccated coconut
500 ml	1 pt	curry sauce made from vegetable stock (page 104)

1 portion provides:

432 kcals/1814 kJ
35.5 g fat of which 7.4 g saturated
23.5 g carbohydrate of which 16.3 g sugars
6.4 g protein
6.7 g fibre

1 Prepare vegetables: cut cauliflower and broccoli into small florets, blanch and refresh; cut peppers into half, remove seeds, cut into 1 cm (½ in) dice; cut carrots into large dice, blanch and refresh; and courgettes into 1 cm (½ in) dice; leave the mushrooms whole; cut aubergines into 1 cm (½ in) dice.
2 Heat the margarine and sweat the onion.
3 Add garam masala, sweat approx. 2 mins and add coconut.
4 Add all vegetables, sweat together for approx. 5 mins.
5 Add the curry sauce, bring to the boil and gently simmer until all the vegetables are cooked but crunchy in texture.
6 Serve in a suitable dish with a wholegrain rice pilaff garnished with flaked almonds, poppadoms and a curry tray with mango chutney.

4 portions

Wholegrain rice pilaff

Page 201, using 100 g (4 oz) rice.

To the basic recipe, after cooking, add 50 g (2 oz) roasted flaked almonds.

24 Tomato savarin filled with cucumber, apple and walnut dressing

400 g	16 oz	can of plum tomatoes	
25 g	1 oz	tomato purée	
25 g	1 oz	agar-agar (gelatine substitute) (page 80)	
125 ml	¼ pt	mayonnaise	
		juice ½ lemon	
		½ green pepper	
		½ yellow pepper	cut in large dice
		3 sticks of celery	
		2 egg whites	
125 ml	¼ pt	whipping cream or natural yoghurt	
		seasoning	

1 portion provides:

289 kcals/1215 kJ
25.8 g fat of which 9.2 g saturated
4.8 g carbohydrate of which 4.7 g sugars
9.8 g protein
1.8 g fibre

1 Purée the tomatoes with their juice to measure 500 ml (1 pt).
2 Bring to the boil, and whisk in tomato purée.
3 Dissolve the agar-agar in hot water, add to the tomatoes and vegetables.
4 Place the mixture in a basin on a bowl of ice, stir until cool.
5 Season, whisk in mayonnaise and lemon juice.
6 Continue to cool until setting point is reached, carefully fold in stiffly beaten whites and whipping cream.
7 Pour into 18–19 cm (7–8 in) savarin mould and set in refrigerator.
8 Unmould onto a suitable serving dish, fill the centre with cucumber, apple and walnut dressing. Decorate with tomato and mint leaves.

Note 25 g (1 oz) soaked leaf gelatine may be used to replace agar-agar, although gelatine is not vegetarian but an animal product.

Cucumber, Apple and Walnut Dressing

		1 small cucumber
		3 dessert apples
		juice of 1 lime
75 g	3 oz	crushed walnuts
250 ml	½ pt	natural yoghurt

1 Peel the cucumber and cut into ½ cm (¼ in) dice.
2 Peel and cut the dessert apples into 2 cm (¾ in) dice, sprinkle with lime juice.
3 Place the cucumber and apple into a basin, add walnuts, bind with natural yoghurt.
4 Use this mixture to fill the centre of the tomato savarin and serve with a green salad of mixed lettuce.

4 portions

25 Vegetable crumble

150 g	6 oz	100% wholemeal flour	crumble topping
100 g	4 oz	butter or margarine	
100 g	4 oz	grated Cheddar cheese	
50 g	2 oz	chopped mixed nuts	
25 g	1 oz	sesame seeds	
600 g	1½ lb	mixed vegetables (swede, turnips, parsnips, potatoes, carrots, etc.)	
100 g	4 oz	onion, finely chopped	
50 g	2 oz	butter or margarine	
25 g	1 oz	100% wholemeal flour	
200 g	8 oz	fresh tomatoes	
250 ml	½ pt	vegetable stock	
125 ml	¼ pt	milk	
		chopped parsley	
		seasoning	

Using hard margarine
1 portion provides:

698 kcals/2931 kJ
49.0 g fat of which 20.3 g saturated
50.4 g carbohydrate of which 12.4 g sugars
18.5 g protein
10.5 g fibre

1 Make crumble by sieving flour and rubbing in butter or margarine.
2 Add grated Cheddar cheese, nuts and sesame seeds.
3 Wash, peel and re-wash vegetables, cut into macedoine.
4 Sweat the onion in the butter or margarine without colour.
5 Add the rest of the vegetables and continue to sweat for 10 minutes.
6 Stir in the flour, add the other ingredients, including the liquid which should be added slowly stirring well between each addition.
7 Bring to boil, reduce heat, cover and simmer for about 15 minutes, until the vegetables are just tender.
8 Transfer to a pie dish. Press the crumble topping over the vegetables and bake in a pre-heated oven at 190 °C (Reg. 5) for about 30 minutes approx., or until golden brown and serve.

4 portions

26 Vegetarian kedgeree

100 g	4 oz	cauliflower
100 g	4 oz	French beans
100 g	4 oz	courgettes
100 g	4 oz	mange-tout
125 ml	¼ pt	sunflower oil
50 g	2 oz	finely chopped onion
		1 clove garlic, crushed and chopped
25 g	1 oz	curry powder
10 g	½ oz	grated root ginger
3 g	⅛ oz	ground cardamom
3 g	⅛ oz	turmeric
100 g	4 oz	basmati rice
180 ml	⅜ pt	vegetable stock
75 g	3 oz	cooked green lentils
500 ml	1 pt	curry sauce (page 104) using veg. stock

1 portion provides:

563 kcals/2367 kJ
39.6 g fat of which 6.3 g saturated
46.4 g carbohydrate of which 11.7 g sugars
8.7 g protein
8.9 g fibre

1 Prepare the vegetables in the following way: cut the cauliflower into small florets, cook in boiling salted water, refresh and drain; top and

tail French beans, cut in half and cook in boiling salted water, refresh, and drain; remove ends from courgettes, peel carefully, cut into 1 cm (½ in) lengths, blanch in boiling salted water, refresh and drain; top and tail mange-tout, leave whole, blanch in boiling salted water for 30 secs, refresh and drain.

2 Heat half the oil in a sauté pan, add the chopped onion and garlic, sweat without colour.
3 Add curry powder, ginger, cardamom and turmeric, sweat for 1 min.
4 Add the basmati rice, stir well. Add boiling vegetable stock, cover with a greased greaseproof paper and lid. Cook in a moderately hot oven, 200–230 °C (Reg. 6–8) until the rice is tender but retains a bite.
5 When cooked remove from oven and stir in cooked lentils.
6 Reheat the vegetables by lightly frying them in the remaining oil, keeping all vegetables crisp.
7 Drain the vegetables, stir into the rice and serve, with the curry sauce.

4 portions

27 Vegetarian lasagne

		10 pieces of wholemeal lasagne
125 ml	¼ pt	sunflower oil
100 g	4 oz	finely chopped onion
		2 garlic cloves, chopped
200 g	8 oz	sliced mushrooms
		seasoning
		2 medium-sized courgettes, cut in 1 cm (½ in) dice
3 g	⅛ oz	oregano
200 g	8 oz	tomato skinned, deseeded and diced
50 g	2 oz	tomato purée
300 g	12 oz	broccoli (small florets)
100 g	4 oz	carrots, cut in ½ cm (¼ in) dice
25 g	1 oz	pine kernels
250 ml	½ pt	béchamel made with skimmed milk and sunflower margarine
50 g	2 oz	grated Parmesan cheese
250 ml	½ pt	natural yoghurt

1 portion provides:

713 kcals/2993 kJ
46.2 g fat of which 8.5 g saturated
54.6 g carbohydrate of which 16.5 g sugars
22.9 g protein
11.8 g fibre

1 Cook the lasagne sheets in boiling salted water until al dente, refresh and drain.
2 Heat half the oil and sweat the onion and garlic.
3 Add the mushrooms and continue to cook without colour. Season.
4 Heat the remaining oil in a sauteuse, add the courgettes and lightly fry; sprinkle with the oregano. Cook until crisp, add tomato concassé and tomato purée.
5 Add the broccoli florets and carrots, previously blanched and refreshed. Mix together with the pine kernels.
6 Make a cheese sauce using the béchamel and half the grated cheese, finish with natural yoghurt.

7 Well grease a suitable ovenproof dish with sunflower oil, place a layer of lasagne in the bottom.
8 Cover with a layer of mushroom, then a layer of lasagne, then the broccoli and tomato mixture, then lasagne, then cheese sauce. Continue to do this finishing with a layer of cheese sauce on the top.
9 Sprinkle with remaining grated Parmesan cheese.
10 Bake in a pre-heated oven at 180 °C (Reg. 4) for approx. 20–25 mins.

4 portions

28 Vegetarian moussaka

50 g	2 oz	finely chopped onion	
		1 clove garlic, chopped	
		4 tablspns sunflower oil	
100 g	4 oz	tvp mince (natural flavour), soaked in cold water 2–3 hours	
200 g	8 oz	tomato skinned, deseeded and diced	
50 g	2 oz	tomato purée	
		pinch oregano	
		seasoning	
500 ml	1 pt	vegetable stock	
5 g	¼ oz	yeast extract	
10 g	½ oz	arrowroot	
400 g	1 lb	potatoes	
		2 large aubergines	
25 g	1 oz	sunflower margarine	Cheese sauce see page 95
25 g	1 oz	wholemeal flour	
250 ml	½ pt	skimmed milk	
25 g	1 oz	Parmesan cheese	
		1 egg yolk	
		2 tablespns natural yoghurt	
50 g	2 oz	grated Parmesan cheese	

1 portion provides:

536 kcals/2249 kJ
29.1 g fat of which 7.0 g saturated
46.2 g carbohydrate of which 11.4 g sugars
25.5 g protein
6.4 g fibre

1 Cook the onion and garlic in the sunflower oil until lightly coloured.
2 Add the drained tvp.
3 Add tomato concassé, tomato purée, oregano and seasoning.
4 Add vegetable stock to cover. Bring to boil, simmer for 5 mins.
5 Add yeast extract, stir well.
6 Dilute arrowroot with a little water and gradually stir into the tvp.
7 Bring back to the boil. Simmer for 2 mins.
8 Cook the potatoes with the skins on, by steaming or boiling. Peel and slice into ½ cm (¼ in) slices.
9 Slice the aubergines into ½ cm (¼ in) slices, pass through wholemeal flour, shallow fry in sunflower oil on both sides, until golden brown. Drain on kitchen paper.
10 In a suitable ovenproof dish arrange layers of tvp mixture and overlapping slices of potato and aubergines.
11 Pour the cheese sauce on top, sprinkle with grated Parmesan cheese.
12 Bake in a pre-heated oven at 190 °C (Reg. 5) for approx. 30 mins.

4 portions

29 Wholemeal vegetarian pizza

300 g	12 oz	wholemeal flour	pizza dough
10 g	½ oz	soya flour	pizza dough
		pinch of salt	pizza dough
180 ml	⅜ pt	warm water at 90 °F/32 °C	pizza dough
10 g	½ oz	fresh yeast	pizza dough
5 g	¼ oz	ascorbic acid	pizza dough
200 g	8 oz	finely chopped onions	
		2 cloves of garlic, crushed	
		4 tablespns sunflower oil	
400 g	1 lb	tomato skinned, deseeded and diced	
50 g	2 oz	tomato purée	
10 g	½ oz	fresh parsley	
10 g	½ oz	fresh chopped basil	
		2 cooked artichoke bottoms	
25 g	1 oz	pine kernels	
10 g	½ oz	sesame seeds	
10 g	½ oz	capers	
		8 green olives	
		8 black olives	
25 g	1 oz	sultanas	
50 g	2 oz	Mozzarella cheese	

1 portion provides:

541 kcals/2272 kJ
26.6 g fat of which 4.8 g saturated
64.0 g carbohydrate of which 13.7 g sugars
17.0 g protein
10.4 g fibre

1. Sieve the flour, soya flour and a pinch of salt into a basin.
2. Warm the water, place in a separate basin with the yeast, disperse the yeast in the warm water, allow sufficient flour to make a light batter, sprinkle a little flour over the ferment, cover with a damp cloth and allow the ferment to break through the flour.
3. When the ferment is ready pour into the rest of the flour.
4. Add the ascorbic acid, incorporate the flour until a smooth elastic dough is obtained.
5. Turn out onto a floured surface and continue to knead the dough until smooth.
6. Return to basin, cover with a damp cloth and allow to prove in a warm place until double in size.
7. Knock back the dough to bring the yeast back into contact with the dough and to equalise the dough.
8. Roll out the dough into rounds, approx. 15 cm (6 in) or in a rectangle, and cover a lightly greased swiss roll tin.
9. Allow to prove for 10 minutes in a warm atmosphere.
10. Bake for 4–5 minutes in a pre-heated oven approx. 200 °C (Reg. 5–6).
11. Sweat the onions and garlic in the oil.
12. Add the tomato concassé and purée. Stir well.
13. Add the chopped parsley and basil. Cook out the tomatoes for approx. 15 minutes. Season.
14. Spread this tomato mixture on the pizza base.
15. Arrange neatly on top the artichoke bottoms into small pieces, sprinkle on the pine kernels, sesame seeds, capers, stoned olives and sultanas.

16 Finally sprinkle with grated Mozzarella cheese.
17 Bake in oven for approx. 15 mins at 200 °C (Reg. 6). Serve very hot.

Note Alternatively a ratatouille mixture, or a variation of it, may be used as a pizza topping with grated cheese.

4 portions

30 Vegetable biryani

400 g	1 lb	Basmati rice
		2 tablesp oil
		½ cinnamon stick } chopped
		4 cardamon pods } chopped
		4 cloves } chopped
100 g	4 oz	sliced onions
		1 clove garlic
		1 green chilli finely chopped
		1 tablesp grated root ginger
600 g	1½ lb	mixed vegetables (carrots, celery, broccoli, cauliflower, French beans)
400 g	1 lb	tomato blanched, deseeded and chopped or canned plum tomatoes
25 g	1 oz	tomato pureé
		chopped coriander leaves

1 Wash, soak and drain the rice.
2 Partly cook the rice in boiling salted water for approx. 3 mins. Refresh and drain well.
3 Heat the oil in a suitable sized pan. Add the cinnamon, cardamon and cloves and sweat for 2 mins.
4 Add the sliced onions, garlic, chilli and ginger. Continue to sweat until soft.
5 Prepare the vegetables: cut the carrots and celery into batons, the cauliflower and broccoli into florets and the French beans into 2.5 cm (1 in) lengths.
6 Add the vegetables and fry for approx. 2–3 mins.
7 Add the tomatoes and tomato purée. Season.
8 Make sure there is sufficient moisture in the pan to cook the vegetables. Usually a little water needs to be added. Ideally the vegetables should cook in their own juices combined with the tomatoes.
9 When the vegetables are partly cooked, layer them in a casserole or suitable pan with the rice.
10 Cover the casserole, finish cooking in a moderate oven (180 °C, 350 °F) for approx. 20 mins. or until the rice is tender.
11 Sprinkle with chopped coriander leaves and serve.

31 Vegetable and nut Stroganoff

		4 tablespns sunflower oil
50 g	2 oz	finely chopped onions
300 g	12 oz	Chinese leaves shredded
		6 sticks celery cut in paysanne
300 g	12 oz	button mushrooms, sliced
200 g	8 oz	mixed nuts – peanuts, cashews, hazelnuts
		1 teaspn paprika
		1 teaspn English or continental mustard
125 ml	¼ pt	white wine
125 ml	¼ pt	unsweetened vegetable creamer or smetana
		seasoning

1 portion provides:

500 kcals/2098 kJ
41.5 g fat of which 7.0 g saturated
12.0 g carbohydrate of which 7.0 g sugars
15.7 g protein
6.4 g fibre

1 Heat the oil and sweat the onions for 2–3 mins.
2 Add the Chinese leaves, celery and mushrooms. Cook for 5 mins.
3 Add the nuts whole. Stir in the paprika and diluted mustard.
4 Add white wine, bring to the boil and simmer for 5 mins.
5 Season. Cool slightly, add heat-stable unsweetened vegetable creamer or smetana. Serve with a dish of plain-boiled wholewheat noodles tossed in sunflower margarine or wholegrain pilaff rice.

32 Vegetarian strudel

125 g	5 oz	wholemeal flour	strudel dough
75 g	3 oz	strong flour	strudel dough
		pinch of salt	strudel dough
25 g	1 oz	sunflower oil	strudel dough
		1 egg	strudel dough
83 ml	⅙ pt	water at 100 °F, 37 °C	strudel dough
200 g	8 oz	large cabbage leaves	
		4 tablespns sunflower oil	
50 g	2 oz	finely chopped onion	
		2 cloves garlic, chopped	
400 g	1 lb	courgettes	
200 g	8 oz	carrots	
100 g	4 oz	turnips	
300 g	12 oz	tomato skinned, deseeded and diced	
25 g	1 oz	tomato purée	
25 g	1 oz	toasted sesame seeds	
50 g	2 oz	wholemeal breadcrumbs	
3 g	⅛ oz	fresh chopped basil	
		seasoning	

1 portion provides:

504 kcals/2117 kJ
27.6 g fat of which 4.0 g saturated
54.1 g carbohydrate of which 10.5 g sugars
14.3 g protein
9.7 g fibre

1 Make strudel paste by sieving the flour with the salt, make a well.
2 Add the oil, egg and water, gradually incorporate the flour to make a smooth dough and knead well.
3 Place in a basin, cover with a damp cloth, relax for 3 minutes.
4 Meanwhile prepare the filling: take the large cabbage leaves, wash and discard the tough centre stalks, blanch in boiling salted water for 2 minutes, until limp. Refresh and drain well in a clean cloth.

5 Heat the oil in a sauté pan, gently fry the onion and garlic until soft.
6 Peel and chop the courgettes into ½ cm (¼ in) dice, blanch and refresh. Peel and dice the carrots and turnips, blanch and refresh.
7 Place the well drained courgettes, carrots and turnips into a basin, add tomato concassé, tomato purée, sesame seeds, breadcrumbs, chopped basil. Mix well, season.
8 Roll out strudel dough to a thin rectangle, place on a clean cloth and stretch until extremely thin.
9 Lay the drained cabbage leaves on the stretched strudel dough, leaving approximately 1 cm (½ in) gap from the edge.
10 Place the filling in the centre. Egg wash the edges.
11 Fold in the longer side edges to meet in the middle. Roll up.
12 Transfer to a lightly oiled baking sheet. Brush with sunflower oil.
13 Bake for 40 minutes approx. in a pre-heated oven at 180–200 °C.
14 When cooked serve hot, sliced on individual plates with a cordon of tomato sauce made with vegetable stock and without bacon.

4 portions

33 **Tomato and courgette tian**

A tian is a country dish which can be made with many different ingredients. It takes its name from the heavy earthenware dish in which it is cooked.

70 mls	⅛ pt	olive or sunflower oil
		1 large onion, finely chopped
		2 cloves garlic, crushed
		1 red pepper, deseeded and finely chopped
200 g	8 oz	courgettes, thinly sliced
		4 large tomatoes, skinned, deseeded and diced
50 g	2 oz	rice, cooked
		3 eggs, beaten
		1 tablespn fresh chopped herbs (parsley, chives, thyme, basil)
25 g	1 oz	freshly grated Parmesan
25 g	1 oz	white or wholemeal breadcrumbs
		salt, pepper

This recipe provides:

1260 kcals/5292 kJ
97.2 g fat of which 20.1 g saturated
56.8 g carbohydrate of which 23.2 g sugars
43.2 g protein
7.0 g fibre

1 Heat the oil and add the chopped onion; sweat without colour.
2 Add garlic, red pepper and courgettes, gently cook for approx. 5–6 mins.
3 Remove from heat, add tomatoes, rice, herbs and seasoning, stir in beaten eggs.
4 Place in a greased earthenware gratin dish, sprinkle with cheese and breadcrumbs.
5 Bake in a pre-heated oven (180 °C, Reg. 4) for approx. 30–35 mins.

4 portions

34 Spiced chick peas *Kabli Channa*

200 g	8 oz	chick peas
50 g	2 oz	butter or oil
100 g	4 oz	finely chopped onion
		½ cinnamon stick
		4 chopped cloves
		2 cloves garlic, crushed
25 g	1 oz	grated root ginger
		2 green chillies finely chopped
		2 teasp ground coriander
150 g	6 oz	tomatoes skinned, deseeded and chopped
		1 teasp tomato purée
		vegetable stock
		1 teasp garam masala
		chopped coriander leaves

1. Wash and soak the chick peas.
2. Cover with fresh water, bring to the boil and gently simmer until tender, approx. 2 hrs.
3. Heat the butter and oil in a suitably sized pan; add the onion and fry until lightly brown.
4. Add the cinnamon, cloves and garlic. Continue to fry for a few seconds.
5. Add the ginger, chillies and ground coriander and fry for a further 5 mins.
6. Add the tomatoes and tomato purée and cook out, reducing most of the moisture.
7. Add the drained chick peas; stir well.
8. Moisten with vegetable stock to barely cover. Bring to the boil and simmer for 10 mins.
9. Add garam masala and stir well.
10. Serve sprinkled with chopped coriander leaves.

4 portions

Clockwise from left: braised onions (p. 427); braised celery (p. 414); braised leeks (p. 432)

17

VEGETABLES

General objectives
To be aware of the variety of vegetables available and to know how they may be prepared, cooked and served.

Specific objectives
To state the principles of vegetable cookery and to explain the classification of vegetables. To describe and produce dishes at a suitable standard. To be able to name and to cut vegetables in the correct sizes.

Vegetables Légumes

Approximate times are given for the cooking of vegetables as quality, age, freshness and size all affect the length of cooking time required. Young, freshly picked vegetables will cook for a shorter time than vegetables allowed to grow older and which may have been stored after picking.

As a general rule all root vegetables are started to cook in cold salted water, with the exception of new potatoes: those vegetables which grow above the ground are started in boiling salted water. This is so that they may be cooked as quickly as possible for the *minimum* period of time so that *maximum* flavour, food value and colour are retained. The use of high speed steam cookers can reduce cooking time, thus helping to retain flavour and goodness. (See note, page 415).

1 **Cuts of vegetables**

The size to which the vegetables are cut may vary according to their use, however the shape does not change.

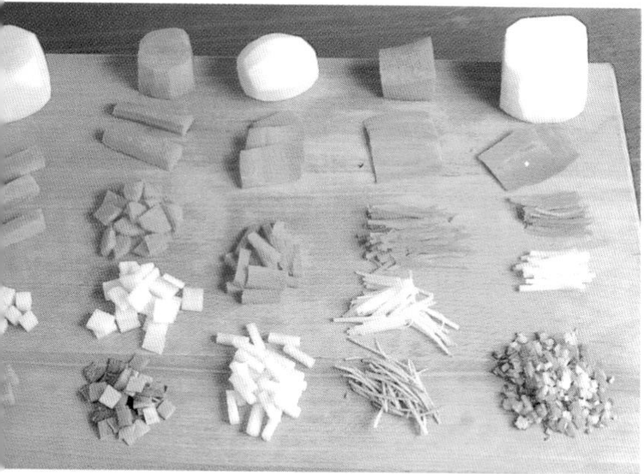

Cuts of vegetables (from left to right): macédoine, paysanne, jardinière, julienne, brunoise

Julienne (strips)

1 Cut the vegetables into 2 cm (1 in) lengths.
2 Cut the lengths into thin slices.
3 Cut the slices into thin strips.

Brunoise (small dice)

1 Cut the vegetables into convenient-sized lengths.
2 Cut the lengths into 2 mm (1/12 in) slices.
3 Cut the slices into 2 mm (1/12 in) strips.
4 Cut the strips into 2 mm (1/12 in) squares.

Macédoine (1/2 cm (1/4 in) dice)

1 Cut the vegetables into convenient lengths.
2 Cut the lengths into 1/2 cm (1/4 in) slices.
3 Cut the slices into 1/2 cm (1/4 in) strips.
4 Cut the strips into 1/2 cm (1/4 in) squares.

Jardinière (batons)

1 Cut the vegetables into 1 1/2 cm (3/4 in) lengths.
2 Cut the lengths into 3 mm (1/4 in) slices.
3 Cut the slices into batons (3 × 3 × 18 mm (1/8 × 1/8 × 3/4 in)).

Paysanne

There are at least four accepted methods of cutting paysanne. In order to cut economically, the shape of the vegetables should decide which method to choose. All are cut thinly.

1 1 cm sided (1/2 in) triangles.
2 1 cm sided (1/2 in) squares.
3 1 cm diameter (1/2 in) rounds.
4 1 cm diameter (1/2 in) rough-sided rounds.

2 · Globe artichokes
Artichauts en branche

Not including sauce
1 portion provides:

8 kcals/32 kJ
0.0 g fat of which 0.0 g saturated
1.4 g carbohydrate of which 1.4 g sugars
0.6 g protein
0.0 g fibre

1. Allow 1 artichoke per portion.
2. Cut off the stems close to the leaves.
3. Cut off approx. 2 cm (1 in) across the tops of the leaves.
4. Trim the remainder of the leaves with scissors or a small knife.
5. Place a slice of lemon at the bottom of each artichoke.
6. Secure with string.
7. Simmer in gently boiling salted water (to which a little ascorbic acid – one vitamin C tablet – may be added) until the bottom is tender (approx. 20–30 min).
8. Refresh under running water until cold.
9. Remove the centre of the artichoke carefully.
10. Scrape away all the furry inside and leave clean.
11. Replace the centre, upside down.
12. Reheat by placing in a pan of boiling salted water for about 3–4 min.
13. Drain and serve accompanied by a suitable sauce, e.g. artichaut en branche sauce hollandaise.

Artichokes may also be served cold, e.g. artichaut en branche sauce vinaigrette.

3 · Artichoke bottoms *Fonds d'artichauts*

1. Cut off the stalk and pull out all the underneath leaves.
2. With a large knife cut through the artichoke leaving only 1½ cm (¾ in) at the bottom of the vegetable.
3. With a small sharp knife, whilst holding the artichoke upside down, peel carefully removing all the leaf and any green part, keeping the bottom as smooth as possible. If necessary smooth with a peeler.
4. Rub immediately with lemon and keep in lemon water or ascorbic acid solution.
5. Using a spoon or the thumb, remove the centre furry part which is called the choke. The choke is sometimes removed after cooking.
6. Artichoke bottoms should always be cooked in a blanc. The recipe for blanc follows.

Fonds d'artichauts are served as a vegetable; they are sometimes filled with another vegetable, e.g. peas, spinach, etc.

When they are served ungarnished they are usually cut into quarters, e.g. fonds d'artichauts sautés au beurre.

4 · Blanc *Blanc*

½ litre	1 pt	cold water
10 g	¼ oz	flour
		juice of ½ lemon
		salt

1 Mix the flour and water together.
2 Add the salt and lemon juice. Pass through a strainer.
3 Place in a pan, bring to the boil, stirring continuously.

Note Alternatively artichokes may be cooked in ½ litre (1 pint) water, 2 vitamin C tablets and 30 ml (1/16 pt) oil and salt.

5 · Purée of Jerusalem artichokes *Topinambours en purée*

600 g	1 lb 8 oz	Jerusalem artichokes
25 g	1 oz	butter
		salt, pepper

1 portion provides:

69 kcals/291 kJ
5.1 g fat of which 3.3 g saturated
4.1 g carbohydrate of which 0.0 g sugars
2.1 g protein
– g fibre

1 Wash, peel and rewash the artichokes.
2 Cut in pieces if necessary. Barely cover with water, add salt.
3 Simmer gently until tender. Drain well.
4 Pass through a sieve, mouli or liquidise.
5 Return to the pan, reheat and mix in the butter and correct the seasoning and serve.

4 portions

6 · Purée of Jerusalem artichokes with cream
Topinambours en purée à la crème

As above, 125 ml (¼ pt) cream or natural yoghurt mixed in before serving.

7 · Jerusalem artichokes in cream sauce
Topinambours à la crème

1 Wash and peel the artichokes and rewash. Cut to an even size.
2 Barely cover with water, add salt and simmer till tender, but do not overcook.
3 Drain well and add ¼ litre (½ pt) cream sauce (page 95).

Note Cream sauce may be made with wholemeal flour, skimmed milk and natural yoghurt.

8 · **Asparagus** *Asperges*

1 portion provides:
138 kcals/580 kJ
12.3 g fat of which 7.8 g saturated
1.7 g carbohydrate of which 1.7 g sugars
5.2 g protein
2.3 g fibre

Allow 6–8 good-sized pieces per portion.
An average bundle will yield 3–4 portions.

1. Using the back of a small knife, carefully remove the tips of the leaves.
2. Scrape the stem, either with the blade of a small knife or a peeler.
3. Wash well. Tie into bundles of approx. 12 heads.
4. Cut off the excess stem.
5. Cook in boiling salted water approx. 15 min.
6. Test if cooked by gently pressing the green part of the stem, which should be tender, but do not overcook.
7. Lift carefully out of the water. Remove the string, drain well and serve.

Serve a suitable sauce separately, e.g. hollandaise or melted butter.

Asparagus are usually served as a separate course. They may also be served cold, in which case they should be immediately refreshed when cooked in order to retain the green colour. Serve with vinaigrette or mayonnaise.

9 · **Asparagus points or tips** *Pointes d'asperges*

Young thin asparagus, approx. 50 pieces to the bundle, known as sprew or sprue.

They are prepared in the same way as asparagus except that when they are very thin removing of the leaf tips is dispensed with. They may be served as a vegetable, e.g. Pointes d'asperges au beurre.

They are also used in numerous garnishes for soups, egg dishes, fish, entrée, cold dishes, salad, etc.

10 · **Fried egg plant** *Aubergine frite*

1 portion provides:
225 kcals/944 kJ
20.0 g fat of which 3.8 g saturated
10.1 g carbohydrate of which 5.9 g sugars
1.9 g protein
5.2 g fibre

1. Allow ½ aubergine per portion.
2. Remove alternate strips with a peeler.
3. Cut into ½ cm (¼ in) slices on the slant.
4. Pass through seasoned flour or milk and flour (à la française).
5. Shake off all surplus flour.
6. Deep fry in hot fat (185 °C). Drain well and serve.

Aubergines may also be shallow fried.

11 · Ratatouille *Ratatouille*

200 g	½ lb	baby marrow
200 g	½ lb	aubergines
200 g	½ lb	tomatoes
50 ml	⅛ pt	oil
50 g	2 oz	onion (finely sliced)
		1 clove garlic, peeled and chopp
50 g	2 oz	red peppers, diced
50 g	2 oz	green peppers, diced
		salt, pepper
		1 teaspn chopped parsley

1 portion provides:

138 kcals/579 kJ
12.6 g fat of which 1.7 g saturated
5.2 g carbohydrate of which 4.6 g sugars
1.3 g protein
2.4 g fibre

Service of and ingredients for stir-fry vegetables

1 Trim off both ends of the marrow and aubergines.
2 Remove the skin using a peeler.
3 Cut into 3 mm (⅛ in) slices.
4 Concassée the tomatoes (peel, remove seeds, roughly chop).
5 Place the oil in a thick bottomed pan and add the onions.
6 Cover with a lid and allow to cook gently 5–7 min without colouring.
7 Add the garlic, the marrow and aubergine slices and the peppers.
8 Season with salt and mill pepper.
9 Allow to cook gently 4–5 min, toss occasionally and keep covered.
10 Add the tomato and continue cooking until all is tender (approx. 20–30 min).
11 Mix in the parsley, correct the seasoning and serve.

4 portions

12 · Stuffed aubergine or egg plant *Aubergine farcie*

		2 aubergines
10 g	½ oz	chopped shallot
100 g	4 oz	mushrooms
		chopped parsley
100 g	4 oz	tomato concassé
		salt, pepper
125 ml	¼ pt	demi-glace

1 Cut the aubergines in two lengthwise.
2 With the point of a small knife make a cut round the halves approx. ½ cm (¼ in) from the edge, then make several cuts ½ cm (¼ in) deep in the centre.
3 Deep fry in hot fat (185 °C) for 2–3 min, drain well.
4 Scoop out the centre pulp and finely chop it.
5 Cook the chopped shallot in a little oil or fat without colouring.
6 Add the well-washed chopped mushrooms.
7 Cook gently for a few minutes.
8 Mix in the pulp, parsley, tomato, and season.
9 Replace in the aubergine skins.
10 Sprinkle with breadcrumbs and melted butter.
11 Brown under the salamander.
12 Serve with a cordon of demi-glace or jus-lié. *4 portions*

13 · Broccoli *Brocolis*

Cook and serve as for any of the cauliflower recipes (page 418). Green and purple broccoli, because of their size, need less cooking time than cauliflower.

1 portion provides:

18 kcals/76 kJ
0.0 g fat of which 0.0 g saturated
1.6 g carbohydrate of which 1.5 g sugars
3.1 g protein
4.1 g fibre

14 · Buttered carrots *Carottes au beurre ou Carottes glacées*

400 g	1 lb	carrots
		salt, pepper
25 g	1 oz	butter
		chopped parsley

1 portion provides:

71 kcals/297 kJ
5.1 g fat of which 3.3 g saturated
5.8 g carbohydrate of which 5.8 g sugars
0.7 g protein
2.8 g fibre

1 Peel and wash the carrots.
2 Cut into neat even pieces or turn barrel shape.
3 Place in a pan with a little salt, a pinch of sugar and butter. Barely cover with water.

4 Cover with a buttered paper and allow to boil steadily in order to evaporate all the water.
5 When the water has completely evaporated check that the carrots are cooked, if not, add a little more water and continue cooking. Do not overcook.
6 Toss the carrots over a fierce heat for 1–2 min in order to give them a glaze.
7 Serve sprinkled with chopped parsley.

4 portions

15 **Purée of carrots** *Purée de carottes*

600 g	1 lb 8 oz	carrots
25 g	1 oz	butter or margarine
		salt, pepper

1 Wash, peel and rewash the carrots. Cut in pieces.
2 Barely cover with water, add salt. Simmer gently until tender.
3 Drain well. Pass through a sieve or mouli.
4 Return to the pan, reheat and mix in the butter, correct the seasoning, and serve.

16 **Vichy carrots** *Carottes Vichy*

1 Allow the same ingredients as for buttered carrots, substitute Vichy water for the liquid.
2 Peel and wash the carrots (which should not be larger than 2 cm (1 in) in diameter).
3 Cut into 2 mm (1⁄12 in) thin slices on the mandolin.
4 Cook and serve as for buttered carrots.

17 **Carrots in cream sauce** *Carottes à la crème*

400 g	1 lb	carrots
¼ litre	½ pt	cream sauce (page 95)
10 g	½ oz	butter or margarine
		salt, pepper

Prepare and cook carrots as for buttered carrots. Mix with the sauce, correct the seasoning and serve.

Note The cream sauce may be made with wholemeal flour, skimmed milk and natural yoghurt.

18 · Stuffed mushrooms *Champignons farcis*

300 g	12 oz	grilling mushrooms
10 g	½ oz	chopped shallot
50 g	2 oz	butter, margarine or oil
25 g	1 oz	breadcrumbs

Using sunflower oil
1 portion provides:

137 kcals/577 kJ
13.1 g fat of which 1.8 g saturated
3.2 g carbohydrate of which 0.3 g sugars
1.9 g protein
2.1 g fibre

1 Peel, remove the stalk and wash well.
2 Retain 8 or 12 of the best mushrooms. Finely chop the remainder with the well washed peelings and stalks.
3 Cook the shallots, without colour, in a little fat.
4 Add the chopped mushrooms and cook for 3–4 min (duxelle).
5 Grill as in the recipe 20.
6 Place the duxelle in the centre of each mushroom.
7 Sprinkle with a few breadcrumbs and melted butter.
8 Reheat in the oven or under the salamander and serve.

19 · Braised celery *Céleri braisé*

		2 heads of celery
100 g	4 oz	carrots, sliced
100 g	4 oz	onion, sliced
		bouquet garni
¼ litre	½ pt	white stock
		salt, pepper
50 g	2 oz	fat bacon or suet
		2 crusts of bread

1 portion provides:

120 kcals/505 kJ
10.2 g fat of which 4.1 g saturated
4.8 g carbohydrate of which 4.5 g sugars
2.8 g protein
3.8 g fibre

1 Trim the celery heads and the root, cut off outside discoloured stalks and cut the heads to approx. 15 cm (6 in) lengths.
2 Wash well under running cold water.
3 Place in a pan of boiling water. Simmer for approx. 20 min until limp. Refresh and rewash.
4 Place the sliced vegetables in a sauté pan, sauteuse or casserole.
5 Add the celery heads whole or cut them in halves lengthwise, fold over and place on the bed of roots.
6 Add the bouquet garni, barely cover with stock and season.
7 Add the fat bacon or suet, the crusts of bread, cover with a buttered greaseproof paper and a tight lid and cook gently in a moderate oven (150–200 °C, Reg. 2–6) for 2 hrs or until tender.
8 Remove the celery from the pan, drain well and dress neatly.

Ingredients for braised vegetables

9 Add the cooking liquor to an equal amount of jus-lié or demi-glace, reduce and correct the seasoning and consistency.
10 Mask the celery, finish with chopped parsley, and serve.

4 portions

Braised celery

20 · Grilled mushrooms *Champignons grillés*

200 g	8 oz	grilling mushrooms
		salt, pepper
50 g	2 oz	butter, margarine or oil

Using sunflower oil
1 portion provides:

119 kcals/499 kJ
12.8 g fat of which 1.7 g saturated
0.0 g carbohydrate of which 0.0 g sugars
0.9 g protein
1.3 g fibre

1 Peel mushrooms, remove the stalks and wash and drain well.
2 Place on a tray and season with salt and pepper.
3 Brush with melted fat or oil and grill on both sides for approx. 3–4 min. Serve with picked parsley.

4 portions

21 · Cabbage *Chou vert*

1 portion provides:

9 kcals/38 kJ
0.0 g fat of which 0.0 g saturated
1.1 g carbohydrate of which 1.1 g sugars
1.3 g protein
2.5 g fibre

1 Cut cabbage in quarters.
2 Remove the centre stalk and outside leaves.
3 Shred and wash well.
4 Place into boiling salted water.
5 Boil steadily until cooked, approx. 10–15 min according to age and type. Do not overcook.
6 Drain immediately in a colander and serve.

Note Overcooking will lessen and the addition of soda will destroy the vitamin content. These points are also true when cooking any green vegetables.

3–4 portions to ½ kg (1 lb)

22 · Spring greens *Choux de printemps*

Prepare and cook as for cabbage for approx. 10–15 min according to age and type. Do not overcook.

3–4 portions to ½ kg (1 lb)

23 · Stir-fry cabbage with mushrooms and beansprouts

		2 tablespns sunflower oil
400 g	1 lb	spring cabbage shredded
		2 tablespns soy sauce
200 g	8 oz	mushrooms
100 g	4 oz	beansprouts
		freshly ground pepper

1 Heat the oil in a suitable pan, i.e. wok.
2 Add the cabbage and stir for 2 mins.
3 Add the soy sauce, stir well. Cook for a further 1 min.
4 Add the mushrooms cut into slices and cook for a further 2 mins.
5 Stir in the beansprouts and cook for 1–2 mins.
6 Stir well. Season with freshly ground pepper and serve.

Note This recipe can be prepared without the mushrooms and/or beansprouts if desired. *4 portions*

24 · Braised cabbage *Choux braisés*

½ kg	1 lb	cabbage
100 g	4 oz	carrot
100 g	4 oz	onion
250 ml	½ pt	white stock
		salt, pepper
		bouquet garni
125 ml	¼ pt	jus-lié

1 Quarter the cabbage, remove the centre stalk and wash.
2 Retain four light green leaves, shred the remainder.
3 Blanch leaves and shredded cabbage 2–3 mins, refresh.
4 Lay the four blanched leaves flat on the table.
5 Place the remainder of the cabbage on the centre of each and season.
6 Wrap each portion of cabbage in a tea-cloth and shape into a fairly firm ball.
7 Remove from the tea-cloth. Place on a bed of roots.
8 Add the stock half way up cabbage, seasoning and bouquet garni.
9 Bring to the boil, cover with a lid and cook in the oven approx. 1 hr.
10 Dress the cabbage in a serving dish.
11 Add the cooking liquor to the jus-lié, correct the seasoning and consistency and strain.
12 Pour over the cabbage and serve.

25 · Braised stuffed cabbage *Choux farcis braisés*

As for braised cabbage with the addition of 25–50 g (1–2 oz) sausage meat placed in the centre before shaping into a ball. This recipe can be prepared using Chinese leaves.

26 Sauerkraut (pickled white cabbage) *Choucroûte*

400 g	1 lb	sauerkraut
50 g	2 oz	onion piqué
50 g	2 oz	carrot
		bouquet garni
		6 peppercorns
		6 juniper berries
250 ml	½ pt	white stock

1 Season the sauerkraut and place in a casserole or pan, suitable for placing in the oven.
2 Add the whole onion and carrot, the bouquet garni and the peppercorns and berries.
3 Barely cover with good white stock.
4 Cook with a buttered paper and lid.
5 Cook slowly in a moderate oven 3–4 hr.
6 Remove the bouquet garni and onion. Cut the onion in slices.
7 Serve the sauerkraut garnished with slices of carrot.

27 Garnished sauerkraut *Choucroûte garni*

This dish is served as an entrée. See page 336.

28 Braised red cabbage *Choux à la flamande*

300 g	12 oz	red cabbage
		salt, pepper
50 g	2 oz	butter
125 ml	¼ pt	vinegar or red wine
50 g	2 oz	bacon trimmings (optional)
100 g	4 oz	cooking apples
10 g	½ oz	castor sugar

1 portion provides:

180 kcals/754 kJ
15.2 g fat of which 8.4 g saturated
7.8 g carbohydrate of which 7.7 g sugars
3.4 g protein
3.2 g fibre

1 Quarter, trim and shred the cabbage. Wash well and drain.
2 Season with salt and pepper.
3 Place in a well-buttered casserole or pan suitable for placing in the oven (not aluminium or iron).
4 Add the vinegar and bacon (if using), cover with a buttered paper and lid.
5 Cook in a moderate oven (150–200 °C, Reg. 2–6) for approx. 1½ hr.
6 Add the peeled and cored apples cut into 1 cm (½ in) dice and sugar. Recover with the lid and continue cooking until tender, approx. 2 hr in all. If a little more cooking liquor is needed use stock.
7 Remove bacon (if used) and serve.

4 portions

29 · **Brussels sprouts** *Choux de bruxelles*

1 Using a small knife trim the stems and cut a cross 2 mm (1/12 in) deep and remove any discoloured leaves. Wash well.
2 Cook in boiling salted water approx. 10–15 mins according to size. Do not overcook.
3 Drain well in a colander and serve.

1 portion provides:
20 kcals/82 kJ
0.0 g fat of which 0.0 g saturated
1.9 g carbohydrate of which 1.8 g sugars
3.1 g protein
3.2 g fibre

1/2 kg (1 lb) will yield 3–4 portions

30 · **Brussels sprouts with butter** *Choux de bruxelles au beurre*

1 Cook and serve as in previous recipe.
2 Brush with 25–50 g (1–2 oz) melted butter.

31 · **Brussels sprouts fried in butter** *Choux de bruxelles sautés au beurre*

1 Cook and drain.
2 Melt 25–50 g (1–2 oz) butter in a frying-pan.
3 When foaming, add the sprouts and toss lightly, browning slightly.

32 · **Brussels sprouts with chestnuts** *Choux de bruxelles limousine*

To every 400 g (1 lb) sprouts add 100 g (4 oz) cooked peeled chestnuts.

33 · **Cauliflower** *Chou-fleur nature*

Allow 1 medium-sized cauliflower for 4 portions.

1 Trim stem and remove outer leaves.
2 Hollow out stem with a peeler. Wash.
3 Cook in boiling salted water approx. 20 min. Do not overcook.
4 Drain well and serve cut into 4 even portions.

1 portion provides:
9 kcals/38 kJ
0.0 g fat of which 0.0 g saturated
0.8 g carbohydrate of which 0.8 g sugars
1.6 g protein
1.8 g fibre

34 · **Buttered cauliflower** *Chou-fleur au beurre*

As for cauliflower, brush with 25–50 g (1–2 oz) melted butter to serve.

35 · **Buttered cauliflower with parsley** *Chou-fleur persillé*

As for buttered cauliflower, sprinkle with chopped parsley.

36 · **Cauliflower fried in butter** *Chou-fleur sauté au beurre*

1 Cut the cooked cauliflower in 4 portions.
2 Lightly colour on all sides in 25–50 g (1–2 oz) butter.

37 · **Cauliflower, cream sauce** *Chou-fleur, sauce crème*

1 Cook and serve as for cauliflower.
2 Accompany with ¼ litre (½ pt) cream sauce in a sauceboat.

38 · **Cauliflower, melted butter** *Chou-fleur, beurre fondu*

As for cauliflower, with a sauceboat of 100 g (4 oz) melted butter (see page 107).

39 · **Cauliflower, hollandaise sauce** *Chou-fleur, sauce hollandaise*

As for cauliflower, accompany with a sauceboat of ⅛ litre (¼ pt) hollandaise sauce (see page 108).

40 · **Cauliflower au gratin** *Chou-fleur au gratin*
or *ou*
41 · **Cauliflower Mornay** *Chou-fleur Mornay*

1 Cut the cooked cauliflower into four.
2 Reheat in a pan of hot salted water (chauffant), or reheat in butter.
3 Place in vegetable dish or on greased tray.
4 Coat with ¼ litre (½ pt) Mornay sauce, if using (see page 95).
5 Sprinkle with grated cheese.
6 Brown under the salamander and serve.

1 portion (au gratin) provides:
150 kcals/632 kJ
10.4 g fat of which 3.9 g saturated
8.6 g carbohydrate of which 3.8 g sugars
6.3 g protein
2.0 g fibre

42 · **Cauliflower polonaise** *Chou-fleur polonaise*

1 Cut the cooked cauliflower into four, reheat in a chauffant or in butter.
2 Heat 50 g (2 oz) butter, add 10 g (½ oz) white or wholemeal breadcrumbs in a frying-pan and lightly brown. Pour over the cauliflower, sprinkle with sieved hard-boiled egg and chopped parsley.

43 · **Sea-kale** *Chou de mer*

1 Trim the roots, remove any discoloured leaves.
2 Wash well and tie into neat bundle.
3 Cook in boiling salted water. Do not overcook, approx. 15–20 min.
4 Drain well, serve accompanied with a suitable sauce, e.g. beurre fondu, hollandaise, etc.

½ kg (1 lb) will yield approx. 3 portions

44 Sea-kale Mornay *Chou de mer Mornay*
or *ou*
45 Sea-kale au gratin *Chou de mer au gratin*

1 Prepare and cook as for sea-kale (recipe 43).
2 Reheat and cut into 5 cm (2 in) lengths, place in a vegetable dish.
3 Coat with ¼ litre (½ pt) Mornay sauce (page 95) and sprinkle with grated cheese.
4 Brown under the salamander and serve.

1 portion provides:
157 kcals/628 kJ
10.4 g fat of which 3.9 g saturated
8.4 g carbohydrate of which 3.6 g sugars
6.1 g protein
1.4 g fibre

46 Marrow *Courge*

All the variations for cauliflower may be used with marrow.

1 Peel the marrow with a peeler or small knife.
2 Cut in half lengthwise.
3 Remove the seeds with a spoon.
4 Cut into even pieces approx. 5 cm (2 in) square.
5 Cook in boiling salted water approx. 10–15 min. Do not overcook.
6 *Drain well* and serve.

1 portion provides:
11 kcals/44 kJ
0.0 g fat of which 0.0 g saturated
2.1 g carbohydrate of which 2.0 g sugars
0.6 g protein
0.9 g fibre

47 Stuffed marrow *Courge farcie*

Various stuffings may be used: 100 g (4 oz) sausage meat or 100 g (4 oz) rice for 4 portions, e.g. cooked rice with chopped cooked meat, seasoned with salt, pepper and herbs; well-seasoned cooked rice with sliced mushroom, tomatoes, etc.

1 Peel the marrow and cut in half lengthwise.
2 Remove the seeds with a spoon.
3 Season and add the stuffing. Replace the two halves.
4 Cook as for braised celery (page 414) allowing approx. 1 hr.
5 To serve, cut into thick slices and dress neatly in a vegetable dish. Baby marrows are ideal for this.

48 Marrow provençale *Courge provençale*

400 g	1 lb	marrow
50 g	2 oz	chopped onion
		1 clove garlic (chopped)
50 g	2 oz	oil or butter
		salt, pepper
400 g	1 lb	tomatoes skinned, deseeded and diced
		chopped parsley

1 Peel the marrow, remove the seeds and cut into 2 cm (1 in) dice.
2 Cook onion and garlic in the oil in a pan for 2–3 min without colouring.
3 Add the marrow, season with salt and pepper.
4 Add the tomato concassé.
5 Cover with a lid, cook gently in the oven or on the side of the stove until tender, approx. 1 hr.
6 Sprinkle with chopped parsley and serve.

49 · **Baby marrow** *Courgette*

Because they are tender, courgettes are not peeled or de-seeded.
1 Wash. Top and tail and cut into round slices 3–6 cm (⅛–¼ in) thick.
2 Gently boil in lightly salted water or steam for two or three minutes. Do not overcook.
3 Drain well and serve.
   a) plain,
   b) brushed with melted butter or margarine and/or sprinkled with chopped parsley.

1 portion provides:
27 kcals/113 kJ
0.1 g fat of which – g saturated
5.9 g carbohydrate of which 0.4 g sugars
1.0 g protein
0.8 g fibre

¾ kg (1½ lb) yields approx. 4 portions

50 · **Shallow-fried courgettes** *Courgettes sautées*

1 Prepare as recipe 49.
2 Gently fry in hot oil or butter for 2 or 3 minutes, drain and serve.

(An example of service of this dish can be seen in the photograph on page 291.)

51 · **Deep-fried courgettes** *Courgettes frites*

1 Prepare as recipe 49.
2 Pass through flour, or milk and flour, or batter and deep fry in hot fat (185 °C). Drain well and serve.

52 · **Courgettes provençale** *Courgettes provençale*

1 Prepare as recipe 49.
2 Proceed as for marrow provençale recipe 48, reducing the cooking time to 5 to 10 minutes.

53 · **Stuffed cucumber** *Concombre farci*

1 Peel the cucumber with a peeler.
2 Cut into 2 cm (1 in) pieces.
3 Remove two-thirds of the centre with parisienne cutter.
4 Cook in boiling salted water for 10 min. Refresh.
5 Fill centre with a duxelle-base stuffing to which may be added chopped cooked meat, rice, tomato, etc.
6 Cover with a buttered paper and reheat in a moderate oven and serve.

54 · **Belgian chicory** *Endive belge à l'étuvée*

Using 25 g butter per ½ kg
1 portion provides:

73 kcals/304 kJ
6.8 g fat of which 4.3 g saturated
1.8 g carbohydrate of which 0.0 g sugars
1.0 g protein
1.0 g fibre

1 Trim the stem, remove any discoloured leaves, wash.
2 Place in a well-buttered casserole or pan suitable to place in the oven.
3 Season lightly with salt and a little sugar if desired.
4 Add the juice of half a lemon to prevent discoloration.
5 Add 25–50 g (1–2 oz) butter per ½ kg (1 lb) and a few drops of water.
6 Cover with a buttered paper and lid.
7 Cook gently in a moderate oven (150–200 °C, Reg. 2–6) approx. 1 hr.
8 Dress and serve.

½ kg (1 lb) will yield 3 portions

55 · **Shallow-fried chicory** *Endive meunière*

Cook the chicory as in previous recipe, drain, shallow fry in a little butter, colour lightly on both sides. Serve with 10 g (½ oz) per portion nut-brown butter, lemon juice and chopped parsley.

56 · **Braised chicory** *Endive au jus*

Cook the chicory as à l'étuvée (recipe 54), when dressed surround with a cordon of jus-lié.

57 · **Leaf spinach** *Epinards en branches*

Using 25 g butter per ½ kg
1 portion provides:

123 kcals/515 kJ
10.8 g fat of which 6.6 g saturated
1.4 g carbohydrate of which 1.2 g sugars
5.2 g protein
6.3 g fibre

1 Remove the stems and discard them.
2 Wash the leaves very carefully in plenty of water several times if necessary.
3 Cook in boiling salted water, approx. 5 min, do not overcook.
4 Refresh under cold water, squeeze dry into a ball.

5 When required for service, place into a pan containing 25–50 g (1–2 oz) butter, loosen with a fork and reheat quickly without colouring, season lightly with salt and mill pepper and serve.

½ kg (1 lb) will yield 2 portions

58 · **Spinach purée** *Epinards en purée*

1 Cook, refresh and drain spinach as above.
2 Pass through a sieve or mouli, or use a food processor.
3 Reheat in 25–50 g (1–2 oz) butter, mix with wooden spoon, correct the seasoning and serve.

59 · **Creamed spinach purée** *Epinards en purée à la crème*

1 As for spinach purée.
2 Mix in 30 ml (⅛ pt) cream, 60 ml (¼ pt) béchamel or natural yoghurt before serving.
3 Serve as for spinach purée and serve with a border of cream.

60 · **Spinach with croûtons** *Epinards aux croûtons*

As for creamed spinach with the cordon of cream and surround with 1 cm (½ in) triangle shaped croûton fried in butter.

61 · **Broad beans** *Fèves*

1 Shell the beans and cook in boiling salted water until tender, approx. 10–15 mins. Do not overcook.
2 If the inner shells are tough they should also be removed before serving.

1 portion provides:
34 kcals/142 kJ
0.4 g fat of which 0.1 g saturated
5.0 g carbohydrate of which 0.4 g sugars
2.9 g protein
3.0 g fibre

½ kg (1 lb) will yield approx. 2 portions

62 · **Broad beans with butter** *Fèves au beurre*

As above, brush liberally with butter.

63 · **Broad beans with parsley** *Fèves persillées*

As for broad beans with butter, then sprinkle with chopped parsley.

64 · **Broad beans with cream sauce** *Fèves à la crème*

Prepare and cook as recipe 61, bind with ¼ litre (½ pt) cream sauce or fresh cream.

65 · Dried beans

E.g. black-eyed, borlotti, butter, haricot, kidney, flageolet beans only require soaking if they have been stored for a long time.

1 If necessary soak in cold water overnight in a cool place.
2 Change the water, refresh.
3 Cover with cold water. Do not add salt (as salt toughens the skin and lengthens the cooking time). Bring to the boil.
4 Skim when necessary.
5 Add 50 g (2 oz) carrot, 50 g (2 oz) onion piqué, 50 g (2 oz) bacon bone or trimmings (optional) and bouquet garni.
6 Simmer until tender. Season lightly with salt.
7 Drain and serve.

½ kg (1 lb) will yield 8 portions

66 · French beans *Haricots verts*

1 Top and tail the beans, carefully and economically.
2 Using a large sharp knife cut beans into strips approx. 5 cm × 3 mm (2 × ⅛ in).
3 Wash.
4 Cook in boiling salted water until tender, approx. 10–15 mins.
5 Do not overcook. Drain well and serve.

1 portion provides:
7 kcals/29 kJ
0.0 g fat of which 0.0 g saturated
1.1 g carbohydrate of which 0.8 g sugars
0.8 g protein
3.2 g fibre

(See page 283 for an example of service.)

½ kg (1 lb) will yield 3–4 portions

67 · French beans with butter *Haricots verts au beurre*

As previous recipe, brush the beans liberally with butter.

68 · French beans tossed in butter *Haricots verts sautés au beurre*

Gently toss the cooked beans in butter over heat without colouring.

69 · French beans with onions *Haricots verts lyonnaise*

400 g (1 lb) cooked French beans with 50 g (2 oz) shallow-fried onions.

70 · Mixed beans *Haricots panachés*

400 g (1 lb) cooked French beans with 100 g (4 oz) cooked flageolet beans.

71 Runner beans

1 portion provides:
19 kcals/80 kJ
0.2 g fat of which 0.0 g saturated
2.7 g carbohydrate of which 1.3 g sugars
1.9 g protein
3.4 g fibre

Wash and string the beans with a small knife, then cut them into thin strips approx. 4–6 cm (2–3 in) long.

Cook in boiling salt water approx. 10 min.

Drain well and serve. Do not overcook.

72 Braised lettuce *Laitue braisée*

		2 large lettuce
50 g	2 oz	carrot (sliced)
50 g	2 oz	onion (sliced)
		salt, pepper
		bouquet garni
125 ml	¼ pt	white stock approx.
50 g	2 oz	fat bacon (optional)
		2 slices stale bread
50 g	2 oz	butter or margarine
60 ml	⅛ pt	jus-lié or demi-glace
		chopped parsley

Using hard margarine 1 portion provides:
243 kcals/1023 kJ
20.9 g fat of which 8.7 g saturated
11.0 g carbohydrate of which 2.7 g sugars
3.6 g protein
2.4 g fibre

1. Wash the lettuce, keeping whole.
2. Place in boiling salted water and cook for 5 min, refresh.
3. Squeeze carefully.
4. Arrange the sliced vegetables in a pan or casserole suitable for placing in the oven.
5. Season lightly, add the bouquet garni and stock to come half-way up the lettuce, add the bacon (if used).
6. Cover with a buttered greaseproof paper and a lid.
7. Cook in a moderate oven (150–200 °C, Reg. 2–6) approx. 1 hr.
8. Remove the lettuce, cut in halves lengthwise, flatten slightly and fold each in half.
9. Meanwhile cut 4 neat heart-shaped croûtons from the bread and fry in butter or margarine to a golden brown.
10. Reduce the cooking liquor from the lettuce with the jus-lié or demi-glace, keeping the sauce thin.
11. Serve the lettuce masked with the thin sauce.
12. Dip the points of the croûtons in the sauce and then into chopped parsley and arrange neatly on or by the lettuce.

73 · Corn on the cob *Maïs*

I portion provides:
154 kcals/646 kJ
2.9 g fat of which 0.5 g saturated
28.5 g carbohydrate of which 2.1 g sugars
5.1 g protein
5.9 g fibre

1 Trim the stem.
2 Cook in boiling water until the corn is tender (approx. 15–20 mins). Do not overcook.
3 Remove the outer leaves and fibres.
4 Serve with a sauceboat of melted butter.

Allow 1 cob per portion

74 · Creamed sweetcorn *Maïs a la crème*

1 Remove the corn from the cooked cobs, drain well.
2 Lightly bind with cream, fresh or non-dairy, béchamel or yoghurt.

75 · Buttered turnips or swedes *Navets au beurre, rutabaga au beurre*

400 g	1 lb	turnips or swedes
		salt, sugar
25 g	1 oz	butter
		chopped parsley

I portion provides:
60 kcals/253 kJ
5.4 g fat of which 3.3 g saturated
2.5 g carbohydrate of which 2.5 g sugars
0.7 g protein
1.9 g fibre

1 Peel and wash the vegetables.
2 Cut into neat pieces or turn barrel shape.
3 Place in a pan with a little salt, a pinch of sugar and butter. Barely cover with water.
4 Cover with a buttered paper and allow to boil steadily in order to evaporate all the water.
5 When the water has completely evaporated check that the vegetables are cooked, if not, add a little more water and continue cooking. Do not overcook.
6 Toss the vegetables over a fierce heat for 1–2 min in order to glaze.
7 Drain well, and serve.

76 · Purée of turnips or swedes *Purée de navets, purée de rutubaga*

600 g	1 lb 8 oz	turnips or swedes
		salt, pepper
25 g	1 oz	butter

1 Wash, peel and rewash the vegetables. Cut in pieces if necessary.
2 Barely cover with water, add salt.
3 Simmer gently until tender. Drain well.
4 Pass through a sieve or mouli, or use a food processor.
5 Return to the pan, reheat and mix in the butter, correct the seasoning and serve.

77 · **Fried onions** *Oignons sautés ou Oignons lyonnaise*

1. Peel and wash the onions, cut in halves, slice finely.
2. Cook slowly in 25–50 g (1–2 oz) fat in a frying-pan, turning frequently until tender and nicely browned, and season lightly with salt.

½ kg (1 lb) will yield approx. 2 portions

Using peanut oil
1 portion provides:

162 kcals/681 kJ
12.9 g fat of which 2.4 g saturated
10.4 g carbohydrate of which 10.4 g sugars
1.8 g protein
2.6 g fibre

78 · **French fried onions** *Oignons frits à la française*

1. Peel and wash the onions.
2. Cut in 2 mm (1/12 in) thick slices, against the grain. Separate into rings.
3. Pass through milk and seasoned flour.
4. Shake off the surplus. Deep fry in hot fat (185 °C).
5. Drain well, season lightly with salt and serve.

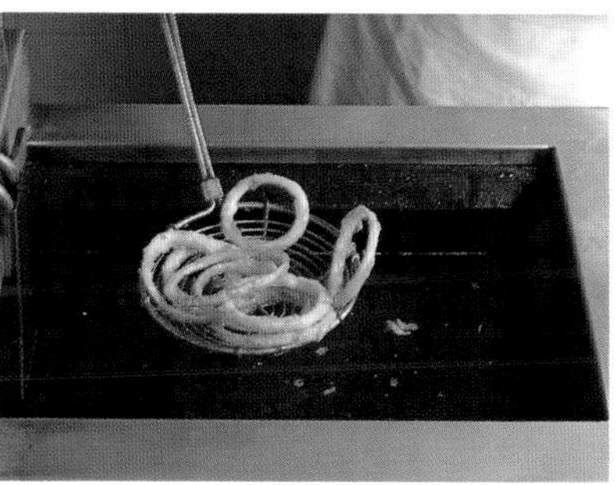

Preparation and cooking of French fried onions

(An example of service of this dish can be found on page 283.)

79 · **Braised onions** *Oignons braisés*

1 portion provides:

58 kcals/245 kJ
0.4 g fat of which 0.1 g saturated
10.9 g carbohydrate of which 10.4 g sugars
3.4 g protein
2.8 g fibre

1. Select medium even-sized onions, allow 2–3 portions per ½ kg (1 lb).
2. Peel, wash and cook in boiling salted water for ½ hr.
3. Drain and place in a pan or casserole suitable for placing in the oven.
4. Add a bouquet garni, half-cover with stock and a lid and braise gently (180–200 °C, Reg. 4–6) in the oven till tender.
5. Drain well and dress neatly in a vegetable dish.
6. Reduce the cooking liquor with an equal amount of jus-lié or demi-glace. Correct the seasoning and consistency and pass. Mask the onions and sprinkle with chopped parsley.

(The service of this dish is illustrated on page 403.)

80 Peas *Petits pois*

Fresh peas

1 portion provides:
62 kcals/260 kJ
0.4 g fat of which 0.1 g saturated
9.8 g carbohydrate of which 3.7 g sugars
5.4 g protein
4.8 g fibre

1. Shell and wash the peas.
2. Cook in boiling salted water with a sprig of mint until tender, approx. 10–15 min. Do not overcook. Drain in a colander.
3. Add 25 g (1 oz) butter and ½ teaspn castor sugar, toss gently.
4. Serve with blanched, refreshed mint leaves.

1 kg (2 lb) will yield approx. 4 portions

Frozen peas

Cook in boiling salted water until tender approx. 5 min. Drain in a colander. Add 25 g (1 oz) butter and ½ teaspn castor sugar, toss gently. Serve with blanched refreshed mint leaves.

¼ kg (½ lb) will yield approx. 4 portions

81 Peas French style *Petits pois à la française*

1 kg	2 lb	peas (in the pod)
		12 spring or button onions
		1 small lettuce
25 g	1 oz	butter
		salt
		½ teaspn castor sugar
5 g	¼ oz	flour

1 portion provides:
123 kcals/515 kJ
5.6 g fat of which 3.4 g saturated
12.9 g carbohydrate of which 5.8 g sugars
5.9 g protein
5.7 g fibre

1. Shell and wash the peas and place in a sauteuse.
2. Peel and wash the onions, shred the lettuce and add to the peas with 10 g (½ oz) butter, salt and the sugar.
3. Barely cover with water. Cover with a lid and cook steadily, preferably in the oven, until tender.
4. Correct the seasoning.
5. Mix the other 10 g (½ oz) butter with 5 g (¼ oz) flour and shake into the boiling peas until thoroughly mixed, and serve.

Note When using frozen peas allow the onions to almost cook before adding the peas.

4 portions

82 · Peas Flemish style *Petits pois à la flamande*

200 g	8 oz	carrots
400 g	1 lb	peas
50 g	2 oz	butter

1 Wash and peel the carrots and cut into batons or dice.
2 Cover with water, season and cook until tender.
3 Meanwhile cook the peas.
4 Drain the peas and carrots.
5 Mix together in pan containing the butter and serve.

4 portions

83 · Sugar peas *Mange-tout*

Mange-tout are a variety of pea which does not have the normal tough fibrous lining to the pod. As the peas are harvested very young they are cooked and served in the pod, all of which is eaten.

1 Top and tail and remove any stringy centre fibre. Wash and drain.
2 Cook in boiling salted water approx. 5 mins, until al dente.
3 Drain well and serve plain or brushed with butter.

½ kg (1 lb) will yield 4–6 portions

84 · Stuffed pimento *Piment farci*

		4 medium-sized red pimentos	
200 g	½ lb	rice (long grain)	pilaff
50 g	2 oz	chopped onion	pilaff
50 g	2 oz	butter	pilaff
		salt, pepper	
50 g	2 oz	carrot (sliced)	
50 g	2 oz	onion (sliced)	
		bouquet garni	
½ litre	1 pt	white stock	

1 portion provides:

308 kcals/1291 kJ
11.4 g fat of which 6.7 g saturated
48.8 g carbohydrate of which 5.3 g sugars
5.4 g protein
3.1 g fibre

1 Place the pimentos on a tray in the oven or under the salamander for a few minutes or deep fry in hot oil (180 °C) until the skin blisters.
2 Remove the skin and stalk carefully and empty out all the seeds.
3 Stuff with a well-seasoned pilaff of rice which may be varied by the addition of mushrooms, tomatoes, ham, etc.
4 Replace the stem.
5 Place the pimentos on the sliced carrot and onion in a pan suitable for the oven, add the bouquet garni, stock, seasoning. Cover with a buttered paper and lid.
6 Cook in a moderate oven (180–200 °C) until tender, approx. 1 hr.
7 Serve garnished with picked parsley.

4 portions

85 · Salsify *Salsifi*

I portion provides:

18 kcals/76 kJ
0.0 g fat of which 0.0 g saturated
2.8 g carbohydrate of which 2.8 g sugars
1.9 g protein
– g fibre

1 Wash, peel and rewash the salsify.
2 Cut into 5 cm (2 in) lengths.
3 Cook in a blanc as for artichokes (recipe 4). Do not overcook.
4 They may then be served as for any of the cauliflower recipes, page 418.
5 Salsify may also be passed through batter and deep fried.

½ kg (1 lb) will yield 2–3 portions

86 · Grilled tomatoes *Tomates grillées*

Using sunflower oil
I portion provides:

29 kcals/121 kJ
1.3 g fat of which 0.3 g saturated
3.5 g carbohydrate of which 3.5 g sugars
1.1 g protein
1.9 g fibre

1 Wash the tomatoes, and remove the eyes with a small knife.
2 Place on a greased, seasoned baking tray.
3 Make an incision 2 mm ($^1/_{12}$ in) cross-shape on the opposite side to the eye and peel back the four corners.
4 Brush with melted fat or oil and season lightly with salt and pepper.
5 Grill under a moderately hot salamander. Serve garnished with picked parsley.

Allow 1 or 2 per portion according to size
½ kg (1 lb) will yield approx. 3–4 portions

87 · Stuffed tomatoes *Tomates farcies*

		8 medium-sized tomatoes	
10 g	½ oz	chopped shallot	duxelle
25 g	1 oz	butter or oil	duxelle
150 g	6 oz	mushrooms	duxelle
		salt, pepper	duxelle
		1 clove garlic, crushed (optional)	duxelle
25 g	1 oz	white or wholemeal breadcrumbs	
		chopped parsley	

1 Wash the tomatoes, remove the eyes.
2 Remove approx. one-quarter of the tomato with a sharp knife.
3 Carefully empty out the seeds without damaging the flesh.
4 Place on a greased baking tray.
5 Cook the shallot in a little oil or butter or margarine without colouring.
6 Add the washed chopped mushrooms, season with salt and pepper, add the garlic if using and cook for 2–3 min.
7 Add a little of the strained tomato juice, the breadcrumbs and the parsley, mix to a piping consistency. Correct the seasoning. At this

stage several variations may be made, e.g. chopped ham, cooked rice, etc., can be added.

8 Place the mixture in a piping bag with a large star tube and pipe into the tomato shells.
9 Replace the tops.
10 Brush with melted fat, season lightly with salt and pepper.
11 Cook in a moderate oven (180–200 °C, Reg. 4–6) approx. 4–5 min.
12 Serve garnished with picked parsley.

88 · **Beetroot** *Betterave*

Select medium sized or small beetroots, carefully twist off the green leaves (do not cut). Well wash in cold water, cover with water and simmer gently until the skin is easily removed by rubbing between the fingers. Do *not* cut or prick with knife as the beetroots will 'bleed' and turn pale. Beetroots may also be cooked in a steamer.

1 portion provides:

22 kcals/92 kJ
0.0 g fat of which 0.0 g saturated
5.0 g carbohydrate of which 5.0 g sugars
0.9 g protein
1.3 g fibre

89 · **Basic tomato preparation** *Tomate concassée*

This is a cooked preparation which is usually included in the normal *mise en place* of a kitchen as it is used in a great number of dishes.

400 g	1 lb	tomatoes
25 g	1 oz	chopped shallot or onion
25 g	1 oz	butter, margarine or oil
		salt, pepper

2 Plunge into *boiling* water 5–10 secs, the riper the tomatoes the less time required. Refresh *immediately*.
2 Plunge into *boiling* water 5–10 secs. Refresh *immediately*.
3 Remove the skins, cut in halves across the tomato and remove all the seeds.
4 Roughly chop the flesh of the tomatoes.
5 Meanwhile cook the chopped onion or shallot without colouring in the butter or margarine.
6 Add the tomatoes and season.
7 Simmer gently on the side of the stove until the moisture is evaporated.

90 · **Braised leeks** *Poireaux braisés*

1 portion provides:
31 kcals/130 kJ
0.0 g fat of which 0.0 g saturated
5.6 g carbohydrate of which 5.4 g sugars
2.3 g protein
2.8 g fibre

1 Cut the roots from the leek, remove any discoloured outside leaves and trim the green.
2 Cut through lengthwise and wash well under running water.
3 Tie into a neat bundle.
4 Place in boiling salted water for 5 min approx.
5 Place on a bed of root vegetables.
6 Barely cover with stock, add the bouquet garni and season.
7 Cover with a lid and cook until tender, approx. ½–1 hr.
8 Remove leeks from pan and fold neatly, arrange in a vegetable dish.
9 Meanwhile add jus-lié to the cooking liquor and correct the seasoning and consistency.
10 Pour the sauce over the leeks.

½ kg (1 lb) of leeks will yield approx. 2 portions

91 · **Boiled leeks** *Poireaux nature*

1 Prepare as for 1–4 recipe 90, cooking for 10–15 minutes approx.
2 Drain well, cut the string and serve plain, or brushed with melted butter.

Leeks may also be served coated with cream or parsley sauce.

92 · **Parsnips** *Panais*

1 portion provides:
56 kcals/235 kJ
0.0 g fat of which 0.0 g saturated
13.5 g carbohydrate of which 2.7 g sugars
1.3 g protein
2.5 g fibre

Wash well. Peel the parsnips and again wash well. Cut into quarters lengthwise, remove the centre root if tough. Cut into neat pieces and cook in salt water till tender. Drain and serve with melted butter or in a cream sauce. They may be roasted in the oven in a little fat or in with a joint.

Parsnips can be cooked and prepared as a purée.

93 · **Pease pudding**

200 g	8 oz	yellow split peas soaked
½ litre	1 pt	water approx.
50 g	2 oz	onion piqué
50 g	2 oz	carrot
50 g	2 oz	bacon trimmings
50 g	2 oz	butter or margarine
		salt, pepper

Using hard margarine 1 portion provides:
304 kcals/1277 kJ
15.6 g fat of which 6.5 g saturated
29.6 g carbohydrate of which 2.3 g sugars
13.1 g protein
6.5 g fibre

1 Place all the ingredients, except the butter and margarine, in a saucepan with a tight-fitting lid.
2 Bring to the boil, cook in a moderate oven (180–200 °C, Reg. 4–6) approx. 2 hrs.
3 Remove onion, carrot and bacon and pass the peas through a sieve or use a food processor.
4 Return to a clean pan, mix in the butter or margarine, correct the seasoning and consistency (this should be firm).

94 Mixed vegetables *Macédoine de légumes, Jardinière de légumes*

100 g	4 oz	carrots
50 g	2 oz	turnips
		salt
50 g	2 oz	French beans
50 g	2 oz	peas

1 portion provides:

14 kcals/58 kJ
0.1 g fat of which – g saturated
2.5 g carbohydrate of which 1.7 g sugars
1.0 g protein
2.1 g fibre

1 Peel and wash the carrots and turnips.
2 Cut into ½ cm (¼ in) dice (macédoine) or batons (jardinière).
3 Cook separately in salted water, do not overcook. Refresh.
4 Top and tail the beans.
5 Cut into ½ cm (¼ in) dice, cook and refresh, do not overcook.
6 Cook the peas and refresh.
7 Mix the vegetables and when required reheat in hot salted water.
8 Drain well, serve brushed with melted butter.

4 portions

95 Fennel *Fenouil*

1 portion provides:

5 kcals/21 kJ
0.0 g fat of which 0.0 g saturated
0.7 g carbohydrate of which 0.7 g sugars
0.6 g protein
2.2 g fibre

The foliage of this plant is a herb of distinctive flavour used in fish cookery and salads. One good-sized bulb will serve 2–4 portions.

1 Trim the bulb, remove the stalks and leaves and wash well.
2 Cook in boiling salted water 15–20 mins approx. Do not overcook.
3 Drain well, cut into portions and serve as for any of the cauliflower recipes on page 418.

Note Fennel may also be braised as for celery, page 414.

96 · Mixed fried vegetables in batter *Légumes en fritot*

cauliflower	fennel	Prepared in small pieces. These vegetables may also be served individually.
broccoli	parsnips	
celery	salsify	
French beans	courgettes	

1. Boil or steam the vegetables (except the courgettes) keeping them slightly firm.
2. Marinade in oil, lemon juice and chopped parsley.
3. Dip in batter (see page 220).
4. Deep fry in hot fat 180 °C until golden brown.
5. Drain and serve.

Fried in peanut oil
1 portion provides:

253 kcals/1062 kJ
16.5 g fat of which 3.6 g saturated
22.7 g carbohydrate of which 2.7 g sugars
4.9 g protein
3.1 g fibre

97 · Ladies fingers (okra) in cream sauce *Okra à la crème*

400 g	1 lb	ladies fingers
50 g	2 oz	butter or margarine
¼ litre	½ pt	cream sauce

Using hard margarine
1 portion provides:

221 kcals/928 kJ
20.2 g fat of which 9.8 g saturated
5.7 g carbohydrate of which 5.7 g sugars
4.4 g protein
3.2 g fibre

1. Top and tail the ladies fingers.
2. Blanch in boiling salted water, drain.
3. Sweat in the margarine or butter until tender, approximately 5–10 minutes.
4. Carefully add the cream sauce.
5. Bring to the boil, correct seasoning and serve in a suitable dish.

Note Okra may also be served brushed with butter or sprinkled with chopped parsley.

Selection of potato dishes (clockwise from left): brioche (p. 440); marquis (p. 440); duchess (p. 439); Anna (p. 450); macaire (p. 446); potato ready to be baked (p. 440); savoury (p. 445); (centre) sauté potatoes with onions (p. 442)

18

POTATOES

General objectives	*Specific objectives*
To know a variety of potato dishes suitable for various catering establishments.	To describe and demonstrate the ways of preparing, cooking and presenting a variety of potato dishes. To be able to state with which main dishes they would be suitable.

Potatoes Pommes de terre

½ kg (1 lb) old potatoes will yield approx. 3 portions.
½ kg (1 lb) new potatoes will yield approx. 4 portions.

Note Old potatoes are used in the recipes except where 'new' is specifically stated.

1 Plain boiled potatoes *Pommes nature*

1. Wash, peel and wash the potatoes.
2. Cut or turn into even-sized pieces allowing 2–3 pieces per portion.
3. Cook carefully in salted water approx. 20 min.
4. Drain well and serve.

Using old potatoes
1 portion provides:

116 kcals/487 kJ
0.1 g fat of which – g saturated
28.6 g carbohydrate of which 0.6 g sugars
2.0 g protein
1.5 g fibre

2 Parsley potatoes *Pommes persillées*

1. Prepare and cook potatoes as for plain boiled.
2. Brush liberally with melted butter and sprinkle with chopped parsley.

Using 10 g butter per portion old pots
1 portion provides:

190 kcals/798 kJ
8.3 g fat of which 5.2 g saturated
28.6 g carbohydrate of which 0.6 g sugars
2.1 g protein
1.5 g fibre

3 · Riced or snow potatoes *Pommes à la neige*

Using old potatoes
1 portion provides:

116 kcals/487 kJ
0.1 g fat of which – g saturated
28.6 g carbohydrate of which 0.6 g sugars
2.0 g protein
1.5 g fibre

1. Wash, peel and rewash the potatoes. Cut to an even size.
2. Cook in salted water.
3. Drain off the water, place a lid on the saucepan and return to a low heat to dry out the potatoes.
4. Pass through a medium sieve or a special potato masher. Serve without further handling.

4 · Mashed potatoes *Pommes purée*

Using old potatoes, butter, whole milk
1 portion provides:

182 kcals/763 kJ
7.1 g fat of which 4.4 g saturated
29.0 g carbohydrate of which 1.1 g sugars
2.4 g protein
1.5 g fibre

1. Wash, peel and rewash the potatoes. Cut to an even size.
2. Cook in salted water.
3. Drain off the water, place a lid on the saucepan and return to a low heat to dry out the potatoes.
4. Pass through a medium sieve or a special potato masher.
5. Return the potatoes to a clean pan.
6. Add 25 g (1 oz) butter per ½ kg (1 lb) and mix in with a wooden spoon.
7. Gradually add warm milk 30 ml (⅛ pt) stirring continuously until a smooth creamy consistency is reached.
8. Correct the seasoning and serve.

5 · Mashed potatoes with cheese *Pommes purée au gratin*

Proceed as for pommes purée, stages 1–6, place in serving dish, then sprinkle with grated cheese and melted butter and gratinate.

6 · Mashed potatoes with cream *Pommes purée à la crème*

Proceed as for pommes purée, stages 1–6, place in serving dish, then surround with a cordon of fresh cream.

7 · Biarritz potatoes *Pommes biarritz*

As for mashed potatoes with the addition, for four portions, of:

50 g	2 oz	diced cooked lean ham
25 g	1 oz	diced red pimento
		chopped parsley

8 Duchess potatoes – basic recipe *Pommes duchesse*

Brioche (p. 440), marquis (p. 440) and duchess potatoes

Using old pots, whole milk, hard marg
1 portion provides:

195 kcals/819 kJ
8.2 g fat of which 3.3 g saturated
28.6 g carbohydrate of which 0.6 g sugars
3.5 g protein
1.5 g fibre

1. Wash, peel and rewash the potatoes. Cut to an even size.
2. Cook in salted water.
3. Drain off the water, place a lid on the saucepan and return to a low heat to dry out the potatoes.
4. Pass through a medium sieve or a special potato masher or mouli.
5. Place the potatoes in a clean pan.
6. Add 1 yolk per ½ kg (1 lb) and stir in vigorously with a wooden spoon.
7. Mix in 25 g (1 oz) butter or margarine per ½ kg (1 lb). Correct the seasoning.
8. Place in a piping bag with a large star tube and pipe out into neat spirals approx. 2 cm (1 in) diameter and 5 cm (2 in) high on to a lightly greased baking sheet.
10. Place in a hot oven (230 °C, Reg. 8) for 2–3 min in order to slightly firm the edges.
11. Remove from the oven and brush with eggwash.
12. Brown lightly in a hot oven or under the salamander.

9 Croquette potatoes *Pommes croquettes*

1. Duchess mixture moulded cylinder shape 5×2 cm (2×1 in).
2. Pass through flour, eggwash and breadcrumbs.
3. Reshape with a palette knife and deep fry in hot deep fat (185 °C) in a frying-basket.
4. When a golden colour drain well and serve.

Using hard marg, fried in peanut oil
1 portion provides:

405 kcals/1699 kJ
25.4 g fat of which 6.6 g saturated
40.8 g carbohydrate of which 1.1 g sugars
6.0 g protein
2.2 g fibre

Croquette potatoes

10 · Galette potatoes *Pommes galette*

Duchess mixture moulded into flat cakes 3 cm (1½ in) diameter, 1 cm (½ in) thick. Shallow fry as for Macaire potatoes (page 446).

11 · Brioche potatoes *Pommes brioche*

Duchess mixture in small brioche or cottage loaf shape, i.e. 2 cm (1 in) diameter ball with a ½ cm (½ in) diameter ball on top pierced completely through with a small knife. Place in a hot oven to firm the surface. Brush with eggwash and brown lightly in a hot oven or under a salamander and serve.

(This dish is illustrated on page 435.)

12 · Almond potatoes *Pommes amandines*

Prepare cook and serve as for croquette potatoes, using nibbed almonds in place of breadcrumbs.

13 · Marquis potatoes *Pommes marquise*

1 Pipe duchess mixture in the shape of an oval nest 5×2 cm (2×1 in).
2 Glaze as for duchess potatoes, 8–10.
3 Place a spoonful of cooked tomato concassée (page 431) in the centre, sprinkle with a little chopped parsley and serve.

Using hard marg, fried in peanut oil
1 portion provides:

473 kcals/1988 kJ
32.3 g fat of which 10.6 g saturated
40.6 g carbohydrate of which 0.8 g sugars
7.8 g protein
2.0 g fibre

14 · Dauphine potatoes *Pommes dauphine*

1 Combine ½ kg (1 lb) duchess potato mixture with ⅛ litre (¼ pt) choux paste (no sugar in the choux paste).
2 Mould cylinder shape 5×2 cm (2×1 in).
3 Deep fry in hot fat (185 °C) and serve.

Using 200 g potato per portion
1 portion provides:

153 kcals/643 kJ
0.2 g fat of which – g saturated
36.5 g carbohydrate of which 0.8 g sugars
3.8 g protein
3.6 g fibre

15 · Baked jacket potatoes *Pommes au four*

1 Select good-sized potatoes and allow 1 per portion.
2 Scrub well, make a 2 mm ($^1/_{12}$ in) deep incision round the potato.
3 Place on a bed of salt on a tray in a hot oven (230–250 °C, Reg. 8–9) for approx. 1 hr. Turn the potatoes over after 30 min.
4 Test by holding the potato in a cloth and squeezing gently; if cooked it should feel soft.

16 · Baked jacket potatoes and cheese *Pommes gratinées*

		4 large potatoes
75 g	3 oz	butter
25 g	1 oz	grated Parmesan

1 Bake the potatoes as for recipe 15.
2 Cut the potatoes in halves, lengthwise.
3 Remove the potato from the skin using a spoon.
4 Place the potato in a basin.
5 Add 50 g (2 oz) butter, season lightly with salt and pepper.
6 Mix lightly with a fork.
7 Refill the potato skin with the mixture.
8 Place on a baking sheet.
9 Sprinkle with grated cheese and the remaining 25 g (1 oz) melted butter.
10 Place in the oven (200 °C, Reg. 6) until golden brown and serve.

Baked potatoes can be served with a variety of fillings and dressings, e.g. cheese, baked beans, coleslaw, and are often served as snacks.

17 · Steamed potatoes *Pommes vapeur*

1 Prepare potatoes as for plain boiled, season lightly with salt.
2 Cook in a steamer and serve.

Using old potatoes
1 portion provides:

116 kcals/487 kJ
0.1 g fat of which – g saturated
28.6 g carbohydrate of which 0.6 g sugars
2.0 g protein
2.9 g fibre

18 · Steamed potatoes in jacket *Pommes en robe de chambre*

1 Select small even-sized potatoes and scrub well.
2 Cook in a steamer or boil in salted water and serve unpeeled.

Using old potatoes
1 portion provides:

116 kcals/487 kJ
0.1 g fat of which – g saturated
28.6 g carbohydrate of which 0.6 g sugars
2.0 g protein
1.5 g fibre

19 · Lorette potatoes *Pommes Lorette*

1 Prepare a dauphine potato mixture (recipe 14).
2 Shape like short cigars.
3 Deep fry in hot fat (185 °C) and serve.

Ingredients for and service of sauté potatoes with onions

20 · Sauté potatoes *Pommes sautées*

1 Select medium even-sized potatoes. Scrub well.
2 Plain boil or cook in the steamer. Cool slightly and peel.
3 Cut into approx. 3 mm (1/8 in) slices.
4 Toss in hot shallow fat in a frying-pan until lightly coloured, season lightly with salt.
5 Serve sprinkled with chopped parsley.

Using old potatoes, sunflower oil
1 portion provides:

297 kcals/1249 kJ
11.4 g fat of which 1.3 g saturated
46.8 g carbohydrate of which 0.4 g sugars
4.9 g protein
1.7 g fibre

(See page 283 for an example of service of this dish.)

21 · Shallow fried potatoes *Pommes sautées à cru*

1 Select medium sized potatoes, wash, peel and rewash.
2 Cut into approximately 3 mm (1/8 in) slices. Wash and dry.
3 Shallow fry in hot fat in a frying pan until cooked and lightly coloured.
4 Drain, season, toss lightly in butter or margarine.
5 Serve sprinkled with chopped parsley.

22 · Sauté potatoes with onions *Pommes lyonnaise*

1 Allow 1/4 kg (8 oz) onion to 1/2 kg (1 lb) potatoes.
2 Cook the onions as for fried onions, page 427.
3 Prepare sauté potatoes as for previous recipe.
4 Combine the two and toss together.
5 Serve as for pommes sautées.

(This dish is illustrated above.)

23 Crisps (game chips) *Pommes chips*

1 Wash, peel and rewash the potatoes.
2 Cut in thin slices on the mandolin.
3 Wash well and dry in a cloth.
4 Cook in hot deep fat (185 °C) until golden brown and crisp.
5 Drain well and season lightly with salt.

Using old potatoes, peanut oil
1 portion (25 g) provides:

101 kcals/424 kJ
9.0 g fat of which 1.7 g saturated
4.9 g carbohydrate of which 0.1 g sugars
0.4 g protein
0.3 g fibre

Crisps are not usually served as a potato by themselves, but are used as a garnish and are also served with drinks and for snacks.

24 Wafer potatoes *Pommes gaufrettes*

1 Wash, peel and rewash the potatoes.
2 Using a corrugated mandolin blade, cut in slices, giving a half turn in between each cut in order to obtain a wafer or trellis pattern.
3 Cook and serve as for crisps.

Deep fried potatoes: background, clockwise from left: fried, matchstick, Pont Neuf, croquette, bataille; foreground, left to right: straw, game chips, wafer

25 Matchstick potatoes *Pommes allumettes*

1 Select medium even-sized potatoes.
2 Wash, peel and rewash.
3 Trim on all sides to give straight edges.
4 Cut into slices 5 cm × 3 mm (2 × ⅛ in).
5 Cut the slices into 5 cm × 3 mm × 3 mm (2 × ⅛ × ⅛ in) strips.
6 Wash well and dry in a cloth.
7 Fry in hot deep fat (185 °C) till golden brown and crisp. Drain.
8 Season lightly with salt and serve.

These may also be blanched as for fried potatoes (recipe 28).

26 · Straw potatoes *Pommes pailles*

Using old potatoes, peanut oil
1 portion (25 g) provides:

101 kcals/424 kJ
9.0 g fat of which 1.7 g saturated
4.9 g carbohydrate of which 0.1 g sugars
0.4 g protein
0.3 g fibre

1 Wash, peel and rewash potatoes.
2 Cut into fine julienne.
3 Wash well and drain in a cloth.
4 Cook in hot deep fat (185 °C) until golden brown and crisp.
5 Drain well and season lightly with salt.

This potato is used as a garnish, usually for grills of meat.

27 · Mignonette potatoes *Pommes mignonette*

1 Prepare, wash and trim as in previous recipe.
2 Cut into 2×½ cm (1×¼ in) slices.
3 Cut into 2×½×½ cm (1×¼×¼ in) strips.
4 Cook and serve as for matchstick potatoes.

These may also be blanched as for fried potatoes (below).

28 · Fried or chipped potatoes *Pommes frites*

Using old potatoes, peanut oil
1 portion provides:

367 kcals/1541 kJ
15.8 g fat of which 2.8 g saturated
54.1 g carbohydrate of which 0.0 g sugars
5.5 g protein
1.5 g fibre

1 Prepare, wash and trim as in previous recipe.
2 Cut into slices 1 cm (½ in) thick and 5 cm (2 in) long.
3 Cut the slices into strips 5×1×1 cm (2×½×½ in).
4 Wash well and dry in a cloth.
5 Cook in a frying-basket without colour in moderately hot fat (165 °C).
6 Drain and place on kitchen paper on trays till required.
7 When required place in a frying-pan and cook in hot fat (185 °C) till crisp and golden.
8 Drain well, season lightly with salt and serve.

29 · Pont Neuf potatoes *Pommes Pont Neuf*

1 Select large even-sized potatoes.
2 Prepare, wash and trim as in previous recipe.
3 Cut into slices 2 cm (1 in) thick, 5 cm (2 in) long.
4 Cut the slices into strips 5×2×2 cm (2×1×1 in).
5 Wash and dry on a cloth.
6 Cook in moderately hot fat (165 °C) without colour. Drain.
7 Heat the fat until almost smoking (185 °C).
8 Re-cook the potatoes to a golden brown.
9 Drain well, season lightly with salt and serve.

30 Bataille potatoes *Pommes bataille*

1 Select large even-sized potatoes.
2 Wash, peel and rewash.
3 Cut into 1 cm (½ in) slices.
4 Cut the slices into 1 cm (½ in) strips.
5 Cut the strips into 1 cm (½ in) dice.
6 Wash and dry on a cloth.
7 Cook as for fried potatoes (recipe 28).

31 Savoury potatoes *Pommes boulangère*

400 g	1 lb	potatoes
100 g	4 oz	onions
		salt, pepper
¼ litre	½ pt	white stock
25–50 g	1–2 oz	butter, margarine or oil
		chopped parsley

Using 25 g hard margarine
1 portion provides:

142 kcals/595 kJ
5.3 g fat of which 2.2 g saturated
22.3 g carbohydrate of which 1.8 g sugars
2.8 g protein
2.4 g fibre

Using 50 g hard margarine
1 portion provides:

187 kcals/787 kJ
10.3 g fat of which 4.4 g saturated
22.3 g carbohydrate of which 1.8 g sugars
2.8 g protein
2.4 g fibre

1 Cut the potatoes into 2 mm (1/12 in) slices on a mandolin. Keep the best slices for the top.
2 Peel, halve and finely slice the onions.
3 Mix the onions and potatoes together and season lightly with pepper and salt.
4 Place in well-buttered shallow earthenware dish or roasting tin.
5 Barely cover with stock.
6 Neatly arrange overlapping slices of potato on top.
7 Add a few knobs of butter or a little oil.
8 Place in a hot oven (230–250 °C, Reg. 8–9) approx. 20 min until lightly coloured.
9 Reduce the heat and allow to cook steadily, pressing down firmly from time to time with a flat-bottomed pan.
10 When ready all the stock should be cooked into the potato. Allow 1½ hr cooking time in all.
11 Serve sprinkled with chopped parsley. If cooked in an earthenware dish, clean the edges of the dish with a cloth dipped in salt, and serve in the dish.

(This dish is illustrated on page 435.)

4 portions

32 Macaire potatoes *Pommes Macaire*

Using hard marg, sunflower oil
This recipe provides:

1047 kcals/4392 kJ
65.7 g fat of which 14.7 g saturated
109.8 g carbohydrate of which 2.7 g sugars
11.4 g protein
10.8 g fibre

1 ½ kg (1 lb) will yield 2–3 portions.
2 Prepare and cook as for baked jacket potatoes (recipe 15).
3 Cut in halves, remove the centre with a spoon, into basin.
4 Add 25 g (1 oz) butter per ½ kg (1 lb), salt and mill pepper.
5 Mash and mix as lightly as possible with a fork.
6 Using a little flour, mould into a roll, then divide into pieces, allowing one or two per portion.
7 Mould into 2 cm (1 in) round cakes, flour lightly.
8 Shallow fry on both sides in very hot oil and serve.

(This dish is illustrated on page 435.)

33 Byron potatoes *Pommes Byron*

1 Prepare and cook as for Macaire potatoes.
2 Using the back of a dessert-spoon make a shallow impression on each potato.
3 Carefully sprinkle the centres with grated cheese. Make sure no cheese is on the edge of the potato.
4 Cover the cheese with cream.
5 Brown lightly under the salamander and serve.

34 Fondant potatoes *Pommes fondantes*

Using old potatoes, hard margarine
1 portion (125 g raw potato) provides:

228 kcals/956 kJ
7.0 g fat of which 2.1 g saturated
39.6 g carbohydrate of which 0.9 g sugars
4.1 g protein
1.5 g fibre

1 Select small or even-sized medium potatoes.
2 Wash, peel and rewash.
3 Turn into eight-sided barrel shapes, allowing 2–3 per portion, approx. 5 cm (2 in) long, end diameter 1½ cm (¾ in), centre diameter 2½ cm (1¼ in).
4 Brush with melted butter, margarine or oil.
5 Place in a pan suitable for the oven.
6 Half cover with white stock, season with salt and pepper.
7 Cook in a hot oven (230–250 °C, Reg. 8–9), brushing the potatoes frequently with melted butter, margarine or oil.
8 When cooked the stock should be completely absorbed by the potatoes.
9 Brush with melted butter, margarine or oil and serve.

35 Crétan potatoes *Pommes crétan*

Fondant potatoes lightly sprinkled with thyme.

36 Champignol potatoes *Pommes champignol*

Fondant potatoes sprinkled with grated Parmesan and Gruyère cheese.

37 Berrichonne potatoes *Pommes berrichonne*

400 g	1 lb	peeled potatoes
25 g	1 oz	butter or margarine
50 g	2 oz	chopped onion
100 g	4 oz	streaky bacon
¼ litre	½ pt	white stock
		chopped parsley

Using old potatoes, hard margarine
1 portion provides:

242 kcals/1018 kJ
15.1 g fat of which 6.0 g saturated
21.6 g carbohydrate of which 1.2 g sugars
6.4 g protein
2.3 g fibre

1 Turn the potatoes barrel shape, 3–4 pieces per portion.
2 Melt the butter in a sauteuse.
3 Add the chopped onion, cover with a lid. Cook for 2–3 min without colour.
4 Add the bacon cut in lardons.
5 Replace the lid and cook gently for 1–2 min without colour.
6 Add the potatoes and sufficient white stock to come half way up the potatoes.
7 Season lightly with salt and pepper, add half the chopped parsley.
8 Replace the lid, cook in the oven (230–250 °C, Reg. 8–9) until tender.
9 Serve sprinkled with chopped parsley.

38 Roast potatoes *Pommes rôties*

Using old potatoes, peanut oil
1 portion (125 g raw potato) provides:

228 kcals/956 kJ
7.0 g fat of which 1.1 g saturated
39.6 g carbohydrate of which 0.9 g sugars
4.1 g protein
1.5 g fibre

1 Wash, peel and rewash the potatoes.
2 Cut into even-sized pieces, allow 3–4 pieces per portion.
3 Heat a good measure of oil or dripping in a roasting tray.
4 Add the well-dried potatoes and lightly brown on all sides.
5 Season with salt and cook in a hot oven (230–250 °C, Reg. 8–9).
6 Turn the potatoes over after approx. 30 min.
7 Cook to a golden brown. Drain and serve.

Cooking time approx. 1 hr.

39 · Château potatoes *Pommes château*

1 Select small even-sized potatoes and wash.
2 If they are of a fairly even size, they need not be peeled, but can be turned into barrel-shaped pieces approx. the size of fondant potatoes.
3 Place in a saucepan of boiling water for 2–3 min, refresh immediately. Drain in a colander.
4 Finish as for roast potatoes (recipe 38).

40 · Rissolée potatoes *Pommes rissolées*

Proceed as for château potatoes, with the potatoes half the size. Cooked potatoes may also be used, in which case they are browned in shallow fat in a frying-pan.

41 · Cocotte potatoes *Pommes cocotte*

Proceed as for château potatoes, but with the potatoes a quarter the size, cooking them in a sauté pan or frying-pan.

42 · Noisette potatoes *Pommes noisette*

1 Wash, peel and rewash the potatoes.
2 Scoop out balls with a noisette spoon.
3 Cook in a little fat in a sauté pan or frying-pan. Colour on top of the stove and finish cooking in the oven (230–250 °C, Reg. 8–9).

½ kg (1 lb) will yield 2 portions

43 · Parisienne potatoes *Pommes parisienne*

1 Prepare and cook as for noisette potatoes.
2 Just before serving, for each ½ kg (1 lb) potatoes melt a tablespoon of meat glaze in a pan, add the cooked potatoes, roll them round so as to give a light overall coating and serve.

44 · Potatoes with bacon and onions *Pommes au lard*

400 g	1 lb	peeled potatoes
100 g	4 oz	streaky bacon (lardons)
100 g	4 oz	button onions
¼ litre	½ pt	white stock (approx.)
		salt and pepper
		chopped parsley

Using old potatoes
1 portion provides:

199 kcals/836 kJ
10.1 g fat of which 3.8 g saturated
22.2 g carbohydrate of which 1.8 g sugars
6.4 g protein
2.5 g fibre

1 Cut the potatoes in 1 cm (½ in) dice.
2 Cut the bacon into ½ cm (¼ in) lardons, lightly fry in a little fat together with the onions, brown lightly.
3 Add the potatoes, half cover with stock, season with salt and pepper.

Cover with a lid and cook steadily in the oven (230–250 °C, Reg. 8–9) approx. 30 min.

4 Correct the seasoning, serve in a vegetable dish and sprinkle with chopped parsley.

45 · **Potatoes in cream** *Pommes à la crème*

1 Cook the potatoes in their jackets in water.
2 Peel and cut into slices.
3 Barely cover with milk, season and allow to simmer for approx. 10 min. Add two tablespoons of cream, toss gently and serve.

Using old pots, single cream, whole milk
1 portion provides:

155 kcals/650 kJ
3.1 g fat of which 1.9 g saturated
30.5 g carbohydrate of which 2.5 g sugars
3.4 g protein
1.5 g fibre

46 · **Maître d'hôtel potatoes** *Pommes maître d'hôtel*

Proceed as for potatoes in cream with the addition of chopped parsley.

47 · **Delmonico potatoes** *Pommes Delmonico*

1 Wash, peel and rewash the potatoes.
2 Cut into 6 mm (1/4 in) dice.
3 Barely cover with milk, season with salt and pepper and allow to cook approx. 30–40 min.
4 Place in an earthenware dish, sprinkle with crumbs and melted butter, brown in the oven or under the salamander and serve.

Using old potatoes, whole milk
1 portion provides:

214 kcals/900 kJ
6.3 g fat of which 3.7 g saturated
37.5 g carbohydrate of which 2.7 g sugars
4.4 g protein
2.0 g fibre

48 · **New potatoes** *Pommes nouvelles*

Method I

1 Wash the potatoes and boil or steam in their jackets until cooked.
2 Cool slightly, peel while warm and place in a pan of cold water.
3 When required for service add salt and a bunch of mint to the potatoes and heat through slowly.
4 Drain well, serve brushed with melted butter and sprinkle with chopped mint or decorate with blanched refreshed mint leaves.

1 portion provides:

91 kcals/383 kJ
0.1 g fat of which – g saturated
22.0 g carbohydrate of which 0.8 g sugars
1.9 g protein
2.4 g fibre

Method II

1 Scrape the potatoes and wash well.
2 Place in a pan of salted boiling water with a bunch of mint and boil

gently until cooked. Approx. 20 min. Serve as above.

3 The starch cells of new potatoes are immature, to help break down these cells new potatoes are started to cook in boiling water.

49 **New rissolée potatoes**
Pommes nouvelles rissolées

Cooked, drained, new potatoes fried to a golden brown in oil or butter.

> Using peanut oil
> 1 portion provides:
>
> 145 kcals/610 kJ
> 6.1 g fat of which 1.1 g saturated
> 22.0 g carbohydrate of which 0.8 g sugars
> 1.9 g protein
> 2.4 g fibre

50 **Parmentier potatoes** *Pommes Parmentier*

1 Select medium to large size potatoes.
2 Wash, peel and rewash.
3 Trim on three sides and cut into 1 cm (½ in) slices.
4 Cut the slices into 1 cm (½ in) strips.
5 Cut the strips into 1 cm (½ in) dice.
6 Wash well and dry in a cloth.
7 Cook in hot shallow fat in a frying-pan till golden brown.
8 Drain, season lightly and serve sprinkled with chopped parsley.

½ kg (1 lb) will yield 2–3 portions

> Using peanut oil
> 1 portion provides:
>
> 433 kcals/1819 kJ
> 33.5 g fat of which 6.3 g saturated
> 32.8 g carbohydrate of which 0.7 g sugars
> 2.3 g protein
> 1.7 g fibre

51 **Anna potatoes** *Pommes Anna*

		oil
600 g	1½ lb	peeled potatoes
25 g	1 oz	butter

1 Grease a pomme anna mould using hot oil.
2 Trim the potatoes to an even cylindrical shape.
3 Cut into slices 2 mm (1/12 in) thick.
4 Place a layer of slices neatly overlapping in the bottom of the mould, season lightly with salt and pepper.

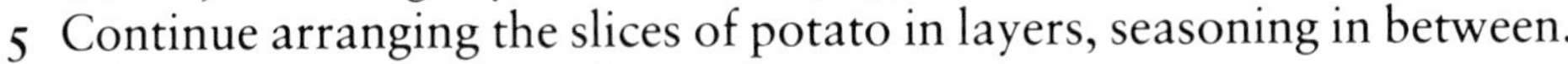

5 Continue arranging the slices of potato in layers, seasoning in between.
6 Add the butter to the top layer.
7 Cook in a hot oven (230–250 °C, Reg. 8–9) for ¾–1 hr, occasionally pressing the potatoes flat.
8 To serve, turn out of the mould and leave whole or cut into four portions.

Uses of meringue: (top) large vacherin; (foreground) small vacherin and examples of presenting meringues (p. 512)

19

PASTRY

General objectives	*Specific objectives*
To know a wide range of pastry recipes and to understand the principles of their preparation.	To describe and demonstrate the variety of dishes in the chapter. To specify the points of care needed and how to recognise faults. To explain the need to weigh accurately and the importance of recipe yield.

Introduction

A simple understanding of the composition of flour is necessary before engaging in pastry work. The recipes in this chapter which refer to strong flour indicate a flour with a high proportion of gluten protein, approximately 12 to 15%. Other recipes indicate a soft flour with a gluten protein content of approximately 8 to 10%. Students are advised to read the section on flour in *The Theory of Catering* page 151.

Hens eggs are graded in seven sizes, in all recipes in this book use grade 3, 60 g. See *The Theory of Catering*.

When baking, ovens must always be pre-heated to the correct temperature before inserting any foods. If continuing baking, allow the oven to heat to regain the correct temperature before inserting successive batches of products.

Pastes

1 **Short pastry** *Pâte à foncé or Pâté à brisée*

200 g	8 oz	flour (soft)
		pinch salt
50 g	2 oz	lard or vegetable fat
50 g	2 oz	butter or margarine
		2–3 tablespns water (approx.)

Using ½ lard, ½ hard marg
This recipe provides:

1493 kcals/6269 kJ
92.6 g fat of which 38.0 g saturated
155.5 g carbohydrate of which 3.1 g sugars
18.9 g protein
7.2 g fibre

1 Sieve the flour and salt.
2 Rub in the fat to a sandy mixture.
3 Make a well in the centre.
4 Add sufficient water to make a fairly firm paste.
5 Handle as little and as lightly as possible.

The amount of water used varies according to: the type of flour, e.g. a very fine soft flour is more absorbent; the degree of heat, e.g. prolonged contact with hot hands and weather conditions.

For wholemeal short pastry use ½ to ¾ wholemeal flour in place of white flour.

Uses: fruit pies, Cornish pasties, etc.

Possible reasons for faults in short pastry:

1 *Hard:*
too much water
too little fat
fat rubbed in insufficiently
too much handling and rolling
over baking.

2 *Soft-crumbly:*	too little water too much fat.
3 *Blistered:*	too little water water added unevenly fat not rubbed in evenly.
4 *Soggy:*	too much water too cool an oven baked for insufficient time.
5 *Shrunken:*	too much handling and rolling pastry stretched whilst handling.

2 · **Puff pastry** *Feuilletage*

200 g	8 oz	flour (strong)
		salt
200 g	8 oz	margarine or butter (or 50 g (2 oz) margarine or butter and 150 g (6 oz) hardened vegetable fat)
125 ml	¼ pt	ice-cold water
		few drops of lemon juice

Using hard margarine
This recipe provides:

2142 kcals/8997 kJ
164.8 g fat of which 70.9 g saturated
150.8 g carbohydrate of which 3.0 g sugars
23.2 g protein
7.4 g fibre

1 Sieve the flour and salt.
2 Rub in 50 g (2 oz) butter or margarine.
3 Make a well in the centre.
4 Add the water, and lemon juice (which is to make the gluten more elastic), and knead well into a smooth dough in the shape of a ball.
5 Relax the dough in a cool place for approx. 30 min.
6 Cut a cross half-way through the dough and pull out the corners to form a star shape.
7 Roll out the points of the star square, leaving the centre thick.
8 Knead the remaining 150 g (6 oz) of butter or margarine to the same texture as the dough. This is most important, if the fat is too soft it will melt and ooze out, if too hard it will break through the paste when being rolled.
9 Place the butter or margarine on the centre square which is four times thicker than the flaps.
10 Fold over the flaps.
11 Roll out approx. 30×15 cm (1×1½ ft), cover with a cloth or plastic, rest for 5–10 min in a cool place.
12 Roll out approx. 60×20 cm (2×⅔ ft), fold both ends to the centre, fold in half again to form a square. This is one double turn.
13 Allow to rest in a cool place approx. 20 min.
14 Half-turn the paste to the right or the left.
15 Give one more double turn, allow to rest 20 mins.

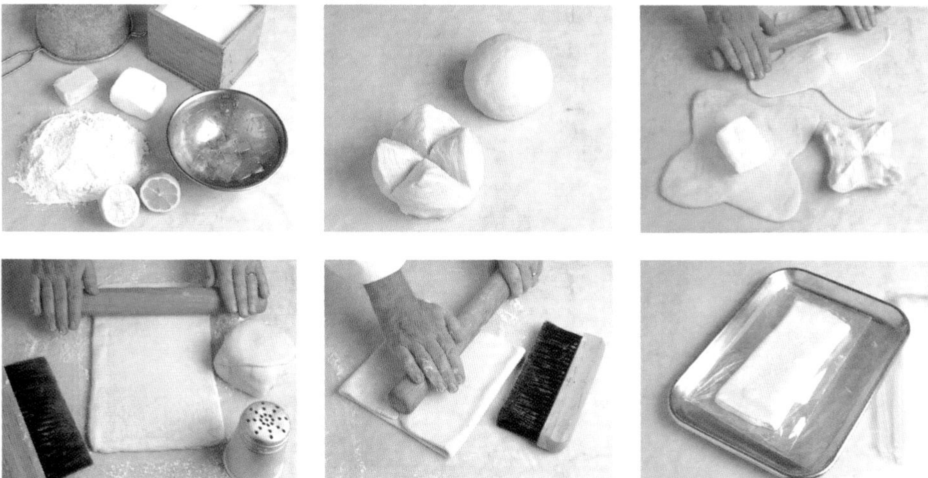

Preparation and making of puff pastry

16 Give two more double turns, allowing to rest between each.
17 Allow to rest before using.

Care must be taken when rolling out the paste to keep the ends and sides square.

The lightness of the puff pastry is mainly due to the air which is trapped when giving the pastry folds during preparation. The addition of lemon juice (acid) is to strengthen the gluten in the flour, thus helping to make a stronger dough so that there is less likelihood of the fat oozing out; 3 g ascorbic or tartaric acid may be used in place of lemon juice. The rise is caused by the fat separating layers of paste and air during rolling. When heat is applied by the oven, steam is produced causing the layers to rise and give the characteristic flaky formation.

50% wholemeal flour may be used.

Uses: meat pies, sausage rolls, jam-puffs, etc. (See page 490 for illustrations of the uses of puff pastry.)

Possible reasons for faults in puff pastry:

1 *Not flaky:* fat too warm thus preventing the fat and paste remaining in layers during rolling
excessively heavy use of rolling pin.

2 *Fat oozes out:* fat too soft
dough too soft
edges not sealed
uneven folding and rolling
oven too cool.

3 *Hard:*	too much water flour not brushed off between rolling over handling.
4 *Shrunken:*	Insufficient resting between rolling overstretching.
5 *Soggy:*	under baked oven too hot.
6 *Uneven rise:*	uneven distribution of fat sides and corners not straight uneven folding and rolling.

3 · Rough puff pastry

200 g	8 oz	flour (strong)
		salt
150 g	6 oz	butter or margarine
125 ml	1/4 pt	ice-cold water
		squeeze of lemon juice or ascorbic or tartaric acid

Using hard margarine
This recipe provides:

1777 kcals/7464 kJ
124.3 g fat of which 53.2 g saturated
150.8 g carbohydrate of which 3.0 g sugars
23.2 g protein
7.4 g fibre

1 Sieve the flour and salt.
2 Cut the fat into 10 g (1/2 oz) pieces and lightly mix them into the flour without rubbing in.
3 Make a well in the centre.
4 Add the liquid and mix to a fairly stiff dough.
5 Turn on to a floured table and roll into an oblong strip, approx. 30×10 cm (12×4 in), keeping the sides square.
6 Give one double turn as for puff pastry.
7 Allow to rest in a cool place, covered with cloth or plastic for approx. 30 min.
8 Give three more double turns, resting between each.
9 Allow to rest before using.

50% wholemeal flour may be used.

4 · Sugar pastry *Pâte à sucre*

		1 egg
50 g	2 oz	sugar
125 g	5 oz	margarine or butter
200 g	8 oz	flour (soft)
		pinch salt

Using hard margarine
This recipe provides:

1872 kcals/7864 kJ
109.8 g fat of which 46.4 g saturated
208.0 g carbohydrate of which 55.6 g sugars
25.7 g protein
7.2 g fibre

Method I

1 Taking care not to over soften, cream the egg and sugar.
2 Add the margarine and mix for a few seconds.
3 Gradually incorporate the sieved flour and salt.

4 Mix lightly until smooth.
5 Allow to rest in a cool place before using.

Method II

1 Sieve the flour and salt.
2 Lightly rub in the margarine to a sandy texture.
3 Make a well in the centre.
4 Add the sugar and beaten egg.
5 Mix the sugar and egg until dissolved.
6 Gradually incorporate the flour and margarine and lightly mix to a smooth paste. Rest paste before using.

50%, 70% or 100% wholemeal flour may be used.

Uses: flans, fruit tartlets.

5 Suet paste

200 g	8 oz	flour (soft)	or self-raising flour
10 g	½ oz	baking-powder	
		pinch salt	
100 g	4 oz	prepared beef suet	
125 ml	¼ pt	water	

This recipe provides:

1524 kcals/6402 kJ
89.3 g fat of which 40.6 g saturated
171.3 g carbohydrate of which 3.0 g sugars
19.3 g protein
7.2 g fibre

1 Sieve the flour, baking-powder and salt.
2 Mix in the suet.
3 Make a well.
4 Add the water.
5 Mix lightly to a fairly stiff paste.

Uses: steamed fruit puddings, steamed jam rolls, steamed meat puddings and dumplings.

Possible reasons for faults in suet paste:

1 *Heavy and soggy:* cooking temperature too low.
2 *Tough:* too much handling, over-cooking.

6 · Choux paste *Pâte à choux*

¼ litre	½ pt	water
		pinch of sugar and salt
100 g	4 oz	butter, margarine or oil
125 g	5 oz	flour (strong)
		4 eggs (approx.)

Using hard margarine
This recipe provides:

1488 kcals/6248 kJ
106.6 g fat of which 43.3 g saturated
99.3 g carbohydrate of which 4.1 g sugars
38.9 g protein
4.5 g fibre

1 Bring the water, sugar and fat to the boil in a saucepan.
2 Remove from heat.
3 Add the sieved flour and mix in with a wooden spoon.
4 Return to a moderate heat and stir continuously until the mixture leaves the sides of the pan.
5 Remove from the heat and allow to cool.
6 Gradually add the beaten eggs, mixing well.
7 The paste should be of dropping consistency.

50%, 70% or 100% wholemeal flour may be used.

Uses: éclairs, cream buns, profiteroles, etc. (Illustrated on page 495.)

Possible reasons for faults in choux paste:

1 *Greasy and heavy:* basic mixture over-cooked.
2 *Soft – not aerated:* flour insufficiently cooked, eggs insufficiently beaten in the mixture, oven too cool, under-baked.

Ingredients for choux pastry

Cakes

7 · Scones

200 g	8 oz	self-raising flour
5 g	¼ oz	baking-powder
		pinch salt
50 g	2 oz	butter or margarine
50 g	2 oz	castor sugar
95 ml	3/16 pt	milk or water (approx.)

Using hard margarine
1 portion provides:

162 kcals/678 kJ
5.8 g fat of which 2.5 g saturated
26.3 g carbohydrate of which 7.5 g sugars
2.7 g protein
1.0 g fibre

1 Sieve the flour, baking-powder and salt.
2 Rub in the fat to a sandy texture.
3 Make a well in the centre.
4 Add the sugar and the liquid.
5 Dissolve the sugar in the liquid.
6 Gradually incorporate the flour, mix lightly.
7 Roll out two rounds 1 cm (½ in) thick.
8 Place on a greased baking sheet.
9 Cut a cross half-way through the rounds with a large knife.
10 Milk wash and bake at 200 °C, Reg. 6 for 15–20 min.

50% wholemeal flour may be used.

The comparatively small amount of fat, rapid mixing to a soft dough, quick and light handling are essentials to produce a light scone.

Further information on the use of baking-powder, page 155, *The Theory of Catering*.

yield: 8 scones

8 · Fruit scones

Add 50 g (2 oz) washed and dried sultanas to the scone mixture.

9 · Small cakes – basic mixture

200 g	8 oz	flour (soft)	or self-raising flour
		level teaspn baking-powder	
		salt	
125 g	5 oz	margarine or butter	
125 g	5 oz	castor sugar	
		2–3 eggs	

Using hard margarine
1 portion provides:

225 kcals/947 kJ
11.6 g fat of which 4.8 g saturated
28.8 g carbohydrate of which 13.4 g sugars
3.3 g protein
0.7 g fibre

Method A – Rubbing In

1 Sieve the flour, baking-powder and salt.
2 Rub in butter or margarine to sandy texture.
3 Add the sugar.
4 Gradually add the well-beaten eggs and mix as lightly as possible until combined.

Method B – Creaming

1 Cream the margarine and sugar in a bowl until soft and fluffy.
2 Slowly add the well-beaten eggs, mixing continuously and beating really well between each addition.
3 Lightly mix in the sieved flour, baking-powder and salt.

In both cases the consistency should be a light dropping one, and if necessary it may be adjusted with the addition of a few drops of milk.

yield: 10 good-sized or 20 small cakes

Possible reasons for faults in cakes:

1 *Uneven texture:* fat insufficiently rubbed in; too little liquid; too much liquid.
2 *Close texture:* too much fat; hands too hot when rubbing in; fat to flour ratio incorrect.
3 *Dry:* too much liquid; oven too hot.
4 *Bad shape:* too much liquid; oven too cool; too much baking-powder.
5 *Fruit sunk:* fruit wet; too much liquid; oven too cool.
6 *Cracked:* too little liquid; too much baking-powder.

10 · Cherry cakes

Add 50 g (2 oz) glacé cherries cut in quarters and 3 to 4 drops vanilla essence to the basic mixture, Method B, and divide into 8–12 lightly greased cake tins or paper cases. Bake in a hot oven (220 °C, Reg. 7) approx. 15–20 min.

11 · Coconut cakes

In place of 50 g (2 oz) flour, use 50 g (2 oz) desiccated coconut and 3 to 4 drops vanilla essence to the basic mixture, Method B, and cook as for cherry cakes.

12 · Raspberry buns

Divide basic mixture, Method A, into eight pieces. Roll into balls, flatten slightly, dip tops into milk then castor sugar. Place on a greased baking sheet, make a hole in the centre of each, add a little raspberry jam. Bake in a hot oven (220 °C, Reg. 7) 15–20 min.

13 · Queen cakes

To the basic mixture, Method B, add 100 g (4 oz) washed and dried mixed fruit and cook as for cherry cakes.

14 · Large fruit cake

125 g	5 oz	butter or margarine
125 g	5 oz	castor sugar
		2–3 eggs
200 g	8 oz	flour
		1 level teaspn baking powder
200 g	8 oz	dried fruit – currants, sultanas
50 g	2 oz	glacé cherries
		½ level teaspn mixed spice
100 g	4 oz	chopped peel
50 g	2 oz	almonds (peeled)

Using hard margarine
This recipe provides:

3355 kcals/14 093 kJ
142.8 g fat of which 50.7 g saturated
504.3 g carbohydrate of which 349.3 g sugars
45.0 g protein
29.3 g fibre

1 Cream fat and sugar till soft and fluffy.
2 Gradually add the beaten eggs, mix well.
3 Fold in the sieved flour and baking powder, washed and dried fruit, chopped cherries, spice and peel, combine lightly.
4 Place in a lightly greased 18 cm (7 in) cake tin lined with greased greaseproof or silicone paper.
5 Place the almonds on top, whole, sliced or chopped.
6 Bake at 170 °C, Reg. 3–4, for approx. 1 hr.
7 Reduce the heat to 150 °C, Reg. 2 for ½ hour.
8 Reduce the heat to 140 °C, Reg. 1 until cooked, approx. ½ hour.

Test by inserting a thin needle or skewer in the centre. If the cake is cooked it should come out clean. If not cooked a little raw cake mixture sticks to the needle.

When baking avoid slamming the oven door, open and close it gently. An inrush of cold air checks the rising and may cause the mixture to rise unevenly.

Moving or shaking the cake before it has set will cause it to sink in the middle. See also pages 463–4.

15 · Rock cakes

200 g	8 oz	flour (soft)	or self-raising flour
5 g	¼ oz	baking powder	
		pinch salt	
75 g	3 oz	margarine or butter	
75 g	3 oz	castor sugar	
		1 large egg	
50 g	2 oz	currants-sultanas	

Using hard margarine
1 portion provides:

217 kcals/913 kJ
8.7 g fat of which 3.6 g saturated
33.6 g carbohydrate of which 14.3 g sugars
3.4 g protein
1.3 g fibre

Use Method A, page 463. Keep the mixture slightly firm. Place with a fork into 8–12 rough shapes on a greased baking sheet, milk or egg wash and bake in a fairly hot oven (220 °C, Reg. 7) approx. 20 min.

Sponges

Possible reasons for faults in sponges:

1 *Close texture:*	underbeating too much flour oven too cool or too hot.
2 *Holey texture:*	flour insufficiently folded in tin unevenly filled.
3 *Cracked crust:*	oven too hot.
4 *Sunken:*	oven too hot tin removed during cooking.
5 *White spots on surface:*	insufficient beating.

16 · Victoria sandwich

100 g	4 oz	butter or margarine
100 g	4 oz	castor sugar
		2 eggs
100 g	4 oz	flour (soft)
5 g	¼ oz	baking-powder

Using hard margarine
This recipe provides:

1635 kcals/6866 kJ
94.3 g fat of which 39.3 g saturated
184.7 g carbohydrate of which 106.6 g sugars
23.3 g protein
3.6 g fibre

1 Cream the fat and sugar until soft and fluffy.
2 Gradually add the beaten eggs.
3 Lightly mix in the sieved flour, and baking-powder.
4 Divide into two 18 cm (7 in) greased sponge tins.
5 Bake at 190–200 °C, Reg. 5–6, approx. 12–15 min.
6 Turn out on to a wire rack to cool.
7 Spread one half with jam, place the other half on top.
8 Dust with icing sugar.

17 · Genoese sponge *Génoise*

		4 eggs
100 g	4 oz	castor sugar
100 g	4 oz	flour (soft)
50 g	2 oz	butter, margarine or oil

Using hard margarine
This recipe provides:

1423 kcals/5978 kJ
65.8 g fat of which 25.6 g saturated
182.8 g carbohydrate of which 106.6 g sugars
36.5 g protein
3.6 g fibre

1. Whisk the eggs and sugar with a balloon whisk in a bowl over a pan of hot water.
2. Continue until the mixture is light, creamy and double in bulk.
3. Remove from the heat and whisk until cold and thick (ribbon stage).
4. Fold in the flour very gently.
5. Fold in the melted butter very gently.
6. Place in a greased, floured Genoese mould.
7. Bake in a moderately hot oven (200–220 °C, Reg. 6–7) approx. 30 min.

18 · Chocolate Genoese *Génoise au chocolat*

75 g	3 oz	flour (soft)
10 g	½ oz	cocoa powder
10 g	½ oz	cornflour
		4 eggs
100 g	4 oz	castor sugar
50 g	2 oz	butter, margarine or oil

Sift the flour and the cocoa together with the cornflour, then proceed as for Genoese sponge.

Possible reasons for faults in Genoese sponges

1. *Close texture:* eggs and sugar overheated
   eggs and sugar underbeaten
   too much flour
   flour insufficiently folded in
   oven too hot.
2. *Sunken:* too much sugar
   oven too hot
   tin removed during cooking.
3. *Heavy:* butter too hot
   butter insufficiently mixed in
   flour overmixed.

19 · Chocolate gâteau *Gâteau au chocolat*

		4 egg chocolate genoese sponge (as previous recipe)
200 g	8 oz	unsalted butter } butter cream
150 g	6 oz	icing sugar } butter cream
50 g	2 oz	block chocolate (melted in a basin in a bain-marie)
50 g	2 oz	chocolate vermicelli or flakes
		stock syrup (recipe no. 21)

Using hard margarine, butter
This recipe provides:

4789 kcals/20 113 kJ
260.9 g fat of which 148.7 g saturated
606.0 g carbohydrate of which 533.2 g sugars
41.6 g protein
4.8 g fibre

1 Cut genoese into three slices crosswise.
2 Prepare butter cream as in recipe 192, and mix in melted chocolate.
3 Lightly moisten each slice of genoese with stock syrup which may be flavoured with kirsch, rum, etc.
4 Lightly spread each slice of genoese with butter cream and sandwich together.
5 Lightly coat the sides with butter cream and coat with chocolate vermicelli or flakes.
6 Neatly smooth the top using a little more butter cream if necessary.

Many variations can be used in decorating this gâteau, chocolate fondant may be used on the top and various shapes of chocolate can be used to decorate the top and sides. The genoese may be made using 50% white and 50% wholemeal flour.

20 · Coffee gâteau *Gâteau moka*

		4 egg genoese sponge (as recipe 17)
200 g	8 oz	unsalted butter } butter cream
150 g	6 oz	icing sugar } butter cream
		coffee essence
50 g	2 oz	toasted, flaked or nibbed almonds
		stock syrup (recipe no. 21)

1 Cut genoese into three slices crosswise.
2 Prepare butter cream as in recipe 192, and flavour with coffee essence.
3 Lightly moisten each slice of genoese with stock syrup which may be flavoured with Tia Maria, brandy etc.
4 Lightly spread each slice with butter cream and sandwich together.
5 Lightly coat the sides with butter cream and coat with almonds.
6 Smooth the top using a little more butter cream if necessary.
7 Decorate by piping the word MOKA in butter cream.
8 Coffee-flavoured fondant may be used in place of butter cream for the top.

21 · Stock syrup

500 ml	1 pt	water
150 g	6 oz	granulated sugar
50 g	2 oz	glucose

1 Boil water, sugar and glucose together, strain and cool.
2 Glucose helps to prevent crystallizing.

22 · Swiss roll

		4 eggs
100 g	4 oz	castor sugar
100 g	4 oz	flour (soft)
		or
250 ml	½ pt	eggs
175 g	7 oz	castor sugar
125 g	5 oz	flour (soft)

This recipe provides:
1058 kcals/4445 kJ
25.3 g fat of which 8.0 g saturated
182.7 g carbohydrate of which 106.5 g sugars
36.5 g protein
3.6 g fibre

1 Whisk the eggs and sugar with a balloon whisk in a bowl over a pan of hot water.
2 Continue until the mixture is light, creamy and double in bulk.
3 Remove from the heat and whisk until cold and thick (ribbon stage).
4 Fold in the flour very gently.
5 Grease a Swiss roll tin and line with greased greaseproof paper.
6 Pour in genoese mixture and bake (220 °C, Reg. 7) approx. 6 min.
7 Turn out on to a sheet of paper sprinkled with castor sugar.
8 Remove the paper from the Swiss roll, spread with warm jam.
9 Roll into a fairly tight roll, leaving the paper on the outside for a few minutes.
11 Remove the paper and allow to cool on a wire rack.

23 · Shortbread biscuits (also page 536)

150 g	6 oz	flour (soft)
		pinch of salt
100 g	4 oz	butter or margarine
50 g	2 oz	castor sugar

Using butter
1 portion provides:
121 kcals/507 kJ
7.0 g fat of which 4.4 g saturated
14.1 g carbohydrate of which 4.6 g sugars
1.2 g protein
0.5 g fibre

1 Sift the flour and salt.
2 Mix in the butter or margarine and sugar with the flour.
3 Combine all the ingredients to a smooth paste.
4 Roll carefully on a floured table or board to the shape of a rectangle or round, ½ cm (¼ in) thick.
5 Place on a lightly greased baking sheet.
6 Mark into the desired size and shape. Prick with a fork.
7 Bake in a moderate oven (180–200 °C, Reg. 4–6) approx. 15–20 min.

yield: 12 biscuits

24 · Piped shortbread biscuits

100 g	4 oz	butter or margarine
100 g	4 oz	icing sugar
		1 egg
150 g	6 oz	flour (soft)

1 Cream the butter or margarine and sugar thoroughly.
2 Add the egg and mix in.
3 Mix in the flour.
4 Pipe on to lightly greased and floured baking sheets using a large star tube.
5 Bake 200–220 °C, Reg. 6–7, approx. 15 min.

yield: 12 biscuits

25 · Sponge fingers *Biscuits à la cuillère*

		4 eggs
100 g	4 oz	castor sugar
100 g	4 oz	flour (soft)

1 Cream the egg yolks and sugar in a bowl until creamy and almost white.
2 Whip the egg whites stiffly.
3 Add a little of the whites to the mixture and cut in.
4 Gradually add the sieved flour and remainder of the whites alternately, mixing as lightly as possible.
5 Place in a piping bag with 1 cm (½ in) plain tube and pipe in 8 cm (3 in) lengths on to baking sheets lined with greaseproof or silicone paper.
6 Sprinkle liberally with icing sugar. Rest for 5 min.
7 Bake in a moderate hot oven (200–220 °C, Reg. 6–7) approx. 10 min.
8 Remove from the oven, lift the paper on which the biscuits are piped and place upside down on the table.
9 Sprinkle liberally with water. This will assist the removal of the biscuits from the paper. (No water is needed if using silicone paper.)

yield: approx. 32 fingers

Yeast Goods

Before using yeast of any kind please refer to pages 155–7 of *The Theory of Catering*, for essential information.

Possible reasons for faults using yeast doughs:

1 *Close texture:*	insufficiently proved	oven too hot
	insufficiently kneaded	too much water
	insufficient yeast	too little water

2 *Uneven texture:*	insufficient kneading oven too cool	over-proving
3 *Coarse texture:*	over-proved, uncovered insufficient kneading	too much water too much salt
4 *Wrinkled:*	over-proved	
5 *Sour:*	stale yeast too much yeast	
6 *Broken crust:*	under-proved at the second stage	
7 *White spots on crust:*	not covered before second proving	

26 · Bread rolls

200 g	8 oz	flour (strong)
5 g	3/8 oz	yeast
125 ml	1/4 pt	liquid (half water, half milk)
10 g	1/2 oz	butter or margarine
		1/4 teaspn castor sugar
		salt

Using white flour, hard marg
1 portion provides:

102 kcals/426 kJ
1.7 g fat of which 0.7 g saturated
19.5 g carbohydrate of which 1.0 g sugars
3.4 g protein
1.1 g fibre

Bread rolls, showing a variety of shapes: (left) with poppy seeds; (right) with sesame seeds

1 Sieve the flour into a bowl and warm in the oven or above the stove.
2 Cream the yeast in a small basin with a quarter of the liquid.
3 Make a well in the centre of the flour, add the dissolved yeast.
4 Sprinkle over a little of the flour, cover with a cloth, leave in a warm place until the yeast ferments (bubbles).
5 Add the remainder of the liquid (warm), the fat, sugar and the salt.
6 Knead firmly until smooth and free from stickiness.
7 Return to the basin, cover with a cloth and leave in a warm place until double its size. (This is called *proving* the dough.)

8 Knock back. Divide into eight even pieces.
9 Mould into desired shape.
10 Place on a floured baking sheet. Cover with a cloth.
11 Leave in a warm place to prove (double in size).
12 Brush carefully with eggwash.
13 Bake in a hot oven (220 °C, Reg. 7) approx. 10 min.

At all times during preparation of the dough extreme heat must be avoided as the yeast will be killed and the dough spoiled.

yield: 8 rolls

27 Wholemeal rolls

As recipe 26 using all wholemeal flour, one teaspoon raw cane sugar in place of castor sugar and all water and no milk.

1 portion provides:

90 kcals/379 kJ
1.6 g fat of which 0.5 g saturated
17.1 g carbohydrate of which 1.2 g sugars
3.4 g protein
2.3 g fibre

28 Bun dough – basic mixture

200 g	½ lb	flour (strong)
5 g	⅜ oz	yeast
125 ml	¼ pt	milk and water, approx.
		1 egg
50 g	2 oz	butter or margarine
25 g	1 oz	castor sugar

Using hard margarine
1 portion provides:

157 kcals/656 kJ
6.4 g fat of which 2.7 g saturated
22.6 g carbohydrate of which 4.0 g sugars
3.6 g protein
1.2 g fibre

1 Sieve the flour into a bowl and warm.
2 Dissolve the yeast in a basin with a little of the liquid.
3 Make a well in the centre of the flour.
4 Add the dispersed yeast, sprinkle with a little flour, cover with a cloth, leave in a warm place until the yeast ferments (bubbles).
5 Add the beaten egg, butter or margarine, sugar and remainder of the liquid. Knead well to form a soft, slack dough, knead until smooth and free from stickiness.
6 Keep covered and allow to prove in a warm place.
7 Use as required.

yield: 8 buns

29 Bun wash

100 g	¼ lb	sugar
125 ml	¼ pt	water or milk

Boil together until the consistency of a thick syrup.

30 · Fruit buns

Using hard margarine
1 portion provides:

173 kcals/728 kJ
6.5 g fat of which 2.7 g saturated
26.9 g carbohydrate of which 8.0 g sugars
3.7 g protein
1.7 g fibre

1. Add 50 g (2 oz) washed, dried fruit (currants, sultanas) and a little mixed spice to the basic mixture (recipe 28).
2. Mould into eight round balls.
3. Place on a lightly greased baking sheet.
4. Cover with a cloth, allow to prove.
5. Bake in hot oven (220 °C, Reg. 7) approx. 15–20 min.
6. Brush liberally with bun wash as soon as cooked.

31 · Hot cross buns

1. Proceed as for fruit buns using a little more spice.
2. When moulded make a cross with the back of a knife, or make a slack mixture of flour and water and pipe on crosses using a greaseproof paper cornet.
3. Allow to prove and finish as for fruit buns.

32 · Bath buns

1. Add to basic bun dough 50 g (2 oz) washed and dried fruit (currants and sultanas), and 25 g (1 oz) chopped mixed peel and 25 g (1 oz) sugar nibs.
2. Proceed as for fruit buns. Pull off into eight rough-shaped pieces.
3. Sprinkle with a little broken loaf sugar or sugar nibs.
4. Cook as for fruit buns.

33 · Chelsea buns

1. Take the basic bun dough and roll out into a large square.
2. Brush with melted margarine or butter.
3. Sprinkle liberally with castor sugar.
4. Sprinkle with 25 g (1 oz) currants, 25 g (1 oz) sultanas and 25 g (1 oz) chopped peel.
5. Roll up like a Swiss roll, brush with melted margarine or butter.
6. Cut into slices across the roll 3 cm (1½ in) wide.
7. Place on a greased baking tray with deep sides.
8. Cover and allow to prove. Complete as for fruit buns.

34 · Swiss buns

1 Take the basic bun dough and divide into eight pieces.
2 Mould into balls, then into 10 cm (4 in) lengths.
3 Place on a greased baking sheet, cover with a cloth.
4 Allow to prove.
5 Bake at 220 °C, Reg. 7, approx. 15–20 min.
6 When cool, glaze with fondant or water icing (see below).

35 · Water icing

200 g	8 oz	icing sugar
		few drops vanilla essence
		2–3 tablespns warm water

1 Pass sugar through a fine sieve into a basin.
2 Gradually mix in warm water with a wooden spoon until the required consistency.

36 · Fondant

200 g	8 oz	loaf sugar
		1 teaspn glucose
125 ml	¼ pt	water

1 Place the water, sugar and glucose in a pan and boil gently. Keep the sides of the pan clean until a temperature of 115 °C (240 °F) is reached.This is assessed by using a special thermometer (saccharometer).
2 Pour on to a lightly watered marble slab. Allow to cool.
3 Using a metal spatula, turn frequently.
4 Finally knead with the palm of the hand till smooth.
5 Keep covered with a damp cloth to prevent a hard surface forming.

To glaze Swiss buns warm sufficient fondant in a saucepan and adjust the consistency with a little syrup (equal quantities of sugar and water boiled together) if necessary. Fondant must not be heated to more than 37 °C (98 °F) or it will lose its gloss, because the sugar crystals increase in size and coarseness, thus reflecting less light and making the surface dull.

37 · Doughnuts

1 Take the basic bun dough (recipe 28) and divide into eight pieces.
2 Mould into balls. Press a floured thumb into each.
3 Add a little jam in each hole. Mould carefully to seal the hole.

Using hard margarine, peanut oil
1 portion provides:

218 kcals/918 kJ
13.3 g fat of which 4.0 g saturated
22.6 g carbohydrate of which 4.0 g sugars
3.6 g protein
1.2 g fibre

4 Cover and allow to prove on a well-floured tray.
5 Deep fry in moderately hot fat (175 °C) approx. 12–15 min.
6 Lift out of the fat, drain and roll in a tray containing castor sugar mixed with a little cinnamon.

38 · **Rum baba** *Baba au rhum*

200 g	8 oz	flour (strong)
5 g	3/8 oz	yeast
125 ml	1/4 pt	milk
50 g	2 oz	currants
		2 eggs
50 g	2 oz	butter
10 g	1/2 oz	sugar
		pinch salt
		1 small glass of rum

Using butter
1 portion provides:

190 kcals/797 kJ
7.6 g fat of which 4.2 g saturated
25.4 g carbohydrate of which 6.4 g sugars
4.9 g protein
1.4 g fibre

1 Sieve flour in a bowl and warm.
2 Cream the yeast with a little of the warm milk in a basin.
3 Make a well in the centre of the flour and add the dispersed yeast.
4 Sprinkle with a little of the flour from the sides, cover with a cloth and leave in a warm place till it ferments.
5 Add the remainder of the warm milk and the washed, dried currants and the beaten eggs, knead well to a smooth elastic dough.
6 Replace in the bowl, add the butter in small pieces, cover with a cloth and allow to prove in a warm place.
7 Add the sugar and salt, mix well till absorbed in the dough.
8 Half fill 8 greased dariole moulds, and allow to prove.
9 Bake in a hot oven (220 °C, Reg. 7) approx. 20 min.
10 Turn out when cooked, cool slightly.
11 Soak carefully in hot syrup.
12 Sprinkle liberally with rum.
13 Brush all over with apricot glaze.

Babas may be decorated with a rose of whipped cream. *8 portions*

39 · **Cream Chantilly** *Crème Chantilly*

This is whipped cream which is sweetened with castor sugar and flavoured with a little vanilla essence.

40 · **Syrup for baba and savarin and marignans**

100 g	4 oz	sugar
		1 bay leaf
		rind and juice of 1 lemon
1/4 litre	1/2 pt	water
		2–3 coriander seeds
		1/2 small cinnamon stick

Boil all the ingredients together and strain.

41 · Savarin paste – basic mixture

200 g	8 oz	flour (strong)
5 g	⅜ oz	yeast
125 ml	¼ pt	milk
		2 eggs
50 g	2 oz	butter
10 g	½ oz	sugar
		pinch salt

1. Sieve flour in a bowl and warm.
2. Cream the yeast with a little of the warm milk in a basin.
3. Make a well in the centre of the flour and add the dissolved yeast.
4. Sprinkle with a little of the flour from the sides, cover with a cloth and leave in a warm place till it ferments.
5. Add the remainder of the warm milk and the beaten eggs, knead well to a smooth elastic dough.
6. Replace in the bowl, add the butter in small pieces, cover with a cloth and allow to prove in a warm place.
7. Add the sugar and salt, mix well till absorbed in the dough.
8. Half fill a greased savarin mould, and prove.
9. Bake in a hot oven (220 °C, Reg. 7) approx. 30 min.
10. Turn out when cooked, cool slightly.
11. Soak carefully in hot syrup (recipe 40).
12. Brush over with apricot glaze (recipe 51).

8 portions

42 · Savarin with fruit *Savarin aux fruits*

Prepare the basic savarin mixture. Prove and cook for approx. 30 min in a large greased savarin mould. Complete in exactly the same way as rum baba including the cream. The rum is optional for savarin. Fill the centre with fruit salad.

8 portions

43 · Marignans *Marignans Chantilly*

1. Marignans are prepared from a basic savarin mixture, cooking them in barquette moulds.
2. After the marignans have been soaked, carefully make a deep incision along one side.
3. Decorate generously with whipped sweetened vanilla-flavoured cream.
4. Brush with apricot glaze.

44 Fruit pies

Apple, blackberry, blackberry and apple, cherry, rhubarb, gooseberry, damson, damson and apple, etc.

400 g	1 lb	fruit
		2 tablespns water
100 g	4 oz	sugar
150 g	6 oz	flour (soft)
35 g	1½ oz	butter or margarine
35 g	1½ oz	lard or vegetable fat
		water to mix

Alternatively, wholemeal short paste may be used

Using white flour, apple
This recipe provides:

1621 kcals/6808 kJ
65.0 g fat of which 26.6 g saturated
260.0 g carbohydrate of which 144.1 g sugars
15.3 g protein
15.0 g fibre

Using 50% wholemeal flour, apple
This recipe provides:

1598 kcals/6709 kJ
65.6 g fat of which 26.7 g saturated
251.1 g carbohydrate of which 144.5 g sugars
17.8 g protein
18.8 g fibre

1. Prepare the fruit, wash and place half in a ½ litre (1 pt) pie dish.
2. Add the sugar and water and the remainder of the fruit.
3. Place a clove in the apple pie.
4. Roll out the pastry ½ cm (¼ in) thick to the shape of the pie dish, allow to relax. Damp the rim of the pie dish and edge the rim with a strip of the pastry.
5. Damp the edge of the pastry.
6. Carefully lay the pastry on the dish without stretching it and firmly seal the rim of the pie. Cut off any surplus pastry.
7. Brush with milk and sprinkle with castor sugar.
8. Place the pie on a baking sheet and bake in a hot oven (220 °C, Reg. 7) for approx. 10 min.
9. Reduce the heat or transfer to a cooler part of the oven and continue cooking for a further 30 min approx. If the pastry colours too quickly cover with a sheet of paper.
10. Clean the pie dish, and serve with a sauceboat of custard ¼ litre (½ pt).

Preparation of fruit for pies, etc.

Apples	Peeled, quartered, cored, washed, cut in slices.
Cherries	Remove the stalks, wash.
Blackberries	Stalks removed, washed.
Gooseberries	Stalks and tails removed, washed.
Damsons	Picked and washed.
Rhubarb	Leaves and root removed, tough strings removed, cut into 2 cm (1 in) pieces, washed.

45 · **Jam tart** (short, sugar or wholemeal paste may be used)

Short Paste

100 g	4 oz	flour (soft)
25 g	1 oz	lard, margarine or vegetable fat
		water to mix
25 g	1 oz	butter or margarine
		salt
		2 tablespns jam

1 Prepare short paste (page 457), mould into a ball.
2 Roll out into a 3 mm thick (1/8 in) round.
3 Place carefully on a greased plate.
4 Cut off any surplus pastry. Neaten the edges.
5 Prick the bottom several times with a fork.
6 Spread on the jam to within 1 cm (1/4 in) of the edge.
7 Roll out any surplus pastry, cut into 1/2 cm (1/2 in) strips and decorate the top.
8 Place on a baking sheet and bake in a hot oven (220 °C, Reg. 7) approx. 20 min.

A jam tart may also be made in a shallow flan ring.

4 portions

46 · **Lemon curd tart**

As recipe 45, using lemon curd, page 486.

47 · **Syrup or treacle tart**

As for jam tart, but spread with:

100 g	4 oz	syrup or treacle
		3–4 drops lemon juice
15 g	3/4 oz	white breadcrumbs or cake crumbs
		1 tablespn water

This recipe provides:

1039 kcals/4364 kJ
42.1 g fat of which 17.9 g saturated
164.2 g carbohydrate of which 81.0 g sugars
11.0 g protein
4.2 g fibre

Warm the syrup or treacle slightly, then mix in the remainder of the ingredients.

48 · **Flans** *Flans*

Allow 25 g (1 oz) flour per portion and prepare sugar pastry (page 460).

1 Grease the flan ring and baking sheet.
2 Roll out the pastry 2 cm (1 in) larger than the flan ring.
3 Place the flan ring on the baking sheet.
4 Carefully place the pastry on the flan ring, by rolling it loosely over the rolling-pin, picking up, and unrolling it over the flan ring.
5 Press the pastry into shape without stretching it, being careful to exclude any air.
6 Allow a ½ cm (¼ in) ridge of pastry on top of the flan ring.
7 Cut off the surplus paste by rolling the pin firmly across the top of the flan ring.
8 Mould the edge with thumb and forefinger. Decorate (a) with pastry tweezers or (b) with thumbs and forefingers, sqeezing the pastry neatly to form a corrugated pattern.

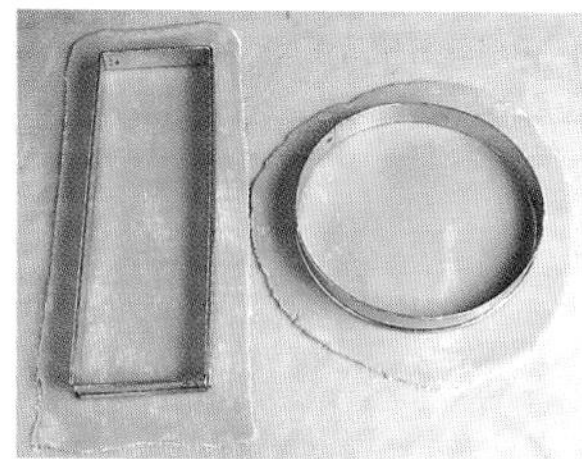

Preparation and making of flan and slice (band)

49 · **Cherry flan – using fresh cherries** *Flan aux cerises*

100 g	4 oz	sugar paste (4 oz flour) (page 460)
200–300 g	4 oz	cherries
50 g	8–12 oz	sugar
	2 oz	2 tablespns red glaze (recipe 59)

1 Line the flan ring, pierce the bottom.
2 Stone the cherries. Arrange neatly in the flan case.
3 Sprinkle with sugar.
4 Bake in a moderately hot oven (200–230 °C, Reg. 6–8) approx. 30 min.
5 Remove ring and eggwash sides. Complete the cooking.
6 Brush with hot red glaze. See Note, recipe 58.

4 portions

50 · Apple flan *Flan aux pommes*

100 g	4 oz	sugar paste (4 oz flour) (page 460)
50 g	2 oz	sugar
400 g	1 lb	cooking apples
		2 tablespns apricot glaze (recipe 51)

1 portion provides:

340 kcals/1428 kJ
13.8 g fat of which 5.8 g saturated
53.8 g carbohydrate of which 0.0 g sugars
3.5 g protein
2.9 g fibre

1 Line flan ring. Pierce the bottom several times with a fork.
2 Keep the best-shaped apple and make the remainder into a purée (see below).
3 When cool place in the flan case.
4 Peel, quarter and wash the remaining apple.
5 Cut in neat thin slices and lay carefully on the apple purée (recipe 52), overlapping each slice. Ensure that each slice points to the centre of the flan then no difficulty should be encountered in joining the pattern up neatly.
6 Sprinkle a little sugar on the apple slices and bake the flan in a moderately hot oven (200–220 °C, Reg. 6–7), 30–40 min.
7 When the flan is almost cooked, remove the flan ring carefully, return to the oven to complete the cooking. Mask with hot apricot glaze.

4 portions

51 · Apricot glaze

Prepare by boiling apricot jam with a little water and passing it through a strainer. Glaze should be used hot.

52 · Apple meringue flan *Flan aux pommes meringué*

Cook as for apple flan, without arranging sliced apples. Pipe with meringue, page 510, using two egg whites. Return to moderately hot oven (200 °C, Reg. 6) to cook and colour meringue, approx. 5 min.

Apple Purée Marmalade de pomme

400 g	1 lb	cooking apples
10 g	½ oz	butter or margarine
50 g	2 oz	sugar

Peel, core and slice the apples. Place the butter or margarine in a thick-bottomed pan, heat until melted, add the apples and sugar, cover with a lid and cook gently until soft. Drain off any excess liquid and pass through a sieve or liquidize.

4 portions

53 Gooseberry flan *Flan aux groseilles*

100 g	4 oz	sugar paste (4 oz flour) (page 460)
100 g	4 oz	sugar
200–300 g	8–12 oz	gooseberries
		2 tablespns apricot glaze

1 Line flan ring and pierce. Sprinkle with sugar.
2 Add the topped and tailed, washed gooseberries.
3 Arrange neatly in the flan case.
4 Sprinkle with the remainder of the sugar.
5 Bake at 200–220 °C, Reg. 6–7.
6 When the flan is almost cooked carefully remove the flan ring and return the flan to the oven to complete the cooking.
7 Mask with hot apricot glaze. See Note, recipe 58.

4 portions

54 Lemon meringue pie (economic recipe)

200 g	8 oz	sugar paste (8 oz flour) (page 460)	
125 ml	¼ pt	water	lemon curd
100 g	4 oz	sugar	lemon curd
25 g	1 oz	cornflour	lemon curd
25 g	1 oz	butter	lemon curd
		1 lemon	lemon curd
		1–2 yolks	lemon curd
		4 egg whites	meringue
200 g	8 oz	castor sugar	meringue

1 portion provides:

434 kcals/1824 kJ
17.5 g fat of which 7.8 g saturated
68.3 g carbohydrate of which 46.3 g sugars
5.2 g protein
1.0 g fibre

1 Line a flan ring and cook blind.
2 Prepare the lemon curd by boiling the water, sugar and zest and juice of lemon to a syrup.
3 Thicken with diluted cornflour, remove from the heat, add the butter and whisk in yolks.
4 Place in the flan case.
5 When set, pipe in the meringue, recipe 127 and colour in a hot oven (220 °C, Reg. 7).

8 portions

Lemon curd (alternative recipe)

		2 eggs, separated
100 g	4 oz	castor sugar
100 g	4 oz	butter
		1 lemon

Cream the egg yolks and sugar in a bowl with a whisk, add the butter, zest and juice of lemon. Place in a bain-marie on low heat and whisk continuously till it thickens (20–30 min).

55 · Baked jam roll

200 g short or wholemeal paste (8 oz flour with ¼ oz baking-powder added when sifting flour, or 8 oz self-raising flour)
2–3 tablespns jam

Using white flour
1 portion provides:

399 kcals/1677 kJ
20.9 g fat of which 8.9 g saturated
50.6 g carbohydrate of which 12.4 g sugars
5.3 g protein
2.2 g fibre

1 Roll out pastry into a rectangle 3 cm×16 cm (12×6 in) approx.
2 Spread with jam leaving 1 cm (½ in) clear on all edges.
3 Fold over two short sides, 1 cm (½ in).
4 Roll the pastry from the top.
5 Moisten the bottom edge to seal the roll.
6 Place edge down on a greased baking sheet.
7 Brush with eggwash or milk. Sprinkle with sugar.
8 Bake in a moderate oven (200 °C, Reg. 6) approx. 40 min.
9 Serve with a sauceboat of jam or custard sauce separately.

4 portions

56 · Baked apple dumplings

200 g	8 oz	short or wholemeal paste (8 oz flour) (page 457)
		4 cloves
100 g	4 oz each	4 small cooking apples
50 g	2 oz	sugar

1 Roll out pastry 3 mm (⅛ in) thick into a square.
2 Cut into four even squares. Damp the edges.
3 Place a whole peeled, cored and washed apple in the centre of each square. Pierce the apple with a clove.
4 Fill the centre with sugar.
5 Fold over the pastry to completely seal the apple, without breaking the pastry.
6 Roll out any debris of pastry and cut neat 2 cm (1 in) fancy rounds and place one on top of each apple.
7 Egg or milk wash and place on a lightly greased baking sheet.
8 Bake in a moderately hot oven (200 °C, Reg. 6) approx. 30 min.
9 Serve with a sauceboat of custard.

4 portions

57 · Dutch apple tart

200 g	8 oz	sugar paste (8 oz flour) (page 457)
400 g	1 lb	cooking apples
100 g	4 oz	sugar
		pinch of cinnamon
		zest of lemon
50 g	2 oz	sultanas

1 Roll out half the pastry 3 mm (1/8 in) thick into a neat round and place on a greased plate or line a flan ring.
2 Prick the bottom several times with a fork.
3 Peel, core and wash and slice the apples.
4 Place them in a saucepan with the sugar and a little water.
5 Partly cook the apples, add the cinnamon and zest of lemon.
6 Add the washed, dried sultanas and allow to cool.
7 Place on the pastry. Moisten the edges.
8 Roll out the other half of the pastry to a neat round and place on top.
9 Seal firmly, trim off excess pastry, mould the edges.
10 Brush with milk and sprinkle with castor sugar.
11 Place on a baking sheet, bake in a moderately hot oven (200–220 °C, Reg. 6–7) approx. 40 min.
12 Remove from the plate carefully before serving.

6–8 portions

58 · **Rhubarb flan** *Flan au rhubarbe*

100 g	4 oz	sugar paste (4 oz flour) (page 457)
100 g	4 oz	sugar
300 g	3/4 lb	rhubarb
		2 tablespns apricot or red glaze

1 Trim the roots and leaves from the rhubarb and remove the tough string. Cut into 2 cm (1 in) pieces, wash and dry thoroughly.
2 Line flan ring and pierce.
3 Sprinkle with sugar.
4 Arrange the fruit neatly in the flan case.
5 Sprinkle with the remainder of the sugar.
6 Bake at 200–220 °C, Reg. 6–7.
7 When the flan is almost cooked, carefully remove the flan ring and return the flan to the oven to complete the cooking.
8 Mask with hot apricot or red glaze.

Note A 1/2 cm (1/4 in) layer of pastry cream or thick custard may be placed in the flan case before adding the rhubarb then complete as above.

4 portions

59 · **Red glaze**

a) Boil sugar and water or fruit syrup with a little red colour and thicken with diluted arrowroot or fecule, re-boil till clear, strain.

or

b) Red jam and a little water boiled and passed through a strainer.

60 · **Plum or apricot flan** *Flan aux prunes ou aux abricots*

100 g	4 oz	sugar paste (4 oz flour) (page 460)
100 g	4 oz	sugar
200–300 g	8–12 oz	plums or apricots
		2 tablespns apricot glaze

1 Line flan ring and pierce. Sprinkle with sugar.
2 Quarter or halve the fruit. Arrange neatly in the flan case.
3 Sprinkle with the remainder of the sugar.
4 Bake at 200–220 °C, Reg. 6–7.
5 When the flan is almost cooked carefully remove the flan ring and return the flan to the oven to complete the cooking.
6 Mask with hot apricot glaze. See Note, recipe 58.

61 · **Soft fruit and tinned fruit flans**

For soft fruit (e.g. strawberry, raspberry, banana) and tinned fruits (e.g. pear, peach, pineapple, cherry), the flan case is lined in the same way, the bottom pierced and then cooked 'blind', i.e. tearing a piece of paper 2 cm (1 in) larger in diameter than the flan ring, place it carefully in the flan case. Fill the centre with dried peas, beans or small pieces of stale bread. Bake at 200–220 °C, Reg. 6–7, approx. 30 min. Remove the flan ring, paper and beans before the flan is cooked through, eggwash and return to the oven to complete the cooking. Add pastry cream and sliced or whole drained fruit. Mask with glaze. The glaze may be made with the fruit juice thickened with arrowroot, approx. 10 g (½ oz) to ¼ litre (½ pt).

62 · **Strawberry flan** *Flan aux fraises*

63 · **Raspberry flan** *Flan aux framboises*

100g	4 oz	sugar paste (using 4 oz flour) (page 460)
200 g	8 oz	fruit
		2 tablespns red glaze

1 Cook the flan blind, allow to cool.
2 Pick and wash the fruit, drain well.
3 Dress neatly in flan case. Coat with the glaze. *4 portions*

64 · **Fruit tartlets**

These are made from the same pastry and the same fruits as the fruit flans. The ingredients are the same. The tartlets are made by rolling out the pastry 3 mm (⅛ in) thick and cutting out rounds with a fluted cutter and neatly placing them in greased tartlet moulds. Depending on the fruit used they may sometimes be cooked blind, e.g. strawberries, raspberries.

65 · Fruit barquettes

Certain fruits (e.g. strawberries, raspberries) are sometimes served in boat-shaped moulds. The preparation is the same as for tartlets.

Tartlets and barquettes should be glazed and served allowing one large or two small per portion.

66 · Jam tartlets

100 g	4 oz	sugar paste (using 4 oz flour) (page 460)
50 g	2 oz	jam

1 Prepare the tartlets as above. Prick the bottom with a fork.
2 Add a little jam in each. Place on a baking sheet.
3 Bake in a moderately hot oven (200–230 °C, Reg. 6–8) 20–30 min.

4 portions

Lemon curd tartlets – prepare as for jam tartlets, using lemon curd.

Syrup or treacle tartlets

100 g	4 oz	syrup or treacle
		3–4 drops lemon juice
15 g	¾ oz	white breadcrumbs
		1 tablespn water

Warm the syrup or treacle slightly, then mix in the remainder of the ingredients. Use in place of jam and proceed as for jam tartlets.

67 · Bakewell tart

200 g	8 oz	sugar paste (using 8 oz flour) (page 460)	
35 g	1½ oz	icing sugar	
50 g	2 oz	raspberry jam	
50 g	2 oz	apricot glaze	
100 g	4 oz	butter or margarine	frangipane
50 g	2 oz	ground almonds	frangipane
		2 eggs	frangipane
100 g	4 oz	castor sugar	frangipane
50 g	2 oz	flour	frangipane
		almond essence	frangipane

Using hard margarine
1 portion provides:

501 kcals/2105 kJ
28.8 g fat of which 11.0 g saturated
57.5 g carbohydrate of which 33.7 g sugars
6.7 g protein
2.2 g fibre

1 Line a flan ring using three-quarters of the paste 2 mm (1/12 in) thick.
2 Pierce the bottom with a fork.
3 Spread with jam and the frangipane.
4 Roll the remaining paste, cut into neat ½ cm (¼ in) strips and arrange neatly criss-cross on the frangipane, trim off surplus paste.
5 Brush with eggwash.
6 Bake in a moderately hot oven (200–220 °C, Reg. 6–7) 30–40 min.
7 Brush with hot apricot glaze.
8 When cooled brush over with very thin water icing.

8 portions

68 · Frangipane for bakewell tart (alternative)

100 g	4 oz	butter
100 g	4 oz	castor sugar
		2 eggs
100 g	4 oz	ground almonds
10 g	½ oz	flour

Cream the butter and sugar, gradually beat in the eggs. Mix in the almonds and flour, mix lightly.

69 · Banana flan *Flan aux bananes*

100 g	4 oz	sugar paste (using 4 oz flour)
125 ml	¼ pt	pastry cream or thick custard
		2 bananas
		2 tablespns apricot glaze

1 portion provides:

369 kcals/1549 kJ
16.0 g fat of which 6.9 g saturated
53.7 g carbohydrate of which 30.3 g sugars
6.0 g protein
2.9 g fibre

Banana flan

1. Cook flan blind, allow to cool.
2. Make pastry cream (page 530) or custard and pour while hot into the flan case.
3. Allow to set. Peel and slice the bananas neatly.
4. Arrange overlapping layers on the pastry cream. Coat with glaze.

4 portions

70 · Mincemeat tart

200 g	8 oz	sugar paste (8 oz flour) (page 460)
200 g	8 oz	mincemeat (page 533)

1. Roll out half pastry 3 mm (⅛ in) thick into a neat round and place on a greased plate.

2 Prick the bottom several times with a fork.
3 Add the mincemeat. Moisten the edges.
4 Roll out the other half of the pastry to a neat round and place on top.
5 Seal firmly, trim off excess pastry, mould the edges.
6 Brush with milk and sprinkle with castor sugar.
7 Place on a baking sheet, bake at 200–220 °C, Reg. 6–7 approx. 40 min and serve.

Puff Pastry Goods

71 · Cream horns

200 g	8 oz	puff pastry (page 458)
½ litre	1 pt	cream
		few drops vanilla essence
50 g	2 oz	jam
50 g	2 oz	castor sugar

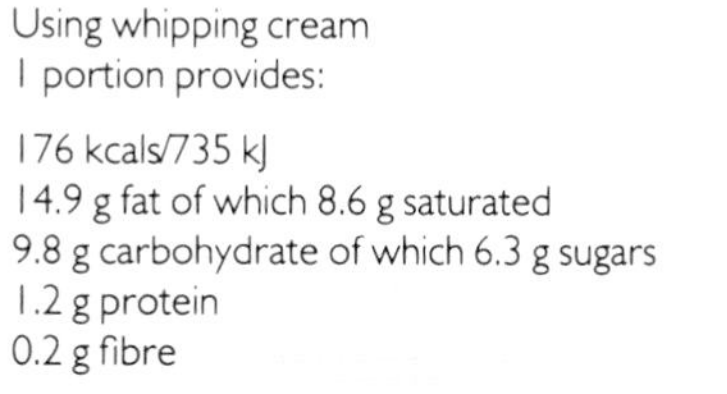
Using whipping cream
1 portion provides:

176 kcals/735 kJ
14.9 g fat of which 8.6 g saturated
9.8 g carbohydrate of which 6.3 g sugars
1.2 g protein
0.2 g fibre

Above: cream horns

Left: preparation of vol-au-vent (p. 490); bouchées (p. 490); cream horns; palmiers (p. 490)

1 Roll out the pastry 2 mm (1/12 in) thick, 30 cm (1 ft) long.
2 Cut into 1½ cm wide (¾ in) strips. Moisten on one side.
3 Wind carefully round lightly greased cream horn moulds, starting at the point and carefully overlapping each round slightly.
4 Brush with eggwash on one side and place on a greased baking sheet.
5 Bake at 220 °C, Reg. 7, approx. 20 min.
6 Sprinkle with icing sugar and return to a hot oven for a few seconds to glaze.
7 Remove carefully from the moulds and allow to cool.
8 Place a little jam in the bottom of each.
9 Add the sugar and essence to the cream and whip stiffly.
10 Place in a piping bag with a star tube and pipe a neat rose into each horn.

yield: 16 horns

72 · Eccles cakes

200 g	8 oz	puff or rough puff pastry (8 oz flour) (page 458)	
50 g	2 oz	butter or margarine	filling
50 g	2 oz	mixed peel	filling
50 g	2 oz	demerara sugar	filling
200 g	8 oz	currants	filling
		pinch mixed spice	filling

1 portion provides:

164 kcals/691 kJ
8.6 g fat of which 3.7 g saturated
22.1 g carbohydrate of which 17.3 g sugars
1.1 g protein
1.4 g fibre

1 Roll out the pastry 2 mm (1/12 in) thick.
2 Cut into rounds 10–12 cm (4–5 in) diameter.
3 Damp the edges.
4 Place a tablespoon of the mixture in the centre of each.
5 Fold the edges over to the centre and completely seal in the mixture.
6 Brush the top with egg white and dip into castor sugar.
7 Place on a greased baking sheet.
8 Cut two or three incisions with a knife so as to show the filling.
9 Bake at 220 °C, Reg. 7, approx. 15–20 min.

yield: 12 cakes

73 · Jam turnovers *Chausson à la confiture*

200 g	8 oz	puff pastry (page 458)
200 g	8 oz	jam

1 Roll out pastry 2 mm (1/12 in) thick.
2 Cut with a fancy cutter into 8 cm diameter (4 in) rounds.
3 Roll out slightly oval 12×10 cm (5×4 in).
4 Moisten the edges.
5 Place a little jam in the centre of each.
6 Fold over and seal firmly.
7 Brush with egg white and dip in castor sugar.
8 Place sugar side up on a greased baking sheet.
9 Bake in a hot oven (220 °C, Reg. 7) approx. 15–20 min.

yield: 12 turnovers

74 · Jam puffs

Ingredients as for jam turnovers

1 Roll out pastry 2 mm (1/12 in) thick.
2 Cut into 14 cm (6 in) rounds. Moisten edges.
3 Place a little jam in the centre of each.
4 Fold over three sides to form a triangle. Finish as for jam turnovers.

yields: 8 puffs

75 · Cream slice *Mille-feuilles*

200 g	8 oz	puff pastry (page 458)
100 g	4 oz	apricot jam
¼ litre	½ pt	pastry cream
200 g	8 oz	fondant or water icing

1. Roll out the pastry 2 mm (1/12 in) thick into an even-sided square.
2. Roll up carefully on a rolling-pin and unroll onto a greased, dampened baking sheet.
3. Using two forks pierce as many holes as possible.
4. Cut in half with a large knife then cut each half in two to form four even sized rectangles.
5. Bake in a hot oven (220 °C, Reg. 7), approx. 15–20 min, turn the strips over after 10 min. Allow to cool.
6. Keep the best strip for the top. Spread pastry cream on one strip.
7. Place another strip on top and spread with jam.
8. Place the third strip on top and spread with pastry cream.
9. Place the last strip on top, flat side up.
10. Press down firmly with a flat tray.
11. Decorate by feather-icing as follows:
12. Warm the fondant to blood heat and correct the consistency with sugar syrup if necessary.
13. Separate a little fondant into two colours and place in paper cornets.
14. Pour the fondant over the mille-feuille in an even coat.
15. Immediately pipe on one of the colours lengthwise in strips 1 cm (½ in) apart.
16. Quickly pipe on the second colour between each line of the first.
17. With the back of a small knife, wiping after each stroke, mark down the slice strokes 2 cm (1 in) apart.
18. Quickly turn the slice around and repeat in the same direction with strokes in between the previous ones.
19. Allow to set and trim the edges neatly.
20. Cut into even portions with a sharp thin-bladed knife, dip into hot water and wipe clean after each cut.

Note At stages 15 and 16 baker's chocolate or tempered couverture may be used for marbling.

yield: 6–8 slices

76 · Apple turnover *Chausson aux pommes*

Proceed as for jam turnover (see page 488), using a dry, sweetened apple purée.

yield: 8 turnovers

77 · Palmiers

Puff pastry trimmings are suitable for these.

1 Roll out the pastry 2 mm (1/12 in) thick into a square.
2 Sprinkle liberally with castor sugar on both sides and roll into the pastry.
3 Fold into three from each end so as to meet in the middle, brush with eggwash and fold in two.
4 Cut into strips approx. 2 cm (1 in) thick, dip one side in castor sugar.
5 Place on a greased baking sheet, sugared side down, leaving a space of at least 2 cm (1 in) between each.
6 Bake in a very hot oven approx. 10 min.
7 Turn with a palette knife, cook on the other side until brown and the sugar caramelised.

Puff pastry goods (from top to foreground): bouchées, vol-au-vent, palmiers, cream horns

Palmiers may be made in all sizes. Two joined together with a little whipped cream may be served as a pastry, small ones for petits fours.

78 · Puff pastry cases *Bouchées et vol-au-vent*

200g	puff pastry (8 oz flour) (page 458)

1 Roll out pastry approx. 1/2 cm (1/4 in) thick.
2 Cut out with a round, fluted 5 cm (2 in) cutter.
3 Place on a greased, dampened baking sheet, eggwash.
4 Dip a plain 4 cm (1 1/2 in) diameter cutter into hot fat or oil and make an incision 3 mm (1/8 in) deep in the centre of each.
5 Allow to rest in a cool place.
6 Bake at 220 °C, Reg. 7, approx. 20 min.
7 When cool remove caps or lids carefully and remove all the raw pastry from inside the cases.

Bouchées are filled with a variety of savoury fillings and are served hot or cold. They may also be filled with cream and jam or lemon curd as a pastry.

Large bouchées are known as vol-au-vent; details of their preparation are on page 361. They may be produced in one, two, four or six portion sizes, and a single sized vol-au-vent would be approximately twice the size of a bouchée. When preparing one and two portion size vol-au-vent the method for bouchées may be followed. When preparing larger sized vol-au-vent it is advisable to have two layers of puff pastry each ½ cm (¼ in) thick sealed together with eggwash. One layer should be a plain round, and the other of the same diameter with a circle cut out of the centre.

yield: 12 bouchée or 6 vol-au-vent cases

79 · **Kiwi slice** *Bande aux kiwis*

1 Cook band blind.
2 When cool add pastry cream.
3 Arrange slices of kiwi fruit on pastry cream.
4 Coat with apricot glaze.
5 Decorate with whipped cream.

Kiwi fruit slice

80 · Jalousie

200 g	8 oz	puff pastry (page 458)
200 g	8 oz	mincemeat (page 538), jam or frangipane (page 486)

1 Roll out one-third of the pastry 3 mm (⅛ in) thick into a strip approx. 25 × 10 cm (10 × 4 in) and place on a greased, dampened baking sheet.
2 Pierce with a fork. Moisten the edges.
3 Spread on the filling, leaving 2 cm (1 in) free all the way round.
4 Roll out the remaining two-thirds of the pastry to the same size.
5 Fold in half lengthwise and, with a sharp knife, cut slits across the fold about ½ cm (¼ in) apart to within 2 cm (1 in) of the edge.
6 Carefully open out this strip and neatly place on to the first strip.
7 Neaten and decorate the edge. Brush with eggwash.
8 Bake at 220 °C, Reg. 7, approx. 25–30 min.
9 Sprinkle with icing sugar and return to a very hot oven to glaze.

8 portions

81 · Pithiviers *Gâteau Pithiviers*

200 g	8 oz	puff pastry (page 458)
		1 tablespn apricot jam
		frangipane (recipe 68) using ½ the recipe

1 Roll out one-third of the pastry into a round 20 cm (8 in), 2 mm (1/12 in) thick, moisten the edges and place on a greased, dampened baking sheet, spread the centre with jam.
2 Prepare the frangipane by creaming the margarine and sugar in a bowl, gradually adding the beaten eggs and folding in the flour and almonds.
3 Spread on the frangipane, leaving a 2 cm (1 in) border round the edge.
4 Roll out the remaining two-thirds of the pastry and cut into a slightly larger round.
5 Place neatly on top, seal and decorate the edge.
6 Using a sharp pointed knife make approximately twelve curved cuts 2 mm (1/12 in) deep radiating from the centre to about 2 cm (1 in) from the edge.
7 Brush with eggwash.
8 Bake at 220 °C, Reg. 78, approx. 25–30 min.
9 Glaze with icing sugar as for jalousie.

8 portions

82 · Mince pies

200 g	8 oz	puff pastry (page 458)
200 g	8 oz	mincemeat (page 533)

1 portion provides:
171 kcals/718 kJ
10.2 g fat of which 4.5 g saturated
17.7 g carbohydrate of which 10.2 g sugars
1.3 g protein
1.0 g fibre

1. Roll out the pastry 3 mm (1/8 in) thick.
2. Cut half the pastry into fluted rounds approx. 6 cm (2½ in) diameter.
3. Place on greased, dampened baking sheet.
4. Moisten the edges.
5. Place a little mincemeat in the centre of each.
6. Cut remainder of the pastry into fluted rounds 8 cm (3 in) diameter.
7. Cover the mincemeat, seal the edges.
8. Brush with eggwash.
9. Bake at 220 °C, Reg. 7, approx. 20 min.
10. Sprinkle with icing sugar and serve warm. Accompany with a suitable sauce, e.g. custard, brandy sauce, brandy cream, etc.

Mince pies may be made with short or sugar pastry.

yield: 8–12 pies

83 · Sausage rolls

200 g	8 oz	puff pastry (page 458)
400 g	1 lb	sausage meat

1 portion provides:
190 kcals/799 kJ
15.9 g fat of which 5.8 g saturated
7.9 g carbohydrate of which 0.2 g sugars
4.3 g protein
0.4 g fibre

1. Roll out pastry 3 mm (1/8 in) thick into a strip 10 cm (4 in) wide.
2. Make sausage meat into a roll 2 cm (1 in) diameter
3. Place on the pastry. Moisten the edges of the pastry.
4. Fold over and seal. Cut into 8 cm (3 in) lengths.
5. Mark the edge with the back of a knife. Brush with eggwash.
6. Place on to a greased, dampened baking sheet.
7. Bake at 220 °C, Reg. 7, approx. 20 min.

yield: 12 rolls

84 · **Fruit slice** *Bande aux fruits, or Tranche aux fruits*

These may be prepared from any fruit suitable for flans.

200 g	8 oz	puff pastry (page 458)
400 g	1 lb	fruit
		sugar to sweeten
		2 tablespns appropriate glaze.

1 portion provides:

183 kcals/767 kJ
7.8 g fat of which 3.4 g saturated
28.6 g carbohydrate of which 21.3 g sugars
1.3 g protein
1.6 g fibre

1 Roll out the pastry 2 mm (1/12 in) thick in a strip 12 cm (6 in) wide.
2 Place on a greased, dampened baking sheet.
3 Moisten two edges with eggwash, lay two 1½ cm (⅜ in) wide strips along each edge.
4 Seal firmly and mark with the back of a knife.
5 Prick the bottom of the slice.
6 Then depending on the fruit used, either put the fruit on the slice and cook together (e.g. apple), or cook the slice blind and afterwards place the pastry cream and fruit (e.g. tinned peaches) on the pastry. Glaze and serve as for flans.

Note Alternative methods are: (i) to use short or sweet pastry for the base and puff pastry for the two side strips; (ii) to use sweet pastry in a slice mould.

8 portions

Choux Pastry Goods

85 · **Eclairs – chocolate** *Eclairs au chocolat*

125 ml	¼ pt	choux paste (recipe 6)
100 g	4 oz	fondant
¼ litre	½ pt	whipped cream
25 g	1 oz	chocolate couverture

1 portion provides:

123 kcals/516 kJ
9.5 g fat of which 5.7 g saturated
8.8 g carbohydrate of which 7.3 g sugars
1.1 g protein
0.1 g fibre

1 Place the choux paste into a piping bag with 1 cm (½ in) plain tube.
2 Pipe into 8 cm (3 in) lengths on to a lightly greased baking sheet.
3 Bake in a moderate oven (200–220 °C, Reg. 6–7), approx. 30 min.
4 Allow to cool.
5 Slit down one side, with a sharp knife.
6 Fill with sweetened, vanilla-flavoured whipped cream, using a piping bag and small tube. The continental fashion is to fill with pastry cream.

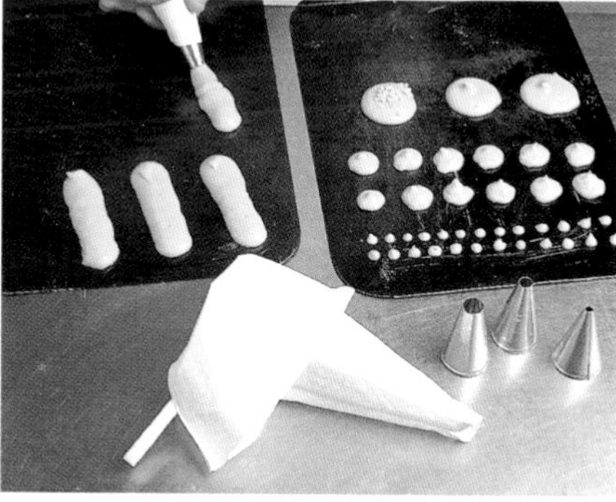

Above: preparation of choux pastry goods; Left: choux pastry goods (clockwise from top): cream buns (p. 496), profiteroles and chocolate sauce (p. 528); coffee and chocolate éclairs (pp. 494–5)

7 Warm the fondant, add the finely cut chocolate, allow to melt slowly, adjust the consistency with a little sugar and water syrup if necessary. *Do not overheat or the fondant will lose its shine.*
8 Glaze the éclairs by dipping them in the fondant, remove the surplus with the finger. Allow to set.

yield: 12 éclairs

86 · **Coffee éclairs** *Eclairs au café*

Add a few drops of coffee essence instead of chocolate to the fondant.

Coffee éclairs may be filled with coffee-flavoured pastry cream, page 528, or whipped non-dairy cream.

87 · **Profiteroles** *Profiteroles*

These are small choux paste buns which can be made in a variety of sizes:
a) pea size – for consommé garnish,
b) double pea size (stuffed) for garnish,
c) half-cream-bun size – filled with cream and served with chocolate sauce.

88 Cream buns *Choux à la crème*

125 ml	¼ pt	choux paste (recipe 6)
25 g	1 oz	chopped almonds
¼ litre	½ pt	whipped cream

1 Place the choux paste into a piping bag with a 1 cm (½ in) plain tube.
2 Pipe out on to a lightly greased baking sheet into pieces the size of a walnut.
3 Sprinkle each with chopped almonds. Cook, split and fill as for éclairs.
4 Sprinkle with icing sugar and serve.

yield: 8 buns

89 Profiteroles and chocolate sauce *Profiteroles au chocolat*

125 ml	¼ pt	choux paste (recipe 6)
¼ litre	½ pt	chocolate sauce (recipe 186)
¼ litre	½ pt	whipped, sweetened, vanilla flavoured cream

1 portion provides:

219 kcals/919 kJ
16.2 g fat of which 9.7 g saturated
16.4 g carbohydrate of which 12.8 g sugars
2.9 g protein
0.2 g fibre

1 Proceed as for cream buns (recipe 88), pipe out half the size and omit the almonds. Fill with cream and dredge with icing sugar.
2 Serve with a sauceboat of cold chocolate sauce.

Alternatively, coffee sauce may be served and the profiteroles filled with non-dairy cream or pastry cream.

90 Choux paste fritters *Beignets soufflés, sauce abricot*

125 ml	¼ pt	choux paste
125 ml	¼ pt	apricot sauce (recipe 175)

1 portion provides:

82 kcals/344 kJ
3.9 g fat of which 1.3 g saturated
11.5 g carbohydrate of which 8.8 g sugars
0.9 g protein
0.2 g fibre

1 Using a tablespoon and the finger, break the paste off into pieces the size of a walnut into a moderately hot deep fat (170 °C).
2 Allow to cook gently for approx. 10–15 min.
3 Drain well, sprinkle liberally with icing sugar.
4 Serve with a sauceboat of hot apricot sauce.

8 portions

Puddings

91 Steamed fruit puddings

Apple, apple and blackberry, rhubarb, rhubarb and apple, etc.

200 g	8 oz	suet paste (recipe 5)
¾–1 kg	1½–2 lb	fruit
100 g	4 oz	sugar
		2 tablespns water

Using apple
1 portion provides:

230 kcals/967 kJ
7.4 g fat of which 3.4 g saturated
41.5 g carbohydrate of which 27.1 g sugars
1.9 g protein
3.0 g fibre

1. Grease the basin.
2. Line, using three-quarters of the paste.
3. Add prepared and washed fruit and sugar. Add 1–2 cloves in an apple pudding.
4. Add two tablespoons water. Moisten the edge of the paste.
5. Cover with the remaining quarter of the pastry. Seal firmly.
6. Cover with greased greaseproof paper, a pudding cloth or foil.
7. Steam for 1½ hr approx. and serve with custard.

6 portions

92 Steamed jam roll

200 g	8 oz	suet paste (recipe 5)
100 g	4 oz	jam

1. Roll out paste into a rectangle 3 cm × 16 cm (12 × 6 in) approx.
2. Spread with jam leaving 1 cm (½ in) clear on all edges.
3. Fold over two short sides, 1 cm (½ in).
4. Roll the pastry from the top.
5. Moisten the bottom edge to seal the roll.
6. Wrap in buttered greaseproof paper and a pudding cloth or foil, tie both ends. Steam for 1½–2 hr.
7. Serve with jam or custard sauce.

6 portions

93 · Steamed currant roll

300 g	12 oz	flour, white or wholemeal	or self-raising flour
10 g	½ oz	baking-powder	
		pinch salt	
150 g	6 oz	chopped suet	
75 g	3 oz	sugar, castor or unrefined	
100 g	4 oz	currants	
185 ml	⅜ pt	water or milk, approx.	

1 Sieve the flour, salt and baking-powder into a bowl.
2 Mix in the suet. Mix in the sugar and currants.
3 Add sufficient water or milk to make a fairly firm dough.
4 Roll in greased greaseproof paper and a pudding cloth or foil. Tie with string at both ends. Steam 1½–2 hr.
5 Remove the cloth and paper and serve with a sauceboat of custard.

Sultanas, raisins or dates may be used instead of currants.

6 portions

94 · Steamed dried fruit pudding

100 g	4 oz	flour, white or wholemeal	or self-raising flour
10 g	½ oz	baking-powder	
		pinch salt	
100 g	4 oz	breadcrumbs	
100 g	4 oz	suet	
100 g	4 oz	sugar, castor or unrefined	
100 g	4 oz	fruit (currants, raisins, dates or sultanas)	
		1 egg	
125 ml	¼ pt	milk, whole or skimmed	

1 Mix all the dry ingredients together. Add the liquid and mix.
2 Place in a greased pudding basin, cover and steam 1½–2 hr.
3 Serve with custard sauce or vanilla sauce.

6 portions

95 · Golden syrup or treacle pudding

150 g	6 oz	flour, white or w'meal	or self-raising flour
10 g	½ oz	baking-powder	
		pinch salt	
75 g	3 oz	chopped suet	
50 g	2 oz	castor or unrefined sugar	
		zest 1 lemon	
		1 egg	
125 ml	¼ pt	milk, whole or skimmed (approx.)	
125 ml	¼ pt	golden syrup or light treacle	

1 portion provides:

313 kcals/1315 kJ
13.0 g fat of which 5.9 g saturated
47.8 g carbohydrate of which 26.6 g sugars
4.3 g protein
0.9 g fibre

1 Sieve the flour, salt and baking-powder into a bowl.
2 Mix the suet, sugar and zest.
3 Mix to a medium dough, with the beaten egg and milk.

4 Pour the syrup in a well-greased basin. Place mixture on top.
5 Cover securely, steam for 1½–2 hr.
6 Serve with a sauceboat of warm syrup containing the lemon juice.

6 portions

96 · Steamed sponge pudding – basic recipe

100 g	4 oz	butter or margarine
100 g	4 oz	castor or soft brown sugar
		2 eggs
150 g	6 oz	flour, white or wholemeal
10 g	½ oz	baking-powder
		few drops of milk

1 Cream the butter or margarine and sugar in a bowl until fluffy and almost white.
2 Gradually add the beaten eggs, mixing vigorously.
3 Sieve the flour and baking-powder.
4 Gradually incorporate into the mixture as lightly as possible keeping to a dropping consistency by the addition of the milk.
5 Place in a greased pudding basin.
6 Cover securely with greased greaseproof paper. Steam for 1–1½ hr.

6 portions

Above: preparation of steamed sponge puddings
Left: steamed sponge puddings (clockwise from left): sultana, chocolate and lemon with chocolate sauce (p. 529), lemon sauce (p. 526) and custard sauce (p. 527)

97 · Vanilla sponge pudding

Add a few drops of vanilla essence to the basic mixture (recipe 96), and serve with a vanilla-flavoured sauce (recipe 187).

98 · Chocolate sponge pudding

Add 25 g (1 oz) chocolate or cocoa powder in place of 25 g (1 oz) flour – that is 125 g (5 oz) flour, 25 g (1 oz) chocolate to basic recipe 96.

Serve with a chocolate sauce (recipe 186).

99 · Lemon sponge pudding

Add the grated zest of one or two lemons, and a few drops of lemon essence to basic recipe 96.

Serve with a lemon (recipe 177) or vanilla sauce.

100 · Orange sponge pudding

Proceed as for lemon sponge pudding, but using oranges in place of lemons.

Serve with an orange sauce (recipe 176) or vanilla sauce.

101 · Cherry sponge pudding

Add 100 g (4 oz) chopped or quartered glacé cherries to recipe 96.

Serve with a custard sauce (recipe 179) or almond sauce (recipe 180).

102 · Sultana sponge pudding

103 · Currant sponge pudding

104 · Raisin sponge pudding

Add 100 g (4 oz) of washed well dried fruit to recipe 96.
Serve with custard sauce, recipe 184.

105 · Soufflé pudding *Pouding soufflé*

185 ml	⅜ pt	milk, whole or skimmed
25 g	1 oz	flour, white or wholemeal
25 g	1 oz	butter or margarine
25 g	1 oz	castor or unrefined sugar
		3 eggs, separated

Using white flour, hard margarine
1 portion provides:

122 kcals/510 kJ
7.6 g fat of which 3.2 g saturated
9.1 g carbohydrate of which 5.9 g sugars
4.8 g protein
0.2 g fibre

1 Boil the milk in a sauteuse.
2 Combine the flour, butter and sugar.
3 Whisk into the milk and re-boil.
4 Remove from heat, add yolks one at a time, whisking continuously.
5 Stiffly beat the whites.

6 Carefully fold into the mixture.
7 Three-quarters fill buttered and sugared dariole moulds.
8 Place in a roasting tin, half full of water.
9 Bring to the boil and place in a hot oven (230–250 °C) 12–15 min.
10 Turn out on to a flat dish and serve with a suitable hot sauce, e.g. custard or sabayon sauce (recipe 184).

6 portions

106 · Orange or lemon soufflé pudding

Flavour the basic mixture (recipe 105) with the grated zest of 1 orange or lemon and a little appropriate sauce. Use the juice in the accompanying sauce.

107 · Cold lemon soufflé *Soufflé milanaise*

10 g	½ oz	leaf gelatine
		2 lemons
		4 eggs, separated
200 g	8 oz	castor sugar
¼ litre	½ pt	whipping or double cream or non-dairy cream

1 portion provides:

330 kcals/1385 kJ
18.6 g fat of which 10.6 g saturated
36.2 g carbohydrate of which 36.2 g sugars
6.7 g protein
0.0 g fibre

1 Prepare a soufflé dish by tying a 8 cm (3 in) wide strip of oiled greaseproof paper around the outside top edge with string, so that it extends 2–4 cm (1–1½ in) above the top of the dish.
2 Soak the gelatine in cold water.
3 *Lightly* grate the zest of the lemons.
4 Squeeze the juice of the lemons into a bowl.
5 Add the lemon zest, yolks, sugar and whisk over a pan of hot water until the mixture thickens and turns a very light colour.
6 Dissolve the gelatine in a few drops of water over heat, mix in, remove from heat.
7 Lightly whisk cream until three-quarters stiff.
8 Stiffly beat the egg whites.
9 Stir the basic mixture frequently until almost on setting point.
10 Gently fold in the cream. Gently fold in the egg whites.
11 Pour into the prepared dish (ref. point 1).
12 Place in refrigerator to set.
13 To serve, remove paper collar and decorate sides with green chopped almonds or pistachio nuts. The top may be similarly decorated or by using rosettes of sweetened vanilla-flavoured whipped cream.

6 portions

108 · Queen of puddings

½ litre	1 pt	milk, whole or skimmed
		3 eggs
50 g	2 oz	castor or unrefined sugar
		vanilla essence
75 g	3 oz	cake or breadcrumbs
25 g	1 oz	butter or margarine
50 g	2 oz	castor sugar for the meringue
50 g	2 oz	jam

1 portion provides:

362 kcals/1522 kJ
14.7 g fat of which 6.8 g saturated
50.0 g carbohydrate of which 41.2 g sugars
10.9 g protein
0.9 g fibre

1 Boil the milk.
2 Pour on to 2 yolks, 1 egg, 50 g (2 oz) sugar and vanilla essence, whisk well.
3 Place the crumbs in a buttered pie dish.
4 Strain the custard on to the crumbs.
5 Bake in a moderate oven in a bain-marie, until set, approx. 30 min.
6 Allow to cool.
7 Stiffly beat the egg whites, fold in the 50 g (2 oz) castor sugar.
8 Spread the warmed jam over the baked mixture.
9 Using a large star tube, pipe the meringue to cover the jam.
10 Brown in a hot oven (220 °C, Reg. 7) and serve.

4 portions

109 · Apple Charlotte *Charlotte aux pommes*

400 g	1 lb	stale bread (white or wholemeal)
100 g	4 oz	margarine or butter
400 g	1 lb	cooking apples
50–75 g	2–3 oz	sugar, castor or unrefined
35 g	1½ oz	breadcrumbs or cake crumbs

Using hard margarine
1 portion provides:

515 kcals/2163 kJ
22.3 g fat of which 9.3 g saturated
74.5 g carbohydrate of which 23.4 g sugars
9.4 g protein
6.1 g fibre

1 Use either one charlotte mould or four dariole moulds.
2 Cut the bread into 3 mm (⅛ in) slices and remove the crusts.
3 Cut a round the size of the bottom of the mould, dip into melted butter or margarine on one side and place in the mould fat side down.
4 Cut fingers of bread 2–4 cm (1–1½ in) wide, and fit overlapping well to the sides of the mould after dipping each one in melted fat. Take care not to leave any gaps.
5 Peel, core and wash the apples, cut into thick slices and three parts cook in a little butter and sugar (a little cinnamon or a clove may be added), and add the breadcrumbs.
6 Fill the centre of the mould with the apple.
7 Cut round pieces of bread to seal the apple in.
8 Bake at 220 °C, Reg. 7, approx. 30–40 min. Remove from mould.
9 Serve with apricot (recipe 175) or custard (recipe 179) sauce.

4 portions

110 · **Apple fritters** *Beignets aux pommes*

400 g	1 lb	cooking apples
150 g	6 oz	frying batter (page 220)
125 ml	¼ pt	apricot sauce (recipe 175)

Fried in peanut oil
1 portion provides:

246 kcals/1034 kJ
10.2 g fat of which 1.9 g saturated
38.9 g carbohydrate of which 25.0 g sugars
2.1 g protein
3.0 g fibre

Apple fritters

1 Peel and core the apples and cut into ½ cm (¼ in) rings.
2 Pass through flour, shake off the surplus.
3 Dip into frying batter.
4 Lift out with the fingers, into fairly hot deep fat (185 °C).
5 Cook approx. 5 min on each side.
6 Drain well, dust with icing sugar and glaze under the salamander.
7 Serve with hot apricot sauce.

4 portions

111 · **Banana fritters** *Beignets aux bananes*

		4 bananas
150 g	6 oz	frying batter (page 220)
125 ml	¼ pt	apricot sauce (recipe 175)

Peel and cut the bananas in half lengthwise then in half across. Cook and serve as for apple fritters (recipe 110).

112 · **Pineapple fritters** *Beignets aux ananas*

		4 rings of pineapple
150 g	6 oz	frying batter (page 220)
125 ml	¼ pt	apricot sauce (recipe 175)

Cut the rings in half, cook and serve as for apple fritters (recipe 110).

113 · Pancakes with lemon *Crêpes au citron*

100 g	4 oz	flour, white or wholemeal
		pinch of salt
		1 egg
¼ litre	½ pt	milk, whole or skimmed
10 g	½ oz	melted butter, margarine or oil
		oil for frying
50 g	2 oz	sugar, castor or unrefined

Using white flour, whole milk, hard marg, peanut oil 1 portion provides:

304 kcals/1275 kJ
16.2 g fat of which 4.8 g saturated
35.5 g carbohydrate of which 16.4 g sugars
6.1 g protein
0.9 g fibre

1 Sieve the flour and salt into a bowl, make a well in the centre.
2 Add the egg and milk gradually incorporating the flour from the sides, whisk to a smooth batter.
3 Mix in the melted butter.
4 Heat the pancake pan, clean thoroughly.
5 Add a little oil, heat until smoking.
6 Add enough mixture to just cover the bottom of the pan thinly.
7 Cook for a few seconds until brown.
8 Turn and cook on the other side. Turn on to a plate.
9 Sprinkle with sugar. Fold in half then half again.

When making a batch of pancakes it is best to keep them all flat one on top of the other on a plate. Sprinkle sugar between each. Fold them all when ready for service, sprinkle again with sugar and dress neatly overlapping on a serving dish. Garnish with quarters of lemon free from pips. Serve very hot, two per portion.

4 portions

114 · Pancakes with jam *Crêpes à la confiture*

50 g	2 oz	warm jam
25 g	1 oz	sugar

Mixture as for recipe 113.
1 Prepare pancakes as in recipe 113. Spread each with warm jam.
2 Roll like a swiss roll, trim the ends.
3 Dredge with castor sugar and serve.

115 · Pancakes with apple *Crêpes normande*

Method I

Cook as for recipe 113 and spread with a hot purée of apple (page 480), then roll up, sprinkle with castor sugar.

Method II

Place a little cooked apple in the pan, add the pancake mixture and cook on both sides. Turn out, sprinkle with castor sugar and roll up.

116 · Pancakes with orange *Crêpes à l'orange*

Proceed as for lemon pancakes (recipe 113), using orange in place of lemon.

117 · Baked apple *Pommes bonne femme*

		4 medium-sized cooking apples
50 g	2 oz	sugar, white or unrefined
		4 cloves
25 g	1 oz	butter or margarine
60 ml	⅛ pt	water

Using hard margarine
1 portion provides:

156 kcals/663 kJ
5.1 g fat of which 2.2 g saturated
29.7 g carbohydrate of which 29.5 g sugars
0.4 g protein
2.7 g fibre

1 Core the apples and make an incision 2 mm (1/12 in) deep round the centre of each. Wash well.
2 Place in a roasting tray or ovenproof dish.
3 Fill the centre with sugar and add a clove.
4 Place 5 g (¼ oz) butter on each. Add the water.
5 Bake in a moderate oven (200–220 °C, Reg. 6–7) 15–20 min approx.
6 Turn the apples over carefully.
7 Return to the oven until cooked, approx. 40 min in all.
8 Serve with a little of the cooking liquor and custard.

4 portions

118 · Stuffed baked apple

Proceed as for baked apples, but fill the centre with washed sultanas, raisins or chopped dates, or a combination of these.

119 · Junket

½ litre	1 pt	milk
10 g	½ oz	castor sugar
		1 teaspn rennet
		grated nutmeg

1 portion provides:

91 kcals/383 kJ
4.8 g fat of which 3.0 g saturated
8.5 g carbohydrate of which 8.5 g sugars
4.1 g protein
0.0 g fibre

1 Warm the milk to blood heat and pour into a glass dish.
2 Add sugar and rennet, stir gently. Leave until set.
3 Sprinkle lightly with nutmeg and serve.

The addition of rennet causes the clotting or coagulation of milk.

4–6 portions

120 · **Fresh fruit salad** *Salade de fruits, Macédoine de fruits*

All the following fruits may be used: dessert apples, pears, pineapple, oranges, grapes, melon, strawberries, peaches, raspberries, apricots, bananas, cherries. All fruit must be ripe.

Allow approx. 150 g (6 oz) unprepared fruit per portion.

50 g	2 oz	castor sugar
		juice of ½ lemon
		1 orange
		1 dessert apple
		1 dessert pear
50 g	2 oz	cherries
50 g	2 oz	grapes
		1 banana

Fresh fruit salad

1. Boil the sugar with ⅛ litre (¼ pt) water to make a syrup, place in a bowl.
2. Allow to cool, add the lemon juice.
3. Peel and cut the orange into segments as for cocktail.
4. Quarter the apple and pear, remove the core, peel and cut each quarter into two or three slices, place in the bowl and mix with the orange.
5. Stone the cherries, leave whole.
6. Cut the grapes in half, peel if required, and remove the pips.
7. Mix carefully and place in a glass bowl in the refrigerator to chill.
8. Just before serving, peel and slice the banana and arrange on top.

Kiwi fruit, plums, mangoes, paw-paws and lychees may also be used. Kirsch, Cointreau or Grand Marnier may be added to the syrup.

4 portions

1 portion provides:

117 kcals/493 kJ
– g fat of which – g saturated
30.3 g carbohydrate of which 29.5 g sugars
0.9 g protein
3.0 g fibre

121 · Fruit fool

Method I Apple, gooseberry, rhubarb etc.

400 g	1 lb	fruit
60 ml	⅛ pt	water
100 g	4 oz	granulated or unrefined sugar

Cook to a purée and pass through a sieve.

25 g	1 oz	cornflour
¼ litre	½ pt	milk, whole or skimmed
25 g	1 oz	castor or unrefined sugar

1 Dilute the cornflour in a little of the milk, add the sugar.
2 Boil remainder of the milk.
3 Pour on the diluted cornflour, stir well.
4 Return to the pan on low heat and stir to the boil.
5 Mix with the fruit purée. The quantity of mixture should not be less than ½ litre (1 pt).
6 Pour into four glass coupes and allow to set.
7 Decorate with whipped sweetened cream or non-dairy cream. The colour may need to be adjusted slightly with food colour.

4 portions

Method II Raspberries, strawberries, etc.

400 g	1 lb	fruit in purée
100 g	4 oz	castor sugar
¼ litre	½ pt	fresh whipped cream

Mix together and serve in coupes.

4 portions

Method III

35 g	1½ oz	cornflour
375 ml	¾ pt	water
100 g	4 oz	sugar
400 g	1 lb	fruit
185 ml	⅜ pt	cream

1 Dilute the cornflour in a little of the water.
2 Boil the remainder of the water with the sugar and prepared fruit until soft.
3 Pass through a fine sieve.
4 Return to a clean pan and re-boil.
5 Stir in the diluted cornflour and reboil. Allow to cool.
6 Lightly whisk the cream and fold into the mixture.
7 Serve as for Method I, points 6 and 7.

122 · Trifle

		1 sponge (3 eggs)
25 g	1 oz	jam
		1 tin fruit (pears, peaches, pineapple)
35 g	1 ½ oz	custard powder } custard
375 ml	¾ pt	milk, whole or skimmed } custard
50 g	2 oz	castor sugar } custard
125 ml	¼ pt	cream (¾ whipped) or non-dairy cream
¼ litre	½ pt	whipped sweetened cream or non-dairy cream
25 g	1 oz	angelica
25 g	1 oz	glacé cherries

Using whole milk, whipping cream
1 portion provides:

543 kcals/2280 kJ
29.1 g fat of which 17.1 g saturated
66.2 g carbohydrate of which 51.3 g sugars
8.2 g protein
1.9 g fibre

1. Cut the sponge in half, sideways, and spread with jam.
2. Place in a glass bowl and soak with fruit syrup.
3. A few drops of sherry may be added.
4. Cut the fruit into small pieces and add to the sponge.
5. Dilute the custard powder in a basin with some of the milk, add the sugar.
6. Boil the remainder of the milk, pour a little on the custard powder, mix well, return to the saucepan and over a low heat stir to the boil. Allow to cool, stirring occasionally to prevent a skin forming, fold in the three-quarters whipped 125 ml (¼ pt) cream.
7. Pour on to the sponge. Leave to cool.
8. Decorate with whipped cream, angelica and cherries.

6–8 portions

123 · Baked alaska *Omelette soufflée surprise*

		4 pieces sponge cake
60 ml	⅛ pt	fruit syrup
		4 scoops vanilla ice-cream
		4 egg whites
200 g	8 oz	castor sugar

1 portion provides:

521 kcals/2190 kJ
16.4 g fat of which 7.3 g saturated
91.3 g carbohydrate of which 81.2 g sugars
7.7 g protein
0.6 g fibre

1. Neatly arrange the pieces of sponge cake in the centre of a flat ovenproof dish.
2. Sprinkle the sponge cake with a little fruit syrup.
3. Place a flattened scoop of vanilla ice-cream on each piece of sponge.
4. Meanwhile stiffly whip the egg whites and fold in the sugar.
5. Use half the meringue and completely cover the ice-cream and sponge. Neaten with a palette knife.
6. Place the remainder of the meringue into a piping bag with a large tube (plain or star) and decorate the omelette.
7. Place the omelette into a hot oven (230–250 °C, Reg. 8–9) and colour a golden brown. Serve immediately.

4 portions

124 · Baked alaska with peaches *Omelette soufflée milady*

Proceed as for recipe 123, adding a little maraschino to the fruit syrup and using raspberry ice-cream instead of vanilla ice-cream. Cover the ice-cream with four halves of peaches.

125 · Baked alaska with pears *Omelette soufflée milord*

Proceed as for recipe 123 adding a little kirsch to the fruit syrup and adding halves of poached pears to the ice-cream.

126 · Poached fruits *Compote de fruits*

400 g	1 lb	fruit	
¼ litre	½ pt	water	sugar or stock syrup
100 g	4 oz	sugar	sugar or stock syrup
		½ lemon	sugar or stock syrup

Using pears
1 portion provides:

126 kcals/531 kJ
0.0 g fat of which 0.0 g saturated
33.5 g carbohydrate of which 33.5 g sugars
0.2 g protein
2.2 g fibre

Apples, pears

1 Boil the water and sugar.
2 Quarter the fruit, remove the core and peel.
3 Place in a shallow pan in sugar syrup.
4 Add a few drops of lemon juice.
5 Cover with greaseproof paper.
6 Allow to simmer slowly, preferably in the oven, cool and serve.

Soft fruits – raspberries, strawberries

1 Pick and wash the fruit.
2 Place in a glass bowl.
3 Pour on the hot syrup.
4 Allow to cool and serve.

Stone fruits – plums, damsons, greengages, cherries

Wash the fruit, barely cover with sugar syrup and cover with greaseproof paper or a lid. Cook gently in a moderate oven until tender.

Rhubarb

Trim off the stalk and leaf and wash. Cut into 5 cm (2 in) lengths and cook as above, adding extra sugar if necessary. A little ground ginger may also be added.

Gooseberries, blackcurrants, redcurrants

Top and tail gooseberries, wash and cook as for stone fruit, adding extra sugar if necessary.

The currants should be carefully removed from the stalks, washed and cooked as for stone fruits.

Dried fruits – prunes, apricots, apples, pears

Dried fruits should be washed and soaked in cold water overnight. Gently cook in the liquor with sufficient sugar to taste.

Note A piece of cinnamon stick and a few slices of lemon may be added to the prunes or pears, one or two cloves to the dried or fresh apples.

4 portions

127 · **Meringue** *Meringue*

		4 egg whites
200 g	8 oz	castor sugar

1 Whip the egg whites stiffly.
2 Sprinkle on the sugar and carefully mix in.
3 Place in a piping bag with a large plain tube and pipe on to silicone paper on a baking sheet.
4 Bake in the slowest oven possible or in a hot plate (110 °C, Reg. ¼). The aim is to cook the meringues without any colour whatsoever.

To gain maximum efficiency when whipping egg whites, the following points should be observed:

a) Eggs should be fresh.

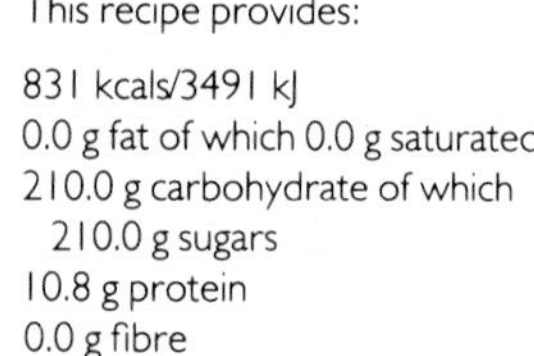

This recipe provides:

831 kcals/3491 kJ
0.0 g fat of which 0.0 g saturated
210.0 g carbohydrate of which
210.0 g sugars
10.8 g protein
0.0 g fibre

Preparation and piping of meringues

b) When separating yolks from whites *no* speck of egg yolk must be allowed to remain in the white; egg yolk contains fat, the presence of which can prevent the white being correctly whipped.

c) The bowl and whisk must be scrupulously clean, dry and free from any grease.

d) When egg whites are whipped the addition of a little sugar (15 g – 4 whites) will assist the efficient beating and lessen the chance of overbeating.

The reason egg whites increase in volume when whipped is because they contain so much protein (11%). The protein forms tiny filaments which stretch on beating, incorporate air in minute bubbles then set to form a fairly stable puffed-up structure expanding to seven times its bulk.

Top: large vacherin; foreground: small vacherin and examples of presenting meringues

128 · **Meringue with whipped cream** *Meringue Chantilly*

1 Allow two meringues per portion.
2 Join together with a little sweetened, vanilla-flavoured whipped cream, or non-dairy cream.
3 Decorate with whipped cream, glacé cherries and angelica, or crystallized violets or roses.

129 · Meringue with strawberries and cream *Vacherin aux fraises*

A vacherin is a round meringue shell piped into a suitable shape so that the centre may be filled with sufficient strawberries, stoned cherries, peaches, apricots etc. and whipped cream to form a rich sweet.

The vacherin may be prepared in one, two, four or larger portion sizes.

		4 egg whites
200 g	8 oz	castor sugar
100–300 g	¼–¾ lb	strawberries (picked and washed)
125 ml	¼ pt	cream (whipped and sweetened) or non-dairy cream

1. Stiffly whip the egg whites.
2. Carefully fold in the sugar.
3. Place the mixture into a piping bag with a 1 cm (½ in) plain tube.
4. Pipe on to silicone paper on a baking sheet.
5. Start from the centre and pipe round in a circular fashion to form a base 16 cm (6 in) then pipe around the edge so as to form approx. 2–3 cm (1–1½ in) high.
6. Bake in a cool oven (110 °C, Reg. ¼) until the meringue case is completely dry. Do not allow to colour.
7. Allow a meringue case to cool then remove from the paper.
8. Spread a thin layer of cream on the base. Add the strawberries.
9. Decorate with the remainder of the cream.

Note a) Melba sauce (recipe 183) may be used to coat the strawberries before decorating with cream.
b) Refer to recipe 127, points *a–d* before whipping the egg whites.

4 portions

130 · Meringue with raspberries and whipped cream *Vacherin aux framboises*

Proceed as in recipe 129 using raspberries in place of strawberries.

Illustrated on page 451.

4 portions

131 · Jam omelette *Omelette à la confiture*

1. Allow 2–3 eggs per portion. Break the eggs into a basin.
2. Beat well with a fork or whisk until the yolks and whites are thoroughly combined and no streaks of white can be seen.
3. Heat the omelette pan. Wipe thoroughly clean with a dry cloth.

Using 2 eggs, hard margarine
1 portion provides:

300 kcals/1260 kJ
20.1 g fat of which 7.4 g saturated
17.3 g carbohydrate of which 17.3 g sugars
13.7 g protein
0.3 g fibre

4 Add 10 g (½ oz) butter or oil. Heat until foaming but not brown.
5 Add the eggs and cook quickly, keeping the mixture moving with a fork until lightly set.
6 Remove from the heat. Add 1 tablespoon warmed jam.
7 Half fold the mixture over at right-angles to the handle.
8 Tap the bottom of the pan to bring up the edge of the omelette.
9 Tilt the pan completely over the serving dish or plate so as to allow the omelette to fall carefully into the centre of the dish.
10 Neaten the shape if necessary. Sprinkle liberally with icing sugar.
11 Brand criss-cross pattern with a red-hot poker or branding iron to caramelise the sugar.

Using 3 eggs, hard margarine
1 portion provides:

381 kcals/1599 kJ
26.1 g fat of which 9.4 g saturated
17.3 g carbohydrate of which 17.3 g sugars
20.5 g protein
0.3 g fibre

(The service of this dish is illustrated on page 175.)

Milk Puddings

132 Baked rice pudding *Pouding de riz*

100 g	4 oz	rice (short or wholegrain)
50 g	2 oz	sugar, castor or unrefined
½ litre	1 pt	milk, whole or skimmed
10 g	½ oz	butter or margarine
		2–3 drops vanilla essence
		grated nutmeg

Using whole milk, hard margarine
1 portion provides:

239 kcals/1006 kJ
7.0 g fat of which 3.9 g saturated
40.7 g carbohydrate of which 19.0 g sugars
5.8 g protein
0.6 g fibre

1 Wash the rice, place in a pie dish.
2 Add the sugar and milk, mix well.
3 Add the butter, essence and nutmeg.
4 Place on a baking sheet, clean the rim of the pie dish.
5 Bake at 180–200 °C, Reg. 4–6, until the milk starts simmering.
6 Reduce the heat and allow the pudding to cook slowly, allowing approx. 1½–2 hr in all.

4 portions

133 Rice pudding

Ingredients as for baked rice pudding.
1 Boil the milk in a thick-bottomed pan.
2 Add the washed rice, stir to the boil.
3 Simmer gently, stirring frequently until the rice is cooked.
4 Mix in the sugar, flavouring and butter (at this stage an egg yolk may also be added). A vanilla pod can be used in place of essence.
5 Pour into a pie dish, place on a baking tray and brown lightly under the salamander.

134 · Semolina pudding

½ litre	1 pt	milk, whole or skimmed
35 g	1½ oz	semolina
50 g	2 oz	sugar, castor or unrefined
10 g	½ oz	butter or margarine
		2–3 drops lemon juice or lemon essence

Using whole milk, hard margarine
1 portion provides:

179 kcals/753 kJ
6.9 g fat of which 3.9 g saturated
25.8 g carbohydrate of which 19.0 g sugars
5.1 g protein
0.3 g fibre

1 Boil the milk in a thick-bottomed pan.
2 Sprinkle in the semolina and stir to the boil.
3 Simmer 15–20 min.
4 Add the sugar, butter flavouring (an egg yolk if desired).
5 Pour into a pie dish. Brown under the salamander.

4 portions

135 · Sago pudding

136 · Tapioca pudding

137 · Ground rice pudding

These are made in the same way as for semolina pudding using sago, tapioca or ground rice in place of semolina and vanilla essence instead of lemon essence.

138 · Empress rice *Riz à l'impératrice*

125 ml	¼ pt	red jelly
½ litre	1 pt	milk, whole or skimmed
50 g	2 oz	rice (short or wholegrain)
75 g	3 oz	sugar, castor or unrefined
		3–4 drops vanilla essence or a vanilla pod
25 g	1 oz	gelatine
25 g	1 oz	angelica
25 g	1 oz	glacé cherries
125 ml	¼ pt	lightly whipped cream or non-dairy cream
		2 egg whites

1 Prepare the jelly and pour into the bottom of a charlotte mould, leave to set.
2 Boil the milk, add the washed rice, simmer until tender.
3 Mix in the sugar, essence (or vanilla pod), gelatine (if leaf gelatine is used soak in cold water) and diced angelica and cherries (which may be soaked in kirsch or maraschino).
4 Allow to cool, stirring occasionally.
5 When setting point is almost reached fold in the whipped cream and stiffly beaten egg whites and pour into the mould.
6 Leave to set in the refrigerator. Turn out carefully and serve.

4 portions

139 · Bread and butter pudding

25 g	1 oz	sultanas
		2 slices of white or wholemeal bread, spread with butter or margarine
		3 eggs
50 g	2 oz	sugar, castor or unrefined
		2–3 drops vanilla essence or a vanilla pod
½ litre	1 pt	milk, whole or skimmed

Using white bread, butter
1 portion provides:

260 kcals/1093 kJ
11.6 g fat of which 5.9 g saturated
30.4 g carbohydrate of which 23.4 g sugars
10.6 g protein
1.0 g fibre

Service of bread and butter pudding

1. Wash the sultanas and place in a pie dish.
2. Remove the crusts from the bread and cut each slice into four triangles, neatly arrange overlapping in the pie dish.
3. Prepare an egg custard as in recipe 140.
4. Strain on to the bread, dust lightly with sugar.
5. Cook and serve as for baked egg custard.

4 portions

140 · Baked egg custard

		3 small eggs
50 g	2 oz	sugar, castor or unrefined
		2–3 drops vanilla essence
½ litre	1 pt	milk, whole or skimmed
		grated nutmeg

1. Whisk the eggs, sugar and essence.
2. Pour on the warmed milk, whisking continuously.
3. Pass through a fine strainer into a pie dish.
4. Add a little grated nutmeg. Wipe the edge of the pie dish clean.
5. Stand in a roasting tray half full of water and cook slowly in a moderate oven at 160 °C, Reg. 3, approx. 45 min to 1 hr.
6. Clean the edges of the pie dish and serve.

Using whole milk
1 portion provides:

186 kcals/780 kJ
8.4 g fat of which 4.3 g saturated
19.0 g carbohydrate of which 19.0 g sugars
8.7 g protein
0.0 g fibre

4 portions

141 Pear Condé *Poire Condé*

75 g	3 oz	rice (short or wholegrain)
½ litre	1 pt	milk, whole or skimmed
50 g	2 oz	sugar, castor or unrefined
		3–4 drops vanilla essence or a vanilla pod
		2 dessert pears
125 ml	¼ pt	apricot glaze
10 g	½ oz	angelica
		2 glacé cherries

Using whole milk
1 portion provides:

309 kcals/1299 kJ
4.9 g fat of which 3.1 g saturated
64.5 g carbohydrate of which 48.3 g sugars
5.7 g protein
2.4 g fibre

1 Cook the rice in the milk, sweeten and flavour. Allow to cool.
2 Peel, core and halve the pears and poach them carefully, leave to cool.
3 Dress the rice either in a glass bowl or on a silver flat dish.
4 Drain the pears and neatly arrange them on top.
5 Coat with apricot glaze. Decorate with angelica and cherries.

Many other fruits may be prepared as a Condé, e.g. banana, pineapple, peach. The rice can be enriched with 10 g (½ oz) butter or margarine and an egg yolk.

4 portions

142 Pineapple créole *Ananas créole*

60 g	2½ oz	rice (short or wholegrain)
½ litre	1 pt	milk, whole or skimmed
50 g	2 oz	sugar, castor or unrefined
		3–4 drops vanilla essence or a vanilla pod
25 g	1 oz	currants
		4 rings pineapple (if fresh, poach in syrup)
125 ml	¼ pt	apricot glaze
50 g	2 oz	angelica

1 Cook the rice in the milk, sweeten and flavour. Allow to cool.
2 Dress the rice in the shape of half a pineapple on a flat dish.
3 Mark the rice with a knife in small diamonds and add a currant in each space.
4 Drain the pineapple and arrange in half slices around the dish.
5 Coat the rice and fruit with warmed apricot glaze (which may be flavoured with kirsch).
6 Decorate the top with the angelica, cut in long thin strips to represent pineapple leaves.

The rice may be enriched as in recipe 133.

4 portions

143 Bread pudding

½ kg	1 lb	stale white or wholemeal bread
125 g	5 oz	sugar, castor or unrefined
125 g	5 oz	currants or sultanas
		½ teaspn mixed spice
75 g	3 oz	margarine
		1 egg

1 Soak the bread in cold water until soft.
2 Squeeze bread dry and place in a bowl.
3 Mix in 100 g sugar and rest of ingredients.
4 Place in a greased baking tray. Sprinkle with 25 g sugar.
5 Bake at 180 °C, Reg. 4, for approx. 1 hr.

144 Cabinet pudding *Pouding cabinet*

100 g	4 oz	plain sponge cake
25 g	1 oz	glacé cherries
25 g	1 oz	currants and sultanas
10 g	½ oz	angelica
½ litre	1 pt	milk, whole or skimmed
		3–4 eggs
50 g	2 oz	castor or unrefined sugar
		2–3 drops vanilla essence or a vanilla pod

Using whole milk, 3 eggs
1 portion provides:

340 kcals/1427 kJ
15.8 g fat of which 7.2 g saturated
40.9 g carbohydrate of which 35.5 g sugars
11.0 g protein
0.7 g fibre

Using whole milk, 4 eggs
1 portion provides:

360 kcals/1512 kJ
17.3 g fat of which 7.7 g saturated
40.9 g carbohydrate of which 35.5 g sugars
12.7 g protein
0.7 g fibre

1 Cut the cake into ½ cm (¼ in) dice.
2 Mix with the chopped cherries and fruits (which can be soaked in rum).
3 Place in a greased, sugared charlotte mould or four dariole moulds. Do not fill more than half-way.
4 Warm the milk and whisk on to the eggs, sugar and essence (or vanilla pod).
5 Strain on to the mould.
6 Place in a roasting tin, half full of water, allow to stand for 5–10 min.
7 Cook in a moderate oven (150–160 °C) approx. 30–45 min.
8 Leave to set for a few minutes before turning out.
9 Serve a fresh egg custard or hot apricot sauce separately.

145 Diplomat pudding *Pouding diplomate*

As for cabinet pudding, but served cold with redcurrant, raspberry, apricot or vanilla sauce.

146 · Cream caramel *Crème caramel*

100 g	4 oz	sugar, granulated or cube	*caramel*
125 ml	¼ pt	water	*caramel*
½ litre	1 pt	milk, whole or skimmed	
		4 eggs	
50 g	2 oz	sugar, castor or unrefined	
		3–4 drops vanilla essence or a vanilla pod	

Using whole milk
1 portion provides:

207 kcals/868 kJ
7.2 g fat of which 3.3 g saturated
30.2 g carbohydrate of which 30.2 g sugars
7.3 g protein
0.0 g fibre

1 Prepare the caramel by placing three-quarters of the water in a thick-bottomed pan, adding the sugar and allowing to boil gently, without shaking or stirring the pan.
2 When the sugar has cooked to a golden brown caramel colour, add the remaining quarter of the water, re-boil until the sugar and water mix, then pour into the bottom of six dariole moulds.
3 Prepare the cream by warming the milk and whisking on to the beaten eggs, sugar and essence (or vanilla pod).
4 Strain and pour into the prepared moulds.
5 Place in a roasting tin half full of water.
6 Cook in a moderate oven (150–160 °C, Reg. 2–3) approx. 30–40 min.
7 When thoroughly cold, loosen the edges of the cream caramel with the fingers, shake firmly to loosen and turn out on to a flat dish or plates.
8 Pour any caramel remaining in the mould around the creams.

6 portions

Cream caramels (with copper sugar boiler and dariol moulds)

147 · Bavarois (basic recipe)

10 g	½ oz	gelatine
		2 eggs, separated
50 g	2 oz	castor sugar
¼ litre	½ pt	milk, whole or skimmed
125 ml	¼ pt	whipping or double cream or non-dairy cream

Using whole milk, whipping cream
1 portion provides:

231 kcals/970 kJ
18.2 g fat of which 10.9 g saturated
11.8 g carbohydrate of which 11.8 g sugars
5.8 g protein
0.0 g fibre

1 If using leaf gelatine, soak in cold water.
2 Cream the yolks and sugar in a bowl until almost white.
3 Whisk on the milk which has been brought to the boil, mix well.
4 Clean the milk saucepan which should be a thick-bottomed one, and return the mixture to it.
5 Return to a low heat and stir continuously with a wooden spoon until the mixture coats the back of the spoon. The mixture must not boil.
6 Remove from the heat, add the gelatine, stir until dissolved.
7 Pass through a fine strainer into a clean bowl, leave in a cool place, stirring occasionally until almost setting point.
8 Then fold in the lightly beaten cream.
9 Fold in the stiffly beaten whites.
10 Pour the mixture into a mould (may be very lightly greased with oil).
11 Allow to set in the refrigerator.
12 Shake and turn out on to a flat dish.

Bavarois may be decorated with sweetened, flavoured whipped cream.

6–8 portions

148 · Orange bavarois *Bavarois à l'orange*

Add grated zest and juice of 2 oranges and 1 or 2 drops orange colour to the mixture, and increase the gelatine by 2 leaves. Decorate with blanched, fine julienne of orange zest, orange segments and whipped cream.

Orange bavarois

149 · **Vanilla bavarois** *Bavarois vanille*

Add a vanilla pod or a few drops of vanilla essence to the milk. Decorate with vanilla-flavoured cream.

150 · **Coffee bavarois** *Bavarois au café*

Proceed as for bavarois with the addition of coffee essence to taste.

151 · **Lemon bavarois** *Bavarois au citron*

As orange bavarois using lemons in place of oranges.

152 · **Lime bavarois** *Bavarois au limon*

As orange bavarois using limes in place of oranges.

153 · **Chocolate bavarois** *Bavarois au chocolat*

Dissolve 50 g (2 oz) chocolate couverture in the milk. Decorate with whipped cream and grated chocolate.

154 · **Strawberry bavarois** *Bavarois aux fraises*

155 · **Raspberry bavarois** *Bavarois aux framboises*

200 g	½ lb	fruit (picked, washed and sieved) yield 60 ml (⅛ pt) of fruit purée
		2 eggs
10 g	½ oz	gelatine
180 ml	⅜ pt	milk, whole or skimmed
50 g	2 oz	sugar, castor or unrefined
125 ml	¼ pt	whipping or double cream or non-dairy cream

Prepare as for the basic recipe (recipe 147). When the custard is almost cool add the fruit purée. Decorate with whole fruit and whipped cream.

4 portions

156 · **Charlotte russe**

A charlotte russe is a vanilla bavarois (recipe 149) set in a charlotte mould which has been lined with sponge fingers (biscuits à la cuillère, recipe 25, page 470). The bottom of the charlotte mould should be lined with fan shaped pieces of finger biscuit. If, in place of fan shaped biscuit, ½ cm (¼ in) of red jelly is used, the charlotte is called charlotte moscovite.

1 Prepare and cook the finger biscuits.
2 Remove on to a cooling grid.

3 Prepare the bavarois.
4 While the bavarois is setting line the bottom of the charlotte mould by either method described in point 5.
5 Trim sufficient biscuits into fan shaped pieces of a length half the diameter of the base of the mould and neatly arrange in the bottom of the mould round side down, *or* pour in sufficient red jelly for a thickness of ½ cm (¼ in).
6 Neatly line the sides of the mould with trimmed finger biscuits, round sides facing outwards (if using a red jelly base, allow this to set first).
7 Pour the bavarois mixture into the lined mould at the last possible moment before setting point is reached.
8 Place the charlotte in the refrigerator to set.
9 To serve, trim any biscuit end which may project above the mould.
10 Carefully turn the charlotte out on to a serving dish (if red jelly base is used dip the bottom of the mould into boiling water for 2–3 seconds, wipe dry and turn out).
11 Decorate the charlotte with whipped sweetened cream (crème Chantilly).

Using whole milk, whipping cream
1 portion provides:

483 kcals/2029 kJ
29.7 g fat of which 16.9 g saturated
44.5 g carbohydrate of which 31.8 g sugars
12.3 g protein
0.6 g fibre

157 White chocolate mousse

125 ml	¼ pt	milk, whole or skimmed
		1 orange, grated zest
150 g	6 oz	white chocolate
		2 eggs
25 g	1 oz	castor sugar
6 g	¼ oz	leaf gelatine
250 ml	½ pt	whipping cream, fromage frais or natural yoghurt

1 Heat the milk to boiling point with the grated zest of the orange.
2 Add the white chocolate and melt. Stir well, away from the heat.
3 Whisk the eggs and sugar together, add the hot milk and return to the sauce pan.
4 Stir on the side of the stove until the mixture coats the back of a spoon but do not boil. Remove from the heat.
5 Add the soaked and squeezed gelatine and bring down to setting point.
6 Fold in the whipped cream or alternative. Carefully and immediately pour into mould.
7 Turn out and use as required.

The mousse can be prepared in individual moulds, turned out onto plates, topped with poached fruit (eg pears, peaches, apricots) or fresh berries (eg loganberries, raspberries, strawberries). It can be coated with a suitable sauce (lemon, orange, lime, strawberry, Grand Marnier, grenadine).

158 · Avocado mousse with poached pear and strawberry sauce

250 ml	½ pt	avocado purée
		½ lemon, juice of
50 g	2 oz	icing sugar
12 g	½ oz	leaf gelatine
125 ml	¼ pt	whipped cream, fromage frais or natural yoghurt
		4 halves poached pear

1 Add the lemon juice to the avocado purée.
2 Mix in the icing sugar.
3 Place the soaked and lightly squeezed gelatine into a small pan. Heat gently until it starts to boil.
4 Carefully add the gelatine to the purée, stirring well.
5 When setting point is reached, carefully fold in the whipped cream or alternative.
6 Pour into individual moulds and place in the refrigerator to set.
7 When set, turn out onto plates and garnish each with half a poached pear carefully fanned.
8 Mask with strawberry sauce.

Strawberry sauce

125 ml	¼ pt	strawberry purée
125 ml	¼ pt	white wine
50 g	2 oz	castor sugar

Mix all the ingredients together and strain.

Alternative fruit purées that can be used in the mousse are peach, apricot, mango, paw paw, strawberry and raspberry.

Alternative sauces include raspberry, peach, apricot, lemon, orange and lime.

Ice-cream

The Ice-cream Regulations 1959 and 1963 require ice-cream to be pasteurised by heating to:

65 °C (150 °F) for 30 minutes or
71 °C (160 °F) for 10 minutes or
80 °C (175 °F) for 15 seconds or
149 °C (300 °F) for 2 seconds (sterilised).

After heat treatment the mixture is reduced to 7.1 °C (45 °F) within 1½ hours and kept at this temperature until the freezing process begins. Ice-cream needs this treatment so as to kill harmful bacteria. Freezing without correct heat treatment does not kill bacteria, it allows them to remain dormant. The storage temperature for ice-cream should not exceed −2 °C. All establishments making ice-cream for sale must be licensed by the local authority Environmental Health Officer.

159 · Vanilla ice-cream *Glace vanille*

		4 egg yolks
100 g	4 oz	castor or unrefined sugar
		vanilla pod or essence
375 ml	¾ pt	milk, whole or skimmed
125 ml	¼ pt	cream or non-dairy cream

Using whole milk, single cream
1 portion provides:

147 kcals/616 kJ
8.1 g fat of which 4.2 g saturated
15.8 g carbohydrate of which 15.8 g sugars
3.5 g protein
0.0 g fibre

1 Whisk the yolks and sugar in a bowl until almost white.
2 Boil the milk with the vanilla pod or essence in a thick-bottomed pan.
3 Whisk on to the eggs, add sugar, mix well.
4 Return to the cleaned saucepan, place on a low heat.
5 Stir continuously with a wooden spoon until the mixture coats the back of the spoon.
6 Pass through a fine strainer into a bowl.
7 Freeze in an ice-cream machine, gradually adding the cream.

8 portions

160 · Coffee ice-cream *Glace au café*

Add coffee essence to taste to the custard after it is cooked.

161 · Chocolate ice-cream *Glace au chocolat*

Add 50–100 g (2–4 oz) of chopped couverture to the milk before boiling.

162 · Strawberry ice-cream *Glace à la fraise*

Add 125 ml (¼ pt) of strawberry pulp in place of 125 ml (¼ pt) of milk. The pulp is added after the custard is cooked.

163 Meringue and ice-cream *Meringue glacée Chantilly*

1 Allow 2 meringues per portion.
2 Join together with a small ball of vanilla ice-cream.
3 Serve in a coupe or ice-cream dish.
4 Decorate with whipped cream.

164 Mixed ice-cream

Balls or spoonfuls of two or more flavoured ice-creams served in individual coupes.

165 Fruit Melba (peach, pear, banana, etc.)

Peach Melba Pêche Melba

		2 peaches
125 ml	¼ pt	vanilla ice-cream
125 ml	¼ pt	Melba sauce (page 528)

1 portion provides:

145 kcals/607 kJ
2.6 g fat of which 1.3 g saturated
30.5 g carbohydrate of which 30.2 g sugars
1.6 g protein
1.3 g fibre

If using fresh peaches they should be dipped in boiling water for a few seconds, cooled by placing into cold water, peeled and halved.

Dress the fruit on a ball of ice-cream in an ice-cream coupe and coat with Melba sauce. May be decorated with whipped cream.

Fresh pears should be peeled, halved and poached. Bananas should be peeled at the last moment.

166 Pear Belle Helene *Poire Belle Hélène*

Serve a cooked pear on a ball of vanilla ice-cream in a coupe. Decorate with whipped cream. Serve with a sauceboat of hot chocolate sauce (recipe 186).

167 Peach cardinal *Pêche cardinal*

Place half a prepared peach on a ball of strawberry ice-cream in a coupe. Coat with Melba sauce; may be decorated with whipped cream and sprinkled with toasted almonds cut in slices.

168 Coupe Jacques

Place in a coupe some fruit salad, on top arrange one scoop of lemon ice-cream and one of strawberry ice-cream. May be decorated with whipped cream.

Water ices Sorbets

169 **Lemon ice** *Sorbet au citron*

200 g	8 oz	sugar
½ litre	1 pt	water
		2 lemons
		1 egg white

1 portion provides:
100 kcals/421 kJ
0.0 g fat of which 0.0 g saturated
26.3 g carbohydrate of which 26.3 g sugars
0.4 g protein
0.0 g fibre

1 Bring the sugar, water and peeled zest of lemons to the boil.
2 Remove from the heat and cool. The saccarometer reading for the syrup should be 18–20° baumé.
3 Add the juice of the lemon.
4 Add the white and mix well.
5 Pass through a fine strainer and freeze.

8 portions

170 **Orange ice** *Sorbet à l'orange*

200 g	8 oz	sugar
½ litre	1 pt	water
		2 large oranges
		1 lemon
		1 egg white

Prepare and freeze as for lemon ice, 18–20° baumé.

171 **Strawberry ice** *Sorbet à la fraise*

200 g	8 oz	sugar
375 ml	¾ pt	water
		1 lemon
125 ml	¼ pt	strawberry purée
		1 egg white

Prepare and freeze as for lemon ice, 18–20° baumé.

172 **Raspberry ice** *Sorbet à la framboise*

200 g	8 oz	sugar
375 ml	¾ pt	water
		1 lemon
125 ml	¼ pt	raspberry purée
		1 egg white

Prepare and freeze as for lemon ice, 18–20° baumé.

173 **Tutti frutti ice** *Glace tutti frutti*

Lemon and strawberry ice with candied fruits.

Sweet Sauces

¼ litre (½ pt) = 4–8 portions

174 · Jam sauce

200 g	8 oz	jam
100 ml	4 oz	water
		2–3 drops lemon juice
10 g	½ oz	cornflour

1 Boil jam, water and lemon juice together.
2 Adjust the consistency with a little cornflour or arrowroot diluted with water.
3 Re-boil until clear and pass through a conical strainer.

175 · Apricot sauce *Sauce abricot*

200 g	8 oz	apricot jam
100 ml	4 oz	water
		2–3 drops lemon juice
10 g	½ oz	cornflour

Proceed as for jam sauce above.

176 · Orange sauce

50 g	2 oz	sugar, castor or unrefined
250 ml	½ pt	water
10 g	½ oz	cornflour or arrowroot
	1–2	oranges

1 Boil the sugar and water.
2 Add the cornflour diluted with water, stirring continuously.
3 Re-boil till clear, strain.
4 Add blanched julienne of orange zest and the strained orange juice.

177 · Lemon or lime sauce

Proceed as for orange sauce using a lemon or lime in place of the orange.

(An example of the service of lemon sauce is illustrated on page 499.)

178 · Syrup sauce

200 ml	8 oz	syrup
125 ml	¼ pt	water
		juice of 1 lemon
10 g	½ oz	cornflour or arrowroot

Bring the syrup, water and lemon juice to the boil and thicken with diluted cornflour. Boil for a few minutes and strain.

179 · Custard sauce

10 g	½ oz	custard powder
250 ml	½ pt	milk, whole or skimmed
25 g	1 oz	castor or unrefined sugar

Using whole milk
This recipe provides:

296 kcals/1245 kJ
9.6 g fat of which 6.0 g saturated
47.2 g carbohydrate of which 38.0 g sugars
8.3 g protein
0.3 g fibre

Custard sauce (served with sultana sponge p. 500)

1 Dilute the custard powder with a little of the milk.
2 Boil the remainder of the milk.
3 Pour a little of the boiled milk on to the diluted custard powder.
4 Return to the saucepan.
5 Stir to the boil and mix in the sugar.

See also recipe 187 .

180 · Almond sauce

10 g	½ oz	cornflour
250 ml	½ pt	milk, whole or skimmed
25 g	1 oz	castor or unrefined sugar
		few drops almond essence

1 Dilute the cornflour with a little of the milk.
2 Boil remainder of the milk. Whisk on to the cornflour.
3 Return to the pan, stir to the boil. Simmer 3–4 min.
4 Mix in the sugar and essence. Pass through a strainer.

181 · Rum or brandy cream

Whipped, sweetened, cream flavoured with rum or brandy.

182 · Rum or brandy butter

Cream equal quantities of butter and sieved icing sugar together and add rum or brandy to taste.

183 Melba sauce *Sauce Melba*

Method I

400 g	1 lb	raspberry jam
125 ml	¼ pt	water

Boil together and pass through a conical strainer.

Method II

400 g	1 lb	raspberries
125 ml	¼ pt	water
100 g	4 oz	sugar, castor or unrefined

Boil ingredients together, cool, liquidise and strain.

Method III

400 g	1 lb	raspberries
200 g	8 oz	icing sugar

Liquidise, pass through a fine sieve and add a little lemon juice.

Note Methods II and III are also known as raspberry cullis – *coulis de framboises.*

184 Sabayon sauce *Sauce sabayon*

		4 egg yolks
100 g	4 oz	castor or unrefined sugar
¼ litre	½ pt	dry white wine

1 Whisk egg yolks and sugar in a 1 litre (2 pt) pan or basin until white.
2 Dilute with the wine.
3 Place pan or basin in a bain-marie of warm water.
4 Whisk mixture continuously until it increases to 4 times its bulk and is firm and frothy.

Sauce sabayon may be offered as an accompaniment to any suitable hot sweet, e.g. pudding soufflé.

Note A sauce sabayon may also be made using milk in place of wine which can be flavoured according to taste, e.g. vanilla, nutmeg, cinnamon.

8 portions

185 · Sabayon with Marsala *Zabaglione alla Marsala*

		8 egg yolks
200 g	8 oz	castor or unrefined sugar
150 ml	⅛ pt	Marsala

1 Whisk egg yolks and sugar in a bowl until almost white.
2 Mix in the Marsala.
3 Place the bowl and contents in a bain-marie of warm water.
4 Whisk mixture continuously until it increases to 4 times its bulk and is firm and frothy.
5 Pour the mixture into glass goblets.
6 Accompany with a suitable biscuit, e.g. sponge finger.

4 portions

186 · Chocolate sauce *Sauce chocolat*

10 g	½ oz	cornflour
250 ml	½ pt	milk
10 g	½ oz	cocoa powder or
25 g	1 oz	chocolate (block)
65 g	1½ oz	sugar
5 g	¼ oz	butter

With cocoa

1 Dilute the cornflour with a little of the milk, mix in the cocoa.
2 Boil the remainder of the milk.
3 Pour a little of the milk on to the cornflour.
4 Return to the saucepan.
5 Stir to the boil.
6 Mix in the sugar and butter.

With chocolate

Shred the chocolate, add to the milk and proceed as above, omitting the cocoa.

187 · Fresh egg custard sauce *Sauce à l'anglaise*

		2 egg yolks (4 if using skimmed milk)
25 g	1 oz	castor or unrefined sugar
		2–3 drops vanilla essence or vanilla pod
250 ml	½ pt	milk, whole or skimmed

Using whole milk
This recipe provides:

397 kcals/1666 kJ
21.7 g fat of which 9.9 g saturated
38.0 g carbohydrate of which 38.0 g sugars
14.7 g protein
0.0 g fibre

1 Mix yolks, sugar and essence in a basin.
2 Whisk on the boiled milk and return to a thick-bottomed pan.
3 Place on a low heat and stir with a wooden spoon till it coats the back of the spoon. Do *not* allow to boil or the eggs will scramble.

188 · Pastry cream *Crème pâtissière*

		2 eggs
100 g	4 oz	castor or unrefined sugar
50 g	2 oz	flour, white or wholemeal
10 g	½ oz	custard powder
½ litre	1 pt	milk, whole or skimmed
		vanilla pod or essence

Using white flour, whole milk
This recipe provides:

1087 kcals/4564 kJ
31.7 g fat of which 16.0 g saturated
176.6 g carbohydrate of which 129.3 g sugars
34.8 g protein
2.1 g fibre

1 Whisk the eggs and sugar in a bowl until almost white.
2 Mix in the flour and custard powder.
3 Boil the milk in a thick-bottomed pan.
4 Whisk on to the eggs, sugar and flour and mix well.
5 Return to the cleaned pan, stir to the boil.
6 Add a few drops of vanilla essence or a vanilla pod.
7 Remove from the heat and pour into a basin.
8 Sprinkle the top with a little castor or icing sugar to prevent a skin forming.

189 · Chocolate pastry cream

Dissolve 100 g (4 oz) of couverture or 50 g (2 oz) cocoa powder in the milk and proceed as recipe 188.

190 · Coffee pastry cream

Add coffee essence to taste and proceed as recipe 188.

191 · Boiled butter cream

		2 No. 2 grade eggs
50 g	2 oz	icing sugar
300 g	12 oz	granulated sugar or cube sugar
100 g	4 oz	water
50 g	2 oz	glucose
400 g	1 lb	unsalted butter

1 Beat eggs and icing sugar until ribbon stage (sponge).
2 Boil granulated or cube sugar with water and glucose to 118 °C (245 °F).
3 Gradually add the sugar at 118 °C to the eggs and icing sugar at ribbon stage, whisk continuously and allow to cool to 26 °C (80 °F).
4 Gradually add the unsalted butter while continuing to whisk until a smooth cream is obtained.

192 · Butter cream

150 g	6 oz	icing sugar
200 g	8 oz	butter

1 Sieve the icing sugar.
2 Cream the butter and icing sugar until light and creamy.
3 Flavour and colour as required.

193 · Rum butter cream

Add rum to flavour and blend in.

194 · Chocolate butter cream

Add melted chocolate, sweetened or unsweetened according to taste.

195 · Christmas pudding

100 g	4 oz	chopped suet
50 g	2 oz	flour, white or wholemeal
100 g	4 oz	stoned raisins
100 g	4 oz	sultanas
50 g	2 oz	mixed peel
50 g	2 oz	currants
5 g	¼ oz	nutmeg
5 g	¼ oz	mixed spice
100 g	4 oz	barbados sugar
100 g	4 oz	breadcrumbs, white or wholemeal
25 g	1 oz	ground almonds
60 ml	⅛ oz	milk, whole or skimmed
		pinch of salt
		2 eggs
		wineglass of stout
		½ wineglass brandy
		½ lemon grated zest and juice
		½ orange grated zest and juice

Using white flour, whole milk
1 portion provides:

485 kcals/2037 kJ
19.6 g fat of which 8.0 g saturated
68.7 g carbohydrate of which 51.4 g sugars
6.4 g protein
4.8 g fibre

1 Mix all the dry ingredients together.
2 Add the liquid and mix well.
3 Leave in a cool place for 3–4 days.
4 Place into greased basins, cover with greased greaseproof paper and steam for 6–8 hr.
5 Serve with rum or brandy cream, rum or brandy butter or custard.

6 portions

196 Christmas cake

400 g	1 lb	butter or margarine
400 g	1 lb	demerara sugar
		10 eggs
		mixed spice
400 g	1 lb	currants
200 g	8 oz	raisins
100 g	4 oz	glacé cherries
400 g	1 lb	sultanas
200 g	8 oz	mixed peel
		glass of brandy or rum
		2 teaspns glycerine
100 g	4 oz	chopped almonds
100 g	4 oz	ground almonds
600 g	1 lb 8 oz	flour (soft)

Using hard margarine
This recipe provides:

11647 kcals/48917 kJ
499.2 g fat of which 171.1 g saturated
1704.2 g carbohydrate of which
1243.4 g sugars
178.6 g protein
120.4 g fibre

1. Cream butter and sugar until light and fluffy.
2. Gradually beat in the eggs, creaming continuously.
3. Mix in spice, fruit, brandy, glycerine and chopped almonds.
4. Fold in ground almonds and flour.
5. Correct consistency with milk if necessary.
6. Line a 24–30 cm (10–12 in) cake tin with silicone paper.
7. Add the mixture, spread evenly.
8. Bake at 160 °C, Reg. 3, for 1½ hours.
9. Reduce heat to 150 °C, Reg. 2, for a further 1½ hours.
10. Reduce heat to 140 °C, Reg. 1, until cooked, approximately ½ to 1 hour.
11. Insert a fine trussing needle or skewer into the centre of the cake, when cooked it should come out clean and free of uncooked mixture.
12. Remove from oven.
13. Allow to set approximately 15 minutes.
14. Remove tin and paper. Allow to cool.
15. Brush with boiling apricot glaze.
16. Cover the side and top with marzipan.
17. Coat with royal icing and decorate.

197 · Marzipan or almond paste

Raw

400 g	1 lb	ground almonds
600 g	1 lb 8 oz	icing sugar
		3–4 yolks
		vanilla

Sift the almonds and sugar, make a well and add the egg yolks and flavouring. Knead well.

Cooked

250 ml	½ pt	water
1 kg	2 lb	castor sugar
400 g	1 lb	ground almonds
		3 yolks
		almond essence

Place the water and sugar in a pan and boil. Skim. When the sugar reaches 116 °C draw aside and mix in the almonds, then add the yolks and essence and mix in quickly to avoid scrambling. Knead well until smooth.

198 · Royal icing

400 g	1 lb	icing sugar
		3 whites of egg
		juice of lemon
		2 dessertspoons glycerine

Mix well together in a basin the sieved icing sugar and the whites of egg, with a wooden spoon. Add a few drops of lemon juice and glycerine and beat till stiff.

199 · Mincemeat

100 g	4 oz	suet (chopped)
100 g	4 oz	mixed peel (chopped)
100 g	4 oz	currants
100 g	4 oz	sultanas
100 g	4 oz	raisins
100 g	4 oz	apples (chopped)
100 g	4 oz	barbados sugar
5 g	¼ oz	mixed spice
		1 lemon grated zest and juice
		1 orange grated zest and juice
		½ wineglass rum
		½ wineglass brandy

Mix the ingredients together, place in jars and use as required.

200 · Petits fours

These are an assortment of small biscuits, cakes and sweets served with coffee after special meals. There is a wide variety of items that can be prepared and when serving petits fours as large an assortment as possible should be offered.

Basically petits fours fall into two categories – dry and glazed. Dry includes all manner of biscuits, macaroons, meringue and marzipan items.

Glazed includes fruits dipped in sugar, fondants, chocolates, sweets, and small pieces of neatly cut genoese sponge covered in fondant.

Dry petits fours

201 · Cats tongues *Langues de chat*

125 g	5 oz	icing sugar
100 g	4 oz	butter
		vanilla essence
		3–4 egg whites
100 g	4 oz	soft flour

1 Lightly cream sugar and butter, add 3–4 drops of vanilla essence.
2 Add egg whites one by one, continually mixing and being careful not to allow the mixture to curdle.
3 Gently fold in the sifted flour and mix lightly.
4 Pipe on to a lightly greased baking sheet using a 3 mm (1/8 in) plain tube, 2½ cm (1 in) apart.
5 Bake at 230–250 °C, Reg. 8–9, for a few minutes.
6 The outside edges should be light brown and the centres yellow.
7 When cooked, remove on to a cooling rack using a palette knife.

202 · Cornets *Cornets*

1 Ingredients and method to stage 3 as for cats tongues, recipe 201.
2 Using a 3 mm (1/8 in) plain tube, pipe out the mixture onto a lightly greased baking sheet into rounds approx. 2½ cm (1¼ in) in diameter.
3 Bake at 230–250 °C, Reg. 8–9, until the edges turn brown and the centre remains uncoloured.
4 Remove the tray from the oven.
5 Work quickly while the cornets are hot and twist them into a cornet shape using the point of a cream horn mould. (For a tight cornet shape it will be found best to set the pieces tightly inside the cream horn moulds and to leave them until set.)

203 · Piped biscuits *Sablés à la poche*

75 g	3 oz	castor or unrefined sugar
150 g	6 oz	butter or margarine
		1 egg
		vanilla or grated lemon zest
200 g	8 oz	soft flour, white or wholemeal
35 g	1 ½ oz	ground almonds

1. Cream sugar and butter until light in colour and texture.
2. Add egg gradually, beating continuously, add 3–4 drops vanilla or lemon zest.
3. Gently fold in sifted flour and almonds, mix well until suitable for piping.
4. Pipe on to a lightly greased and floured baking sheet using a medium-sized star tube (a variety of shapes can be used).
5. Some can be left plain, some decorated with half almonds or neatly cut pieces of angelica and glacé cherries.
6. Bake in a moderate oven at 190 °C, Reg. 5 for approximately 10 min.
7. When cooked, remove on to a cooling rack using a palette knife.

204 · Almond biscuits

		1 ½ egg whites
100 g	¼ lb	ground almonds
50 g	2 oz	castor or unrefined sugar
		almond essence
		1 sheet rice paper
		glacé cherries and angelica.

This recipe provides:

800 kcals/3361 kJ
53.5 g fat of which 4.2 g saturated
62.4 g carbohydrate of which 62.4 g sugars
21.2 g protein
14.4 g fibre

1. Whisk the egg whites until stiff.
2. Gently stir in the ground almonds, sugar and 3–4 drops almond essence.
3. Place rice paper on a baking sheet.
4. Pipe mixture using a medium star tube into shapes.
5. Decorate with neatly cut diamonds of angelica and glacé cherries.
6. Bake at 180–200 °C, Reg. 4–6, for 10–15 min.
7. Trim with small knife to cut through rice paper and place on to a cooling rack using a palette knife.

205 · Shortbread biscuits

100 g	4 oz	soft flour, white or wholemeal
100 g	4 oz	rice flour
100 g	4 oz	butter or margarine
100 g	4 oz	castor or unrefined sugar
		1 egg (beaten)

1 Sieve the flour and rice flour into a basin.
2 Rub in the butter until the texture of fine breadcrumbs.
3 Mix in the sugar.
4 Bind the mixture to a stiff paste using the beaten egg.
5 Roll out 3 mm (1/8 in) using castor sugar, prick well with a fork and cut into fancy shapes.
6 Place biscuits on a lightly greased baking sheet.
7 Bake in moderate oven at 180–200 °C, Reg. 4–6, until golden brown (approx. 15 min).
8 Remove with a palette knife on to a cooling rack.

(Another recipe is given on page 469.)

206 · Glazed fruits

1 Dates stoned, stuffed with marzipan (left yellow or lightly coloured pink or green) and rolled in castor sugar.

2 Grapes (in pairs left on the stalk
Tangerines in segments } passed through a syrup prepared as follows:

Syrup

400 g	1 lb	sugar
50 g	2 oz	glucose
50 g	2 oz	water
		juice of 1 lemon

1 Boil sugar, glucose and water to 160–165 °C (310–315 °F).
2 Add lemon juice, shake in thoroughly, remove from heat.
3 Pass fruits through this syrup using a fork and place them on to a lightly oiled marble slab to cool and set.

Marzipan (page 533) can be coloured and moulded into a variety of shapes. They can then be either rolled in castor sugar or glazed by dipping in a syrup as in previous recipe.

207 · **Praline** *Praline*

Praline is a basic preparation used for flavouring items such as gâteaux, soufflés, ice-creams and many other sweets.

100 g	4 oz	almonds	peeled
100 g	4 oz	hazelnuts	peeled
60 ml	⅛ pt	water	
200 g	8 oz	sugar	

1 Lightly brown the almonds and hazelnuts in an oven.
2 Cook the water and sugar in copper or thick-bottomed pan until the caramel stage is reached.
3 Remove the pan from the heat.
4 Mix in the nuts.
5 Turn out the mixture on to a lightly oiled marble slab.
6 Allow to become quite cold.
7 Crush to a coarse texture using a rolling pin.
8 Store in an airtight container.

The cooking of sugar

208 · **Boiled sugar**

Sugar is boiled for a number of purposes – in pastry work, bakery and sweet-making. Loaf (lump) sugar is generally used, placed in a copper saucepan or sugar boiler and moistened with sufficient cold water to melt the sugar (approx. ⅛ litre per ¼ kg) and allowed to boil steadily without being stirred. Any scum on the surface should be carefully removed, otherwise the sugar is liable to granulate. Once the water has evaporated the sugar begins to cook and it will be noticed that the bubbling in the pan will be slower. It is now necessary to keep the sides of the pan free from crystallised sugar; this can be done either with the fingers or a piece of damp linen. In either case the fingers or linen should be dipped in ice water or cold water, rubbed round the inside of the pan and then quickly dipped back into the water.

The cooking of the sugar then passes through several stages which may be tested with a special sugar thermometer or by the fingers (dip the fingers into ice water, then into the sugar and quickly back into the ice water).

Note To prevent the granulation of sugar a tablespoon of glucose or a few drops of lemon juice per 400 g (1 lb) may be added before boiling.

Degrees of cooking sugar

Small thread (104 °C)

When a drop of sugar held between thumb and forefinger forms small threads when the finger and thumb are drawn apart. Used for stock syrup.

Large thread (110 °C)

When proceeding as for small thread the threads are more numerous and stronger. Used for crystallising fruits.

Soft ball (116 °C)

Proceeding as above, the sugar rolls into a soft ball. Used for making fondant.

Hard ball (121 °C)

As for soft ball, but the sugar rolls into a firmer ball. Used for making sweets.

Small crack (140°C)

The sugar lying on the finger peels off in the form of a thin pliable film which sticks to the teeth when chewed. Used for meringue.

Large crack (153 °C)

The sugar taken from the end of the fingers when chewed breaks clean in between the teeth, like glass. Used for dipping fruits.

Caramel (176 °C)

Cooking is continued until the sugar is a golden brown colour. Used for crème caramel.

Black-jack

Cooking is continued until the sugar is deeply coloured and almost black. Water is then added and the black sugar is allowed to dissolve over a gentle heat. Used for colouring.

Welsh rarebit (p. 548); devils on horseback (p. 542); Scotch woodcock (p. 547); mushrooms on toast (p. 543)

20

SAVOURIES

General objectives	*Specific objectives*
To know the variety of savouries available and to understand where and how they are served.	To state the preparation, cooking and presentation of each savoury and to demonstrate them at a satisfactory standard.

Service of Savouries

Savouries may be garnished with a sprig of parsley. The crusts should always be removed from the bread, which may be white or wholemeal, and after toasting may be spread with butter or margarine.

Savouries must always be served very hot.

1 · Anchovies on toast

50 g	2 oz	anchovies
10 g	½ oz	butter or margarine
		2 slices toast
		cayenne pepper

Using butter
1 portion provides:

91 kcals/384 kJ
4.8 g fat of which 1.8 g saturated
8.1 g carbohydrate of which 0.5 g sugars
4.5 g protein
0.7 g fibre

Neatly arrange the anchovy fillets on half slices of buttered toast from which the crusts have been removed, reheat slowly under the salamander, sprinkle with a little cayenne pepper.

2 · Angels on horseback *Anges à cheval*

		8 live oysters (removed from the shell)
		4 rashers of streaky bacon (thinly batted out)
		cayenne pepper
		2 slices toast
10 g	½ oz	butter or margarine

1 Wrap each raw oyster in half a rasher of thin streaky bacon.
2 Place on a skewer then on a baking tray.
3 Grill gently on both sides for a few minutes.
4 Sprinkle with cayenne.
5 Cut the trimmed, buttered toast into four neat rectangles.
6 Place two oysters on each and serve.

3 · Toast baron *Croûte baron*

50 g	2 oz	grilling mushrooms
		4 rashers streaky bacon
50 g	2 oz	beef marrow
		2 slices toast
10 g	½ oz	butter or margarine

Using butter
I portion provides:

200 kcals/836 kJ
16.0 g fat of which 7.3 g saturated
7.9 g carbohydrate of which 0.5 g sugars
6.4 g protein
0.9 g fibre

1 Peel and wash the mushrooms. Brush with a little fat.
2 Season lightly with salt. Place on a baking tray.
3 Grill on both sides for a few minutes.
4 Grill the bacon on both sides.
5 Cut the marrow into ½ cm (¼ in) thick slices.
6 Simmer gently in a little stock or water for a few minutes.
7 Remove and drain.
8 Cut and trim the buttered toast into four neat rectangles.
9 Arrange on top of the mushrooms, bacon and marrow.
10 Sprinkle with cayenne and serve.

4 · Devils on horseback *Diables à cheval*

		8 well-soaked or cooked prunes
50 g	2 oz	chopped chutney
		4 rashers streaky bacon (thinly batted out)
10 g	½ oz	butter or margarine
		2 slices toast
		cayenne

Using butter
I portion provides:

179 kcals/754 kJ
9.5 g fat of which 4.3 g saturated
18.1 g carbohydrate of which 10.6 g sugars
6.5 g protein
2.4 g fibre

1 Stone the prunes carefully. Stuff with chutney.
2 Wrap each one in half a thin rasher of bacon.
3 Place on a skewer and on a baking sheet.
4 Grill on both sides under a salamander.
5 On each rectangle of buttered toast place two prunes.
6 Sprinkle with cayenne and serve.

5 · Devilled kidneys on toast

		4 sheep's kidneys
		salt
50 g	2 oz	butter or margarine
125 ml	¼ pt	sauce diable (page 100)
		2 slices toast

Using butter
I portion provides:

188 kcals/791 kJ
12.0 g fat of which 7.1 g saturated
8.9 g carbohydrate of which 0.9 g sugars
11.4 g protein
0.7 g fibre

1 Prepare kidneys as for sauté.
2 Season and quickly fry in (1½ oz) butter in a frying-pan.
3 Drain in a colander.
4 Add to the boiling sauce diable, do not reboil.
5 Mix in and serve on buttered rectangles of toast.

6 · Mushrooms on toast

150 g	6 oz	grilling mushrooms
10 g	½ oz	butter or margarine
		2 slices of toast

1 Peel and wash the mushrooms. Place on a baking tray.
2 Season lightly with salt, brush with melted fat.
3 Gently grill on both sides for a few minutes.
4 Cut and trim the buttered toast into rectangles.
5 Neatly arrange the mushrooms on the toast.
6 Sprinkle with cayenne and serve.

7 · Curried shrimps or prawns on toast

125 ml	¼ pt	curry sauce (page 104)
150 g	6 oz	picked shrimps or prawns (peeled)
		2 slices toast
10 g	½ oz	butter or margarine

1 Boil the curry sauce. Add the shrimps or prawns. Simmer 2–3 min.
2 Dress on rectangles or round-cut pieces of buttered toast and serve.

8 · Curried shrimp bouchées *Bouchée indienne*

150 g	6 oz	picked shrimps (peeled)
125 ml	¼ pt	curry sauce (page 104)
		4 bouchées (3 cm (1½ in) diameter)
25 g	1 oz	chopped chutney

1 Place the shrimps in boiling curry sauce. Simmer 2–3 min.
2 Meanwhile warm the bouchées through in a moderate oven.
3 Fill the bouchées. Place a little chutney on each.
4 Replace the lids and serve.

9 · Fried ham and cheese savoury *Croque monsieur*

		4 slices cooked ham
		8 slices Gruyère cheese
		8 slices thin toast
50 g	2 oz	clarified butter, margarine or sunflower oil

Using butter
1 portion provides:

370 kcals/1554 kJ
23.0 g fat of which 14.1 g saturated
22.8 g carbohydrate of which 2.7 g sugars
19.1 g protein
1.7 g fibre

1 Place each slice of ham between two slices of cheese, then between two slices of lightly toasted bread.
2 Cut out with a round cutter.
3 Gently fry on both sides in clarified butter or oil and serve.

10 · **Toast Derby** *Croûte Derby*

100 g	4 oz	chopped cooked lean ham
125 ml	¼ pt	béchamel
		cayenne pepper
10 g	½ oz	butter or margarine
		2 slices toast
		2 pickled walnuts

Add the ham to the boiling sauce, simmer for 2–3 min, season with a little cayenne, spread on the four rectangles or round-cut pieces of buttered toast. Place half a pickled walnut on each.

11 · **Chopped ham on toast** *Canapé yorkaise*

100 g	4 oz	cooked lean ham
250 ml	½ pt	béchamel
		cayenne
10 g	½ oz	butter or margarine
		2 slices toast

1 Cut eight neat, thin diamonds of ham for decoration.
2 Cut the remainder into small neat dice.
3 Bind with boiling béchamel. Simmer 2–3 min.
4 Season with cayenne.
5 Dress on rectangles or round-cut buttered toast.
6 Place two diamonds of ham on each and serve.

12 · **Curried ham on toast** *Croûte radjah*

100 g	4 oz	chopped cooked lean ham
125 ml	¼ pt	curry sauce (page 104)
10 g	½ oz	butter or margarine
		2 slices toast
25 g	1 oz	chopped chutney

Simmer the ham in the curry sauce for 2–3 min. Dress on buttered rectangles or rounds of toast. Add a little chutney on each and serve.

13 · **Kippers on toast** *Canapé yarmouth*

		2 small kippers
10 g	½ oz	butter or margarine
		2 slices toast
		cayenne

Using hard margarine
1 portion provides:

103 kcals/434 kJ
4.9 g fat of which 1.5 g saturated
8.1 g carbohydrate of which 0.5 g sugars
7.2 g protein
0.7 g fibre

1 Remove all skin and bone from the kippers.
2 Trim into four neat even pieces. Place on a baking tray.
3 Grill gently on both sides for a few minutes.
4 Dress on trimmed rectangles of buttered toast.

5 Sprinkle with cayenne and serve.

The kippers may also be cooked whole, the skin and bone removed, the flesh flaked, then piled on to the toast.

14 · Soft roes on toast

		6 soft roes
10 g	½ oz	butter or margarine
		2 slices toast
		cayenne

1 Pass the roes through seasoned flour.
2 Shake off all surplus flour.
3 Then either shallow fry on both sides in hot fat or grill.
4 Dress on rectangles of buttered toast, sprinkle with cayenne and serve.

15 · Devilled soft roes *Laitances Méphisto*

		4 short pastry barquettes
150 g	6 oz	soft roes (herring)
125 ml	¼ pt	sauce diable (page 100)

The barquettes are warmed through in the oven and filled with the soft roes cooked as in the previous recipe and mixed with sauce diable then served.

16 · Mushroom and soft roes on toast *Canapé quo vadis*

75 g	3 oz	grilling mushrooms
75 g	3 oz	soft roes
10 g	½ oz	butter or margarine
		cayenne

Cook the mushrooms (recipe 6) and soft roes (recipe 14) as indicated and dress neatly on rectangles of buttered toast, sprinkle with cayenne and serve.

17 · Haddock on toast

200 g	8 oz	trimmed smoked haddock fillet
10 g	½ oz	butter or margarine
		2 slices toast
		cayenne

Using hard margarine
1 portion provides:

96 kcals/402 kJ
2.6 g fat of which 1.0 g saturated
8.1 g carbohydrate of which 0.5 g sugars
10.5 g protein
0.7 g fibre

1 Cut and trim the fish into four neat rectangles.
2 Place on a baking tray with a little butter on top.
3 Grill gently on both sides for a few minutes.
4 Place on the trimmed rectangles of buttered toast.
5 Sprinkle with cayenne and serve.

18 · Haddock and bacon on toast

150 g	6 oz	skinned smoked haddock fillet
		4 rashers streaky bacon (thinly batted out)
10 g	½ oz	butter or margarine
		2 slices toast
		cayenne

1 Cut and trim the fish into four neat rectangles.
2 Fold each one in a thin rasher of bacon.
3 Place on a baking tray.
4 Grill gently on both sides for a few minutes.
5 Place on a buttered rectangle of toast.
6 Sprinkle with cayenne and serve.

19 · Smoked haddock on toast *Canapé hollandaise*

200 g	8 oz	smoked haddock fillet
250 ml	½ pt	milk and water (approx.)
10 g	½ oz	butter or margarine
		2 slices toast
		1 hard-boiled egg
		cayenne

1 Poach the fish in the milk and water.
2 Flake into small pieces. Remove any skin.
3 Pile on to rectangles or round-cuts of buttered toast.
4 Place two slices of egg on each.
5 Sprinkle with cayenne and serve.

20 · Creamed haddock and pickled walnut on toast *Canapé Ivanhoë*

200 g	8 oz	smoked haddock fillet
250 ml	½ pt	milk and water (approx.)
125 ml	¼ pt	béchamel
		cayenne
10 g	½ oz	butter or margarine
		2 slices toast
		4 cooked mushrooms or 4 slices pickled walnut

1 Poach the fish in the milk and water. Remove all the skin.
2 Mix in the boiling béchamel. Season with cayenne.
3 Spread on rectangles or round-cuts of buttered toast.
4 Place a mushroom or a slice of pickled walnut on each and serve.

21 · Creamed haddock on toast

Proceed as for Canapé Ivanoë, omitting the mushroom or walnut.

22 · Creamed haddock and cheese on toast *Canapé Ritchie*

Proceed as for Canapé Ivanhoë, omitting the mushroom or walnut. Instead, sprinkle with grated cheese and lightly brown under the salamander.

23 · Chicken liver and bacon on toast *Canapé Diane*

		4 trimmed chicken livers
		4 rashers streaky bacon (thinly batted out)
		cayenne
10 g	½ oz	butter or margarine
		2 slices toast

Using hard margarine
1 portion provides:

173 kcals/728 kJ
10.2 g fat of which 3.9 g saturated
8.4 g carbohydrate of which 0.0 g sugars
12.7 g protein
0.7 g fibre

1 Roll each half liver in half a rasher of thin bacon.
2 Place on a skewer, then on a baking tray.
3 Grill gently on both sides for a few minutes.
4 Sprinkle with cayenne.
5 Cut the trimmed, buttered toast into four rectangles.
6 Place two livers on each and serve.

24 · Scotch woodcock

		2–3 eggs
		salt, pepper
35 g	1½ oz	butter or margarine
		2 slices toast
5 g	¼ oz	anchovy fillets
5 g	¼ oz	capers

Using hard margarine
1 portion provides:

145 kcals/611 kJ
10.6 g fat of which 4.2 g saturated
8.1 g carbohydrate of which 0.5 g sugars
5.1 g protein
0.8 g fibre

1 Break the eggs into a basin. Season with salt and pepper.
2 Thoroughly mix with a fork or whisk.
3 Place 25 g (1 oz) of butter in a small thick-bottomed pan.
4 Allow to melt over a low heat.
5 Add the eggs and cook slowly, stirring continuously until *lightly* scrambled. Remove from the heat.
6 Spread on four rectangles or round-cut pieces of buttered toast.
7 Decorate each with two thin fillets of anchovy and four capers and serve.

Note Adding 1 tablespoon cream or milk when eggs are almost cooked will help prevent overcooking.

25 · Welsh rarebit

25 g •	1 oz	butter or margarine
10 g	½ oz	flour, white or wholemeal
125 ml	¼ pt	milk, whole or skimmed
100 g	4 oz	Cheddar cheese
		1 egg yolk
		4 tablespns beer
		salt, cayenne
		Worcester sauce
		English mustard
10 g	½ oz	butter or margarine
		2 slices toast

Using hard margarine
1 portion provides:

256 kcals/1074 kJ
18.6 g fat of which 9.7 g saturated
11.9 g carbohydrate of which 2.4 g sugars
10.1 g protein
0.7 g fibre

1 Melt the butter or margarine in a thick-bottomed pan.
2 Add the flour and mix in with a wooden spoon.
3 Cook on a gentle heat for a few minutes without colouring.
4 Gradually add the cold milk and mix to a smooth sauce.
5 Allow to simmer for a few minutes.
6 Add the grated or finely sliced cheese.
7 Allow to melt slowly over a gentle heat until a smooth mixture is obtained.
8 Add the yolk to the hot mixture, stir in and immediately remove from the heat.
9 Meanwhile, in a separate pan boil the beer and allow it to reduce to ½ tablespoon.
10 Add to the mixture with the other seasonings.
11 Allow the mixture to cool.
12 Spread on the four rectangles of buttered toast.
13 Place on a baking sheet and brown gently under the salamander and serve.

Note a) Cheese contains a large amount of protein which will become tough and strongly if heated for too long or at too high a temperature.

b) A low-fat Cheddar may be used instead of the traditional full-fat variety.

26 · Buck rarebit

Prepare Welsh rarebit and place a well-drained poached egg on each portion.

27 · Sardines on toast

		8 sardines
10 g	½ oz	butter or margarine
		2 slices toast
		cayenne

1 If the sardines are large enough and firm enough, they should be skinned and boned.
2 Arrange on rectangles of buttered toast.
3 Reheat carefully under the salamander.
4 Sprinkle with cayenne and serve.

28 · **Mushroom, bacon and olive on toast** *Canapé Fédora*

		2 rashers streaky bacon
75 g	3 oz	grilling mushrooms
10 g	½ oz	butter or margarine
		2 slices toast
		4 stoned olives

1 Grill the bacon and mushrooms.
2 Dress neatly on four rectangles of buttered toast.
3 Place an olive on each. Sprinkle with cayenne and serve.

29 · **Mushroom and bacon on toast**

Proceed as for canapé Fédora, but without the olive.

30 · **Mushroom, tomato and pickled walnut on toast** *Canapé Nina*

75 g	3 oz	grilling mushrooms
		2 tomatoes
		2 pickled walnuts
10 g	½ oz	butter or margarine
		2 slices toast
		cayenne

1 Grill the mushrooms.
2 Peel the tomatoes and cut into thick slices.
3 Season and grill gently.
4 Cut the walnuts into thick slices.
5 Dress neatly on rectangles of buttered toast.
6 Sprinkle with cayenne and serve.

31 · **Savoury flan**

Line a 12 cm (6 in) flan-ring with short paste and proceed as in recipe 32, or vary the filling by using lightly fried lardons of bacon (in place of ham), chopped cooked onions and chopped parsley.

A variety of savoury flans can be made by using imagination and experimenting with different combinations of food e.g. Stilton and onion; salmon and cucumber; sliced sausage and tomato etc.

32 · Cheese and ham savoury flan *Quiche lorraine*

100 g	4 oz	rough puff, puff or short pastry
50 g	2 oz	chopped ham
25 g	1 oz	grated cheese
		1 egg
125 ml	1/4 pt	milk
		cayenne, salt

This recipe provides:

704 kcals/2955 kJ
48.4 g fat of which 22.6 g saturated
38.1 g carbohydrate of which 6.5 g sugars
31.6 g protein
1.8 g fibre

1. Lightly grease four good-size barquette or tartlet moulds.
2. Line thinly with pastry.
3. Prick the bottoms of the paste two or three times with a fork.
4. Cook in a hot oven (230–250 °C, Reg. 8–9) for 3–4 min or until the pastry is lightly set.
5. Remove from the oven, press the pastry down if it has tended to rise.
6. Add the chopped ham and grated cheese.
7. Mix the egg, milk, salt and cayenne thoroughly.
8. Strain into the barquettes.
9. Return to oven (200–230 °C, Reg. 6–8) and bake gently till nicely browned and set, approx. 15–20 min.

33 · Cheese straws *Paillettes au fromage*

100 g	4 oz	puff or rough puff paste
50 g	2 oz	grated cheese
		cayenne

This recipe provides:

610 kcals/2562 kJ
48.1 g fat of which 24.1 g saturated
28.7 g carbohydrate of which 0.6 g sugars
17.4 g protein
1.4 g fibre

1. Roll out the pastry 60×15 cm (24×6 in).
2. Sprinkle with cheese and cayenne.
3. Give a single turn, that is, fold the paste one-third the way over so that it covers the first fold.
4. Roll out approx. 3 mm (1/8 in) thick.
5. Cut out four circles approx. 4 cm (2 in) diameter.
6. Remove the centre with a smaller cutter leaving a circle approx. 1/2 cm (1/4 in) wide.
7. Cut the remaining paste into strips approx. 8×1/2 cm (3×1/4 in).
8. Twist each once or twice.
9. Place on a lightly greased baking sheet.
10. Bake in a hot oven (230–250 °C, Reg. 8–9) for approx. 10 min until a golden brown.
11. To serve place a bundle of straws into each circle.

Note 50% white and 50% wholemeal flour can be used for the pastry.

34 · Cheese soufflé *Soufflé au fromage*

25 g	1 oz	butter or margarine
15 g	¾ oz	flour
125 ml	¼ pt	milk
		3 egg yolks
		salt, cayenne
50 g	2 oz	grated cheese
		4 egg whites

Using hard margarine
This recipe provides:

767 kcals/3223 kJ
60.2 g fat of which 28.2 g saturated
17.6 g carbohydrate of which 6.1 g sugars
39.7 g protein
0.5 g fibre

1 Melt the butter in a thick-bottomed pan.
2 Add the flour and mix with a wooden spoon.
3 Cook out for a few seconds without colouring.
4 Gradually add the cold milk and mix to a smooth sauce.
5 Simmer for a few minutes.
6 Add one egg yolk, mix in quickly; immediately remove from heat.
7 When cool, add remaining yolks. Season with salt and pepper.
8 Add the cheese.
9 Place the egg whites and a pinch of salt in a scrupulously clean bowl, preferably copper, and whisk until stiff.
10 Add one-eighth of the whites to the mixture and mix well.
11 Gently fold in the remaining seven-eighths of the mixture, mix as lightly as possible. Place into a buttered soufflé case.
12 Cook in a hot oven 220 °C, Reg. 7 for approx. 25–30 min.
13 Remove from the oven, place on a round flat dish and serve *immediately*.

35 · Cheese fritters *Beignets au fromage*

125 ml	¼ pt	water
50 g	2 oz	butter or margarine
60 g	2½ oz	flour, white or wholemeal
		2 eggs
50 g	2 oz	grated Parmesan cheese
		salt, cayenne

1 Bring the water and butter or margarine to the boil in a thick-bottomed pan. Remove from the heat.
2 Add the flour, mix with a wooden spoon.
3 Return to a gentle heat and mix well until the mixture leaves the sides of the pan.
4 Remove from the heat. Allow to cool slightly.
5 Gradually add the eggs, beating well.
6 Add the cheese and seasoning.
7 Using a spoon, scoop out the mixture in pieces the size of a walnut, place into deep hot fat (185 °C).
8 Allow to cook with the minimum of handling for approx. 10 min.
9 Drain and serve sprinkled with grated Parmesan cheese.

36 · Pizza

200 g	8 oz	flour, strong white or wholemeal
		pinch of salt
12 g	½ oz	margarine
5 g	¼ oz	yeast
125 ml	¼ pt	water or milk at temperature of 75 °F
5 g	¼ oz	castor sugar
100 g	4 oz	onions
		2 cloves garlic, crushed
60 ml	⅛ pt	sunflower oil
200 g	8 oz	canned plum tomatoes
100 g	4 oz	tomato purée
3 g	⅛ oz	oregano
3 g	⅛ oz	basil
10 g	½ oz	sugar
10 g	½ oz	cornflour
100 g	4 oz	mozzarella cheese

Using wholemeal flour
1 portion provides:

910 kcals/3823 kJ
47.1 g fat of which 13.1 g saturated
103.0 g carbohydrate of which 20.8 g sugars
24.8 g protein
5.9 g fibre

Using 50% wholemeal flour
1 portion provides:

895 kcals/3758 kJ
47.6 g fat of which 13.1 g saturated
97.1 g carbohydrate of which 21.1 g sugars
26.5 g protein
8.4 g fibre

1. Sieve the flour and the salt. Rub in the margarine.
2. Disperse the yeast in the warm milk or water, add the castor sugar. Add this mixture to the flour.
3. Mix well, knead to a smooth dough, place in a basin covered with a damp cloth and allow to prove until doubled in size.
4. Knock back, divide into two and roll out into two 18 cm (7 in) discs. Place on a lightly greased baking sheet.
5. Sweat the finely chopped onions and garlic in the sunflower oil until cooked.
6. Add the roughly chopped tomatoes, tomato purée, oregano, basil and sugar. Bring to boil and simmer for 5 min.
7. Dilute the cornflour in a little water, stir into the tomato mixture and bring back to the boil.
8. Take the discs of pizza dough and spread approx. 125 g (5 oz) of filling on each one.
9. Sprinkle with grated mozzarella cheese or lay the slices of cheese on top.
10. Bake in a moderately hot oven, 180 °C (Reg. 4), for approx. 10 mins. Serve hot or cold.

Note The pizza dough may also be made into rectangles so that it can be sliced into fingers for buffet work.

This is a basic recipe and many variations exist, some have the addition of olives, artichoke bottoms, prawns, mortadella sausage, garlic sausage, anchovy fillets, etc. A vegetarian pizza recipe is on page 398.

INDEX